AGAINST THE PRESIDENT

Kenneth Branagh
The Kennedys and Cuba
Kennedy: The New Frontier Revisited
Missiles in Cuba
The Cuban Missile Crisis

AGAINST THE PRESIDENT

Dissent and Decision-Making
in the White House:
A Historical Perspective

BY

MARK J. WHITE

CHICAGO   IVAN R. DEE

2007

www.ivanrdee.com

Library of Congress Cataloging-in-Publication Data:
White, Mark, 1965–
  Against the president : dissent and decision-making in the White House :
a historical perspective / Mark White.
    p. cm.
  Includes bibliographical references and index.
  ISBN-13: 978-1-56663-744-2 (pbk. : alk. paper)
  ISBN-10: 1-56663-744-9 (pbk. : alk. paper)
    1. United States—Politics and government—1933–1945. 2. United States—
Politics and government—1945–1989. 3. United States—Politics and
government—Decision making—Case studies. 4. Presidents—United States—
Decision making—Case studies. 5. Political leadership—United States—Case
studies. 6. Presidents—United States—History—20th century. I. Title.
E743.W54 2007
973.917—dc22

                                                    2007016032

For my mother

ACKNOWLEDGMENTS

I WISH to thank Ivan Dee for his superb editing of the manuscript, and the many archivists who assisted my research on this project. Parts of Chapters 1 and 2 were published in *The Maryland Historian* 23 (Fall/Winter 1992). My thanks to this journal for permission to reprint.

I am also grateful for the assistance of archivists at the Franklin Roosevelt, Harry Truman, Dwight Eisenhower, John Kennedy, and Lyndon Johnson presidential libraries; the Library of Congress and the National Archives; Princeton University and Yale University; the Roosevelt Study Center in Middleburg, the Netherlands, and the Public Record Office in London; and the various other archives I visited.

CONTENTS

AGAINST THE PRESIDENT

Introduction

▬

"The dissenter is every human being at those
moments of his life when he resigns momentarily
from the herd and thinks for himself."
—ARCHIBALD MACLEISH, 1956

NOT SINCE the 1960s, when American soldiers were bogged down
in Vietnam, has the role played by the United States on the world stage
been so controversial. With the merits of the war in Iraq contested by
leading politicians in America and elsewhere, as well as at the grass
roots, the issue of whether George W. Bush should have taken an alternative approach to the challenge posed by Saddam Hussein has become salient. That Bush might have decided on a different policy has
been made clear by the revelation that his respected secretary of state,
Colin Powell, had reservations about going to war.

On August 5, 2002, Powell expressed his concerns to Bush at a
White House meeting also attended by Condoleezza Rice, the national
security adviser. He told the president that war might destabilize other
governments in the region, and emphasized the difficult responsibility
that would be his once Saddam had been overthrown: "You are going to
be the proud owner of 25 million people," Powell warned. "You will
own all their hopes, aspirations and problems. You'll own it all." As Iraq
had no experience of democracy, he added, "you need to understand

that this is not going to be a walk in the woods." "What should I do?" Bush asked. "What else can I do?" Internationalize the Iraq situation, Powell replied, and work through the United Nations. A month later Powell confronted Vice President Dick Cheney: the unilateral use of American force against Iraq would, he predicted, create a storm of protest from other countries. And going to war could lead to all sorts of dangerous and unanticipated consequences. From the perspective of 2007, Powell's dissent appears strikingly prescient.[1]

This book considers the question of alternatives to American foreign policy in its historical context. I have examined the response of American presidents, from Harry Truman to Lyndon Johnson, to dissent within their own administrations on key national security issues. Historians writing on the cold war have often explored the relationships between presidents and the advisers—such as George Kennan, Dean Acheson, and Henry Kissinger—who most influenced them. History, it is often said, tends to be about winners. That claim can certainly be made about writings on recent U.S. foreign policy. Despite occasional biographies of individual dissenters, there has been little attempt to consider the phenomenon of dissent in the White House, and how leaders such as Dwight Eisenhower and John Kennedy responded to it.[2]

The stories of these episodes and the implications of these dissenters' ideas are revealing. They represent the road less traveled. They show the range of options that have been made available to the nation's leaders. They shed light on the nature of presidential decision-making. They sometimes expose and challenge the assumptions on which U.S. diplomacy has been based. They have implications for policymakers today.

Spanning the two decades from the beginnings of the cold war to America's entry into the Vietnam War, this study examines the dispute between Harry Truman and his advisers Harry Hopkins and Joseph Davies over the Polish question; the disagreements between Truman and Henry Wallace in 1945–1946 on how best to meet the challenge posed by the Soviet Union; Charles Wilson's attempt to persuade Dwight Eisenhower not to commit the United States to the defense of South Vietnam; Adlai Stevenson's disagreements with John Kennedy on policy toward Cuba; and George Ball's quest to prevent Lyndon Johnson from going to war in Vietnam.

A number of factors determined my selection of these dissenters and episodes. I wanted to write not, for example, about members of Congress but about officials who were part of the administration (Davies was technically an exception, but Truman used him as an emissary to speak to Stalin) and who thus had an opportunity to influence presidential policy directly. I wanted to consider major, not peripheral, figures. Hopkins had been Franklin Roosevelt's closest adviser and Davies his ambassador to the Soviet Union. Wallace had been vice president; Wilson was Eisenhower's secretary of defense; Stevenson had been a two-time presidential candidate; Ball was the number two man in the State Department. The stature of these dissenters therefore indicated at least the possibility of their impact on U.S. diplomacy. The selection of the contentious issues in the book has been governed by a desire to tackle some of the vital aspects of American foreign policy during the early years of the cold war: the fate of Eastern Europe, the Soviet challenge, the Bay of Pigs and the Cuban missile crisis, and the Vietnam War.

Various aides encouraged their presidents to adopt a tougher approach to cold war issues. I do not include these harder-line officials because, while they promoted different cold war strategies, they generally shared the same assumptions as the presidents under whom they worked—that the seriousness of the threat posed by Moscow and its Communist allies was severe, that the "domino theory" was valid, and that the Communist bloc was monolithic. In this sense these truculent advisers were not dissenters: they did not disagree with the fundamental beliefs underpinning U.S. foreign policy. Men such as Wallace and Stevenson, however, did. They both contested the premises of American diplomacy and recommended different policies.

The story of this struggle between presidents and dissenters begins in Poland, as World War II drew to a close and the cold war was about to begin.

PART I

Truman, Hopkins, Davies, and the Polish Question

CHAPTER 1

The Ghost of FDR

—

"One reason I'm glad to be here and am glad to
offer all the assistance I can is because I'm
confident that you will continue to carry out the
policies of Franklin Roosevelt."—HARRY HOPKINS,
speaking with Harry Truman, April 14, 1945

ON THURSDAY, April 12, 1945, President Franklin Delano Roosevelt, the man who had heroically combatted the polio virus that had robbed him of the use of his legs, the leader who had injected hope into a nation crippled by economic collapse, the statesman who had orchestrated a monumental military effort to defeat fascism on three continents, died of a massive brain hemorrhage in Warm Springs, Georgia.

"Confused, shocked, stunned," was how one American official described the reaction among his colleagues to FDR's death. The response throughout the nation mirrored that of Roosevelt's friends and advisers. As one State Department official, Dean Acheson, told his son, Roosevelt's passing

> was a major shock throughout the country. . . . It was impressive, as the news of his death went out, to see the effect on people everywhere. . . . As you listened to the conversations on the street car and on the street, you began to realize . . . the tremendous place which the Government and the Presidency, and particularly the

late President, played in the lives of everybody. There were millions of people in practically a parent relationship in the psychological sense, and the sudden shock of his death leaves people completely at sea.[1]

An aching sense of loss was the dominant emotion not only in the United States but elsewhere. Consumed by grief, British Prime Minister Winston Churchill went to the House of Commons where he asked the Members to take the unprecedented step of adjourning as a mark of respect to the memory of a foreign statesman; the Members consented unanimously. The response in Moscow was also unprecedented. A crowd of four hundred, including many senior Soviet officials, attended the memorial service for FDR held in the U.S. embassy.[2]

As soon as he heard the news, Joseph Davies dashed to the White House and witnessed the arrival of Roosevelt's vice president, Harry S. Truman, looking "strained but grim." That evening, as the news sank in, Davies pondered the implications in discussions with close friends: "What kind of a President would Truman make? Whom would he rely on?" As midnight came, Davies in his journal reflected on the enormity of the loss: "Tragedy hit the world and all of us today. This afternoon the President died at Warm Springs, Georgia. It is one of the greatest and most costly of war casualties."[3]

Harry Hopkins, lying ill in a Rochester, Minnesota, hospital at the time of FDR's passing, was no less crestfallen. He dealt with the devastation by firing off a series of messages, as if to dissipate his grief by articulating it. "I still find it difficult to believe that our gallant friend has gone," he confessed to Churchill. "I want you to know," he wrote Stalin, "that I feel that Russia has lost her greatest friend in America." And to FDR's successor in the White House: "Of one thing I am very sure that yesterday the heavens opened wide their gates to receive his noble and generous spirit."[4]

The grief felt by Davies and Hopkins was heartfelt because their relationships with Roosevelt had been so close. A lawyer from Wisconsin, Davies had studied at the university there, practiced privately, and married well before cutting his teeth in politics with a young Franklin Roosevelt as a member of Woodrow Wilson's administration. After losing a

Senate election in Wisconsin in 1918, accompanying Wilson to the Versailles peace conference, and returning in the 1920s to the law (from which he made a fortune), Davies resumed his political career during Roosevelt's presidency. He became vice chairman of the Democratic National Committee when Roosevelt ran for reelection in 1936, and later that same year FDR named him ambassador to the Soviet Union. Davies's time as ambassador is controversial, for while in Moscow he developed what was clearly a naive, overly sanguine view of Stalin's Russia. That view was propagated in Davies's published memoir, *Mission to Moscow*, and in a 1943 film based on that work. He left Moscow in the summer of 1938 to become ambassador to Belgium and minister to Luxembourg, but he held to his central belief that the United States and the Soviet Union must develop closer relations. He saw this as a way of helping counter the German-Italian-Japanese alliance. Through his close association with Franklin Roosevelt during these years, Davies developed a genuine affection for the man.[5]

Hopkins was even more strongly bonded to Roosevelt. Indeed, with the exception of John and Robert Kennedy, there was probably no closer relationship between president and adviser in twentieth-century American history. The partnership was forged during Roosevelt's time as governor of New York when Hopkins—who hailed from Iowa, attended Grinnell College, and moved to New York City where he became a social worker—spearheaded the effort to extend relief to the unemployed in the state, a role he reprised nationally when FDR reached the White House. In the midst of the Great Depression, Hopkins supervised an array of New Deal relief programs, most notably the Works Progress Administration. In effect he helped millions of Americans find work. With the death of Louis Howe in 1936 and the fall from favor of James A. Farley, Hopkins became Roosevelt's most intimate confidant and influential adviser. In May 1940 he accepted an invitation to dinner at the White House—and never left. At Roosevelt's insistence he took up residence in two rooms in the East Wing, the larger of which had been used by Abraham Lincoln to sign the Emancipation Proclamation. Joined in 1942 by his third wife, Louise Macy, in these small but historically vibrant surroundings, they would dine with Franklin or Eleanor Roosevelt or both about five times a week.

During the war Hopkins became FDR's closest adviser on foreign policy, serving as his personal envoy to Churchill, Stalin, and other world leaders, playing a key role in running the Lend Lease program, and accompanying the president to major wartime conferences.[6]

There were many reasons why Roosevelt bestowed this privileged status on Hopkins. He respected Hopkins's abilities, appreciated his loyalty, valued his disinterest in publicity. There was also an empathetic note to the relationship: the president crippled by polio admired Hopkins's stoicism in combating a series of illnesses.[7]

A major feature of the collaboration between Roosevelt and these two advisers was the building of a partnership with Stalin in order to defeat Hitler. When Germany invaded the Soviet Union in June 1941, Hopkins and Davies advocated an alliance with Moscow, arguing that the Lend Lease aid sent to Britain be extended to the Russians. To that end, Hopkins journeyed to Moscow for talks with Stalin. Having pressed for a close Soviet-American relationship since his ambassadorship in Moscow, Davies now found that circumstances gave his arguments a credibility they had earlier lacked. He helped convince Hopkins of the importance of supporting the Russians, and served as an intermediary between the White House and the Soviet embassy in Washington. In 1943 Davies undertook a special mission to Moscow to talk with Stalin on Roosevelt's behalf.[8]

With Roosevelt's passing, both Hopkins and Davies wondered whether Truman would continue FDR's policies, particularly in relations with Stalin. The presidency had been thrust upon Truman at an especially sensitive moment in Soviet-American relations. With the end of World War II and a victory over Nazi Germany close at hand, attention was shifting to a cluster of controversial postwar issues, including the degree of Russian influence in Eastern Europe, occupation policies in a defeated Germany, and the mechanics of organizing the United Nations.

The challenge facing Truman was immense, and his background did not suggest that he was well equipped to meet it. Born in 1884 in Missouri, his early years had been undistinguished. He worked for many years as a farmer, but the haberdashery he established in 1919 in Kansas City went broke. His service as an army captain on the battlefields of Europe in World War I, however, revealed genuine leadership potential. Truman's political rise came on the back of his dubious association with Thomas J. Pendergast, boss of the Democratic party political machine in Kansas City. Pendergast, who was later convicted for income tax evasion, backed Truman in 1922 in the race for county commissioner, which he won, and then again in 1934 when he ran for a U.S. Senate seat. During Truman's first term in the Senate he voted consistently for New Deal policies but remained a largely anonymous figure. In his second term, however, Truman chaired a special committee that did good work in identifying corruption in military procurement without jeopardizing the overall military buildup needed during the war. The senator from Missouri had many virtues: he worked hard, had common sense, and was politically astute. But he had developed no expertise in international affairs. Once selected as the Democratic vice presidential candidate in 1944, such expertise would have been exceedingly useful, as it was soon clear that the president was so ill that he might not live through a fourth term. Catapulted into the presidency on FDR's death, Truman suddenly had to confront a welter of problems having to do with winning the war and establishing a peace.[9]

Of these issues it was Eastern Europe, and particularly the fate of postwar Poland, that became the greatest source of tension between Moscow and Washington. The end of the war, as with its beginning, was thus marked in Europe by conflict over Poland. At the onset of his presidency, it was Truman's biggest headache.

The Polish question had evolved out of the circumstances of the war. To escape from invading Germans and Russians, members of the Polish government and military had fled to France and Britain in the autumn of 1939, finally establishing a government-in-exile in London. Britain and the United States recognized it and established diplomatic links. But relations between the Polish government-in-exile and the Soviet Union, the nation that had initially cooperated with Nazi Germany and seized huge areas of eastern Poland, were strained. This tension continued even after the Nazi invasion of the Soviet Union in June 1941.[10]

At the Teheran Conference in late 1943, Stalin and Churchill agreed that after the war Poland's borders should be moved westward, with the old Curzon Line constituting the eastern boundary and the

Oder River forming the western border. Hence the Soviet Union would acquire a large part of eastern Poland. Roosevelt expressed sympathy with this plan but was unwilling to participate in any decision, explaining to Stalin his desire not to alienate the Polish-American vote in the 1944 presidential election. As the war drew to a close, therefore, the specifics of Polish territorial change had yet to be agreed upon.[11]

Of even greater urgency was the debate over the future Polish government. Determined to enhance Soviet security after the war, Stalin had resolved that any Polish administration must be loyal to him. Accordingly, he began to sponsor in Moscow a new Polish government, the Communist-dominated Union of Polish Patriots, in opposition to the London government-in-exile. In April 1943 he terminated relations with the London Poles when, after the Nazis accused the Red Army of murdering thousands of Polish army officers in the Katyn forest (a claim that has since been authenticated), the government-in-exile demanded an international inquiry into these events. By July 1944 the Russian-backed Polish government declared Lublin to be the new Polish capital, and by the end of the year Stalin officially recognized the Lublin administration as the legitimate government of Poland. In early 1945 the major Polish problem and the key issue in general between the Allies was how to reconstitute the postwar Polish government. Would the London or the Lublin Poles receive Allied blessing?[12]

Roosevelt did not impose himself on the Polish question until early 1945. Concerned perhaps about the Polish-American vote in the 1944 presidential election, he had remained decidedly taciturn to that point. In February 1945 FDR met with Churchill and Stalin at Yalta, where they attempted to reconcile their differences over Poland. Paradoxically, the agreements forged at Yalta formed the basis of Soviet-American disagreement over the next five months. Supporting the principle of self-determination, Roosevelt called for a Polish provisional government that would be representative of the leading nonfascist parties, to be replaced later by a freely elected government. But Stalin demanded that the provisional government be based on the Lublin Poles. The Yalta Declaration on Poland was supposed to reconcile these differences. As a compromise which permitted all participants to interpret it as they chose, the agreement was necessarily ambiguous. It stated that the

Lublin government should be "reorganized on a broader democratic basis with the inclusion of democratic leaders from Poland itself and from Poles abroad. The new Government should then be called the Polish Provisional Government of National Unity." This government was to be committed to free elections. Whether this clause implied that the provisional government was to be dominated by the Lublin government, which would be merely "reorganized," or whether the Lublin Poles were to be a minority in a "new Government," was the ambiguity that fueled Soviet-American antagonism.[13]

It was also decided at Yalta that the eastern border of Poland should, with minor modifications, be the Curzon Line. It was further agreed that Poland should be compensated by "substantial accessions of territory in the north and west," though no particular line was specified.[14]

Superseding the territorial question as the second most difficult Polish problem by the spring of 1945 was the procedural issue of *how* to establish the provisional government. The Yalta agreement had said that Soviet foreign minister Vyacheslav M. Molotov and the U.S. and British ambassadors to the Soviet Union, W. Averell Harriman and Sir Archibald Clark-Kerr, would meet as a commission in Moscow to set up the provisional government. This was to be done by consulting "in the first instance in Moscow with members of the present [Lublin] Provisional Government and with other Polish democratic leaders from within Poland and from abroad [namely the London Poles]." When the Moscow commission began its work in late February, Molotov argued that the Lublin Poles should be allowed to veto the suggestions of Harriman and Clark-Kerr for the London Poles and the non-Lublin Poles inside Poland to be invited to the Moscow commission for consultation. He pointed out that the Yalta agreement stipulated that the Lublin Poles (or Warsaw Poles, as they became known) were to be consulted by the Moscow commission "in the first instance." The Americans and the British strongly disagreed with this interpretation.[15]

From the Yalta Conference until his death, Roosevelt approached the Polish question in an accommodating spirit. That is not to say he was unconcerned by Soviet stonewalling tactics in the Moscow commission. "Averell [Harriman] is right," he grumbled at a luncheon in late March. "We can't do business with Stalin. He has broken every one of the promises he made at Yalta." But his overall view was that he had to accept Russian control of Poland and the rest of Eastern Europe in the short term in order to hold the wartime alliance intact; thorny problems in Allied relations could be sorted out later. FDR was "trying to convince himself," an adviser noted at the time of the president's death, "that the Russians would be satisfied if their outer barriers in Eastern Europe were secure."[16]

When Churchill, irritated by Molotov's position, urged FDR to confront Stalin, the president was reluctant. On March 29 he told Churchill that "if we attempt to evade the fact that we placed, as clearly shown in the agreement, somewhat more emphasis on the Lublin Poles than on the other two groups from which the new Government is to be drawn I feel we will expose ourselves to the charge that we are attempting to go back on the Crimean decision."[17]

But on April 1 Roosevelt did take issue with Stalin over Poland. "The part of our agreements at Yalta which has aroused the greatest popular interest and is the most urgent," he informed the Soviet leader, "relates to the Polish question." He warned Stalin that "any such solution which would result in a thinly disguised continuance of the present Warsaw regime would be unacceptable." While Roosevelt did not mind the Warsaw Poles meeting first with the commission, he believed the Poles nominated by Harriman and Clark-Kerr should not be subject to a veto by the Warsaw Poles, as Molotov had insisted. The president also asked Stalin to ensure "the maximum of political tranquility" in Poland, and to allow American and British representatives to visit the country.[18]

Compared with FDR's general handling of the Polish problem, this message was an anomaly. It elicited a sharp rejoinder. A week later Stalin claimed that the United States and Britain had "departed from the principles of the Crimea Conference" by refusing to accept the Warsaw government as the "kernel" of the new provisional government. The Polish government, he asserted, should be established on similar lines to Tito's Yugoslav government, already recognized by the United States, the composition of which was three-quarters Communist and one-quarter non-Communist.[19]

Roosevelt's general approach was neatly summarized in his last message to Churchill before his death. Reacting to the prime minister's concern over Stalin's Polish policies, he wrote: "I would minimize the general Soviet problem as much as possible because these problems, in one form or another, seem to arise every day and most of them straighten out."[20]

Where Roosevelt had used a velvet glove in his dealings with Stalin over the Polish question, Truman initially preferred an iron fist. He left the Soviet leader in no doubt as to his utter dissatisfaction, particularly with Stalin's idea of using the Yugoslav arrangement as a model for the Polish government. He adopted this position in part because he did not wish to say how much influence the Warsaw Poles should wield in the new government in order to uphold the Yalta accord, which specified that the composition of the Polish provisional government should not be decided until the Moscow commission had consulted with a group of Poles. But Truman also rejected the Yugoslav model on the grounds that it would perpetuate in Poland a Communist-dominated government, subservient to Moscow.

Ignorant about contemporary international relations, Truman relied heavily on advice—and the State Department, often bypassed by Roosevelt, was more than willing to supply it. The day after FDR's death it provided Truman with a comprehensive memorandum on United States foreign relations, alerting him to existing difficulties over Poland. "The present situation relating to Poland is highly unsatisfactory," the State Department warned, "with the Soviet authorities consistently sabotaging Ambassador Harriman's efforts in the Moscow commission to hasten the implementation of the decisions at the Crimea conference."[21]

Despite this caveat, Truman rejected a proposal from Churchill to pressure Stalin by issuing a joint public statement detailing their objections to his policies. Determined to obtain Russian assistance in the war against Japan, Truman warned Churchill of "the effect it [a public statement] will have on our political and military collaboration with the Soviet Union." Truman preferred a private message to Stalin and proposed a text. Churchill accepted it with one minor modification, and on April 18 it was delivered to the Soviet leader.[22]

In their message Truman and Churchill asserted that the main issue dividing the Allies was "whether or not the Warsaw Government has the right to veto individual candidates for consultation. No such interpretation in our considered opinion can be found in the Crimea decision." To get the Polish question moving, they named the Poles with whom the Moscow commission should consult. The group comprised four Warsaw Poles, one party leader from within Poland not linked to the Warsaw government, and three London Poles (including Stanislaw Mikolajczyk, former leader of the government-in-exile). These individuals were to suggest other Polish leaders who might be consulted by the Moscow commission before a provisional government was established. Truman and Churchill also objected to the Yugoslav model but, seeking to uphold the Yalta Declaration, refused to say how the new government should be constituted.[23]

As a verdant president grappled with the foreign policy problems he had inherited from Roosevelt, Harry Hopkins continued to battle ill health. But he soon had the opportunity to sound Truman out about these issues. Rising from his sickbed on Friday, April 13, he flew from Rochester to Washington to attend the funeral services for FDR the following day. Truman sent word that he wished to see Hopkins.[24]

That same Friday, Secretary of State Edward R. Stettinius made sure the new president understood the crucial role Hopkins had played under FDR. He told Truman that Hopkins had "an extremely important and unique relationship as far as foreign relations were concerned, inasmuch as he was the one person who really thoroughly understood the various ramifications and the relations between Roosevelt and Churchill and Stalin." When Stettinius proposed that he take advantage of Hopkins's special knowledge of wartime diplomacy, Truman responded that he had "the greatest regard for Hopkins, he is a grand friend, and I plan to use Hopkins to the limit of his strength."[25]

Perhaps "a grand friend" was overstating it, but relations between Truman and Hopkins had always been cordial. They had met in Kansas City in 1933, collaborating in the provision of relief for the unemployed. After his election to the Senate, Truman came to regard Hopkins as an ally in encouraging White House action on matters affecting Truman's home state of Missouri. Hopkins was especially considerate in the wake of Truman's selection in 1944 as the Democratic party vice-presidential candidate, providing the nominee with an in-depth analysis of Roosevelt's views on issues and individuals. In his dealings with Hopkins, Truman never ceased to be impressed by his candor. "He always told the truth," Truman once remarked. "Never tried to fool you." Perhaps underlying their solid relationship was the sense of much in common: humble beginnings, Midwestern roots, humility despite advancement.[26]

When Hopkins came to his office on the morning of Saturday, April 14, Truman was thus genuinely pleased to see him. "How do you feel, Harry?" he asked as they shook hands. "Terrible," Hopkins confessed. Truman was not surprised. Hopkins's appearance was shocking. "I hope you don't mind my calling you in at this time," the president explained, "but I need to know everything you can tell me about our relations with Russia—all that you know about Stalin and Churchill and the conferences at Cairo, Casablanca, Teheran, and Yalta." He was happy to be of assistance, Hopkins replied, because he felt certain that Truman would continue FDR's policies. Perhaps this was a caution to the new president to think twice before breaking with the foreign policy he had inherited from Roosevelt, a caveat that Joseph Davies and Henry Wallace would soon repeat.[27]

Hopkins proceeded to review the international situation for Truman's benefit. Unlike many other American officials at the time, Hopkins was upbeat about Yalta—"we got much farther on the political side than we anticipated," he had told a friend—and not unduly worried about relations with Moscow. The gist of his comments to Truman was that he should be able to deal with the Soviet leader: "Stalin is a forthright, rough, tough Russian. He is a Russian partisan through and through, thinking always first of Russia. But he can be talked to frankly." The meeting ended with Hopkins informing Truman of his plan to retire, and Truman, according to his memoirs, insisting he wanted to keep Hopkins on board, health permitting.[28]

As Hopkins departed, a throng of reporters gathered, anxious to learn the purpose of his return to Washington. He explained in a barely audible voice that he had come simply to say farewell to Roosevelt and to pay his respects to Truman. The new president, Hopkins declared, would "get what he deserves—the support of all the American people in this time." Asked whether he was ready to be a part of the Truman team, Hopkins, sensibly, kept his cards close to his chest.[29]

As for what a Truman presidency would mean for American foreign policy and his own role in government, Hopkins speculated on these matters the following day with two British officials, Foreign Minister Anthony Eden and Lord Halifax, ambassador to Washington. In a telegram to Churchill, Halifax reported that Hopkins "judged the President's death to have created a completely new situation in which we should be starting from scratch." In addition, Hopkins

> could certainly not carry on in his present job. Truman probably would not want him, and Harry anyhow would not do it. Truman's methods would be quite different from those of F.D.R.: he would conduct his own business, and there would be no room for Harry's particular line of usefulness. They had mentioned the future in a talk they had yesterday, but not much more than to say that they must talk again when Harry was well.[30]

This contemporaneous account gives a different sense of the Hopkins-Truman meeting than that provided by Truman in his memoirs. In his talk with Eden and Halifax, Hopkins implied that Truman would tug American foreign policy in new directions, and that this would diminish his own importance as he was seen as the living embodiment of FDR's policies. Hopkins was right—in the short term. Spurred on by Averell Harriman and others, Truman decided to confront the Russians over Poland in his meeting with Molotov on April 23. What Hopkins did not anticipate is that Truman would revert to Rooseveltian tactics during the second month of his presidency in a way that made Hopkins a key player once again. In this transformation of Truman, Joseph Davies played an important role.

The tension generated by the Polish problem peaked when Molotov stopped off in Washington on April 22 on his way to the San Francisco conference that would establish the United Nations Organization. (Stalin had initially refused to send Molotov but agreed to do so as a gesture of goodwill after FDR's death.) The Soviet foreign minister's visit forced Truman to decide quickly how to handle the Russians, particularly on the Polish question. Would he accommodate them, as FDR had, or would he take a new, tougher stance? In framing an answer to that question, Truman sounded out his advisers: he called an Oval Office meeting for noon on Friday, April 20, with Harriman, Stettinius, Soviet expert Charles E. Bohlen, and Undersecretary of State Joseph C. Grew. Frustrated by Molotov's obstinacy on the Moscow commission, Harriman began the discussion by claiming that Russia was carrying out two policies simultaneously—one of cooperation with the United States and Britain, the other of territorial expansion. Claiming that "a barbarian invasion of Europe" was under way, Harriman called for "a reconsideration of our policy and the abandonment of the illusion that for the immediate future the Soviet Government was going to act in accordance with the principles which the rest of the world held to in international affairs." He believed Truman could be more confrontational without sundering the wartime alliance because Stalin needed American aid to rebuild the Russian economy. During Harriman's presentation, Truman interjected several times to declare his resolve. He was "not in any sense afraid of the Russians," intended "to be firm but fair since . . . the Soviet Union needed us more than we needed them," and felt that "on important matters . . . we should be able to get 85 percent [of what we want]."[31]

Moving on to the Polish question, Harriman said Stalin had learned from the Warsaw Poles that implementation of the Yalta agreements would signal the end of Communist rule in Poland. When the ambassador asked about the importance of the Polish question for American participation in the United Nations, Truman said that failure to settle the issue would mean that "the treaty of American adherence to a world organization would not get through the Senate." And he was prepared to tell Molotov that "in words of one syllable." Truman concluded the discussion by once again insisting he would be "firm in his dealings with the Soviet Government."[32]

Truman received Molotov two days later, on the evening of Sunday, April 22, at Blair House. Following earlier advice from Stettinius, the president expressed his respect for Stalin and the Soviet Union, and his interest in sustaining the partnership forged with Moscow by FDR. Molotov, who conveyed Stalin's personal greetings, said he was pleased to hear that. As the conversation turned to the Yalta decisions, Truman observed that the most challenging problem arising from the implementation of those agreements was Poland. Stressing the importance of this issue to American public opinion, he declared that "in its larger aspects the Polish question had become for our people the symbol of the future development of our international relations." This might be so, Molotov replied, but the issue was even more important to the Soviet Union because it bordered on Poland. Carrying out the Yalta agreements would resolve the issue, he added. As their discussion drew to a close, Truman proposed that they drink to Stalin's health. Molotov amended the toast, saying they should drink to Truman and Churchill as well as the Soviet leader. The president added to the convivialities by saying he hoped to see Stalin soon, and perhaps to visit Russia. Molotov said Stalin was also eager to meet Truman. The first Truman-Molotov meeting had been cagey but courteous. The civility appropriate for this sort of diplomatic exchange would be conspicuously absent from their meeting the following day.[33]

Davies had the opportunity to speak with Molotov on Monday, April 23, at the Soviet embassy, before this next encounter. Molotov helped Davies understand the seriousness with which the Russian leadership viewed the passing of FDR. The Kremlin believed Roosevelt had been committed to Soviet-American cooperation, Molotov reported, but feared that Truman was ignorant of the intricacies of recent developments. As an example, Molotov cited the Polish question. The Russian need for a friendly Poland had been understood by Roosevelt, but with his death "there was threatened wide disagreement now" on this matter. Davies tried to assuage the anxieties of Molotov, whom he had known for years, saying that Truman was pragmatic and honest, and would be fair if Molotov fully explained Soviet concerns to him.[34]

At 2 p.m. that same day, Truman prepared for his second talk with Molotov by again consulting his advisers. It was the most important meeting of his presidency to that point, for it would determine Truman's initial approach to the Russians. Reporting that his own talks with Molotov and Eden since the previous evening had been unproductive, Stettinius warned that "the Soviet Government intended to try to enforce upon the United States and British Governments this puppet government of Poland." A disgruntled Truman responded that "our agreements with the Soviet Union so far had been a one way street and that could not continue; it was now or never. He intended to go on with the plans for San Francisco and if the Russians did not wish to join us they could go to hell." Secretary of War Henry L. Stimson urged caution, contending that very few countries in the world interpreted democracy in the same way as the United States. "The Russians," he added, "perhaps were being more realistic than we were in regard to their own security."[35]

Secretary of the Navy James V. Forrestal, however, claimed that the Russians felt they could dominate Eastern Europe with impunity, and concluded that "if the Russians were to be rigid in their attitude we had better have a showdown with them now rather than later." Harriman, Stettinius, and Gen. John R. Deane, head of the American military mission in Moscow, endorsed this uncompromising approach. Adm. William D. Leahy and Gen. George C. Marshall, on the other hand, supported Stimson's plea for moderation. Marshall reminded his colleagues that the United States still "hoped for Soviet participation in the war against Japan at a time when it would be useful for us." With his advisers divided, Truman decided to back the hard-liners: he would give Molotov a tongue-lashing he would never forget.[36]

In that famous April 23 meeting with Molotov, which took place at 5:30 p.m. in the Oval Office, Truman, as he later put it, "went straight to the point," explaining his regret at the lack of progress in the talks between Molotov, Eden, and Stettinius. He declared his unwillingness to accept any Warsaw government that did not represent all democratic forces in Poland. He groused about the Soviet failure to consult with Poles other than those from the Warsaw government. He also noted that "legislative appropriation was required for any economic measures in the foreign field and that he could not hope to get these measures through Congress unless there was public support for them"—implying that Russian reluctance to play ball on the Polish question would result in an American refusal to grant the Soviet Union a postwar loan. (In January 1945 Moscow had requested a $6 billion loan to help rebuild its war-torn economy.) Truman moreover dismissed Molotov's preference for the Yugoslav precedent, demanded that Moscow carry out its agreements on Poland, and concluded that Soviet-American relations could not be conducted "on the basis of a one way street."[37]

Interpreter Charles Bohlen lavished praise on Truman's tactics: "How I enjoyed translating Truman's sentences! They were probably the first sharp words uttered during the war by an American President to a high Soviet official." Leahy, also present, found Truman's approach "more than pleasing." According to Truman, Molotov himself revealed: "I have never been talked to like that in my life." Nevertheless Truman's methods proved ineffective. At the meeting he handed Molotov a message for Stalin, making clear that he and Churchill had gone as far as they could in accommodating the Soviet leader on the Polish question. In his response the next day, Stalin unflinchingly maintained that the Polish provisional government should be based on the Warsaw Poles, and that Truman and Churchill should endorse the Yugoslav model.[38]

The setting for the discussion of the Polish question now shifted from Washington to San Francisco, where the conference to launch the United Nations opened on April 25. Here Molotov sought to obtain the admission of the Soviet republics of Ukraine and White Russia into the new organization, but Truman's representative, Stettinius, made that conditional upon Soviet cooperation on the Polish question. When Molotov argued that the Warsaw government be allowed to attend the San Francisco Conference, other delegates objected. On May 3 Molotov informed Stettinius and Clark-Kerr that sixteen Polish underground leaders had been arrested for illegal activities behind Red Army lines. The next day Stettinius and Eden agreed that talks on Poland must be suspended until their governments had received an explanation from Stalin.[39]

Along with most of his advisers, Truman soon came to view the Polish question as a symbol of the viability of a Soviet-American partnership after the war. The president had explained to Molotov in their April 22 meeting that "in its larger aspects the Polish question had become for our people the symbol of the future development of our international relations." If Stalin proved unaccommodating over Poland, thought Truman, the prospects for cordial relations between Washington and Moscow were grim. To understand why he defined Poland as *the* symbolic issue in the spring of 1945 is to identify the roots of his growing conviction that the Soviet Union was a major threat. So why was Poland of such deep importance to Truman? The question can be answered only speculatively, for Truman never elaborated.[40]

One possible explanation is economic: to prevent a postwar depression Truman sought markets, including Poland's, to absorb the wartime increase in American production. Undoubtedly Washington was determined to assume the economic leadership of the world in order to ensure free trade, equal access to raw materials, and the lowering and removal of tariffs, in line with long-established U.S. aims. Indeed the July 1944 Bretton Woods Conference, the extension in 1945 of the Reciprocal Trade Agreements Act of 1934, and, later, the American loan to Britain in exchange for the ending of the system by which goods from the British Empire were given tariff advantages over American products, were all milestones on the road to that Open Door world.[41]

But all that does not explain why Soviet control of Poland was more troubling to Truman than any other issue in the spring of 1945. The market and natural resources of Poland were not vastly more alluring than those of any other country, region, or bloc. On the contrary, if the quest for the Open Door was the key consideration, the issue of greatest symbolic importance would have been the opening of the British Empire to American trade on equal terms with the British, for this held the greatest potential for expansion of American commerce. It was no surprise, then, that while Truman and his advisers mentioned the issue of the Open Door in Poland in the spring of 1945, they did not emphasize it.

Another explanation for Truman's concern over Poland is his fear that failure to prevent Russian domination of Poland would alienate Americans of Polish descent, and this in turn would damage his prospects at the polls. For Roosevelt this had been a clear consideration. But for Truman in April 1945 the situation was quite different. Of overriding importance to him was simply coping as best he could with the many problems he suddenly faced. The last thing on his mind was winning the 1948 election, and hence the possibility of alienating the Polish constituency in the United States was not particularly important to him. Consequently Truman and his advisers did not dwell on the sensibilities of Polish Americans, though they did stress to Russian officials the relevance of the Polish question to American public opinion in general.[42]

Did Russian control of Poland offend Truman's principles, especially his commitment to self-determination? This theory does not explain why Truman regarded the fate of Poland as more important than that of other Eastern European countries, such as Romania, where signs of incipient Soviet domination were equally apparent by April 1945. Moreover the depth of Truman's commitment to self-determination as a principle of universal applicability would appear suspect given his negligible effort to pressure Britain into dismantling its gargantuan empire.[43]

A far more convincing explanation is that for Truman, the Polish question became central to his evaluation of whether Stalin would pose as great a threat to the balance of power after World War II as Adolf Hitler had before it. As the historian Gaddis Smith has argued, American officials at the time were "driven by the Ghost of Hitler." That is to say, the impact of Hitler was so profound that Truman and other U.S. officials automatically equated Stalin with Hitler, and interpreted Soviet intentions as echoes of Nazi Germany's belligerent foreign policy. This fear, and the conviction that Stalin must not be appeased as Hitler had been, toughened Washington's policy toward Moscow. U.S. Ambassador to Poland Arthur Bliss Lane expressed the view of many when he argued that "appeasement or apparent appeasement can be as dangerous to United States interests in 1945 as it actually was in 1940 and 1941."[44]

Linking the Soviet Union with Nazi Germany was the way Truman and many of his advisers conceptualized international relations in 1945. Within this framework, Poland took on special significance. German expansion during World War II had begun with the invasion of Poland. Perhaps, Truman pondered, Stalin's desire to control Poland would also be the prologue to sustained Soviet expansion. Hence the president believed that Stalin could prove he was not inspired by the same unquenchable avarice that had motivated Hitler by acting honorably on the Polish question.

Among the leading figures in the West, only Churchill, with his great powers of perspicacity, was able to articulate why the issue of Poland had acquired this significance. "Neither we nor the Americans have any military or special interest in Poland," he wrote to Stalin on April 28, 1945. "[But] we saw in the Nazi treatment of Poland a symbol of Hitler's vile and wicked lust of conquest and subjugation." Truman endorsed Churchill's message.[45]

When Truman thought of Poland in the spring of 1945, therefore, he thought of Hitler too. This explains why he regarded the Polish question as a symbol; and the accompanying belief that Stalin must not be appeased as Hitler had been in the 1930s explains why Truman was so tough over Poland in April 1945.

If the legacy of Hitler hardened Truman's response, the ghost of Franklin Roosevelt had precisely the opposite effect—and in May 1945 the influence of the latter began to dominate Truman's thinking. On becoming president, Truman had succeeded a political colossus. The only American president elected for third and fourth terms, Roosevelt had brought the United States through what were, apart from the Civil War, the greatest challenges in its history—depression and World War II. The legacy produced an obvious pressure on Truman to secure his own legitimacy by continuing FDR's policies. In foreign affairs, the hallmark of Roosevelt's approach had been a partnership with the Soviet Union against fascism. Truman believed he could not ignore this way of handling the Russians.

Samuel I. Rosenman, one of FDR's closest advisers, once recalled that Truman

was overawed, particularly at the beginning [of his presidency], about the responsibility, the authority, and most of all, the lonesomeness of the job. In addition to that, he was committed to the proposition that as long as he was President only by virtue of Roosevelt's death, and that he never would be an Acting President or President if it weren't for the fact that Roosevelt had selected him, and that Roosevelt's policies were the things which gained overwhelming approval at the polls. He was very conscious of those facts; and every time he took a step he would say to himself: "I wonder what Roosevelt would have done? Would he think this is the right thing?" You know, he had a picture on the wall of Roosevelt that he could see just by turning, and he frequently said to me, "I'm trying to do what he would like."

Joseph Grew noticed the same tendency in Truman as it related to foreign policy: the new president "felt bound by his predecessor's commitments and to a large extent by the general policy of continuing to 'get along' with our difficult ally."[46]

In addition to the pressure exerted on Truman as Roosevelt's successor, individuals dedicated to FDR sought to persuade the new president to continue Roosevelt's foreign policy. This group included Henry Stimson, Secretary of the Treasury Henry Morgenthau, Jr., Secretary of Commerce Henry Wallace—and Joseph Davies and Harry Hopkins. Davies and Hopkins, as we shall see, influenced the formulation and implementation of Truman's foreign policy in the late spring of 1945. After they departed the scene, Henry Wallace led the effort to convince Truman of the value of a close relationship with the Russians.

Truman, then, was subject to diametrically opposed forces: the legacies of Hitler and Roosevelt. While the first promoted a tougher U.S. policy toward Moscow, the second encouraged a more cooperative line. Truman's own personal instincts favored a harder line, for he brought to the presidency a deep suspicion of the Soviet Union. "Russian Godless Pervert Systems won't work," he declared on one occasion. But in the spring of 1945 he did not feel bold enough to discard Roosevelt's foreign policy by breaking permanently with Stalin. While some of Truman's advisers managed, despite contradictory pressures on American diplomacy, to support either a consistently accommodating approach toward Moscow (Davies, Hopkins, Stimson, Wallace) or a consistently uncompromising one (Grew, Forrestal, Leahy, and the influential Republican senator from Michigan, Arthur H. Vandenberg), the president did not. The result was vacillation in Truman's foreign policy in 1945—at times confrontational, at other times conciliatory. On no issue was this equivocation more apparent than the Polish question. After reading the Russians the riot act at the start of his presidency, Truman reverted for a time to a cooperative,

Rooseveltian policy. In this shift Truman was much influenced by Davies.[47]

Within three weeks of Roosevelt's death, Davies began an extensive dialogue with Truman on how best to handle Russia. The new president had wasted little time in asking Davies to visit him in order to chew the cud on international affairs, but on April 15 Davies wrote to Truman to apologize for not having taken up his invitation, as his health had been poor. He now availed his services to Truman. "The Russian situation . . . now confronts you immediately," and "there are things with which I alone am familiar, and which you are entitled to know. They would be of value to you. . . . I am at your command." Four days later, Truman replied: "As soon as you are physically able to do it, I will appreciate it very much if you will come to see me so we can discuss the Russian situation."[48]

This Davies soon did. Just out of hospital, he went to the White House on the morning of April 30. Truman opened their meeting by describing the shock of suddenly being thrust into a position of such awesome responsibility. While Truman felt well versed on domestic issues, he said, "the international situation was complex, difficult, and he wanted to get all the information he could," particularly about Russia. Davies proceeded to paint in broad brush strokes the history of wartime relations between America, Russia, and Britain, emphasizing that Stalin had trusted Roosevelt more than Churchill, partly because of the legacy of Anglo-Russian imperial rivalry. America's diplomatic role, as defined by FDR, was to mediate between Moscow and London in order to sustain the wartime alliance. "Now Roosevelt was gone," Davies warned the president, and "[the Russians] feared that this policy [of cooperation with the Soviet Union] might be changed."[49]

Included in Davies's assessment was an interpretation of the Polish question radically different from the one Truman had received from the likes of Harriman. Rather than portraying Soviet policy as expansionist, Davies argued that it was difficult for Stalin to accept an administration in Poland in which officials from the Polish government-in-exile in London were prominent because they had been members of the prewar Polish government that had hated the Soviet Union. Davies went on to emphasize the importance of Poland to Russian security: "Poland might be the corridor through which Soviet forces might have to defend themselves."[50]

Davies was unaware of the treatment meted out by Truman to Molotov on April 23. A candid Truman now filled Davies in: he might have been "too frank," as he had told Molotov "where he got off" on certain issues. When Davies showed concern, a sheepish Truman asked: "Did I do right?" The gist of Davies's answer was, no—Truman's abrasive performance might have convinced Stalin that with the death of FDR the United States had joined Britain on an anti-Russian crusade. Conciliatory perhaps to the point of disingenuity, as he often was when listening to opinions he did not altogether share, Truman thanked Davies for his honesty, saying America and Russia must "get along together" for the sake of world peace. He also asked that they talk again.[51]

What Davies attempted at this meeting, and others later, was to persuade Truman to return to Roosevelt's policy of cooperation. And he succeeded. "After an unfortunate start with Molotov," as Davies put it, "President Truman appeared to revert to the Roosevelt-Hull policy of Big Three Unity." Truman shelved the hard-line policies he had initially favored, including those on the Polish question. After refusing to accept the formation of a pro-Soviet Polish government in April, the president took steps in May which produced exactly that result. The culmination of this policy shift came when Truman sent Hopkins to Moscow to see Stalin, and dispatched Davies to London to talk with Churchill. This represented a dramatic switch in Truman's foreign policy, as he had selected precisely the people whom he knew would not adopt the same uncompromising approach he had used in his meeting with Molotov. No Truman adviser was more favorably disposed toward the Soviet Union than Davies, and Hopkins, as FDR's right-hand man, was the personification of Roosevelt's foreign policy.[52]

Davies alone did not persuade the president to change tack. Harriman, who had second thoughts after urging Truman to confront Molotov, and Bohlen also played important roles. And Truman himself was coming to doubt the wisdom of his earlier truculence. Perhaps abandoning Rooseveltian diplomacy so quickly had been too risky—and besides it had not worked. Stalin was showing no signs of shifting ground on the Polish question.

Still, the influence exerted by Davies in this period should not be underestimated. There is good reason for thinking that Truman took his advice seriously. At the time he did not view Davies, as others did, as a dangerous, pro-Soviet fanatic. On the contrary, he treated Davies respectfully. On May 21, for example, he told Davies of the atomic bomb project, a matter of such obvious delicacy that it can be safely assumed he would have confided it only to a person he trusted. Davies's insistence that he was not seeking a post in the new administration must have made Truman regard his advice as especially disinterested. It is also probable that Davies planted the seeds of the idea that he be sent to London to see Churchill. In their talk on April 30, Davies told Truman that in November 1944 FDR had asked him to undertake a mission to London to settle some differences with Churchill before the Yalta Conference, but ill health had prevented him from making the trip. In dispatching Davies to London, Truman may have thought he was carrying out Roosevelt's own plan.[53]

As Davies encouraged Truman to offer an olive branch to Stalin, Harriman and Bohlen worked to the same end by developing a plan to send Hopkins to Moscow, and then selling it to the president. FDR had been the essential reference point for Davies in his April 30 meeting with Truman, the argument being that Truman had erred by giving Molotov the impression he did not share Roosevelt's friendly attitude toward Russia. In similar fashion, Harriman and Bohlen put forward the notion of Hopkins as a nexus between the present and the Rooseveltian past.

The Harriman-Bohlen plan was hatched on May 9 during a conversation on a flight from San Francisco to Washington. As the two men contemplated the deterioration in Soviet-American relations since Yalta, Bohlen observed that "if Roosevelt were alive, he would undoubtedly think of sending Harry Hopkins to see Stalin." Harriman agreed, realizing it was an initiative Stalin would find agreeable as he had spoken of his respect for Hopkins. He had appreciated Hopkins's trip to Moscow in July 1941 while in poor health, and he was aware of the closeness of the Hopkins-Roosevelt relationship. While all this boded well for the success of a Hopkins mission to Moscow, Harriman wondered whether Hopkins would be up for such an undertaking.[54]

To find out, he went with Bohlen to visit Hopkins in the small Georgetown house he was renting. They found Hopkins in bed, desperately ill. Harriman made the case that Hopkins should see Stalin to demonstrate that Truman had not abandoned Roosevelt's policies. FDR's alter ego was buoyed by the idea: he would be happy to see Stalin.[55]

All that was required now was Truman's consent. When Harriman saw the president, he argued that Hopkins should be sent to Moscow because he was "a link between Roosevelt and Stalin." Thinking perhaps of Hopkins's health, Truman demurred, asking why Harriman himself could not undertake the trip. Hopkins would be a more suitable choice, the ambassador insisted, because he had been "very close to Roosevelt . . . [and so] would be in a better position to impress on Stalin that we intended to carry out the Roosevelt policies." Truman remained unconvinced. In a subsequent telephone conversation with Stettinius he said he was thinking of dispatching Harriman to Moscow.[56]

The president's uncertainty on this matter was evident in his meeting with Davies on May 13. Earlier that day, Davies had learned more from Supreme Court Justice Felix Frankfurter, another Roosevelt confidant, of the division within the Truman administration between hardliners and moderates such as Stimson. Frankfurter urged Davies to contact Stimson and other like-minded officials so they could coordinate their efforts at winning over Truman. Davies refused, saying he was not up to it physically, but he agreed with Frankfurter's proposal that he call the president to arrange a meeting in which he could express his concerns about Soviet-American relations. When Davies called, Truman said he should come over right away.[57]

Davies found Truman working in the Oval Office in his shirtsleeves, surrounded by papers and books that had just been unpacked. It was Mother's Day, and Truman thought Davies should meet his "Mama," a mere ninety-three years old. Davies found her to be "as bright as a squirrel." She explained that she had come "to see that 'Harry' was started right." Davies no doubt viewed the purpose of his visit in much the same way.[58]

Truman began their discussion on matters of substance by indicating his concern over relations with the Russians. After reading a letter he had written the president the preceding day calling for a policy of patience with Moscow, and then cordial correspondence he had recently exchanged with Molotov, Davies provided Truman with a detailed account of wartime relations between the Big Three, fleshing out the comments he had made in their meeting on April 30. As on that occasion, Davies's basic point was to emphasize Stalin's trust in Roosevelt.[59]

Moving on to recent events, Truman asked whether Molotov's visit had been designed to "make trouble." Davies thought not, claiming that "Molotov came over for only one purpose—to size up the situation personally, and to appraise the new President." In other words, the Russians wanted to see if American foreign policy would change now that Roosevelt was gone. Thinking out loud about his next move, Truman asked Davies to travel to Moscow to speak with Stalin, thus showing he had yet to settle on Hopkins as the man for that mission. Davies declined, saying his doctors would never allow him to go. Courteously, Truman said he wanted Davies to be a member of his "official family," to which Davies responded that he could not accept a permanent post but was prepared to "pinch hit" if required. As for what could be done to smooth Soviet-American relations, Davies said another meeting of the Big Three would be a good idea, as it would provide Truman and Stalin with an opportunity to establish a rapport. He volunteered to cable Stalin with this proposal. Truman told him to do just that.[60]

The meeting between these two Midwesterners finally drew to a close after more than six hours of discussion. Truman had been exceedingly hospitable: he had insisted that Davies have dinner with the Truman family, and to round things off the two men drank Scotch. They had both enjoyed the evening, and the conviviality of the occasion may explain in part Truman's subsequent decision to send Davies to London for talks with Churchill.[61]

The next day, May 14, Davies fired off a cable to Stalin via Molotov, as authorized by Truman. In it he asserted that "a frank, personal, heart-to-heart talk" between Truman and Stalin would clear up "many of these matters which threaten misunderstandings." Accordingly, Davies proposed another Big Three conference, adding his personal opinion that it would be beneficial for Truman and Stalin to meet without Churchill in the day or two before the conference formally began.[62]

As Stalin mulled over Davies's message, Truman was finally coming around to the idea that Hopkins was the man for the mission to Moscow, not Harriman or Davies. Although James F. Byrnes, soon to be appointed the new secretary of state, advised against sending Hopkins, Cordell Hull backed the plan—and his advice appears to have settled the matter for the president. Truman asked Hopkins to call on May 19.[63]

At that meeting Truman asked Hopkins to visit Stalin in order to settle the disagreements that had arisen over the Yalta accords. Hopkins was to inform Stalin that Truman was "anxious to have a fair understanding with the Russian Government—that we never made commitments which we did not expect to carry out to the letter—[and that] we expected him to carry his agreement out to the letter and we intended to see that he did." The president said Hopkins could use whatever approach he deemed appropriate—"a baseball bat" or "diplomatic language"—though he must have realized that Hopkins's preference would be for speaking softly. Truman concluded by instructing Hopkins to convey to Stalin his interest in a meeting, perhaps in America, as Roosevelt had already been to Yalta in the Soviet Union. Stalin would be "royally entertained" in the United States, the president promised. The only problem, he added in characteristically self-deprecating fashion, was that Stalin might be nominated for president. That very day Truman sent a message to Stalin, asking him to receive Hopkins for talks. Stalin accepted immediately.[64]

In contemplating the state of Big Three relations as he prepared for his trip to Moscow, Hopkins was no more suspicious of Stalin than he was of Churchill. In fact he told Harriman, Bohlen, and Forrestal on May 20 that he was "skeptical about Churchill, at least in the particular of [the] Anglo-American-Russian relationship . . . it was of vital importance that we not be maneuvered into a position where Great Britain had us lined up with them as a bloc against Russia to implement England's European policy." It was the comment of a man who, despite his closeness to Churchill, was as wary of British imperial traditions as of potential Soviet expansion.[65]

On the advice of his aide Stephen Early, Truman decided to complement Hopkins's mission to Moscow by dispatching Davies to London. This, the president thought, would give a pleasing symmetry to the whole enterprise: a friend of Stalin to speak with Churchill, a friend of Churchill to talk with Stalin. When Truman informed Davies of this plan at a White House meeting on May 21, Davies's initial reaction was to suggest as an alternative that Hopkins see Churchill on his way back from Moscow. Truman rejected that idea, saying this would give Stalin the unfortunate impression that Hopkins was reporting to Churchill on the talks in Moscow.[66]

The president told Davies that the main objective of his mission would be to advance preparations for another Big Three conference, and to persuade Churchill to accept the idea of a private Truman-Stalin meeting before the tripartite session began. Churchill should know, Truman further explained, that "there could be no question of any double-crossing so far as we were concerned, and [that all] he wanted [was] an opportunity to talk with Stalin to size him up, as Churchill had." Truman also told Davies that he did not wish to schedule the conference until July, by which time he hoped the testing of the atomic bomb would be completed. Implicitly Truman was saying that the atomic bomb would be a valuable diplomatic tool at the next Big Three meeting. Ignorant of the atomic project, Davies was, as he put it in his journal, "startled, shocked and amazed" by the information about this new weapon.[67]

At Truman's insistence, Davies and Hopkins met for lunch on May 22 to exchange ideas before leaving for Europe. Hopkins told Davies that he would emphasize to Stalin how American public opinion had been adversely affected by recent developments in the Polish controversy, particularly the Russian arrest of the underground leaders. While this would be worthwhile, Davies agreed, Hopkins's main objective should be to convince the Russians that "they could safely trust us [the United States and Britain] not to doublecross or 'gang up' on them." Hopkins said he thought that was probably right. Hopkins would find Stalin "very direct and effective," Davies predicted, "if he believed you were on the level." So the important thing for Hopkins was to be candid and forthright. For his part, Hopkins warned Davies that Churchill was likely to "blow off" and give him "an earful." Davies would need to listen patiently, and be firm. The prime minister, Hopkins felt, was "big enough" to understand the need for a Truman-Stalin meeting before the opening of the next Big Three conference. Equipped with each other's advice, Davies and Hopkins parted.[68]

The next day the White House released a statement announcing the Hopkins-Davies missions. On the eve of this enterprise, Truman was positive about its prospects. He told Stettinius of his "great confidence that Harry would be able to straighten things out with Stalin. . . . He had hopes now that the Hopkins mission was going to unravel a great many things and that by the time he met with the Big Three that most of our troubles would be out of the way."[69]

Hopkins left Washington on May 23, arriving in Paris the next day. After meeting with Harriman, he lunched with Gen. Dwight Eisenhower, before departing for Moscow. Flying over the war-ravaged landscape of Germany with his wife, Bohlen, and Harriman, Hopkins landed in Moscow on the evening of May 25. Harriman immediately arranged a Kremlin meeting with Stalin for the following evening.[70]

Davies, meanwhile, was making the more picturesque journey to London. Leaving Washington on the morning of Thursday, May 24, his plane arrived that afternoon in Goose Bay, Labrador, where twenty-foot snowdrifts had not melted. Continuing on during a beautiful, clear night, Davies and his party flew over Donegal Bay, then the hills and valleys of Wales, before landing at Bodvington Airfield in England. Commander Thomas, a special assistant to the prime minister, greeted Davies with the news that Churchill was in conference and would call later. That Churchill did, inviting Davies to Chequers, his country seat, for the weekend. Having spent the past month trying to influence Truman's handling of Churchill and Stalin, Davies now had the opportunity to implement the president's foreign policy himself.[71]

CHAPTER 2

Talking with Churchill and Stalin

—

"[Stalin] gives the impression of a strong mind
which is composed and wise. His brown eye is
exceedingly kindly and gentle. A child would like
to sit in his lap and a dog would sidle up to him. It
is difficult to associate his personality and this
impression of kindness and gentle simplicity with
what has occurred here in connection with these
purges and shootings of the Red Army generals,
and so forth."—JOSEPH DAVIES, letter to his
daughter, 1936

JOSEPH DAVIES drove to Chequers on a rainy Saturday afternoon
with the U.S. Ambassador to Britain, John G. Winant. He was greeted
by Churchill's daughter and son-in-law, and by some of the prime minister's aides, but not by Churchill himself, who had called a general
election and was spending the day campaigning in his constituency.
Shortly after Davies's arrival, Churchill burst in with his wife. The
group chatted around the fireplace, and then Churchill showed Davies
to his room. After dinner, with Davies seated next to Churchill, a few
short films were shown for the entertainment of the group. It was not

until 11 p.m. that Churchill and Davies moved to the prime minister's library for talk.[1]

This first Churchill-Davies meeting proved to be a bruising encounter. Both men were passionate, frank, and combative. Davies began by conveying a message from Truman to the prime minister: the president was worried by the growth of tensions in recent weeks between Moscow, London, and Washington. To compose these differences, another Big Three meeting was imperative. There the Russians could be disabused of the idea Truman suspected they had developed—that the British and Americans were beginning to "gang up" on them. If Truman and Stalin could meet first, before being joined by Churchill, this might have the desired effect.[2]

The prime minister's initial response to this proposal seemed tolerant. During the course of the discussion, however, he turned savagely against it. He claimed to be "surprised and hurt" by the idea that Britain be excluded from the first meeting with the Soviet leader after the victory over Germany. That was a shoddy way for the United States to treat a faithful ally. He could never agree to a plan that implied that a Soviet-American deal was to be made behind British backs. At that provocative statement, Davies rose, moved to the fireplace, and declared that although he was a guest in Churchill's house, he "could not do other than resent such an imputation as to the President of the United States." Sensing he had gone too far, Churchill declared he was only thinking of the impression that Truman's plan would make on public opinion.[3]

But the prime minister would not change the position he had now taken. As he put it in his memoirs, "I would not agree in any circumstances to what seemed to be an affront, however unintentional, to our country after its faithful service in the cause of freedom from the first day of the war." Once the three leaders arrived they would be at liberty to arrange informal meetings at the start of the conference in any binary combination they desired. But there could be no formal talks from which the British were excluded.[4]

Continuing to spar, Davies noted that Churchill was a natural thespian. He showed "all the flashes of his great genius," the envoy wrote in his diary, "change of pace, from humor to seriousness; from high indignation to impulsive and generous graciousness." Davies was struck by the way a sense of control underpinned all of Churchill's emotional vicissitudes.[5]

Beyond the issue of the next Big Three conference, the conversation was dominated by a sharp exchange over the Russians. Churchill depicted Moscow's foreign policy in the darkest hues: Stalin's occupation policies in liberated areas were unacceptable as communism was being imposed on these countries, and with it the nefarious aspects of the Soviet system—secret police forces and Gestapo tactics. In a variation on the phrase he would later popularize, he spoke of a "steel curtain" being "clamped down" on Eastern Europe. Exploring the implications of the situation, Churchill suggested that American troops must remain in Europe after the war, otherwise the continent would be vulnerable to invasion by the Red Army. Moreover it was vital that those U.S. forces which had advanced more than a hundred miles east of the agreed-upon line for the American occupation zone in Germany not withdraw. They would be a useful bargaining chip in dealings with the Russians.[6]

Appalled by these comments about Soviet policy, Davies replied by reminding Churchill of the hostility that the Soviet government had endured from the international community in the years between the two world wars: Churchill's support for intervention in the Russian Civil War in an attempt to quash the Bolshevik Revolution; the Anglo-American delay during World War II in opening a second front in the west to alleviate Nazi pressure on the Soviet Union. Davies went so far as to compare Churchill's anti-Soviet diatribe to the "doctrine . . . [of] Hitler and Goebbels." The nub of Davies's argument was that the prime minister's distrust of Stalin was, first of all, dangerous because it threatened the Big Three unity upon which postwar peace depended; and, second, unwarranted because as a general rule the Russians had acted in good faith. As for Churchill's proposals on American troops in Europe, Davies thought them impractical. U.S. forces would have to retire to their occupation zone, and the weight of American public opinion would prevent the long-term deployment of U.S. forces in Europe. The issue of Russian trustworthiness was one on which Churchill and Davies would have to agree to disagree.[7]

Their views were also diametrically opposed on the Polish question. Davies spoke of the disappointment among Soviet leaders over

> the attitude of Britain and the U.S. in failing to recognize the reasonableness, justice, and fairness of the Soviet position as to Poland, when there would be no Poland at all, except for the power of the Russian army; [and] of their feeling that they had not received the same consideration in the Polish matter from their Allies which they had extended, even as against their convictions, in "going along" with Britain and the U.S. in the recognition of Vichy in Africa, Badoglio and the King in Italy, and the domination of Britain in Greece.

This was a view Churchill could not endorse.[8]

During their discussion the prime minister fortified himself with a brandy. After Davies's stinging criticisms, he no doubt needed one. For his part, the frail envoy drank a special chemical soup. As Churchill reflected on their meeting, he thought it best if they exchanged memoranda detailing their opposing views or sent a joint telegram to Truman. Davies said either arrangement would be acceptable.[9]

After five and a half hours of conversation, both men were ready to call it a night. Escorting Davies to his bedroom door, Churchill said he had enjoyed conversing with someone "with so remarkable and unusual a perspective on events." Davies took it as a compliment, but it was clearly tinged with sarcasm. "Goodnight," Churchill added, "to the great American Envoy." "Goodnight to you, Sir," reciprocated Davies, "the greatest Englishman of all time, who lived what Shakespeare dreamed, and who translated into deeds what England's greatest had taught." A little after 4:30 a.m. Davies climbed into a four-poster bed and, as he put it in a letter to his wife Marjorie, "sank into sleep 'four fathoms deep.'"[10]

Rising at 10 a.m., Davies ate breakfast before going in his dressing gown to the prime minister's room. Churchill, who had evidently enjoyed the sleep of the just, was sitting up in bed, reading cables. He appeared to Davies "as bright as a button. I must have looked like the wrath of God. He didn't even have a wrinkle"—a testament, no doubt, to the therapeutic properties of alcohol and cigars. Davies noticed that

Churchill was "still irked and troubled," reflecting once again on the Russian threat to Europe, and the folly of withdrawing American troops from the continent.[11]

When Davies left Churchill's room for lunch, he was not joined by the prime minister for another hour. Unbeknownst to Davies, an exasperated Churchill had called his foreign secretary to tell him of his talks with Davies, including his violent opposition to Davies's proposal for a preliminary Truman-Stalin meeting at the next Big Three conference. Davies, Eden recorded, had plainly "made an unfavourable impression" on the prime minister. The foreign secretary told Churchill that Davies was nothing but "a vain amateur" who might well have transmitted Truman's message inaccurately. Churchill asked Eden to meet with Davies so that he could make his own assessment of the American envoy. Eden agreed.[12]

By the time Churchill joined his wife, Davies, the Duke of Westminster, and other guests for lunch, his equanimity had not been restored. Once again he railed against the Russian menace. Davies decided to bite his tongue this time, as others were present. But he was profoundly concerned. He felt certain reports of Churchill's anti-Soviet statements would find their way back to Russian officials. Davies could account for the prime minister's behavior only by considering the upcoming general election in Britain. Perhaps Churchill wished to generate a Red Scare in order to win, highlighting the Communist threat abroad in order to discredit the Labour party at home.[13]

Lunch was followed by photographs in the garden, after which prime minister and envoy became embroiled in yet another argument over the Russians, this one lasting an hour. They agreed to meet again, however, this time at Downing Street.[14]

The Chequers talks between Churchill and Davies produced no meeting of minds. In retrospect, this was inevitable, for their views on the Soviet Union differed sharply. While Churchill was deeply suspicious, Davies was, to put it charitably, well disposed. Put more bluntly, he was naive, even foolish about the reality of Stalin's Russia. Davies's observations were not entirely fanciful. A number of the factors he cited in explaining why Stalin had good reason to be suspicious of the Western powers were valid. In suggesting that postwar Russian influence in

Eastern Europe was probably inevitable, the American envoy was being realistic. The inconsistency in Davies's outlook, however—and the reason why Churchill was justified in feeling vexed—was that it involved a deep appreciation of Soviet fears but an almost total absence of understanding of British concerns. As Churchill pointed out in a memorandum he wrote on May 27, "The freedom, independence, and sovereignty of Poland was a matter for which the British people went to war, ill-prepared as they were. It has now become a matter of honour with the nation and Empire."[15]

On Monday, May 28, Davies went for lunch at Eden's apartment on the top floor of the Foreign Office. Churchill had wanted Davies to repeat to the foreign secretary the arguments he had made over the weekend. When the American envoy proceeded to do just that, Eden emphasized that the idea of Truman and Stalin negotiating without Churchill present was unacceptable. Realizing that the British would not yield on this matter, Davies now requested that the plan for an exchange of memoranda or a joint telegram to Truman be scrapped, thereby affording him the opportunity to explain to the president in person the outcome of his mission. This, Davies probably calculated, would enable him to put a favorable gloss on his trip to London.[16]

Davies was happy with his talk with Eden, whom he found charming and fair-minded. But Davies's sentiments were not reciprocated. "My impression was not more favourable than the Prime Minister's," Eden said of his lunch with the envoy.[17]

The next Churchill-Davies meeting had been scheduled for that evening, but business in the House of Commons caused it to be postponed until the following day. This change of plan allowed Davies to take up an offer of supper from the Lord Privy Seal, Max Beaverbrook. After failing to convince Churchill and Eden to view Soviet policy with less suspicion, the talk with Beaverbrook provided a much needed fillip. British distrust of Russia had been on the rise, Beaverbrook reported, and hence Davies's visit had been to the good, as "there can be no peace without Russia in it."[18]

His morale thus boosted, Davies called at the Foreign Office the following morning, Tuesday, May 29, for a second meeting with Eden. The foreign secretary reported that he and Churchill could accept

Davies's proposal that the plan for an exchange of aide-mémoire or a telegram to Truman be shelved. Once again the two men came away with very different perceptions of their encounter. Davies thought Eden had been "tolerant and fair and disposed to agree with my point of view. . . . It was an interesting discussion." He could not have been more wrong. In his diary, a disenchanted Eden wrote: "Further long talk with Davies. It didn't amount to more than an appeal for Russia. He is the born appeaser and would gladly give Russia all Europe, except perhaps us, so that America might not be embroiled. All the errors and illusions of Neville C[hamberlain]., substituting Russia for Germany."[19]

Davies now went to 10 Downing Street for his final meeting with Churchill. Before a coal fire in a small sitting room, the two protagonists reiterated the arguments they had made over the weekend. Their differences remained, but at least Churchill was in a better frame of mind. Once again Davies was impressed by the prime minister. "He is sui generis, among the great men I have known," Davies wrote the next day. While he admired Churchill's personal gifts, he was less enthusiastic about the ends to which he used them. "Above all he is first, last, and all the time an Englishman. England and the Empire, is I believe, more to him than either Peace or the Rights of Humanity or the World."[20]

At the close of their discussion, Churchill insisted on accompanying Davies through the corridors to the outer door of the annex to 10 Downing Street, along the way observing that the paintings on the walls were his own handiwork. On reaching Davies's car, they bid farewell.[21]

On May 30 Davies saw Soviet Ambassador to Britain Fedor Gusef to emphasize the importance he attached to Big Three unity, and then drove through and was moved by the devastated area around St. Paul's Cathedral. The following morning he took a flight from London to Frankfurt for talks with Dwight Eisenhower, then moved on to Paris before departing for Washington. He arrived back in the nation's capital on Sunday, June 3.[22]

Davies's mission demonstrated the change in Truman's foreign policy since late April. Initially the new president had been tougher with the Russians than had his predecessor, particularly on the Polish question. This aligned Washington solidly with London, as Churchill had been urging FDR to confront Stalin over Poland. By reverting to a more accommodating, Rooseveltian approach in May and June, and by enlisting the services of an FDR devotee like Davies, Truman reestablished the gap that had existed between the foreign policies of Britain and the United States in Roosevelt's final days. The Americans once again were prepared to compromise with Stalin to an extent that Churchill thought undesirable. Of course these Anglo-American differences appeared especially great during the talks between Churchill and Davies because of the envoy's distinctive representation of the U.S. position. In other words, his gloss on Truman's foreign policy was more sympathetic to the Russians than it would have been if the president had presented the administration's case. Nevertheless Truman was interested at this point in papering over the differences between Moscow on the one hand and Washington and London on the other in a way that Churchill was not.

The Churchill-Davies talks had centered on relations with Russia in general rather than on Poland in particular. That thorny issue was a focus of the discussions between Stalin and Truman's second envoy, Harry Hopkins. These Moscow meetings proved crucial in ending the impasse over the Polish question—but the progress was the result of American concessions rather than reciprocal compromise. It was not a matter of cynicism or naiveté on Hopkins's part. He believed the democratic rights of Poles to be important, and he harbored no illusions about Stalin's commitment to a free and independent Poland. More likely Hopkins suspected, as Roosevelt had, that tolerating a Russian sphere of influence in Eastern Europe, at least in the short term, was needed to preserve Big Three unity while the war was still on, and to increase the chances for postwar peace and stability.

The first meeting between Stalin and Hopkins, who were assisted by Molotov and Harriman, took place in the Kremlin on the evening of May 26. In his opening presentation on recent developments in Soviet-American relations, Hopkins highlighted the role played by public opinion in the United States. A few months earlier, Hopkins explained, there had been strong support among the American people for

FDR's policy of supporting the Soviet Union. But public opinion had begun to turn against the Russians during the past six weeks. This had disturbed Truman, who wished "to continue President Roosevelt's policy of working with the Soviet Union."[23]

In identifying the reasons for this alarming shift in public sentiment, Hopkins emphasized "our inability to carry into effect the Yalta Agreement on Poland." That, Stalin interjected, was not the fault of Russia, which wanted "to have a friendly Poland," but of a British government intent on reviving "the system of *cordon sanitaire* on the Soviet border." In the conciliatory fashion that would be the hallmark of his approach to these Moscow talks, Hopkins assured Stalin that "neither the Government nor the people of the United States had any such intention," and that the Truman administration wanted "a Poland friendly to the Soviet Union and in fact desired to see friendly countries all along the Soviet borders." "If that be so," Stalin commented, "we can easily come to terms in regard to Poland."[24]

Hopkins then introduced the other issues he wished to explore with Stalin in their talks: the upcoming Berlin conference, establishment of a control council for Germany, and Soviet entry into the war against Japan. He added that he would be happy to address any matters of concern to Stalin. The Soviet leader said there would be several. Toward the end of this discussion, Harriman explained to Stalin the significance of Truman's selection of Hopkins as envoy. Hopkins, as Stalin knew, "had not only been very close to President Roosevelt but personally was one of the leading proponents of the policy of cooperation with the Soviet Union." In other words, Harriman was saying, Truman had chosen Hopkins as a gesture of goodwill to the Russians and as a sign that FDR's friendly approach had not been abandoned.[25]

In their second meeting the following evening, May 27, Hopkins asked Stalin to identify the issues that troubled him. Candidly, the Soviet leader claimed that the American attitude toward the Russians had cooled once victory against Germany had drawn near, as indicated by the invitation of Argentina to the San Francisco Conference, the abrupt termination of Lend Lease aid to the Soviet Union, and U.S. handling of the Polish question. Stalin said he was worried by Washington's refusal to accept what was patently clear from the Yalta agreement on Poland, that "the present government was to form the basis of the new."[26]

"The question of Poland per se," Hopkins explained, "was not so important as the fact that it had become a symbol of our ability to work out problems with the Soviet Union." He assured Stalin that Washington had "no special interests in Poland and no special desire to see any particular kind of government," and "would accept any government in Poland which was desired by the Polish people and was at the same time friendly to the Soviet Government." Hopkins did not broach the problem inherent in this view, namely that a democratically created Polish government might well be hostile to the Russians. He went on to say that the Truman administration and the American people suspected the Soviet Union of trying to reestablish Poland with the help of the Warsaw government but without the involvement of the United States. Accordingly he asked Stalin to "put his mind to the task of thinking up what diplomatic methods could be used to settle this question, keeping in mind the feeling of the American people."[27]

A disingenuous Stalin declared that he had no intention of interfering in Polish internal affairs or of excluding American participation. He asked Hopkins to take into account Soviet security interests in Poland. "In the course of twenty-five years the Germans had twice invaded Russia via Poland," he observed. "Neither the British nor American people had experienced such German invasions which were a horrible thing to endure and the results of which were not easily forgotten." Hence the postwar Polish government would have to be friendly to its Russian neighbors.[28]

To speed a solution to the Polish problem, Stalin recommended that the procedural issue of *how* to set up the new provisional government be bypassed. Instead he and Hopkins would simply decide to include four or five non-Communist officials in a Polish government that would comprise eighteen or twenty members. After consulting Molotov, Stalin said the number would have to be four, as this was the maximum acceptable to the Warsaw Poles.[29]

Here Stalin offered nothing new. Under his plan, the new Polish government would be roughly three-quarters Communist, one-quarter non-Communist. Once more, this was the Polish question settled according to the Yugoslav model, which had been his post-Yalta position all along. Hopkins said he would need time to ponder Stalin's proposal.[30]

Perhaps because Stalin looked to circumvent the procedural issue raised at Yalta, Hopkins was wary. In reporting to Truman, he said he would try to get Stalin to clarify his position. "Under any circumstances," he warned, "I am sure that the Polish matter cannot be settled while I am here." As things turned out, it was not—but the search for an agreement was greatly advanced.[31]

That Hopkins was willing to go a long way in meeting Stalin's demands on Poland was clear from a discussion he held around this time with George Kennan, at this time still a relative unknown on the American embassy staff in Moscow but only months away from becoming one of America's most revered thinkers on foreign affairs. Invited to Spaso House, the American embassy, to offer Hopkins his opinion on Stalin's proposal for a Polish settlement, Kennan said it was the best deal that could be extracted from the Russians. But he did not think the proposal should be accepted, as the Truman administration should not be saddled with any sense of shared responsibility for whatever Stalin planned to do in Poland. "Then you think it's sin," Hopkins interjected, "and we should be agin it." "That's just about right," Kennan replied. "I respect your opinion," Hopkins responded. "But I am not at liberty to accept it."[32]

On May 30 Stalin and Hopkins once again put their heads together on the Polish question. Hopkins spelled out what the United States meant by democracy in Poland: freedom of speech and religion, the right of public trial and habeas corpus, and freedom of political expression for all nonfascist parties, among other things. But he also sought to allay Stalin's concerns. As he had explained in their earlier meetings, the United States opposed the imposition of a cordon sanitaire around the Soviet Union and would work for a Polish government friendly to Moscow. There were fresh assurances too. Washington had "no economic interests of substantial importance in Poland," Hopkins said. And he went on to concede what had never before been acknowledged by American officials, that "President Roosevelt and now President Truman had always anticipated that the members of the present Warsaw regime would constitute a *majority* of the new Polish Provisional Government. He said he wished to state that without equivocation." In fact, however, Truman had earlier avoided judgment on the matter in order to uphold the Yalta agreement, which declared that the Moscow commission should make this determination in consultation with Polish leaders, and had rejected a Yugoslav model that would give Communists a decisive majority in the new Polish government.[33]

After offering these olive branches, Hopkins made a specific proposal: he and Stalin should discuss the names of eight or ten Poles to be invited to the Moscow commission for discussions leading to the establishment of a new provisional government. In effect Hopkins was sidestepping Stalin's May 27 recommendation that they decide for themselves the composition of the Polish government. Stalin agreed, and he and Hopkins and Harriman then began to discuss the Poles to be brought to Moscow. Stalin said that apart from officials of the Warsaw government, eight Poles should be invited—five from Poland, three from London. In the report he sent Truman that evening, Hopkins described the progress as "encouraging. It looks as though Stalin is prepared to return to and implement the Crimea [Yalta] decision and permit a representative group of Poles to come to Moscow to consult with the Commission."[34]

At a Kremlin meeting the next day, Hopkins presented a list of the Poles to be invited to Moscow. It included three from London (among them Mikolajczyk) and five from Poland who were not in the Warsaw government, in addition to the Warsaw Poles. On Stalin's behalf, Molotov proposed a different list, though of the same numerical composition. Hopkins asked for time to consider this proposal and confer with Washington.[35]

Hopkins then raised the issue that had caused so much controversy at the San Francisco Conference: the fate of the sixteen arrested Polish underground leaders. This matter plainly worried Hopkins, calling into question Stalin's sense of fair play; and he proceeded to tell Stalin that the episode had sparked concern among the American public and contributed to recent tensions in Soviet-American relations. Stalin countered that these Poles had committed crimes against the Red Army, and that "any government would have taken the same course as had the Soviet Government." When Hopkins asked whether all the men were charged with the same offense, Stalin advised they were not. Some had merely operated illegal radio transmitters, others had committed more serious crimes. That being the case, argued Hopkins, could not Stalin at least release those charged with minor offenses to ensure that this matter did not impede progress on the central issue of the Poles to be brought to the Moscow commission. Hopkins's request hinted at a threat. A refusal to release any of the arrested leaders could result in a U.S. decision to reject the Russian list of Poles to be invited to Moscow. Seeing where Hopkins was headed, Stalin said he did not see the connection between the two issues. While "it might be possible to treat them [the arrested Poles] with leniency . . . they would have to stand trial."[36]

Reporting this exchange, Hopkins urged Truman to accept Stalin's proposal on the Poles to be brought to Moscow, as "it carries out the Yalta Agreement in all its essential aspects." He conveyed his concerns about the arrested Poles, pledging to pressure Stalin to promise an amnesty for those charged merely with operating illegal radio transmitters. Hopkins also declared his intention to use the quid pro quo he had suggested earlier. He would tell Stalin that fair treatment of those charged with minor offenses would enhance the chances of acceptance of his list of Poles from the United States, Britain, and Mikolajczyk.[37]

Hopkins's opportunity to do just that came at the dinner given by Stalin in the envoy's honor in the Kremlin's Catherine the Great ballroom on the night of June 1. It appears that the Soviet leadership had in mind a male-bonding, alcohol-imbibing evening, as Harriman's and Hopkins's wives received rather curious invitations saying they could come "if they wanted to." In apparent deference to the female presence, the vodka bottles were removed from the table early in the evening. With forty guests seated around one long table, Molotov supplied the toasts. At the end of the dinner the Russian hosts played a newsreel of the May Day parade. When Harriman spoke of his admiration for a particular horse shown in the footage, Stalin announced that he would like to give the ambassador two Russian horses. A few days later the Harrimans received photographs of the two horses they would soon receive.[38]

After these festivities, Hopkins managed to have a private word with Stalin about the arrested-Poles issue. As he had promised Truman, he told Stalin that "we would have no great difficulty with getting the [Soviet] list approved of names who might come to Moscow to consult with the Moscow Commission, if this business could be settled." He urged the release of those charged with minor offenses, maintaining that "our whole relationship was threatened by the impasse over Poland." But neither Hopkins's forceful approach nor the evening's conviviality diminished Stalin's resolve. His position remained the same as the day before: all the arrested Poles would be tried, though the men accused of the more trivial crimes could expect lenient treatment.[39]

Truman, meanwhile, was in excellent spirits. Concerned less with the issue of the arrested Poles, he had been thrilled to learn that Stalin had produced a list of Poles for consultation that was acceptable to Hopkins. Accordingly, on June 1 he approved the list in a telephone conversation with Hopkins. Truman wrote to Churchill the same day, requesting his endorsement of the list, as "this represents a very encouraging positive step in the long drawn-out Polish negotiations." He also asked the prime minister to seek Mikolajczyk's approval of the Poles to be invited. Although suggesting modifications, Mikolajczyk accepted the Hopkins-Stalin proposal.[40]

Indicative of Hopkins's accommodating approach to the negotiations in Moscow was the fact that by June 3 he had concluded that American acceptance of the list of Poles should not be made conditional on equitable Soviet treatment of the arrested underground leaders. He advised Truman to adopt the same position. The president consented, though he instructed Hopkins to continue to do all he could for the arrested Poles.[41]

Churchill accepted the Hopkins-Stalin deal on the Poles to be brought to Moscow for consultation—but without enthusiasm. "Hopkins' devoted efforts have produced a break in the deadlock," the prime minister acknowledged in a June 4 message to Truman. Churchill went on, however, to present the president with a realistic appraisal of what this meant in terms of overall progress on the Polish question:

> While it is prudent and right to act in this way at this moment [i.e., to accept the Hopkins-Stalin list of Poles] I am sure you will agree with me that these proposals are no advance on Yalta. They are an advance upon the deadlock, but we ought by now, according to Yalta and its spirit, to have had a representative Polish Government formed. All we have got is a certain number of concessions for outside Poles to take part in the preliminary discussions, out of which hopeful improvements in the Lublin Government may be made. I cannot feel therefore that we can regard this as more than a milestone in a long hill we ought never to have been asked to climb. I think that we ought to guard against any newspaper assumptions that the Polish problem has been solved, or that difficulties between the Western democracies and the Soviet Government on this matter have been more than relieved. Renewed hope and no rejoicing is all we can indulge in at the moment.

Churchill's somber view of the Moscow talks was warranted. Hopkins and Stalin had settled neither of the two principal issues raised by the Yalta Declaration on Poland: the establishment of a provisional government more representative than the Warsaw administration, and the holding of free elections. Agreement had been achieved only on the process by which the first of those goals could be reached.[42]

At their final Kremlin meeting on June 6, Hopkins and Stalin agreed to exact terms on the Poles to be invited to Moscow. The identity of one of the London Poles was left unresolved, but otherwise loose ends were tied. Hopkins again emphasized the importance of the arrested-Poles issue to American public opinion, saying he hoped that Stalin "could find his own way to accommodate this feeling and take it into consideration." Without committing himself, Stalin merely stated that he would take Hopkins's observations "fully into consideration."[43]

The two men discussed a range of other issues during the meeting. Toward the end, Hopkins thanked Stalin for "the many kindnesses and courtesies" he and his wife had received while in Moscow, and said their stay had been "a great pleasure." "Our two countries had so much in common that they could find a way to work out their problems," Hopkins added, and the Moscow meetings had "left him with renewed assurances on that point."[44]

After leaving Moscow on June 7, Hopkins stopped in a few European cities before heading home. In Berlin he visited Hitler's office in the Chancellery and surveyed the destruction caused by the bombing of the city. Meeting with Dwight Eisenhower in Frankfurt, Hopkins summarized his talks with Stalin and discussed the Big Three conference set for Berlin. Following his discussion with Eisenhower, Hopkins concluded that Truman should reject Churchill's proposal that Allied troops who had advanced into the Soviet sector in Germany remain there as a bargaining chip for negotiations with the Russians. Accepting Hopkins's advice, Truman informed Churchill of his decision on this matter. Hopkins arrived back in Washington on June 12, having acquired a viral infection en route. In newsreels of his return to the United States, his appearance was shocking.[45]

General enthusiasm for the results of the Hopkins-Stalin talks, among both administration officials and the American public, must have been a source of solace for the emaciated envoy upon his return. "Harry's visit has been more successful than I had hoped," Harriman told Truman. "The task assigned to you . . . has been gloriously fulfilled for the benefit not only of this nation, but the whole world," enthused one of the many letters of congratulations received by Hopkins. Max Beaverbrook praised him even more ecstatically: "You are the greatest diplomat of our age."[46]

On June 13 Truman received reports from Hopkins and Davies in person. By this time Davies had been back in Washington for ten days, had spoken with the president and several other officials, and had produced both a short and a long report on his discussions with Churchill and Eden. When Davies joined Truman for breakfast on the 13th on the south portico of the White House, overlooking the Jefferson and Washington memorials, he found the president "looking very well— keen and fit." They were joined a few minutes later by Hopkins and Admiral Leahy. Truman was in good spirits. "He had cured two invalids," he joked. "He was afraid that he might have killed them off; but he found he had cured them."[47]

In their reports Hopkins and Davies covered a range of issues, including the upcoming Berlin conference, China, and the UN. On the Polish question, Hopkins told Truman that the stalemate had ended. A statement inviting the agreed-upon list of Poles to the Moscow commission had been released the day before. Hence a settlement to the Polish problem was "in the works."[48]

After breakfast Truman, Leahy, and the two envoys went to the Oval Office for pictures. A group of photographers came and went. Later in the morning the president held a press conference at which he made a statement on the Hopkins-Davies missions and fielded questions. Truman described the results of their meetings with Stalin and Churchill as "completely satisfactory and gratifying."[49]

If Truman anticipated an easy ride from the press corps on the Polish question, he was to be sorely disappointed. With clinical efficiency, the journalists hit all the vulnerable areas in Truman's position. What about the Poles who had been arrested? They had not been released, the president acknowledged, but "every effort" was being made on their behalf. Since Stettinius had asserted at the San Francisco Conference that negotiations leading to a new Polish government had to be postponed until the arrested-Poles issue had been resolved, had the position of the U.S. government changed? It had been "modified," Truman conceded. Had "there been any change in American policy which has caused the Russians to change their position on the Polish issue"? There had not, Truman insisted. Instead, "There has been a very pleasant yielding on the part of the Russians to some of the things in which we are interested."[50]

As the probing on Poland persisted, an exasperated Truman gave the press a piece of his mind: "What we are trying to do is to get the situation worked out that has been causing us a lot of embarrassment. And for God's sake, don't you go muddying it all up so as to make it worse! . . . don't upset the applecart. Say we have made some progress and that I believe that we can get results that will do what we want, which is a free Polish Government." The president clearly wanted the press to lavish praise on his Hopkins-Davies initiative.[51]

Whatever the limits of their accomplishments, Truman's two emissaries had made progress toward a resolution of the Polish issue—Hopkins by securing an agreement with Stalin on the Poles to be brought to Moscow, Davies by impressing on Churchill the determination of the Truman administration to sustain its partnership with the Soviet Union for at least a while longer, regardless of British reservations. The momentum generated by the Hopkins-Davies missions bore fruit during the next three weeks. On June 16 those Poles invited to Moscow began discussing the composition of the Polish provisional government, reaching an agreement that was reported to the commission five days later. The president of the Presidium, in which sovereignty technically rested, was to be the Communist leader Boleslaw Bierut, though three non-Warsaw Poles were to be included. But of the twenty positions in the executive, where real power would lay, only six were to be held by non-Communists. In other words, the new Polish administration was to be formed on essentially the same basis as the Yugoslav government, three-quarters Communist and one-quarter non-Communist—the model previously described by Truman as unacceptable. In addition to their numerical superiority in the new government, Communists were to provide the minister for internal security, a crucial position which controlled the secret police. They would also run the army.[52]

In reporting these arrangements to Washington, Harriman confessed that they had been made because "all the non-Lublin Poles are so concerned over the present situation in Poland that they are ready to accept any compromise which gives some hope for Polish independence and individual freedom." Still, Harriman was "much relieved" that a deal had been struck and saw "no reason why we should not accept it." Both Truman and the State Department thought likewise, enabling the Moscow commission to release on June 23 a communiqué describing the composition of the new Polish provisional government.[53]

As this agreement was being forged, the sixteen arrested Polish underground leaders went on trial in Moscow. Of the sixteen, one was released, three were acquitted, and twelve were found guilty and sentenced to imprisonment for terms ranging from four months to ten years. Hopkins's plea to Stalin for leniency may have had some impact on the sentencing of these Poles, but it was marginal at best.[54]

Despite this disappointment, the final establishment of a new Polish administration went forward. The Polish prime minister Edward B. Osobka-Morawski announced that the provisional government had been formed on the basis of the Moscow commission's recommendations, and so requested American recognition. With the encouragement of Grew and Harriman, Truman decided to grant it. He suggested to Churchill that they recognize the Polish government on July 3. The prime minister asked for a twenty-four-hour delay to give the London government-in-exile time to arrange its own dissolution. Truman thought this was not appropriate because it would clash with American Independence Day (perhaps an implicit acknowledgment that the new Polish government, heavily weighted in favor of pro-Soviet Poles, was hardly that of an independent nation). Hence Truman and Churchill extended recognition to the Polish provisional government on July 5, 1945.[55]

After this the Polish question moved to the back burner in Soviet-American relations. Although the Yalta Declaration provided that the new Polish administration should hold free elections, the problem of establishing the provisional government had become for American officials the Polish question in itself. While the Yalta agreement had provided for an American role, as a member of the Moscow commission, in the creation of the provisional government, no similar U.S. involvement in the holding of free elections had been stipulated.

At the Potsdam Conference in the summer of 1945, the American delegation extracted a vacuous commitment that the Polish government would hold free elections. But there was no reference in the official protocol to Soviet responsibility for these elections. After Potsdam the Truman administration continued to call for free elections in Poland, but to no avail. By the second half of 1945 the Polish question was no longer the issue that defined and symbolized Soviet-American discord. It was rapidly superseded by a number of other problems, such as the need to establish the Romanian, Bulgarian, and Italian peace treaties, the issue of international control of atomic energy, and the reconstruction of postwar Germany.[56]

Truman's handling of the Polish question suggests that at the start of his presidency he neither completely reversed nor dutifully continued Franklin Roosevelt's conciliatory approach to the Russians. Rather, he vacillated between those two alternatives. Implementing a new, tougher policy in April, exemplified by his stormy encounter with Molotov, he shifted to a far more accommodating approach in May, resulting in the Hopkins-Davies missions. Truman did stiffen American policy when he concluded at the start of 1946 that the Soviet Union was incorrigibly aggressive and that the United States needed therefore to oppose Moscow at every juncture. But in 1945 he was not yet confident enough to stamp his personal imprint on American foreign policy. Shaped by the conflicting legacies of Hitler and Roosevelt—that of FDR championed by Hopkins and Davies—Truman's diplomacy was characterized at first by uncertainty rather than coherence.

As the Polish controversy subsided, Davies and Hopkins departed the scene. Davies was a minor member of the American delegation at Potsdam. But his influence was on the wane, especially when in early 1946 Truman decided to abandon altogether the conciliatory policies toward the Russians that Davies had been promoting. Never again did he have the sort of access to or influence over Truman that he had enjoyed in the spring of 1945.[57]

On July 2, 1945, Hopkins, exhausted by long service to the nation during one of the most extraordinary and demanding periods in its history, retired from government. As he explained in a letter to a friend, "I simply came to the conclusion that I had to get well again." "I know there is still much work to be done in this world," he continued. "Among other things, I feel the winning of the peace is going to be just about as difficult as winning the war." Hopkins, who died of hemachromatosis in New York in January 1946, never lived to see the full truth of that statement.[58]

Hopkins and Davies had dissented from the hard-line approach to the Russians adopted by Truman at the start of his presidency; at least in the short term, their dissent proved effective. In the spring of 1945 FDR's legacy was still fresh, Soviet-American wartime cooperation ongoing, and the cold war no more than an embryonic struggle, and in that context the views of Hopkins and Davies were influential. Their advice to Truman and their missions to Moscow and London ensured that the Polish question did not break up the Soviet-American partnership. By early 1946, however, the outlines of the cold war were clearer, the desire for cooperation in both Washington and Moscow practically nonexistent. From that point on, officials who contested American foreign policy would often find themselves impotent, lone voices against a cold war consensus that would remain rigid for more than four decades. Henry Wallace was the first dissenter to confront that reality.

PART II

Truman, Wallace, and the Soviet Challenge

CHAPTER 3

Troubled by Truman

———

"That was one of the biggest things wrong with
Harry Truman, that he wasn't Franklin Roosevelt.
With Roosevelt you'd have known he was
President even if you hadn't been told. You'd have
known he was head of whatever he wanted to be
head of. He looked imperial, and he acted that
way, and he talked that way.
Harry Truman, for God's sake, looked and acted
and talked like—well, like a failed haberdasher. He
certainly wasn't any Roosevelt, and another trouble
with him, for people like me anyway, was that he
wasn't Henry Wallace."—MERLE MILLER,
Plain Speaking, 1973

W HEN Harry Truman made the short trip to Union Station,
Washington, in the late morning of Saturday, April 14, 1945, to escort
Franklin Roosevelt's body to the White House, he asked to accompany
him Secretary of Commerce Henry A. Wallace and James F. Byrnes,
both of whom had hoped to be chosen as FDR's vice-presidential running mate at the Democratic convention in 1944. Had either succeeded,
that man would have become president of the United States on Roosevelt's death, not Truman. "I knew," Truman explained, "that they both
thought they ought to be sitting where I was. A lot of other people in

the country also thought so, and so I thought asking them was the proper thing to do, and I did it."[1]

At the White House funeral for Roosevelt in the afternoon, Senator Arthur Vandenberg sat directly behind Wallace. The secretary of commerce, Vandenberg wryly observed in his diary entry that day, had "missed the Presidency by just three months. I wonder what was going through his head!"[2]

Despite failing to secure the nomination as Roosevelt's running mate in 1944, and hence the presidency itself in 1945, Wallace's career had been one of substantial accomplishment. Born in Iowa in 1888, Wallace, like Truman, emerged from the farmlands of the Midwest. But, unlike Truman, he soon became a rising star of rural America. The newspaper owned by his family, *Wallace's Farmer*, grew popular and influential. After receiving a degree in animal husbandry at Iowa State College, Wallace made such notable innovations in agriculture as the development of hybrid corn for commercial use. As well as farming a plot of land, he wrote for *Wallace's Farmer* and, following the appointment of his father as President Warren G. Harding's secretary of agriculture, took over as editor of the newspaper in 1921.[3]

For much of the next two decades, Wallace devoted his efforts to helping American farmers cope with the agricultural depression that set in after World War I, and in particular with the twin problems of overproduction and low prices for farm products brought about by slackened demand from Europe after the war. He supported the McNary-Haugen bill that was introduced in Congress to assist farmers. Outraged when President Calvin Coolidge twice vetoed the bill, Wallace switched his political allegiance from the Republican party, which his family had traditionally supported, to the Democrats. Having met Roosevelt in the summer of 1932, Wallace campaigned energetically for the Democratic ticket that year and was rewarded by appointment as secretary of agriculture. He used this position to implement his vision for rural America. Among a cluster of reforms he introduced was the landmark Agricultural Adjustment Act of 1933, in which farmers received payments for curtailing output in order to reduce surpluses and raise prices. The general view is that Wallace was an outstanding secretary of agriculture.[4]

That track record and his popularity in the farm states in part explain Roosevelt's decision to select Wallace as his running mate in the 1940 election campaign. Already popular with the left wing of the Democratic party, Wallace's position as vice president allowed him to sustain a high public profile after America entered World War II. He undertook various overseas missions for Roosevelt, including one to Soviet Asia in 1944, which deepened his interest in international issues.[5]

In addition to his convictions about the best course for American farmers, Wallace developed strong beliefs on a number of other issues. Expansion of U.S. trade, and of world trade in general, became an important element in his thinking. Viewing it initially as a way to help American farmers, he came to see it as more than that: lower tariffs and greater international commerce would bring about a more united world. Good relations between the United States and the Soviet Union were also essential for international harmony, he believed.[6]

As the end of World War II came into view, Wallace's career suffered an ignominious setback. At the Democratic convention in the summer of 1944, Wallace failed to be renominated as the vice-presidential candidate once Roosevelt made it clear that he could accept either Harry Truman or Supreme Court Justice William O. Douglas on the ticket. It appears FDR had been swayed by various figures in the Democratic party who believed that if Wallace remained on the ticket, Roosevelt's chances of victory in the presidential election would be severely damaged. Crestfallen, Wallace nonetheless campaigned hard for the Democratic ticket that fall. His reward was a position in the cabinet as secretary of commerce. He was just coming to grips with his new job when the tragic news arrived from Warm Springs on April 12, 1945.[7]

Roosevelt's death represented a double blow for Wallace. Not only did he mourn the passing of a dazzling, inspirational, progressive political leader, he also had to live with the fact that he had failed to become president by the slenderest of margins. For the next year and a half, that circumstance hampered relations between Truman and Wallace. Differences of style between the two men meant that their relationship was never likely to be cordial: Truman's earthiness and Wallace's enigmatic qualities were as compatible as oil and water. But the fact that Wallace had come so close to securing the office that Truman now held made their dealings even more difficult. Wallace—and certainly his friends and political allies—felt he would have been a more worthy successor to Roosevelt. This left the new president with a problem of legitimacy. Knowing the views of Wallace and his supporters put Truman on his guard.

Wallace's principal fear during the days following FDR's death was that Truman would end the New Deal. Had he himself been catapulted into the presidency, Wallace believed, he would have dedicated himself to the energetic pursuit and fulfillment of Roosevelt's objectives. But with Truman in the White House, it was unclear whether the new administration would be similarly committed to Roosevelt's legacy. Truman might implement different kinds of policies, directed less toward progressive change at home and cooperation with the Soviet Union abroad.

The occasion of Roosevelt's burial at his family's Hyde Park estate in the Hudson Valley on Sunday, April 15, sparked Wallace's concerns over this issue. Aboard FDR's internment train from Washington to New York State, Wallace sensed that Roosevelt's old advisers lacked the cohesion and determination necessary to mold the new president.

> The Cabinet members were all together in Car Six. Morgenthau was completely tired out and had almost nothing to say. Ickes was bent over and aged—and had plenty to say, most of it uncomplimentary to the new President and his friends. Stettinius was obviously ill at ease and uncertain, as Henry Morgenthau put it, "nervous as a witch." Harold Ickes was picking on Mrs. Ickes with the querulous, semi-humorous remarks of an ageing man. The cord which had bound the Cabinet had snapped.[8]

On the train journey back to Washington, Wallace noticed that George Allen and Ed Pauley, whom Wallace viewed as unsavory political operators, were in Truman's compartment. "Knowing Pauley's oil record in California and his activities at the Chicago convention," Wallace later reflected,

> I also knew that an era of experimental liberalism had come to an end—and that trouble lay ahead. Having worked with a man [like

Roosevelt] who in his prime had genuine spiritual lifting power, I was overcome with sadness as I thought of what the Pauleys would do to a man like Truman. I remembered the New York TIMES Sunday piece of last January—in which Truman gloried in his own political opportunism. I fear the Pauleys and Allens are in the saddle.

For much of the next year and a half, Wallace continued to worry that Truman's ascent to power signaled the dissolution of the New Deal.[9]

Anxious to familiarize himself with the details of the wartime situation, busy preparing for Molotov's trip to Washington, Truman was unable to meet with Wallace for another two weeks. On the morning of April 27, however, the secretary of commerce arrived at the White House for talks with the new president—to share ideas and attempt to establish the ground rules for their new relationship.[10]

Wallace used the meeting to explain to Truman the nature of his relationship with FDR: they had been very close and had disagreed on only two issues—the 1937 attempted reform of the Supreme Court, and the transfer of control of forestry matters from the Department of Agriculture to the Department of the Interior. "I had served him loyally," Wallace told Truman, "and he had backed me up completely."[11]

After stressing his close association with Roosevelt, Wallace touched on the international scene. Expressing his belief that there were a number of people in China and Poland who wished to see the United States embark upon a war with the Soviet Union, Truman assured Wallace, "That must not be." The president also responded sympathetically to Wallace's complaint that "while my relations with Roosevelt had been of the finest . . . there had been some people around Roosevelt who apparently were conniving against me. I told him I was prepared to serve him as loyally as I had Roosevelt, provided he wanted me to do so." Truman stated emphatically that he did, and he "spoke very vigorously about connivers, saying that he was against them and that he was going to get rid of them as soon as he could." He went on to say that although disagreements were inevitable, "he certainly would be above board with all the cards on the table."[12]

In the course of their conversation, Stettinius called Truman from San Francisco, where the meeting to organize the United Nations was being held, to grouse about Soviet intransigence on the question of which of the victorious powers should supply the senior presiding officer to the conference. Wallace noticed that Truman "spoke very emphatically against the Russians, saying it was always the custom to have the host country furnish the presiding officer." For Wallace, this proved to be a portentous episode—a sign of the stiffening in Truman's attitude toward the Soviet Union that would become more apparent in later months.[13]

Summing up his early impressions of the new president from this meeting, Wallace noted that "Truman was exceedingly eager to agree with everything I said. He also seemed eager to make decisions of every kind with the greatest promptness. Everything he said was decisive. It almost seemed as though he was eager to decide in advance of thinking." As he left the White House, a group of journalists asked Wallace about his talk with Truman. He told them they had "understood each other perfectly."[14]

Truman's affability toward Wallace at this meeting was not contrived. Finding his feet, as he was in the early days of his presidency, Truman was keen to keep a figure with the stature and experience of Wallace within the cabinet. As two authorities on Wallace put it, he "commanded the loyalty of a sizable portion of the Democratic Party, its labor and liberal elements, and Truman, the good politician, recognized his value to party unity."[15]

Despite Truman's friendliness, Wallace grew increasingly worried that his dream of a stable postwar world, underpinned by a constructive Soviet-American partnership, would be lost. That dream could be realized, Wallace believed, because the two emerging superpowers had more in common than appeared to be the case: neither had colonies or wished to acquire them, and both used technology to raise living standards for their poor. While Wallace acknowledged that the Soviet system did not furnish the liberties provided by America's democracy, he was hopeful that the Russian government would gradually permit more individual freedom. The best way to counter communism's appeal, he thought, was to demonstrate that capitalism worked better, not by adopting hostile policies toward Russia. Wallace was naive about the prospects for greater political freedom in Stalin's Russia, but his commitment to cordial Soviet-American relations was linked less to his view of the Soviet system and more to his conviction that Washington and Moscow simply had to get along if peace were to be maintained after the war.[16]

Getting along would not be easy, Wallace believed. He suspected that a number of groups within the United States, including the press, army, and big business, were moving to the right. Moreover a general anti-Soviet sentiment seemed to Wallace to be percolating through Washington. On Sunday, May 6, at a picnic, he found that "several people spoke in horrified tones of Russia and especially of the disappearance of the sixteen members of the Polish underground. More and more it begins to look like the psychology is favorable toward our getting into war with Russia. This must not be. It seems incredible that our people should drift toward this whirlpool which will inevitably end in world Communism."[17]

Wallace's observations reveal a major flaw in his thinking: he yearned for an American foreign policy on a high moral plane, respectful of human rights, but seemed relatively unconcerned about the extent to which Soviet foreign policy was equally principled. He should have been troubled by the plight of the arrested Polish underground leaders. That lack of consistency reduced the appeal of his dissent as it developed over the coming months.

To Wallace, the unfortunate counterpart to an escalating sentiment against the Soviet Union was Truman's harder-line policy toward Moscow. Wallace suspected that Averell Harriman was the architect of this truculent approach, a belief confirmed on May 1 when late at night Harriman briefed a small group of influential Americans, including Wallace and several distinguished journalists such as Walter Lippmann, on the state of Soviet-American relations. In a remarkable exposition, delivered against the backdrop of the ongoing San Francisco Conference, Harriman began by declaring, "I have come to the conclusion that on long range policies there is an irreconcilable difference or differences between the United States and Great Britain on the one hand and Russia on the other." "The difference," he explained, "is this: Russia apparently intends to pursue a policy of Marxian penetration wherever she can to build up her own security system to protect her socialist system to protect her socialist conception and we want a world of free nations and peoples."[18]

In essence, Harriman argued that though Stalin seemed to be working for postwar peace through the establishment of the United Nations, he was simultaneously pursuing a policy of expansion in Eastern Europe. His failure to carry out the Yalta agreements on Poland was the clearest indication of this. Harriman suggested that Truman respond by using the Russian desire for American economic aid as a diplomatic weapon: "I would apportion that credit out piecemeal, demanding in return concessions on the political field."[19]

Dismayed by Harriman's argument, Wallace wrote in his diary: "At this stage let me say—I have never been so hopelessly sick at heart with any American diplomat as I am with Harriman." His suspicion was that British diplomats, determined to curtail Soviet influence in Europe, had been exerting an insidious influence over American officials such as Harriman. "In reality," Wallace wrote, "you have here rivalry in Europe between Britain and Russia. . . . We thus are the sonsabitches in the eyes of the Russians now by playing Britain's game—we are in complete subservience to Britain at the present moment—Eden and Stettinius are Siamese twins out here [in San Francisco]—and the Russians know it."[20]

Toward the end of Harriman's talk, Wallace interjected on behalf of FDR's policy of cooperation with Moscow: "Has our policy toward Russia changed—changed since Roosevelt—changed to lines of resistance and hostility in view of your conclusions that our long range policies clash and can't be resolved." "Oh, no," Harriman replied, "we must not leave Russia out of the world picture. We must go on working with Russia." "But it is obvious," Wallace observed privately, "there is a change." "We certainly need a Roosevelt now," he added, "or even [a secretary of state such as Cordell] Hull."[21]

Concerned that he had unduly heightened alarm about the state of Soviet-American relations, Harriman hastily convened another meeting the next day, May 2, with a number of those who had gathered the night before. He wished to make clear, he said, that he did not feel the present situation was hopeless. A general agreement with the Russians was both possible and desirable. Wallace, however, remained unimpressed. Recalling his encounters with Harriman in early May, he noted:

He is perhaps more nearly the father of our present Russian policy than any other single person. There is the group of the Riga boys in the State Department who have had very great influence, but Harriman has pointed out the anti-Russian approach very early and completely. I would say that Harriman, since the fall of 1944, has been more responsible than any single individual for the course followed with respect to Russia. He arrived at a certain approach long before Truman knew what he was going to do.[22]

What made Wallace certain that Harriman had succeeded in persuading Truman to take a tougher stand with the Russians was the conduct of the American delegation at the San Francisco Conference. At a May 3 dinner party at Wallace's home, the guests included Adlai Stevenson, who had been working for Truman on UN matters at San Francisco. Noticing that Stevenson seemed agitated, Wallace asked him to stay behind at the end of the evening. Stevenson, it turned out, was upset by Nelson Rockefeller's insistence that Argentina, a nation with a reactionary government, be brought into the United Nations because it would function as a close American ally. The result, he thought, would be that "Russia will look at the United States and say, 'There is the United States with twenty American republics plus Liberia plus the Philippines, representing a total of twenty-three votes in the Assembly. Add in the other Latin nations and the British Commonwealth and where does it leave Russia?'" Stevenson thought this made it inevitable that the Russians would feel obliged "to play their own game," and hence an era of international rivalry rather than cooperation through the UN would begin.[23]

Stevenson's comments distressed Wallace, for he believed that postwar stability depended in large measure on a United Nations that functioned well. The new international organization could help to ensure peace, promote free trade, and ameliorate living standards throughout the world. Soviet-American cooperation was essential, however, if the UN were to realize its potential.[24]

On May 7 Wallace talked with a friend, Creekmore Fath, who told him about the argument Rockefeller had made before Congress that the entry of Argentina into the UN was a great coup because of that country's hostility toward the Soviet Union. Fath's account meshed with the one he had heard four days earlier from Stevenson, so Wallace decided to move to counter Rockefeller's pro-Argentinian, anti-Soviet strategy. In Fath's presence he called Dick Gilbert of the Office of Price Administration, whom he knew to be close to Harry Hopkins. As a result of their conversation, Fath went to see Gilbert, and Gilbert subsequently spoke to Hopkins on the matter of Rockefeller's support for Argentina at San Francisco. Although nothing material appears to have developed from Wallace's intervention, it was the first time he had felt compelled to act against what he perceived as the increasingly anti-Soviet orientation of the Truman administration. It would not be the last.[25]

A chief reason for Wallace's anxiety over the new anti-Russian mood was his belief that it served American economic interests poorly. As with many policymakers at the time, Wallace was deeply concerned about the possibility that the end of the war would reduce production and bring on a depression as severe as that of the 1930s. Indeed, in 1945 Wallace published *Sixty Million Jobs*, which presented a plan for preventing mass unemployment in the United States after the war. Part of the solution to America's potential economic problems, Wallace believed, was to find more markets. Hence he used his position as secretary of commerce to energize his department's foreign trade offices, and to push for an extension of the Reciprocal Trade Agreements Act to ensure that international commerce would avoid a revival of the protectionism that had been in fashion after World War I. Unlike most other officials, however, his desire to expand trade encouraged Wallace to work for cordial relations with the Soviet Union on the grounds that it had the potential to become a major market for American goods. Trade with Russia would augment levels of production and employment at home, and thus play an important role in averting a depression.[26]

Interest in the Russian market was a major element in Wallace's thinking throughout the late spring of 1945. After the May 1 meeting with Harriman, for instance, he commented that the lack of concern for Soviet needs "is amazing—considering the fact that Russia is a vital market to trade expansion which we must have after the war to prevent unemployment reaching several millions in this country." In order to increase Soviet-American trade, Wallace thought it would be a good idea if he were to lead a special trade mission to the Soviet Union that would include prominent names from General Electric, Westinghouse, U.S. Steel, and J. P. Morgan. Internal discussions within the Department of Commerce strengthened Wallace's desire for larger markets overseas. On May 16 he was told that by 1946 seven million Americans would be unemployed, a forecast he found sobering.[27]

Although Wallace's concern over the anti-Soviet outlook of many U.S. officials—and the consequences of this attitude for the American economy—was great, he did not assume that the new president was the root cause of the changing mood in Washington. But he did continuously evaluate Truman as a worthy successor to FDR, and, in particular, sought to determine if the new president was interested in maintaining a constructive partnership with Russia. His conclusions in the spring of 1945 were mixed. On the one hand, he was impressed by Truman's decisiveness, and when Wallace expounded on the need for amicable Soviet-American relations, he usually found Truman in accord. On the other hand, Wallace suspected that when Truman expressed goodwill toward Moscow he was not showing his true hand, that he was in fact deeply suspicious of Stalin. Wallace defined his own role in pedagogical terms: because Truman was unschooled in the ways of international affairs, Wallace would tutor the president on the importance of sustaining the close relationship with the Soviet Union that Roosevelt had developed. That education would hopefully serve as a corrective to the advice being offered by the likes of Harriman.

In mid-May Wallace had another opportunity to evaluate Truman during a one-on-one discussion. Before that meeting, various other encounters had fortified Wallace's determination to keep Soviet-American relations friendly, reminded him of Roosevelt's legacy, and prompted him to question Truman's attitude.

On the evening of May 16 Wallace joined members of Roosevelt's family and a few close aides to the late president for a dinner party hosted by Fred Vinson, then director of the Office of War Mobilization. With a tongue loosened by drink, Grace Tully, FDR's secretary, complained about how "the Truman organization had treated the Roosevelt White House staff." Apparently ten of FDR's Secret Service men and his chauffeur had been dismissed. Tully also groused about the lack of consideration she herself had received, and repeated several times that she was sorry that Wallace was not in the White House.[28]

Anna Boettiger, Roosevelt's daughter, spoke about her meeting with Truman earlier in the day in which he had told her that all his aides had advised him to take a hard line with the Russians. When Wallace asked how the president felt about that, Boettiger said her impression was that he thought this approach was a mistake. By way of implicit criticism, however, she stated that one of her father's great accomplishments was the development of a solid relationship with the Soviet Union. "It was obvious," wrote Wallace, "she feels the new President has not done well on this front." The general sense that Truman was an unworthy successor to FDR permeated the entire discussion. "I just can't call that man President," Tully told Wallace again and again.[29]

The following afternoon Wallace attended a reception given by Russian officials in Washington. He noticed there were virtually no senior American officials present, and it seemed the Soviet personnel had recently changed as well. "The whole atmosphere," Wallace bleakly observed, "reminded me somewhat of that which existed back in 1940 when Russia was so unpopular in the United States." The wife of Andrei Gromyko, the Soviet ambassador, spoke earnestly to Wallace, arguing that the entire future of Soviet-American relations depended on him. Wallace said he would do all he could.[30]

His concerns over the Russian question were no doubt intensified by a conversation three hours later at a dinner given by his sister, Mary Bruggmann. Morgenthau, present that evening, asserted that it was vitally important to complete the defeat of Japan by encouraging a prompt Soviet entry into the war in the Far East. The Treasury secretary complained about American officials who exaggerated minor differences with Moscow so as to generate discord between the two allies. Wallace gathered that Morgenthau, "like so many others, feels that the greatest danger in the United States at the present time is our relationship with Russia."[31]

Changing tack, Morgenthau reminisced about Roosevelt, recalling his last evening alive. He explained how grateful he was to be able to share that time with FDR. Roosevelt had been in excellent spirits, eating copious amounts of caviar and imbibing two cocktails. His state of mind had been impressively lucid. The only clue to his health was the fact that he had been unable to pour the cocktail accurately from the shaker into the glass, and so Morgenthau had done it for him. In the aftermath of FDR's death, his admirers, like Morgenthau and Wallace, found solace in their memories of the man. They seemed so much more appealing than the impressions of his successor.[32]

It was the next day, May 18, when Wallace had another opportunity to shape Truman's thinking. After a 2 p.m. cabinet meeting at which Wallace alerted his colleagues to the potential of widespread U.S. unemployment after the war, he stayed behind for a chat with the president. When Truman explained how concerned he was by the relationship with Moscow, Wallace interjected that he must not accept State Department advice unquestioningly. Truman made clear that he had already developed a lack of faith in State's competence, and, moreover, that he planned to install a new secretary of state in the near future—a reference to James Byrnes's imminent appointment.[33]

Analyzing the international situation, Truman pointed out that the Russians had reneged on their treaty commitments at Yalta. Although he had made sure that his communications with Stalin were always amiable, American representatives had been barred from entering Soviet-occupied countries in Eastern Europe. "The Russians," Truman concluded, "were like people from across the tracks whose manners were very bad." He proceeded to discuss the need to continue courting the Soviets so as to ensure their entry into the war against Japan, but Wallace's overall impression was that "Truman was still committed to the doctrine of acting tough with Russia."[34]

Eleven days later, on the morning of May 29, Wallace went to the White House for another private discussion with the president. The meeting had been arranged so that Truman could approve the text of a speech his secretary of commerce would soon make. Truman was in a positive frame of mind. Hopkins was in Moscow by then, and his talks with Stalin had begun. Early reports on their discussions were promising. Truman appeared genuinely optimistic about the prospects for Soviet-American relations.[35]

As Truman went over the text of Wallace's speech, he came across a number of references to the continuity between his policies and Roosevelt's. Truman already knew that ardent New Dealers such as Wallace liked to use FDR as a barometer for measuring the worth of his own presidency. Paying homage to the memory of Roosevelt in private meetings like this was an easy way for Truman to placate New Deal liberals, and he had no qualms about doing that, even though his endorsement of FDR did not convey his true feelings toward the Soviets—namely that their motives, priorities, and policies had at the very least to be questioned. Nonetheless he approved all of Wallace's comments emphasizing his own commitment to FDR's legacy. When the president read the sentence, "President Truman is following the Roosevelt policy," he affirmed: "I certainly am. I have conferred with all who knew anything about his policy, including the immediate members of his family, and I am doing everything I can to carry it out."[36]

Truman said he was happy with the success that Hopkins seemed to be enjoying in his talks with the Soviet leader. By sending Hopkins to Moscow, he told Wallace, "he had straightened out a fundamental misconception of Stalin and [he was now certain] that Stalin was going to come along all right now." Wallace inferred that Truman, because of the Hopkins mission, "now feels much more kindly toward the Russians than he did before." To impress upon Wallace his reluctance to antagonize Stalin, Truman explained that he had refused several times to meet with Churchill, feeling that he should talk to Stalin first before seeing the British leader.[37]

In many ways this May 29 meeting set the tone for future encounters between Wallace and Truman. Wallace would try to convince Truman of the need for sound relations with Stalin, and Truman would insist he did not need convincing. In fact the president's feelings toward the Soviet Union were ambivalent, and by 1946 that ambivalence would be converted into a deep and enduring distrust. Contrary to Truman's "shoot from the hip" image, he was often less than candid with others. His lack of frankness in dealing with Wallace obscured the differences between the two men and helped sow the seeds for later misunderstandings in their relationship—and its eventual rupture. Wallace could read between the lines: he knew that some of Truman's comments about the need to stay on good terms with the Russians did not square, for example, with his decision in early May to terminate Lend Lease aid to the Soviet Union so abruptly. Nonetheless it was difficult for Wallace to gauge Truman's true feelings about relations with Moscow from their conversations.

If Wallace's meetings with Truman caused him to doubt whether the new president shared Roosevelt's outlook on foreign policy, those concerns were amplified by various contacts with Wallace's liberal friends. Their fears about Truman increased his own, and their belief that liberal leaders needed to take concerted action to influence the president's policies strengthened Wallace's determination to do just that.

An example of Wallace's dialogue with the liberal wing of the Democratic party was his May 30 conversation with the head of the National Farmers Union, James Patton. Patton said he was about to leave Washington for a while, but that he did not wish to go until he had imparted some advice to Wallace. The last time they had met, Patton had suggested that Wallace maintain a low profile. Now he had changed his mind. Wallace should move to center stage, and his credibility in the country and in the party meant that his enemies would be able to do nothing about it. Patton said it was time "for the liberal leaders to start talking." Eleanor Roosevelt, he said, "wants to see Mr. Wallace, himself and others sometime in August—to get together, quite off the record." Patton added that Wallace must "not let the mast drop too low here—thinks HAW [Wallace] has the boys in the corner—they don't dare do anything about HAW."[38]

The most intriguing evidence for the split that was emerging between Truman and the New Dealers during this period comes from covert FBI wiretaps of former FDR aide and Washington lawyer Thomas (Tommy the Cork) Corcoran. Corcoran's telephone conversations reveal the extent to which Washington insiders believed that Truman was breaking with the New Dealers. On the morning of June 13, in a wide-ranging discussion with Alabama senator Lister Hill, Corcoran concentrated on the marginalization of liberal Democrats since the death of FDR. "It was funny last night," he told Hill. "I was out at PHIL DOUGLAS' with . . . ICKES . . . myself and some others, and I couldn't help saying to myself, 'Well, here's a bunch of guys, this is just about the time you left for the coast last year, it was three weeks before the [1944 Democratic] convention, here's a bunch of guys that had the world in their hands last year, and now they're just a bunch of political refugees." At a party he had recently attended, Corcoran continued, he had seen "Henry Wallace; I saw all these liberals . . . and I thought what a helpless bunch of sheep."[39]

Analyzing how Wallace had lost the vice-presidential nomination at the convention, Hill and Corcoran concluded that Wallace's stars were on the wane:

Hill: Well doesn't he know that he's completely boxed off now?

Corcoran: He ought to. He's a captive if ever I saw a captive.

Hill: Did you ever see one more boxed off than he is?

Corcoran: No.

Hill: Why he's out of this picture to a fare-thee-well.

Corcoran: That's right.

Hill: Sure, sure.[40]

While it was premature for Corcoran and Hill to write Wallace's political obituary, they were correct in highlighting the increasing isolation of the secretary of commerce and other New Deal liberals. Wallace himself was aware of the trend. Evidence, such as the changing composition of the cabinet, was overwhelming. With alacrity, Truman had removed many of the officials he had inherited from Roosevelt. On May 23 he announced no less than three new appointments: Tom C. Clark would replace Francis Biddle as attorney general, Lewis B. Schwellenbach would take over from Frances Perkins at Labor, and Clinton P. Anderson would succeed Claude R. Wickard as secretary of agriculture. The changes were to take effect June 30. Capping the administrative revolution of early summer 1945 was the appointment of Byrnes as successor to Stettinius as secretary of state, and the replacement of Morgenthau at Treasury with Fred Vinson. Twelve weeks after Roosevelt's death, Wallace at Commerce and Harold Ickes at Interior were the only remaining well-known New Dealers left in the cabinet. As secretary of war, Henry Stimson had become Wallace's only natural ally on foreign policy issues, and Ickes was his one potential supporter in domestic affairs.[41]

July 6 was the occasion of the first cabinet meeting for Byrnes, Clark, Anderson, and Schwellenbach. Although he had felt obliged to tender his resignation the day before, Morgenthau was also present. His imminent departure at Treasury sobered Wallace. "It seems now as though the Roosevelt flavor has completely gone out of the Cabinet," he groused to Frances Perkins later that month. One more FDR man was on his way out; the New Deal appeared to be ending. The tide had shifted, and for the rest of his political career Wallace would be swimming against it.[42]

Despite his increasing isolation within the administration, Wallace was not yet despondent. The Hopkins and Davies missions had pleased him immensely. They had demonstrated that with Truman as president, Soviet-American cooperation was still possible, and that the United States would not automatically align itself with Britain against Stalin. After the return of the envoys from Moscow and London, Wallace fired off a letter to Joe Davies. "Congratulations to you and Harry Hopkins," he enthused, "on the great service you have rendered to the world during the past two months." A week later Wallace called Davies to discuss the situation in Yugoslavia, Soviet-American relations, and Hopkins's health. Wallace concluded their conversation by saying he was delighted that Truman had asked Davies to attend the Potsdam Conference and was "very glad" that he had served as ambassador to the Soviet Union.[43]

Despite the success of the Hopkins-Davies missions, Wallace's general outlook in the early summer of 1945 was one of concern over the course of Truman's policies. On balance it seemed that the new president was abandoning the Rooseveltian idea of cooperating with the Soviet Union. If Wallace was to have any realistic hope of persuading Truman to ignore the hard-line advice he was receiving from advisers like Harriman and Navy Secretary James Forrestal, he had to convert his proscription of Truman's diplomacy into a prescription—a set of foreign policy recommendations. In the fall of 1945, Wallace decided to build those proposals around one issue: the atomic bomb.

CHAPTER 4

The Bomb

—

"[At the luncheon of the American Council,
Edward C.] Carter made a most interesting talk
with regard his trip to Russia. He said he was in
Moscow at the time the atomic bombs fell on
Japan. He said that [former Soviet foreign
minister Maxim] Litvinov told him after the
second atomic bomb fell, 'Those are the only two
atomic bombs that will ever fall. With this power
in the hands of the United States it is bound to be
used for peace and not for destruction.'"
—Henry Wallace, diary entry, October 30, 1945

O N AUGUST 6, 1945, President Truman and Secretary of State
Byrnes sat down to lunch below the deck of the *Augusta*, the ship that
carried the American delegation to the Potsdam Conference back to
the United States. Capt. Frank Graham, the White House Map Room
watch officer, entered the mess to hand the president a decoded message from Secretary of War Stimson: "Results clear-cut successful in all
respects. Visible effects greater than in any test." On a map accompanying the message, Graham had circled the city of Hiroshima with a
red pencil. Grabbing Graham's hand, Truman declared: "This is the
greatest thing in history." A few minutes later another message arrived:
"Big bomb dropped on Hiroshima August 5 at 7:15 P.M. Washington

time. First reports indicate complete success which was even more conspicuous than earlier test." Truman rose from the table, turned to Byrnes, and said, "It's time for us to get home."[1]

Asked in later years about his feelings when the atomic bomb was dropped on Hiroshima, Wallace confessed that he could not accurately recall. "It's funny," he mused, "that with regard to some of the most significant things like that your mind's a complete blank." Although Wallace had been anxious about whether the bomb would be a military success, and hence relieved when it proved to be so, he was appalled by the death of so many people. The event seemed to leave him numb. Realizing that the atomic bomb would cast a shadow over international affairs, he knew that coming to terms with its meaning and implications would be a prerequisite for a stable postwar world. "With nearly everyone who came in to see me," Wallace wrote in his diary on August 7, "the first topic of conversation was the atomic bomb. Everyone seemed to feel that a new epoc [sic] in the world's history had been ushered in. The scramble for the control of this new power is going to be one of the most unusual struggles the world has ever seen."[2]

The bombing of Hiroshima was not the first Wallace had heard of the atomic bomb. He had been aware of the secret American nuclear effort for a number of years. In 1939 and early 1940 he had sifted through early scientific literature on nuclear fission and its possibilities for the invention of a new weapon of unprecedented power. He became aware of the importance that Roosevelt attached to this issue in the summer of 1940 when Vannevar Bush, president of the Carnegie Institution and head of the National Defense Research Committee established by Roosevelt to explore the opportunities for atomic development, came to speak to Wallace. FDR, Bush said, wanted Wallace to know about the work that was being done. Bush explained that the basic science was sufficiently advanced to suggest that "it was probable a bomb could be made of very great power." But he warned that German experts were familiar with much of the same basic information as American scientists, and he wanted Wallace's advice on "whether we should go full steam ahead." Wallace and Bush felt the same way: the United States must produce an atomic bomb before Nazi Germany did.[3]

Wallace's participation in the incipient development of the bomb was most active during the period from the summer of 1941 to September 1942. He was a member of a senior policy group charged with making recommendations to FDR about the nuclear project. The group met in Wallace's room in the Senate Office Building on December 16, 1941, just nine days after the Japanese attack on Pearl Harbor. The decision was made "to push full steam ahead" with work on the atomic bomb. Although Wallace appears not to have attended more of these committee meetings, he did receive updates from Bush. Throughout this period he remained convinced of the project's importance and did all he could to promote it. "I strengthened Roosevelt's belief," he recalled, "that it was something to put the money into. It was a rather daring thing to siphon off that amount of money—two billion dollars or so. It was an amount which was very small at the start, but which expanded and expanded and it was essential to maintain Roosevelt's faith that he should take the risk and do it."[4]

Wallace's close involvement in the development of the atomic bomb ended in September 1942 with the appointment of Maj. Gen. Leslie R. Groves as the executive officer responsible for running what became known as the Manhattan Project. Once the project had been launched, no important policy decisions remained to be made. So for the last three years of the war Wallace's role in the American race for the atomic bomb was limited.[5]

But if the vice president's administrative responsibilities diminished, his personal interest in atomic energy, and particularly its possible peacetime applications, increased. A key stimulus to his interest was a December 1943 meeting with Boris Pregel, president of the Canadian Uranium Company. Pregel told Wallace that recent French experiments with radium refining had produced a more effective fertilizer and manure as well as various agriculturally useful by-products. Market garden crops in France, Pregel explained, had increased by one-third as a result of these new methods. Wallace, ever the avid agronomist, immediately called Eugene Auchter, director of scientific research in the Department of Agriculture, to arrange for him to meet Pregel. Having obtained some of the by-products for his own use, Wallace experimented with them in his garden in Washington between

1944 and 1946. As the war drew to a close, Wallace, unlike other officials aware of the Manhattan Project, was as much interested in the peacetime applications of atomic energy as he was in its use as a weapon of war.[6]

Thus when Truman ordered the dropping of the bombs on Hiroshima and Nagasaki, Wallace was not altogether pessimistic about the dawning of the atomic age. The idea that Japan was crippled and on the verge of surrender, and hence that the dropping of the bombs was not required to end the war against Japan (the argument championed in the 1960s by the scholar Gar Alperovitz), did not occur to Wallace at the time. He had always believed that, within the context of the war, the successful development and use of the atomic bomb was logical and desirable. Truman's decision to use the new weapon against Japan did not seem at all objectionable to him.[7]

Rather than ponder the question of whether the bombs should have been dropped, in the days after Hiroshima Wallace concentrated on the potentially beneficial peacetime uses of atomic energy. Pregel, by now Wallace's mentor on the subject, continued to reinforce his interest. On August 8 he gave Wallace two newspaper articles from 1941 in which he had stressed the value of utilizing radioactive materials in agriculture. "We can look forward," Pregel had claimed, "to unlimited peace, power and fuel, an indefinite supply of raw materials, comfort for all with a minimum of labor—those things that should remove the causes of poverty, envy and greed, make wars unthinkable and usher in a golden age for human beings."[8]

Wallace began to see his mission in the field of atomic energy as the transmission of ideas he received from Pregel and others to senior officials in the administration. On August 21 he wrote to Truman himself, enclosing a letter from Robert M. Hutchins of the University of Chicago, in which the chancellor discussed the need for Truman to utilize experts who were aware of atomic energy's social and economic implications. Truman thanked Wallace for the letter, saying that while he was concerned about the "Atomic situation," he felt it could be "worked out on a practical basis so its usefulness for the welfare of the world can be brought out." In an obvious reference to Stalin, he added that it was fortunate the atomic secrets were in the hands of the United States "rather than some other people we could name." Truman suggested that he discuss the atomic question with Wallace "one of these days."[9]

In the late summer of 1945 Wallace continued to evaluate Truman and gauge the general mood in Washington. He still suspected that Truman favored a less accommodating approach toward the Soviet Union. After attending the August 10 cabinet meeting, in which surrender terms for Japan were discussed, Wallace wrote that while it was clear to him that future peace hinged on "our ties of friendship with Russia," it was equally obvious that "the attitude of Truman, Byrnes and both the War and Navy Departments is not moving in this direction. Their attitude will make for war eventually."[10]

Determined to present an alternative to what seemed to Wallace Truman's increasingly hostile approach to the Russians, the secretary of commerce attempted in September to offer one to the president. Sharing the secret of atomic energy with Moscow, he told Truman, was the best way to sustain close Soviet-American relations. Wallace was aided in this endeavor by Henry Stimson. Nearing the end of one of the most distinguished careers in American political history, the man who had been secretary of state under Herbert Hoover and secretary of war to William Howard Taft, Franklin Roosevelt, and Truman urged the president to use America's atomic knowledge generously as a gesture of goodwill to the Russians, thereby stabilizing international politics in the postwar era.

On September 11 Stimson furnished Truman with a lengthy memorandum on the subject. At the Potsdam Conference he had told the president it might be unwise to share the atomic bomb with the Soviet Union until its police state had been reformed through the promotion and protection of individual rights. Now he informed Truman, in a letter accompanying his memorandum, that "any demand by us for an internal change in Russia as a condition of sharing in the atomic weapon would be so resented that it would make the objective we have in view less probable." Moreover he felt that the close superpower relationship that would develop through cooperation on the atomic bomb would speed the political changes needed in the Soviet system.[11]

In the memorandum Stimson noted that in "many quarters" in the United States the atomic bomb was viewed as a tool with which to off-

set "the growth of Russian influence on the continent." Such an attitude, he argued, would only bolster Stalin's determination to acquire
the weapon. "To put the matter concisely," Stimson continued, "I consider the problem of our satisfactory relations with Russia as not
merely connected with but as virtually dominated by the problem of
the atomic bomb." If the United States did not offer the Soviets a reasonable solution to the atomic problem, and if "[we] merely continue
to negotiate with them, having this weapon rather ostentantiously on
our hip, their suspicions and their distrust of our purposes and motives
will increase." "The chief lesson I have learned in a long life," Stimson
added, "is that the only way you can make a man trustworthy is to trust
him; and the surest way to make him untrustworthy is to distrust him
and show your distrust."[12]

The secretary of war proposed that Truman consult with the
British, then offer to enter into an arrangement with Stalin,

> the general purpose of which would be to control and limit the use
> of the atomic bomb as an instrument of war and so far as possible
> to direct and encourage the development of atomic power for
> peaceful and humanitarian purposes. Such an approach might
> more specifically lead to the proposal that we would stop work on
> the further improvement in, or manufacture of, the bomb as a mil-
> itary weapon, provided the Russians and the British would agree to
> do likewise.[13]

Truman paid close attention to Stimson's memorandum. This, he
knew, was not the advice of the New Deal left but of a seasoned statesman who had provided bipartisan service to the nation. "Stimson was
an honest man," Truman wrote in later years. "He had the ability to express his views in plain language. I respected and trusted him." For
Wallace, therefore, Stimson was a more than useful ally.[14]

The debate within the Truman administration over the atomic
bomb climaxed in late September. On Tuesday the 18th the subject was
taken up by the cabinet at a White House luncheon. Truman opened
the discussion by announcing that while he wished to keep secret the
technology of the bomb, he thought it would be helpful to share the
principles of atomic energy with the Soviet Union and other countries

in the United Nations. The whole matter, he informed his colleagues, would be examined in depth by the cabinet three days hence.[15]

Disagreeing with Truman, Secretary of Agriculture Clinton Anderson reported the finding of a recent Gallup poll that 80 percent of the American people wanted the United States to retain the atomic secrets. Forrestal supported Anderson, saying he was "violently opposed to any disclosure." As expected, Stimson and Wallace endorsed Truman's recommendations. Wallace argued that as countries like the Soviet Union and France would soon develop atomic weapons themselves, an attempt by the United States to preserve its atomic monopoly would represent an unhelpful "Maginot Line" attitude. "It was impossible," he explained, "to bottle [other countries'] scientists up in the way some people seem to think." In a simplification of Wallace's views, Forrestal noted in his diary that the secretary of commerce was "very strongly in favor of making full disclosure to the Russians."[16]

As promised, the president devoted the entire Friday, September 21, cabinet meeting, one of the most acrimonious and controversial of the Truman presidency, to a discussion of the atomic bomb. With his resignation due to take effect at the end of the day, Stimson used the occasion of his last cabinet meeting to reiterate the arguments he had made in his September 11 memorandum. Asked by Truman to open the discussion, Stimson observed that the question of the atomic bomb was intimately linked to the general issue of Soviet-American relations. World peace, he suggested, depended on the ability of Washington and Moscow to reach a general understanding. Such a relationship was possible because their two countries had been traditionally close. The Russian outlook during the American Civil War and its willingness to sell Alaska to the United States in 1867 were two clear examples of past cooperation between the two nations. Scientists in the War Department had told him the Russians would soon acquire the atomic secrets anyway. That being the case, the Truman administration might as well harvest the goodwill that would be generated by sharing the scientific principles behind the atomic bomb. As in his correspondence with Truman, Stimson stated that in matters of diplomacy, trust had to be offered in order to be received.[17]

Stimson's presentation sharply divided his colleagues. While Dean Acheson, Postmaster General Robert E. Hannegan, Abe Fortas, and several other officials expressed their support, Vinson, Attorney General Tom Clark, Forrestal, and Anderson were appalled by the idea of sharing atomic secrets with the Russians. Forrestal, who Wallace felt "took the most extreme attitude of all," read out a memorandum he had produced in consultation with other Navy Department officials. In it he argued forcefully against the transmission of atomic information to the Russians: the American people were not in favor of such an altruistic gesture, and, besides, it was not yet clear whether the Soviet Union could be trusted.[18]

After Forrestal and Anderson had spoken, Wallace entered the fray. In his diary entry for the meeting, Forrestal wrote that in his presentation on the atomic bomb, Wallace was, "Completely, everlastingly and wholeheartedly in favor of giving it to the Russians." When Forrestal's diary was published after his suicide in 1949, that statement created a storm of controversy. Wallace, by then out of public life, characterized it as "a lie." In a phone conversation with journalist Arthur Krock, he accounted for Forrestal's remark by citing his mental deterioration which, he thought, was probably incipient as early as September 1945.[19]

Forrestal's description of the cabinet meeting did indeed distort what Wallace said. Wallace asked Truman precisely what was the subject he wished to discuss. Truman replied that he wanted advice on whether "the scientific information regarding atomic energy should be shared with the other members of the United Nations." Divulging the factory techniques involved in making an atomic bomb was not, the president stated, what he had in mind. Having established that, Wallace proceeded to argue that other nations' scientists would inevitably acquire more knowledge about atomic issues. For that reason he "advocated strongly the interchange of scientific information but *not* the interchange of techniques or 'Know Hows.'" So although Wallace supported the idea that the scientific principles behind atomic energy should be disseminated, he did not recommend handing over the military secrets of the atomic bomb. The distinction between atomic energy and the atomic bomb was one Wallace would continue to make in the fall of 1945. Forrestal's diary entry misrepresented Wallace's position by failing to convey the subtleties of his argument.[20]

To Wallace's dismay, an account of the September 21 cabinet meeting was leaked to the press. The *New York Times* misleadingly reported the next day that Wallace had sponsored a proposal designed to reveal atomic bomb secrets to the Soviet Union. But the *Times* account failed to explain that Stimson, not Wallace, had introduced the original plan to share atomic secrets. It failed to mention that Wallace had highlighted the importance of keeping the technical knowledge needed to produce the bomb. It ignored the fact that a majority of the officials present agreed with Wallace (and Stimson).[21]

Perhaps most important, the press either did not reveal or was unaware that Truman himself concurred in Wallace's view. During the meeting the president had said he favored "an interchange of scientific knowledge." "Relationships are improving between Russia, Great Britain and ourselves," he added. "In order to achieve a lasting peace, we must maintain a mutual trust." In a letter home on September 22, Truman offered his private view of the previous day's cabinet meeting. It had been "stormy," he told his wife Bess, but "very helpful." He listed the officials who were for "free interchange of scientific knowledge," and those opposed. "Anyway," he explained, "I'll have to make a decision and the 'Ayes' will have it even if I'm the only Aye. It is probably the most momentous one I'll make." In other words, Truman, like Wallace, thought sharing the secrets of atomic energy, but not the atomic bomb, made sense.[22]

This showed that the president's outlook was not yet consistently distrustful toward Moscow. He was willing in 1945 to consider conciliatory gestures, as with his decision in the spring to send Hopkins and Davies on diplomatic missions to smooth Soviet-American relations.

Wallace did not believe it was the president who had spoken to the press about the September 21 cabinet meeting. The real culprit, he thought, was Appointments Secretary Matthew J. Connelly, who had taken notes at the meeting. Wallace was almost certainly correct that Truman had not leaked to the press, for he and Truman had agreed with each other at the meeting. More likely, the hard-line Forrestal rather than Connelly was the source.[23]

For Wallace, the cabinet leak was highly disconcerting. It confirmed his suspicion that an alliance had developed between various political figures and the press with a view to ousting him from Truman's cabinet. "I felt at that time," he recalled,

> that it was the beginning of a rolling snowball. . . . I could see what was coming. I felt quite sure of that. My impression was that there were certain people outside of government who were determined to destroy my political influence and that this was just to be the first of a series of incidents. I felt that very strongly.
>
> The people inside government would be essentially those that had worked against me at the 1944 [Democratic] Convention. . . . Those outside would be the group that favored the Nazis prior to Pearl Harbor. I'm referring particularly to the various newspapers that had fought me at all times.
>
> The newspapers that fought me did so fundamentally because they believed I stood for a type of the capitalistic system which did not automatically center power in a select group. I think that accounts for why the Chicago *Tribune*, the Hearst press, the New York *Times*, and the Scripps-Howard press, have continually done all they can to discredit me. . . .
>
> These papers, affiliated with the Republicans, believe that I had quite a bit to do with Roosevelt's victory in 1932 because of influence with the farmers, and so they began at once, after I was Secretary of Agriculture to use every means they could to destroy me. [*Chicago Tribune* publisher] Colonel [Robert R.] McCormick sent reporters out to Des Moines at once to see what they could get to throw against me. I got that from my friends on whom these reporters called. I think they succeeded in some degree, though I did have a large following. . . .

Wallace's analysis of the forces arrayed against him may have been excessively conspiratorial, but large sections of the political community and the press were indeed antagonized by his views, positioned as these views were on the left of the mainstream. Wallace would have been naive to ignore that reality.[24]

His public embarrassment over the September 21 cabinet meeting did not cause Wallace to modify his views on the atomic question. Truman had asked each member of the cabinet to submit in writing his opinion on Stimson's proposals, and on September 24 the secretary of commerce obliged. Once again he told Truman that the prompt sharing of scientific information about atomic energy would help prevent the division of the world into antagonistic blocs. He reiterated his contention that it was impossible for the United States to prevent other nations from developing their own atomic bombs. Hence, Wallace concluded, "I support Henry Stimson in his proposal for the free interchange of scientific information concerning atomic energy."[25]

From October to December 1945 Wallace continued to worry that British influence and the advice received by Truman from many of his aides were helping solidify an anti-Soviet consensus in the administration. Wallace attempted to offer the president an alternative view. In proposing policies aimed at keeping the Russians sweet, Wallace continued to encourage Truman to share the secrets of atomic energy, as he had in September. He also urged the president to make sure that America's atomic program was placed under the control of civilian officials, and not the military. As Truman had not yet adopted an unequivocally anti-Soviet approach, he remained open to Wallace's ideas during the last few months of 1945.

Personal meetings and memoranda were the means by which Wallace sought to influence the president. On October 15 he brought to the White House a memorandum he had written entitled, "The Significance of the Atomic Age." In it Wallace argued that the American monopoly of the atomic bomb made "the United States appear to the world as the greatest potential aggressor nation." Consequently an arms race might well be triggered in which other nations sought to catch up and then overtake the United States. The outcome, Wallace warned, could be "the end of humanity."[26]

On a more positive note, he argued that the advent of the atomic age could transform American society if the civilian applications of nuclear energy were profitably exploited. New sources of power, a twenty-hour workweek, higher standards of living—all these were now within the nation's grasp. "We can enter in the near future into a golden age of abundance," Wallace enthused.

> It is as if God were saying to us, "Enter now into the land of abundance and enjoy all its fruits sharing joyously with one another of the riches which are there for everyone. I shall make it possible for you in five years to learn and apply what otherwise would have taken you 500 years. You are now living in the year 2545 and I expect you to live according to the social rules of abundance of 2545, not according to the social rules of scarcity of 1745. If you do not understand the social rule of abundance, I shall turn this power or light and peace into a power of darkness and war and the final state of men will be ten times as miserable as it ever has been."

Accordingly, Wallace called for a reorientation of Truman's approach, with a greater emphasis on the civilian rather than the military applications of atomic energy. The United States, he suggested, should produce no more atomic bombs while persuading other nations to resist the temptation to develop their own nuclear weaponry.[27]

It was one of Wallace's more opaque offerings, and it revealed a religious strand in the tapestry of his thinking, not only on the atomic bomb but on Soviet-American relations in general. His personal journey of faith had included a deep interest in theosophy. In his call for international harmony, for understanding between America and Russia, a spiritual dimension could be identified. Often it was implicit, but at times he spoke openly of the connection, as he saw it, between the spiritual and the political. "To prevent atomic energy from destroying mankind," he declared in the summer of 1946, "it is essential that there be a psychic revolution, a profound change in the moral values and thinking habits of people the world over. . . . I say that Christian morality, not as practiced during the last nineteen hundred years, but as Jesus himself taught it, has finally become the most practical thing in the world."[28]

When Truman read Wallace's October 15 memorandum, he told his secretary of commerce that "he agreed with it throughout" and that "this was what he had been trying to say right along in the statements which he had made." Placating Wallace further, Truman added that

"Stalin was a fine man who wanted to do the right thing." When Wallace claimed that Britain was trying to drive a wedge between Washington and Moscow, Truman said that was his reading of the situation too. The president also expressed his concern over Stalin's health. If the Soviet leader retired, he speculated, there would be a battle for power between Molotov and Zhukov, and, of the three, he much preferred doing business with Stalin. Uncle Joe was "an honest man who is easy to get along with—who arrives at sound decisions." This meeting must have buoyed Wallace's spirits, but Truman had no doubt exaggerated the extent to which he agreed with Wallace's views.[29]

Wallace's close contacts with the scientific community continued to shape his views on atomic energy. On October 19, for example, he took an early morning stroll with an extremely agitated J. Robert Oppenheimer, the scientist most responsible for producing the atomic bomb. "I never saw a man in such an extremely nervous state as Oppenheimer," observed Wallace. "He seemed to feel that the destruction of the entire human race was imminent." Oppenheimer complained about Secretary of State Byrnes, remarking that he "felt that we could use the bomb as a pistol to get what we wanted in international diplomacy." That approach would not work, Oppenheimer argued, because the Russians would acquire their own nuclear weapons in the very near future. "The eventual slaughter of tens of millions of [sic] perhaps hundreds of millions of innocent people," was, Oppenheimer feared, a distinct possibility. "The guilt consciousness of the atomic bomb scientists," Wallace concluded from the meeting, "is one of the most astounding things I have ever seen."[30]

On October 23 the physicist Edward U. Condon furnished Wallace with a memorandum outlining the next steps to be taken in order to bring about international control of the bomb. Finding it useful, Wallace passed it on to Truman three days later. On October 24 the economist Alexander Sachs supplied the secretary of commerce with information that may have caused him to question the motives behind the decision to drop the atomic bombs on Japan. Sachs said that his and Roosevelt's original idea was that the first bomb would be dropped in the presence of representatives from all neutral nations. Then a second atomic bomb would be dropped on an island off the coast of Japan, after warning the Japanese government to remove their civilian population from it. "Our moral prestige in the world," Sachs lamented, "is very low as a result of the way we used the bomb." He went on to assail General Groves, claiming that he was "very ambitious, intelligent, and a Fascist."[31]

Wallace relayed these kinds of concerns to Truman. After an October 26 cabinet meeting in which Byrnes reported on the recent London Council of Foreign Ministers, Wallace stayed behind for another private conversation with the president. He passed Condon's memorandum on international control of atomic weaponry to Truman, who read part of it and then assured Wallace that he was acting on this issue. He planned to invite Britain's new prime minister, Clement Attlee, and his foreign minister, Ernest Bevin, to the United States to discuss atomic energy, after which he would broach the matter with the Russians. Wallace liked the idea, saying it was necessary because "at the moment the prestige and leadership of the United States were definitely on the skids."[32]

As well as encouraging Truman once again to transfer the "moral burden" of atomic energy secrets to the United Nations, Wallace attempted at this meeting to revise the president's views on two other matters. The first was the question of whether the loan requested by the Russians should be granted to help rebuild the Soviet economy. The terms for a loan to Britain had been worked out by this time, and Wallace now told Truman that a loan to the Russians should be granted "proportionate to their needs comparable to the loan made to the British." He went on to explain why it was in America's self-interest to have an economically stable Soviet Union:

> I said to the President there was grave danger that during the next ten years Russia might hang as a specter over the world economy in the same way as Nazi Germany did during the decade of the thirties. I said it would be possible to prevent that and we should do everything possible to prevent it. I said if we didn't prevent it we would inevitably have from five to ten million people continuously unemployed because of the fear of World War III that would be engendered in the hearts of the business men and especially the investing public.[33]

Wallace also urged Truman to reassess Soviet policies in Eastern
Europe. "The Russian attitude in the Balkan states," Wallace claimed,
"was not so greatly different from our attitude with regard to Mexico
and Cuba." It was inevitable that Russia would exert the same sort of
controlling influence over its Eastern European neighbors that the
United States had exerted over countries in its own backyard. Truman
agreed that "Russia was always talking about a cordon sanitaire."[34]

In this conversation Wallace broadened his analysis of Soviet-
American relations. International control of atomic energy was not the
only tool for reducing tensions between the emerging superpowers.
Granting the Russians a loan and developing a realistic view of Stalin's
policies in Eastern Europe were two other means. And Truman, it
seemed to Wallace, found his arguments persuasive. The president
"talked as though he completely agreed with me and as though the
thing he most wanted in the world was an understanding with Russia
which would make impossible a third world war."[35]

As Truman had not yet decided in the autumn of 1945 to abandon
the idea of cooperation with Stalin, he took note of Wallace's advice.
On the atomic bomb question, moreover, Wallace made headway: Truman would withdraw his backing for the May-Johnson bill, which
stressed the military applications of atomic energy and called for military officials in influential positions on the control board that was to be
created. Instead he came to support the McMahon bill, which emphasized the civilian uses of atomic energy and the principle of UN control. With the backing of Truman, Wallace, and a number of atomic
scientists, Congress passed the McMahon bill in August 1946.[36]

Despite his sympathy for Wallace's views on atomic energy, Truman
was not prepared—as Wallace appeared to be—to bend over backward
to accommodate Stalin. In particular, he did not privately believe that
Russian policy in Eastern Europe could be explained away as similar to
U.S. influence in Latin America. Truman was justified in thinking that
way: it would have been remiss of him not to recognize that the Red
Army controlled half of Europe. That Wallace did not acknowledge
this point was a major shortcoming in his outlook on Soviet-American
relations.

In the following weeks Wallace continued to promote the sharing of atomic energy secrets and a loan to the Soviet Union. In private talks with the president, at cabinet meetings, and in a speech at Madison Square Garden he urged Truman to make sure he, not General Groves, retained ultimate control of atomic weaponry in the United States, and he called for the sharing of atomic energy secrets with other nations as well as the effective exploitation of their peacetime uses.[37]

Throughout late 1945, Wallace's concern over the direction of American diplomacy and his determination to fashion an alternative set of policies for Truman were heightened by his links with liberal allies and his contacts with Soviet officials. In late October he attended a private dinner at which Eleanor Roosevelt was also present. "She seems," Wallace noted, "to have the same slant on the various international and atomic bomb issues that I have." On November 7 Harold Ickes told Wallace he shared his view that a small group of scientists, industrialists, and War Department officials were trying insidiously to gain control of atomic energy. When Wallace spoke to Joe Davies two weeks later, the former ambassador supplied an interpretation of the international scene that meshed with his own: unfortunately, Davies said, the British had persuaded the United States to implement a hard-line policy toward Moscow.[38]

At an October 24 luncheon, an official from the Soviet embassy, Anatole B. Gromov, explained to Wallace that Moscow was perplexed by U.S. support for an undemocratic Argentinian government at the same time it insisted on democracy in Eastern Europe. The approval of a loan to Britain but not the Soviet Union was also troubling. And the issue of the atomic bomb and the hard-line stance of Byrnes since becoming secretary of state were further irritants to Moscow. Gromov's enumeration of Soviet fears must have confirmed Wallace's belief in his own reading of the international situation.[39]

On December 29, as the new year approached, Charles Bruggmann, his brother-in-law, told Wallace about a recent discussion with friends who had visited Ireland. Several Jesuit priests, who were present at a function they attended, made clear that they were anxious to foster a war between the United States and the Soviet Union. Later that day Wallace pondered this information and listed all the groups he believed were trying to promote conflict between America and Russia:

> In addition to a small group in the Catholic hierarchy there is also a small group among the English tories and a small group in the American army . . . , a small group among the American big business hierarchy, a substantial group among the Chinese Nationalists, the London Poles and in general the more wealthy people who live in the countries close to Russia. Also there is a small group in the Navy . . . ; also there should be included in this group a very strong element in the Republican Party. All of these people feel that it is only by the United States whipping Russia that they have a chance to maintain their present position in life.

As 1945 shaded into 1946, Wallace would focus even more sharply on what he perceived as a crystallizing consensus in the West, especially in the upper echelons of the Truman administration, in favor of a tougher policy toward Moscow.[40]

CHAPTER 5

Fighting the
Cold War Consensus

―――

"Unless Russia is faced with an iron fist and strong
language another war is in the making. Only one
language do they understand—'how many
divisions have you?'"—HARRY TRUMAN,
January 5, 1946

IN EARLY 1946 Washington came around to the twin ideas that Stalin could not be trusted and that Truman needed to get tough. Uncertain at the start of his presidency about whether to break with Roosevelt's policy of getting along with the Russians, Truman now resolved to do just that. Other officials who had vacillated in 1945, notably Byrnes and Harriman, also decided to choose confrontation over cooperation with Moscow. Those who had already suggested a more hard-line approach intensified their advocacy.[1]

Changes in personnel to the Truman team accentuated this shift. With Morgenthau's resignation as secretary of the treasury, Stimson's retirement two months later, and the departure of several New Dealers, by the fall of 1945 Harry Wallace was, along with Harold Ickes, almost the only Truman adviser intent on sustaining the wartime partnership with the Soviet Union. The evaporation of those factors that had encouraged Truman and other officials to promote good relations with Moscow also contributed to a frostier U.S. approach toward the Russians. As Japan had been defeated by August 1945, there was no longer a need to placate Stalin in order to ensure he entered the war in the Far East. As the legacies of Rooseveltian cooperation and the Soviet military sacrifice during World War II drifted farther into the past, their impact on the thinking of Truman and his advisers diminished. The necessity and appropriateness of cooperation with Stalin were no longer apparent.

The specific factors that brought Truman to this conclusion included a delayed response to the fact that Eastern Europe, and particularly the Polish problem, had not been solved to his liking. But of great importance was the Iranian issue, which emerged in late 1945 and by March 1946 had developed into what some regard as the first full-blown cold war crisis. The Russian failure to uphold a previous commitment by evacuating northern Iran within six months of the end of World War II troubled Truman. Uppermost in his mind was the question of whether Stalin had territorial ambitions beyond Eastern Europe. The Soviet leader's meddling in Iran seemed to indicate that he did. For Truman, the parallel between postwar Soviet and prewar Nazi foreign policy was now clear. This time the response would need to be something more robust than appeasement.

The first sign that Truman was jettisoning the policy of cooperation with the Russians, inherited from Roosevelt, was the letter he wrote and allegedly read to James Byrnes on January 5, 1946, in the wake of the Moscow Foreign Ministers' Conference. Not only had Byrnes failed to keep him regularly informed of developments at the conference, Truman complained, he had been too willing to accept Soviet demands. After lamenting Stalin's policies in Romania and Bulgaria, Truman argued that "we ought to protest with all the vigor of which we are capable against the Russian program in Iran. There is no justification for it." He also claimed that Stalin "intends an invasion of Turkey and the seizure of the Black Sea Straits to the Mediterranean." At the end of the letter is Truman's famous remark: "I'm tired of babying the Soviets."[2]

This is a controversial episode, for Byrnes later refuted the claim by Truman in his memoirs that he had berated his secretary of state in this way. "Some years later," Byrnes wrote, "a statement was published that at this time . . . there was a serious difference between the President and me over the decisions at the Moscow Conference . . . there was no basis for the statement." Two pieces of information, however, support Truman's version. On January 13, 1946, Harriman noted that he had "had a long talk with [Postmaster General] Fred Walker in which he told me of Truman's dissatisfaction at Byrnes' plowing ahead without consultation." On March 22 Stettinius noted in his diary that Bernard Baruch, a key figure in the shaping of American policy on atomic energy, had told him that "Byrnes and the President had a very serious clash a couple of months ago." Moreover there is no doubt that Truman did write the memorandum at about this time (a stenographic copy of it exists). Even if Truman had not read the letter to Byrnes, it was an accurate representation of his attitude toward Stalin in early 1946. Truman's account of the fracas with Byrnes may have been spicier than it needed to be, but the evidence, including the change in Byrnes's approach to the Soviets, seems to verify Truman's version of events. Truman himself remained in no doubt as to the significance of his exchange with his secretary of state: "My memorandum to Byrnes . . . was the point of departure of our policy."[3]

Once Truman had decided to abandon the notion of a postwar partnership with the Russians, it did not take long for Byrnes, his most prominent adviser on foreign policy, to fall into line—though it would take a little needling and nudging from Republican senator Arthur Vandenberg, who viewed Stalin's policies as a grave threat to the West. In short, Vandenberg believed that Byrnes had been too soft with the Soviets. That was the clear implication of his Senate speech on February 27, in which he posed the rhetorical question, "What is Russia up to now?" "We ask it in Manchuria," he continued, "we ask it in Eastern Europe and the Dardanelles. We ask it in Italy. . . . We ask it in Iran. We ask it in Tripolitania." The Soviet-American partnership was only viable, he concluded, "if the United States speaks as plainly as Russia does; if the United States just as vigorously sustains its own purposes and its ideals upon all occasions as Russia does." Although Vandenberg did not mention Byrnes by name, most observers managed to read between the lines. *Time* interpreted the speech as "a clear challenge to Secretary of State, Byrnes," and the *New York Times* pointed out that "while he did not mention James F. Byrnes . . . Mr. Vandenberg indicated by sharp implication that he saw a lack of American leadership."[4]

Sensing that this criticism was eroding his credibility, and aware that Vandenberg's public pronouncements jibed with Truman's private comments, Byrnes decided it was time to bid farewell to the spirit of compromise that had guided his diplomacy at the Moscow Conference. He revealed his new approach on February 28, the day after Vandenberg's address, in a speech to the Overseas Press Club. "No power has a right to help itself to alleged enemy properties in liberated or ex-satellite countries before a reparation settlement has been agreed upon by the Allies," he declared in obvious reference to Soviet occupation policies. "We have not and will not agree to any power deciding for itself what it will take from these countries." Byrnes went on to say that "we cannot allow aggression to be accomplished by coercion or pressure, or by subterfuges such as political infiltration."[5]

It was clear that Byrnes would now be using an iron fist rather than kid gloves in his dealings with the Russians; and that was very much to the liking of Truman (and Vandenberg). On receiving an advance copy of the speech, Truman wrote to Byrnes: "Jim, I've read it and like it— A good speech! I've marked some phrases I particularly like." With Byrnes now on board as well as Truman, the anti-Soviet bandwagon in Washington gathered momentum.[6]

Lingering doubts among Truman's advisers about the wisdom of getting tough with Stalin were largely removed by a series of developments in early 1946. The first of these was the "election speech" delivered by Stalin on February 9, in which he urged the Russian people to strive to rebuild the war-torn Soviet economy. Rapid growth was vital, he argued, because the instability of the capitalist world meant that future war was a possibility.[7]

Stalin's target audience had been domestic, but his speech created a stir internationally, especially in Washington. Charles Bohlen believed it resuscitated "all the harsh and antagonistic elements of Bolshevism," while Acheson felt that Stalin had expressed "with brutal clarity the Soviet Union's postwar policy. . . . He [had] concluded that no peaceful international order was possible." To Truman and his advisers, the significance of Stalin's speech was clear: if he had no faith that America and Russia could get along, why should they?[8]

Two days after the "election speech," the full Yalta accords, including the secret protocol on the territorial concessions to be made to Stalin in the Far East in return for Soviet entry into the war against Japan, were made public. Viewed uncharitably, it appeared that a tired Roosevelt had "sold out" to Stalin as part of a surreptitious deal. The policy of cooperation with the Russians was thus further discredited. Only five days after this, the Canadian government announced the arrest of twenty-two atomic spies working for Moscow. No doubt the Canadian spy scandal perturbed Truman and his advisers. To U.S. policymakers, it seemed to be shocking evidence of Russian deceit.[9]

On February 22 George Kennan sent his now-famous "Long Telegram" from Moscow, where he was chargé d'affaires in the American embassy, to Washington. "For eighteen long months," Kennan recalled, "I had done little else but pluck people's sleeves, trying to make them understand the nature of the phenomenon with which we in the Moscow embassy were daily concerned. Now, suddenly, my opinion was being asked. . . . They had asked for it. Now, by God, they would have it." In his dispatch, Kennan depicted the Soviet Union in the darkest hues. "We have here a political force committed fanatically to the belief that with the United States there can be no permanent modus vivendi," he asserted, "that . . . our traditional way of life be destroyed, the international authority of our state be broken, if Soviet power is to be secure." Because it rigidly adhered to the notion of capitalist encirclement, he argued, the Soviet Union did not believe a long-term cooperative relationship with the United States was possible.[10]

Kennan's telegram had "a deep effect on thinking within the government," noted Acheson. So helpful did Forrestal find the telegram that he had it mimeographed and sent to all cabinet members who dealt with foreign and military matters. "My reputation," recalled Kennan, "was made." As he perceived, his telegram's success was linked to the receptive mood of administration officials. "It was one of those moments," he wrote, "when Washington . . . was ready to receive a given message." Truman and his advisers had already concluded that they needed to get tough with the Russians. Kennan provided them with the intellectual foundation and precise terminology for that new policy.[11]

For his part, Henry Wallace thought the policy had been in the making for some time, in fact since Roosevelt's death. But his dealings with various people during the early months of 1946—social as well as political contacts—left him with the feeling that support for a hard-line policy toward Moscow was growing even stronger.

A dinner hosted by the columnist Joseph Alsop on the evening of January 2 gave Wallace just that impression. Leaving the women for some after-dinner banter, the men at the party turned to the Soviet question. Where Alsop and William S. Gaud, executive assistant to Secretary of War Robert Patterson, argued that Truman needed to be tougher with Stalin, Wallace and Supreme Court Justice Hugo Black stressed the importance of maintaining good relations with Moscow. Gaud said the United States needed to "kick the Russians in the balls" by opposing their expansionist policies at every juncture. Wallace implied that some Soviet ambitions were reasonable, saying "the Russians were entitled to free access through the Dardanelles" as "they had been promised this in World War I." Gaud called that argument "crap." Wallace replied that Gaud's comments had been "crap." "Well, then," Gaud observed, "we are even." Later in the conversation, Alsop asserted that Russia was comparable to Nazi Germany in the nature of its government and its aggressive foreign policy.[12]

Writing in his diary later that evening, Wallace concluded: "There is only one logical action that can be taken if the Alsop point of view is adhered to and that is to provoke a war with Russia as soon as possible."[13]

Beyond the belligerence of Alsop and Gaud, what worried Wallace about the conversation was the journalist's connections. He believed that Alsop "played very closely with the State Department boys and with the boys in the War Department." So perhaps Alsop expressed his opinions with such confidence because he knew they were shared by people in high places.[14]

A luncheon with former ambassador to the Soviet Union William C. Bullitt on February 12 also troubled Wallace. Bullitt said that though he was a loyal Democrat and liked Wallace's views on domestic policy, he thought his foreign policy outlook was "pretty bad," that it included a lot of the ideas embraced by Joe Davies. Wallace admitted that his views were close to Davies's. He went on to explain that his basic aim was to avoid World War III and to raise the standard of living throughout the underdeveloped regions of the world.[15]

The conversation then turned to Stalin's "election speech." Bullitt was highly critical of it, but Wallace considered it no more than an understandable response to the decision made by the American military to ring the Soviet Union with bases in places like Iceland, Alaska, and Okinawa. "We were challenging him," Wallace claimed, "and his speech was taking up the challenge."[16]

When Bullitt claimed that the Russians had already assimilated Romania, Wallace said he did not think so. Displaying what in retrospect appears to be a striking naiveté, he argued that Soviet policymakers had a completely different approach to Eastern Europe than they did to the Baltic states such as Lithuania. "The Balkan states had never been a part of Russia," he stated, "and . . . I certainly did not think it was Communist policy to impose the Communist economic system on the Balkans." This was Wallace at his most blinkered. Stalin was carving out an empire in Eastern Europe, and that represented a serious matter for the United States.[17]

As with the Alsop conversation, Wallace regarded his talk with Bullitt as significant. The former ambassador was well connected, and Wallace assumed he was part of a coterie of officials and Washington insiders pushing Truman to get tough with Stalin. "Bill unquestionably is a part of some group," he believed. "Who are the members of his group I don't know."[18]

Adding to Wallace's sense that both American foreign policy and the composition of the Washington power structure was shifting to the right was the continued loss or departure in early 1946 of men who had been close to FDR. At the end of January Harry Hopkins died. In early February Secretary of the Interior Ickes resigned over Truman's nomination of Ed Pauley as his new undersecretary of the navy. Viewing him as an unprincipled operator, Ickes testified before the Senate Naval Affairs Committee that Pauley, who had extensive oil interests, had once told him that a lot of money could be raised for the Democratic party campaign coffers in California should the Justice Department decide not to bring the tidelands oil deposits into the federal domain. Indicating his continued support for Pauley at a February 7 press conference, Truman said Ickes might be mistaken in his view of Pauley. Regarding that as a vote of no confidence, Ickes resigned. Since Truman's arrival in the White House, resignation, dismissal, retirement, and death had removed the New Dealers one by one. By mid-February 1946, a mere ten months after FDR's death, Wallace—as a leading light of the New Deal left—felt completely isolated.[19]

The anti-Soviet trend in Washington was furthered by Churchill's "iron curtain" speech delivered in Fulton, Missouri, on March 5. After an introduction by Truman in which he asked the former prime minister to speak candidly, Churchill declared that world peace had been jeopardized by Soviet expansionism. "From Stettin in the Baltic to Trieste in the Adriatic, an iron curtain has descended across the continent," he lamented. "Behind that line lie all the capitals of the ancient states of central and eastern Europe." Churchill called for "a special relationship between the British Commonwealth and Empire and the United States," in which they would use the American monopoly of the atomic bomb to counter Russian aggression. With FDR's death, Churchill was the most celebrated figure to emerge from World War II in the West, and the approach he suggested helped legitimize Truman's already hardening foreign policy outlook.[20]

That worried Wallace. He fervently believed that if the United States sided with Britain against the Soviet Union, it would exacerbate tensions by heightening Soviet suspicions of the West. Instead Washington should serve as neutral arbiter of Anglo-Russian disagreements. Wallace's view was influenced, as J. Samuel Walker has written, by "his long-standing Anglophobia."[21]

On March 5 Wallace explained his concerns at a dinner party hosted by Dean and Alice Acheson, and attended by the Walter Lippmanns, the Charles Bohlens, and Australian ambassador Dick Casey and his wife. Instead of building a military alliance with Britain, as Churchill had proposed, the United States should work toward disarmament, "including inspection of atomic bomb facilities and supplies." In any case, Wallace added, to have two key members of the United

Nations gang up against a third would undermine that organization. Casey was not persuaded. "We might as well talk about a trip to the moon," he said of Wallace's disarmament proposal.[22]

Wallace went on to say of the "iron curtain" speech that he

> didn't see how these warlike words of Churchill now could have any more real influence on the Russians than his warlike attitude toward the Bolsheviks had in 1919. . . . The American people were not willing to send American boys anywhere to fight now; that certainly the Russians did not want to fight anybody now; that in all probability the situation would finally work out on a basis that would cause the Russians completely and utterly to distrust us; . . . that it would cause the Russians to engage in a race with us in the making of atomic bombs; that while they might be a long way behind us at the present time they would have enough bombs to destroy us fifteen years hence; that with the Russians completely distrusting us because of the way we had handled them they would not scruple fifteen years hence to drop bombs on us without warning; that they would have no hesitation in continuing their fifth column activities in all the nations of the world; that they could use these fifth columnists effectively to destroy our form of government.[23]

What disturbed Wallace about Churchill's speech was also the possibility that Truman agreed with its general thrust. At a press conference on March 8 the president said he did not know beforehand what Churchill had intended to say in his Fulton address. Asked to comment on the contents of the speech, he declined.[24]

The president's response squared with what he told Wallace on March 12 during a private discussion at the White House. He "had not seen Churchill's speech in advance," the president claimed. Wallace said that Churchill had insulted Truman by making such a reckless address with him on the platform. He also told Truman an anecdote about a discussion between Churchill and Roosevelt in which he had participated: when the prime minister suggested the creation of an Anglo-Saxon alliance, FDR did not endorse the proposal. Wallace had then announced that he vehemently opposed such an idea: an Anglo-Saxon alliance would alienate the rest of the world. A better policy would be for the United States to develop "a regional sphere of influence" with its Latin American neighbors. Churchill, Wallace recalled, "turned up his nose at this and said that as a painter he knew that when you mixed the colors you got a dirty brown." It was "just like Churchill to make a crack like that," Truman commented. During the rest of their discussion, Wallace argued that Truman should help arbitrate disputes between London and Moscow rather than side with Britain against the Russians.[25]

But Wallace received other information indicating that Truman had in fact read and approved the "iron curtain" speech before Churchill delivered it. He noted, for example, a March 6 *New York Times* report which claimed that, "A fortnight ago the former Prime Minister made a trip to Washington to talk over what he meant to say; so it is not to be supposed that the Missourian made any objection to the Britisher's appeal for a 'fraternal association of the English-speaking powers.'" That Truman appeared to share Churchill's hard-line views left Wallace indignant.[26]

It seems certain that Truman had indeed seen the "iron curtain" speech beforehand. According to Churchill himself, Truman read it, saying that "it was admirable and would do nothing but good though it would make a stir." Truman did not espouse Churchill's proposal for a special Anglo-American atomic partnership, but he probably found the speech's general anti-Soviet tone more pleasing.[27]

A meeting on March 14 with Eleanor Roosevelt reinforced Wallace's concerns about Churchill's address. She was "very much put out with Churchill," Wallace noticed, "and feels that Churchill took advantage of Truman in a most terrible way." Her late husband had enjoyed a cordial relationship with Churchill because they had many common interests, such as a passionate love for ships and the sea. But, she added, "Roosevelt never had any illusions as to Churchill when peace came."[28]

After the meeting with Eleanor Roosevelt, Wallace saw Walter Bedell Smith, who had been appointed Harriman's replacement as ambassador to the Soviet Union. Their discussion was important because it represented the start of a concerted effort by Wallace to counter Churchill's "iron curtain" speech by arguing that a delegation should be sent to Moscow to boost Soviet-American trade and, in this way, maintain friendly relations between the emerging superpowers. In other words, Wallace developed a strategy that appealed to American economic self-interest in order to undercut the move toward a harder-line approach to the Russians that Churchill's speech had capped. To promote this plan, Wallace cleared with Smith a memorandum that he was about to give Truman. After reading it, Smith said he thought a trip by Wallace to the Soviet Union might be a good idea. Wallace replied that he would like to do that but thought the proposal needed careful consideration.[29]

Wallace handed the memorandum to Truman the next day, March 15. In it the secretary of commerce expressed the hope that Smith's arrival in Moscow would break "the present diplomatic deadlock in U.S.-Soviet relations." That goal would be easier for the new ambassador to achieve, however, if a dialogue were initiated with the Russians on economic matters. "We know," Wallace asserted, "that much of the recent Soviet behavior which has caused us concern has been the result of their dire economic needs and of their disturbed sense of security." "I think we can disabuse the Soviet mind," he continued, "and strengthen the faith of the Soviets in our sincere devotion to the cause of peace by proving to them that we want to trade with them and to cement economic relations with them." To that end, Wallace suggested that Truman send a delegation to Moscow to begin negotiations.[30]

Attached to the memorandum was a note to Truman in which Wallace explained that he had already discussed this matter with Smith, who had indicated his interest in taking along a copy of the letter when he left for Moscow on March 20. Wallace asked Truman to initial his approval of the memorandum and to pass it on to Smith.[31]

After Truman had finished reading the memorandum, Wallace told Truman that Smith had suggested he visit the Soviet Union at some point. But he did not wish to go, he said, and he certainly thought it inappropriate for him to go unless the State Department as well as Smith endorsed the idea. Truman said he too would like Wallace to go to Moscow. At that point Wallace became wary and backed away from the proposition. Later he revealed his suspicion that Truman and

Smith wanted him to visit the Soviet Union in order to destroy him politically. He had been scarred by a trip to Soviet Asia in 1944 that had been exploited by those critics who accused him of having left-wing sympathies. "All these people that urged me to go to Russia [in the spring of 1946]," Wallace reflected, "were really asking me to sign my political death warrant."[32]

Wallace's attempt to discredit Churchill's analysis of the international situation and to promote Soviet-American trade moved from the private to the public sphere on March 19 when he delivered a speech in honor of Averell Harriman at a dinner given by the American Society for Russian Relief. Wallace told the assembled guests that it was essential to maintain peace between the superpowers. He called, as Nikita Khrushchev would during the 1950s, for a peaceful Soviet-American competition to see which system could best improve the quality of life for its peoples and those in other countries.[33]

Wallace concluded his address by challenging the concepts embraced by Churchill—and by *Time*'s Henry Luce. The United States, he contended, must make it clear to the Russians that it had no intention of creating an anti-Soviet alliance. Referring to *Time*'s characterization of the U.S. role in the world, as well as Churchill's ideas, Wallace declared, "We are opposed to any ideas of 'The American Century' or the 'Anglo-Saxon Century.' The common people of the world will not tolerate any recrudescence of imperialism even under enlightened Anglo-Saxon atomic bomb auspices. If the English-speaking people have any destiny at all, it is to serve the world, not to dominate it." As in the memorandum he gave Truman, he argued that the development of "maximum trade between the two countries" was the best way for Washington and Moscow to preserve good relations.[34]

By March 1946, however, Truman had decided to get tough with Stalin. Hence he was less sympathetic to Wallace's proposals than he had been during the fall of 1945 over the question of atomic energy. For that reason he decided against giving Wallace's memorandum to Smith to take to Moscow. On March 20 he wrote to Wallace thanking him for his letter on the trade mission. Without saying whether he had handed it to the new ambassador, he told Wallace that he had talked to

Smith and felt that he was leaving for Moscow with "the right attitude in mind" and so would help improve Soviet-American relations.[35]

Truman, though, had not banked on Wallace checking again with Smith. When Wallace did so, he found that Truman had not given Smith his memorandum; so he wrote to Truman on March 21, asking him about this. "I wondered if this was an oversight," he queried, "or if you felt it would be unwise for him to have this letter." At the end of a cabinet meeting the next day, Truman assured Wallace that he would send his memorandum on to Smith. He indicated that he had been unable to give it to Smith the last time he saw him because Byrnes was present and would not have approved. The more plausible explanation, however, is that the president now felt certain that the conciliatory foreign policy advocated by Wallace, and encapsulated in his memorandum, was not in American interests. "I ignored this letter of Wallace's," recalled Truman. "I had expressed my policy to Bedell Smith and had suggested the approach he should take to the Kremlin. I could see little to be gained from the Wallace proposal."[36]

If the development of Soviet-American trade was the main antidote prescribed by Wallace to counteract Churchill's bleak vision of a world divided by an iron curtain, a sensible approach to the question of the atomic bomb was a secondary alternative. Throughout the early months of 1946, Wallace continued to argue, as he had during the previous fall, that more attention must be paid to the peacetime applications of atomic energy.

Much of Wallace's concern with this issue centered on the atomic bomb tests scheduled by the Navy Department. In a memorandum on February 8, Wallace urged Truman to appoint a civilian committee to oversee the tests, thereby preventing the military from interpreting their results simply to further its own interests. In mid-March, at the same time he was promoting a trade mission to Moscow, Wallace argued that two of the three atomic bomb tests planned by the Navy Department should be canceled. All the tests could in fact be called off, he claimed, if a "really effective inspection service" were established to make sure that no other nations acquired nuclear weapons. In the end, Truman decided to conduct the first test in July rather than May, and to delay the other two indefinitely.[37]

The other atomic issue on Wallace's agenda in the spring of 1946 was the McMahon bill, by which Congress was to establish a commission to supervise atomic development in the United States. What concerned Wallace was the Senate Committee on Atomic Energy's adoption on March 13 of the Vandenberg amendment to the bill. That amendment provided for a military board, consisting of War and Navy Department officials, with which the new atomic commission would be obliged to consult. To Wallace this was unacceptable, and he told Truman just that. "The issue," he said to the president, "is simply whether there shall be civilian or military control over atomic energy." He thus urged Truman to oppose the Vandenberg amendment, and encouraged others, like Eleanor Roosevelt, to do the same. In the end, Vandenberg was compelled to fashion a revised amendment that curtailed the authority of the military board.[38]

The hard-line consensus—against which Wallace was now fighting an uphill battle—solidified among Truman and his advisers as a consequence of the Iranian crisis. This controversy was rooted in Moscow's reluctance to remove its troops from northern Iran, and the support it appeared to give to a separatist movement (the Tudeh party) in the Iranian province of Azerbaijan. Truman suspected Stalin of attempting to incorporate Azerbaijan into the Russian sphere of influence. The Soviets, along with the British and Americans, had promised to withdraw their troops, which had occupied northern Iran during the war, by March 2, 1946. Unlike its allies, the Soviet Union failed to do this, and in response Byrnes dispatched a note to Moscow three days later requesting immediate withdrawal of Russian soldiers from Iran. Reacting to reports of Soviet troop movements toward Teheran, Iraq, and Turkey, Byrnes exclaimed, "Now we'll give it to them with both barrels." On March 8 he demanded an explanation of recent troop movements from his Soviet counterpart, but failed to elicit a response.[39]

The crisis was resolved on April 4 when the Soviet and Iranian governments announced that Russian troops would be withdrawn in early May, and that Iranian sovereignty over Azerbaijan would be restored. It was also agreed that the Soviet Union would receive oil concessions from Iran—though the Majlis, the Iranian parliament, later repudiated this part of the settlement.[40]

To Truman, the Iranian crisis confirmed the correctness of his interpretation of Stalin's foreign policy as expansionist. The eventual Soviet withdrawal from Iran seemed also to demonstrate that the uncompromising approach adopted by Byrnes had been effective. He had talked tough, and the Russians had backed down. For Truman the lesson was clear: a tough approach was the best way to restrain Stalin.

Wallace's general lack of concern with the Iranian crisis was curious. In a memorandum to Truman on March 20, he argued that the UN Security Council should take up the Iranian question in order to "localize the issues and not precipitate a general break" with the Russians. Somewhat cryptically, he called for negotiations and "a Potsdam Agreement for the Middle East." But Wallace failed to consider Stalin's motives in Iran. While Wallace's attempt to promote Soviet-American trade was a reasonable position, his failure to incorporate Stalin's conduct over the Iranian question into his overall view of Soviet foreign policy was not. Stalin's domination of Eastern Europe, though plainly reprehensible, could be explained by Russian security fears. On many occasions in the past, most recently during World War II, Eastern Europe had been the corridor through which hostile powers had passed on their way east. The same reason could not be cited in explaining Soviet policies toward Iran.[41]

The emergence of the anti-Soviet consensus in the Truman administration in early 1946 set Wallace apart from his colleagues more clearly than before. He still thought a Soviet-American partnership was viable and essential; Truman and his advisers were increasingly certain it was not. For the most part these differences were apparent only behind closed doors. At some point, however, the divergence between Wallace and his colleagues on foreign policy was sure to become public knowledge. The controversy over the cabinet discussion of the atomic issue in September 1945 had first alerted the American people to the tension between Wallace and other administration officials. On May 20, 1946, a Joseph Alsop article in *Life* magazine informed them afresh of the chasm that now separated the secretary of commerce from his fellow cabinet officers.

The origin of this report lay in Wallace's March 21 conversation with Ruben Karlsted of the Associated Press. Karlsted had told Wallace on that occasion that the Scandinavian countries were looking forward to an American military withdrawal from Iceland. When Wallace said he thought they wanted a U.S. base in Iceland as protection from the Russians, Karlsted assured him that was not the case. Wallace then revealed his private belief that "it would be better for the peace of the world if the United States could be pulled out of Iceland; that undoubtedly the Russians looked on it as a direct threat against them." The Scandinavian journalist agreed, saying Icelanders felt that the presence of American troops violated their sovereign rights. Wallace emphasized to Karlsted that his own remarks on Iceland were made "as a private citizen and not as a member of the United States government."[42]

Karlsted, however, conveyed Wallace's views to Alsop; and the very next day, in a private meeting, Alsop upbraided Wallace for his stance on Iceland. Two months later he wrote the article in *Life*, revealing to the American public Wallace's hitherto private views on the American base in Iceland.[43]

The Alsop article sparked a flurry of press comment about Wallace in the late spring and early summer of 1946. Newspaper reports emphasized his acrimonious relations with other political figures and speculated that he might leave the cabinet and mount a challenge to Truman for the 1948 Democratic presidential nomination. Cold war politics and domestic politics were becoming entwined.

Typical of the media coverage was a piece in the *Chicago Tribune* in late May, entitled "Hint Wallace May Resign to Fight Truman," claiming that Wallace had been so angered by Truman's decision to introduce a bill granting him coercive powers to deal with the coal and railroad strikes (by, for example, drafting strikers into the army) that he was contemplating resignation and seeking his party's presidential nomination two years hence. A week before, the *Tribune* reported, Wallace had reiterated his backing for Truman in 1948. When asked whether he felt the same way after Truman's introduction of the labor bill, Wallace had apparently said, "No comment." The article went on to say that Democratic National Chairman Hannegan would do all he could to prevent a Truman-Wallace split because it would produce "a desperate battle for the nomination and presage the bolt of the left wingers in the election if the President should be nominated to succeed himself."⁴⁴

A *New York Herald Tribune* article by Bert Andrews, meanwhile, highlighted Wallace's isolation on international affairs. Whereas Truman, Byrnes, and Vandenberg agreed on the need for firmness in dealing with Russia, Andrews stated on June 2, Wallace and Florida senator Claude Pepper did not. Those two figures, said Andrews, should either support the administration policy or keep quiet. Twelve days later the *Wall Street Journal* reported that "Wallace's pose as a Soviet authority irks the State Department."⁴⁵

In addition to the reports on Wallace's isolation within the Truman administration, rumors circulated that a third party, spearheaded by Wallace, might form. On June 14 he confronted the issue directly in a St. Louis speech organized by the Liberal Voters League of St. Louis and the National Citizens Political Action Committee. "In recent weeks," he told his audience, "there has been considerable talk about the need for a third party. Now let us analyze this talk bluntly and realistically." Wallace then proceeded to dismiss the idea. The Democratic party, he insisted, was still a viable vehicle for progressive change; and besides, a third party would ensure the election of "a reactionary Republican" in 1948.⁴⁶

As Wallace prepared for the political season ahead—the fall campaign for the 1946 congressional elections, in which he intended to participate fully—he was well aware of his precarious position with Truman and the extent to which the public knew about it.

In his diary on July 16 he wrote: "Today, on the second anniversary of the [Democratic Party] Chicago convention, I couldn't help thinking that so many of the men in the Roosevelt entourage who worked hard for Truman at Chicago are now nearly all out of the government in Washington. Some of them have died; practically all of the others have left for one reason or another." In the Truman administration, Wallace was alone. Two months later he would be out.⁴⁷

CHAPTER 6

Eleven Days in September

—

"I want to go on record now for the sake of my
grandchildren and great grandchildren as
indicating that if there is war with Russia the
criminals will be those who beat the tom-toms for
war in 1946. There will also be blame attached to
those who were so blind they could not see."
—HENRY WALLACE, diary entry,
September 18, 1946

O N THE afternoon of July 18, 1946, Henry Wallace entered the
White House for a meeting with President Truman. After discussing
the upcoming congressional elections, Wallace turned to the question
of Soviet-American economic relations. During the fall of 1945, he had
argued that a loan should be granted to Stalin, and in the spring of
1946 he had advocated a dramatic expansion in trade between the
superpowers as a way of countering the anti-Soviet consensus that was
forming in Washington. Now he returned to that theme. "There
might come a time sometime during the next five or six months," Wallace said, "when it would be very important to world peace and world
trade to be in a position to loan Russia a little money."[1]

Appeasing his secretary of commerce, Truman declared, "We don't
have any aggression whatever in our plans against Russia." Although
this might be the case, said Wallace, that was not how the Russians per-

ceived the situation "because of the way in which the United States was handling the atomic bomb, because of its air bases all over the world."[2]

Truman then showed Wallace a dispatch he had received from Ambassador Smith in Moscow on the prevailing economic difficulties in White Russia and the Ukraine. "We could," the president concluded, "be a great help to Russia if Russia would only let us help her. But she is continuously suspicious of us." Wallace responded by renewing his case that a cordial relationship with the Soviet Union was in America's self-interest: "I told him that we were much concerned with Russia because it had a great deal to do with the future volume of world trade." Pledging to provide the president with a letter on the Soviet situation when they saw each other again five days later, Wallace asked Truman to consider passing it on to Byrnes.[3]

Wallace made good on his promise when on July 23 he handed Truman a memorandum on relations with Russia. He had worked on it diligently, in consultation with several colleagues in the Commerce Department, before producing the final version. When Wallace said the letter would not receive approval from "those who believed that war with Russia was inevitable," Truman indicated that he disagreed with those pessimists and promised to read it carefully and to discuss it with Wallace later.[4]

Wallace's July 23 letter neatly summarized the policy ideas he had developed over the past fifteen months. Arguing that America's fundamental goal should be the avoidance of another war, he suggested that recent U.S. policies did not further that objective. Other nations, by which he meant the Soviet Union, were troubled by Truman's defense initiatives. Putting himself in Stalin's shoes, he asked: "How would it look to us if Russia had the atomic bomb and we did not, if Russia had 10,000-mile bombers and air bases within a thousand miles of our coast lines and we did not?"[5]

No lasting security was to be found, Wallace reasoned, in either an attempt to preserve America's atomic monopoly or an attack on the Soviet Union before it acquired nuclear weapons. The first approach was unsound because Moscow would soon have the bomb anyway, and even if the United States still enjoyed a massive strategic superiority over the Soviets, it would be meaningless because even a few nuclear weapons would be sufficient to inflict immense damage upon industrial and population centers in the United States. The second strategy would not work because a Red Army invasion of continental Europe would follow any American nuclear strike on the Soviet Union. What would Truman do then? Drop atomic bombs on the cities of Europe?[6]

Moving on to the policies he thought would help preserve the peace, Wallace argued that international control of atomic energy was the most important goal. The problem with the Truman administration's latest offer on this issue, the Baruch Plan, was its stipulation that the Soviet Union and other nations refrain from developing their own atomic weapons and agree to a system of inspections before Washington would consider sharing the secrets of atomic energy. Instead, Wallace argued, the United States "must be prepared to reach an agreement which will commit us to disclosing information and destroying our bombs at a specified time or in terms of specified actions by other countries, rather than at our unfettered discretion." At all costs, he added, an "atomic bomb race" must be avoided.[7]

The development of Soviet-American economic relations was, in Wallace's opinion, another way to promote superpower harmony. Pondering whether Truman might grant Moscow a loan, he argued that the expansion of trade between their two nations "might well help to clear away the fog of political misunderstanding."[8]

In addition to sharing the secrets of atomic energy and promoting closer commercial ties, Wallace made a number of other recommendations. The Truman administration must attempt to resolve issues fairly. "Most of us," Wallace explained by way of example, "are firmly convinced of the soundness of our position when we suggest the internationalization and defortification of the Danube or the Dardanelles, but we would be horrified and angered by say [a] Russian counter-proposal that would involve also the internationalizing and disarming of Suez or Panama." Wallace also called for an effort to counter the anti-Soviet propaganda spread by "certain individuals and publications" in the United States. And he suggested that Truman decide against further increases in military spending. It would antagonize other nations, and anyway, "We are by far the most powerful nation in the world, the only

Allied nation which came out of the war without devastation and much
stronger than before the war."9

"I think that progressive leadership," Wallace concluded, "along
the lines suggested above would represent and best serve the interests
of the large majority of our people, would reassert the forward looking
position of the Democratic Party in international affairs, and, finally,
would arrest the new trend towards isolationism and a disastrous
atomic world war."10

Wallace's letter was not entirely convincing. Most important he
failed to provide the sort of critique of Soviet policy in Eastern Europe
and Iran that he made of Truman's foreign and defense policies. His
analysis lacked balance. Nonetheless it was his most carefully crafted
presentation on foreign policy since Truman had become president.
When the Navy Department tried in September to discredit the ideas
developed by Wallace in his July 23 letter, one official privately told
Forrestal that his arguments "are quite obviously the result of long
consideration and reasoning and probably can not be easily brushed
aside."11

On the morning of July 24 Truman tossed Wallace's memorandum
across his desk to his naval aide Clark Clifford. "Read this carefully,
then come back and talk to me about it. It looks as though Henry is going to pull an 'Ickes.'" Truman's speculation worried Clifford because
the controversy preceding the resignation of Ickes in February 1946
had been damaging to the administration.12

Returning to his office, Clifford called in his assistant, George M.
Elsey, and read Wallace's letter aloud. The secretary of commerce,
Clifford predicted to Elsey, "was preparing . . . for a public break with
the President by positioning himself as a 'man of peace.'" In later years
Clifford would argue that Wallace's letter should have forced Truman
to resolve the dilemma presented by Wallace's markedly different approach to foreign policy and his continued presence in the administration. But after evaluating it for three days with Clifford, Truman could
not decide on an appropriate response. He told Clifford that he did not
trust Wallace, but at the same time he asked him to show the letter to
Byrnes, as Wallace had requested. Clifford obliged, carrying the letter
in person to the secretary of state. Byrnes was about to leave for the

Paris Peace Conference and had time to read it only with a cursory eye.[13]

Truman finally wrote to Wallace two weeks later, confirming that he had read his letter. Without endorsing or refuting Wallace's arguments, he simply said he appreciated the time Wallace had taken to articulate his views. "I have been giving this entire subject a great deal of thought," he added, "and I shall continue to do so." Although Truman had promised to discuss Wallace's letter with him further, he did not propose a meeting. "Apparently," Wallace commented privately, "he doesn't wish to talk."[14]

One of the reasons Truman felt he could not break with Wallace over the letter, even though the views expressed in it were plainly at odds with his own, was the secretary of commerce's enduring popularity with many Americans and the political strength this implied. A Gallup poll indicated that Wallace was the seventh most admired man in the world. Truman was third, Churchill came fifth, and James Byrnes was tenth. So even though opinion polls also showed that the public had—unlike Wallace—become increasingly suspicious of the Soviet Union in 1946, Truman still had to tread carefully.[15]

Most important, the president and his advisers recognized that Wallace was a hero to liberal Democrats and, moreover, that he was viewed by many as the only remaining link between the Truman and Roosevelt presidencies. As Clifford later acknowledged:

> Our failure to come to terms with the dangers posed by Wallace stemmed, in part, from our own inexperience. But it was also based on a political reality. With the exception of Eleanor Roosevelt, Wallace was the leading liberal in the nation in 1946, the embodiment of the link between the Truman administration and the New Deal. The new President determined that he would try to live with Wallace rather than alienate the large constituency he still retained among liberals and farmers.

It is all too easy, in the case of Wallace, to read history backward. His later break with the Democratic party seemed so reckless and his defeat as the Progressive candidate in the 1948 presidential election so ignominious that it is easy to assume that in 1946 he was already a political irrelevancy, or close to it. But that was far from the truth, and Truman knew it. Hence his reluctance to part with Wallace that summer.[16]

August proved to be the calm before the storm. No cabinet meetings took place between August 2 and September 6. On August 16 the president departed on the *Williamsburg* yacht for a Bermuda vacation. Wallace left Washington with his wife on August 29 for an official visit to Mexico. He returned early on the morning of Tuesday, September 10.[17]

Just over three hours later he went to the White House for a meeting with Truman that had been arranged before the president had left on his cruise. According to the record of Truman's appointments, his talk with Wallace began at 11 a.m. and finished at 11:15—the time set for a meeting with Joe Davies. Wallace's diary also indicates that his talk with Truman started at 11 a.m. The secretary of commerce's next meeting was at noon, presumably back in the Department of Commerce. Wallace's personal record thus does not supply a time for the end of his meeting with Truman. These details would later prove to be important as Truman and Wallace provided conflicting accounts of their talk that day.[18]

In his memoirs Truman claimed that the meeting lasted fifteen minutes and was dominated by a discussion of various Commerce Department and world food board matters. Only just before he departed, according to the president, did Wallace mention that he would speak in New York on September 12, arguing that the United States should adopt neither a pro-British nor an anti-Soviet outlook. Truman said he thought Wallace would help New York Democrats in the congressional elections by his appearance. "There was, of course," Truman wrote, "no time for me to read the speech, even in part."[19]

In his diary entry, which unlike Truman's memoir was dictated at the time, Wallace provided a fuller version of the meeting. At the start of their conversation he had talked about various matters arising from his trip to Mexico. After that, Wallace "went over page by page with him my Madison Square Garden speech to be given on September 12th. Again and again he said, 'That's right'; 'Yes, that is what I believe.' He didn't have a single change to suggest. He twice said how deeply he appreciated my courtesy in showing him my speech before I gave it." According to Wallace, Truman pointed to no inconsistency between his address and the hard line recently taken by James Byrnes in a speech in Stuttgart on September 6. Moreover the president spoke optimistically about the future, saying that Soviet-American relations were "much more peaceful than the newspapers would have us believe." Expressing concern about the state of Stalin's health, Truman implied that he would rather deal with the present Soviet dictator than Molotov.[20]

In later years Wallace added to his record of the meeting by explaining that he wondered at the time whether Truman saw the contradiction between this speech and the foreign policy being implemented by Byrnes:

> I can't explain Truman on matters of that sort. I don't know whether it's lack of information or a feeling that if you let things drift everything will wash out—let the political forces bang away at each other. . . . It may be that that's his technique for handling political situations—turn the forces loose and let them kill each other off and I'll back them all and stand on the sidelines. Maybe that's his formula, I don't know. That's the only way I know how to explain his capacity to be on the side of everybody.[21]

When Truman claimed in his memoirs that he hadn't time to read even part of Wallace's address, he was being disingenuous. A brisk reading of the speech takes ten or eleven minutes. Given that their meeting apparently lasted about a quarter of an hour, there was perhaps just sufficient time for the president to have read it all, and for the two men to have touched on the other matters they discussed on that occasion. Even if there had not been enough time for a careful reading of the entire address, at the very least Truman could have read a good deal of it closely and examined a few sections in a superficial way. It seems clear, therefore, that Truman did gain a precise sense of the content of the speech from his meeting with Wallace.[22]

The controversy generated by the Madison Square Garden speech was magnified by the president's prior, public endorsement. During a White House press conference on Thursday, September 12, the issue of Wallace's address that evening arose when a journalist revealed that

"In the middle of the speech are these words, 'When President Truman read these words, he said that they represented the policy of this Administration.'" "That is correct," Truman responded. "My question is, does that apply just to that paragraph, or to the whole speech?" "I approved the whole speech." When asked whether he thought Wallace's speech was at odds with the foreign policy being carried out by Byrnes, Truman replied emphatically, "I do not." "They are," he added, "exactly in line."[23]

Behind the scenes, Truman's advisers viewed Wallace's speech with less equanimity. The consensus at a meeting of officials convened in Acting Secretary of State Will Clayton's office just two hours before Wallace was due to speak was that the address should be canceled or modified. That view was passed on to press secretary Charlie Ross at the White House, who in turn alerted the president. But Truman seemed unalarmed. He told Ross that he had granted Wallace permission to deliver the speech for "its political effect in New York." While it might irritate Byrnes, the address would cause no lasting damage. Besides, Truman pointed out, it was too late in the day to call off the speech.[24]

After his conversation with Ross, the president went to a party thrown by Clark Clifford. It was one of Truman's beloved poker evenings, and he seemed untroubled by events in New York. He told the guests that although the State Department was anxious about Wallace's speech, he himself thought it was "no big deal."[25]

Delivered on the evening of September 12 under the joint auspices of the Independent Citizens' Committee of the Arts, Sciences, and Professions and the National Citizens Political Action Committee, Wallace's Madison Square Garden address was designed to accomplish two objectives. First, he hoped that it would energize left-wing groups in New York, thereby increasing the turnout of the Democratic vote in the November elections. Second, he wished to present in public many of the arguments he had been making in private to Truman on the need for Soviet-American cooperation.[26]

Wallace later revealed that by the time of his speech at Madison Square Garden he had already decided to leave the administration, if necessary, over the "peace issue." "Ever since Morgenthau and Ickes had left," he explained, "I figured it was only a question of months until I'd be getting out. I did want to get out on a basis which would help bring about an understanding between the United States and Russia, and insure peace. I wanted to dramatize peace." He did not think his September 12 address would be the event that caused his break with Truman. Nonetheless, "if it hadn't been this speech it would have been another one."[27]

"Tonight, above everything else," Wallace explained to his Madison Square Garden audience, "I want to talk about peace—and how to get peace," especially as the development of the atomic bomb had made the securing of that objective more essential than ever before. New York governor Thomas E. Dewey, he noted, had suggested that a military alliance with Britain be the basis of American foreign policy. But supporting the British would provoke the Russians, Wallace said, and lead to war. Moving to the most controversial aspect of the speech, because of the presidential endorsement therein, Wallace—as planned—told the crowd, "I am neither anti-British, nor pro-British; neither anti-Russian, nor pro-Russian. And just two days ago, when President Truman read these words, he said that they represented the policy of his administration."[28]

In prescribing an American foreign policy that would keep the peace with the Soviets, Wallace suggested that the United States must understand "the Russian character," shaped, as it had been, by the experience of numerous invasions. And American policymakers must resist the temptation to "get tough" with the Soviets. "Getting tough," Wallace maintained, "never brought anything real in the long run—whether for schoolyard bullies or businessmen or world powers. The tougher we get, the tougher the Russians will get."[29]

Wallace's most important recommendation concerned Stalin's policies in Eastern Europe. In the preceding months and particularly in his letters to Truman in March and July, he had asserted that an expansion of Soviet-American trade and international control of atomic energy would be the most helpful steps toward improved relations between Washington and Moscow. It was clear, however, that the main bone of contention had been Russian expansion in Eastern Europe. Wallace now dealt with the issue directly.

Adopting a spheres-of-influence approach, he argued that the Truman administration must accept Soviet control of Eastern Europe just as other nations had tolerated U.S. hegemony in the Western Hemisphere. "On our part," he proposed, "we should recognize that we have no more business in the political affairs of Eastern Europe than Russia has in the political affairs of Latin America, Western Europe and the United States." "Whether we like it or not," he continued, "the Russians will try to socialize their sphere of influence, just as we try to democratize our sphere of influence."[30]

Wallace's speech provoked a mixed reaction. "Your address furnishes the chart and compass for the ship of state," enthused Josephus Daniels, an old Roosevelt hand, in a telegram sent the next day, while the American Veterans Committee told Wallace that he had given "new hope to those of us who still think that peace between the United States and Russia is possible." Other observers, including a majority of the press, were less enthusiastic. James Reston of the *New York Times*, for example, emphasized the contradiction between Wallace's recommendations and the actual policies being implemented by the Truman administration. Mocking the claim made by the president in his press conference, Reston wrote that Truman "seems to be the only person in the capital who thinks that Mr. Wallace's proposals are 'in line' with Mr. Truman's or Mr. Byrnes'."[31]

Like Reston, many Washington insiders pondered the impact of Wallace's speech on Byrnes, then laboring in Paris with Senator Vandenberg and Senator Tom Connally at a meeting of the Council of Foreign Ministers. In a phone conversation on September 13, Harold Ickes asked Tom Corcoran about Byrnes's likely response to Wallace's speech: Corcoran said his information was that he "would raise hell." "I'll bet Jimmy's been burning up the wire," Ickes speculated. "Well," Corcoran interjected, "he's been burning up himself if he hasn't been burning up the wires." They agreed that the speech had damaged both Wallace and Ickes. Claude Pepper, who had spoken at the same Madison Square Garden rally, would, they thought, replace Wallace as the champion of the Democratic left. As for the president, Ickes wondered whether he could now be the party's presidential candidate in 1948. "I don't know if they'll [sic] be enough left of Truman to put on a ticket," he told Corcoran.[32]

Truman himself was acutely aware of the damage. He told his staff on the morning after Wallace's speech that he had committed a "grave blunder." After what Clifford described as a "heated discussion" on whether to release a statement about the Wallace situation, Truman decided to wait. The political storm that was brewing might blow over.[33]

By the next day, Saturday, September 14, it was clear that the tempest was only gathering momentum. The press continued to dissect the increasingly strained triangular relationship between Truman, Wallace, and Byrnes. "We realized," Clifford wrote later, "it was essential to issue a statement in time to make the first editions of the Sunday newspapers." With other advisers, Clifford helped draft one at great speed.[34]

With the press gathered around his table, Charlie Ross read the statement in which the president sought to correct what he called the false impression he had given in his press conference a few hours before Wallace's speech. "The question was answered extemporaneously," Truman explained, "and my answer did not convey the thought that I intended it to convey." With what *Time* magazine would later characterize as a "clumsy lie," the statement went on to say that Truman had meant he "approved the right of the Secretary of Commerce to deliver the speech. I did not intend to indicate that I approved the speech as constituting a statement of the foreign policy of this country." Truman added, "There has been no change in the established foreign policy of our Government."[35]

This final comment was designed in part to smooth the ruffled feathers of the American delegation in Paris. To Byrnes, Vandenberg, and Connally, Wallace's speech and Truman's prior endorsement of it were inconsistent with and therefore jeopardized the hard-line policy they were pursuing. Although Byrnes decided against making a public statement, his colleagues did speak to the press. Connally observed that at a time when American officials were working "for peace in the world there should be no controversy or bickering or strife at home." Vandenberg implied that the Wallace episode threatened the bipartisan support that Truman's foreign policy had recently enjoyed. The situation, he warned, "requires unity within the Administration itself. We can only cooperate with one Secretary of State at a time."[36]

For Truman, this was a low point in his presidency. In a letter home on Sunday, September 15, he expressed his feelings to Bess. It had been a beautiful morning, he told his wife, and he had slept until 6:30 a.m., having gone to bed at two. He had originally intended to get away for the weekend, but because the weather had turned cold and his political difficulties, including "Henry Wallace's fiasco," had mounted, he had decided to stay at the White House. "This place gets more and more uncomfortable," Truman complained. "It seems that no one can be trusted any more to deal squarely with the facts as they are. . . . Wallace now seems to have his eye on 1948 . . . and of course Byrnes has the pouts."[37]

After spending the weekend with his sister just outside New York, Wallace returned to Washington on Monday morning and phoned Truman to clear the air. He said he entirely understood the reasons for the president's public statement, and he suggested that the controversy could have beneficial repercussions: it might bring out the liberal vote in the congressional elections, and the speech itself would prevent Republicans from accusing the Democrats of warmongering. Wallace continued to offer an optimistic analysis of the situation, but Truman cut him short and got straight to the point: "Let's you and I have a session on this to see what we can do without cutting the ground from under Byrnes. I think it can be done. I don't want to get in another position like I am in now. I don't want to hurt anyone—either you or Byrnes." When Wallace pointed out that the Democratic party was well known for its diversity of opinion, Truman reiterated that Byrnes's position at Paris must not be undermined—and, implicitly, he meant not undermined by Wallace.[38]

The secretary of commerce apologized for the fact that so many people had assumed his comment at Madison Square Garden about Truman's approval had referred to the entire address rather than, as was the case, only two sentences. Truman interjected, "It was nobody's fault but mine." At the end of their conversation they agreed to meet to explore these issues in greater depth.[39]

In retrospect, Truman's references to his secretary of state during this phone conversation were ominous for Wallace. To many pundits it was clear that the president would be compelled to choose between Byrnes and Wallace. And the political factors involved did not bode well for the Iowan. As Wallace later observed:

> Truman may have been convinced politically that the cost of break-ing with Byrnes was greater than the cost of breaking with me. I think that was probably the way it finally shaped up in his mind. I don't think he had a high esteem for Byrnes at this time . . . but the combination of Vandenberg and Byrnes and Connally—two of them Senators and one of them a former Senator and all three of them known to Truman when he was a Senator for many years—was just too much for him. So he swung over to their point of view. He didn't really want to do it but he was forced into it.[40]

Although Wallace had sounded hopeful during his phone conver-sation with Truman, he was in fact deeply worried about the situation, and felt the need to release a public statement on September 16. "I stand upon my New York speech," he declared. Noting that both the left and the right had attacked his address, he insisted he would con-tinue to work for "a just and lasting peace and I shall, within the near future, speak on this subject again." That final pledge was important. As one journalist wrote, it forced Truman to choose between Wallace and Byrnes.[41]

For Wallace and the White House, Tuesday, September 17, was dominated by discussion of what had been revealed the previous day. The columnist Drew Pearson had obtained a copy of Wallace's private July 23 letter to Truman, and intended to publish it. That morning Charlie Ross explored the issue with other White House officials. When the question was put to him, "Shouldn't the letter be realeased [sic] to all newsmen, and not let a bastard like Pearson scoop them?" Ross thought it was a good idea. Accordingly, he called Wallace to sug-gest that he release the letter himself in order "to cut the ground from under" Pearson. Wallace consented: "All right. We will do it."[42]

That afternoon another White House meeting, this one attended by Truman, convened to discuss the Wallace-Pearson issue. When

Ross and Clayton argued that it made sense to release the July 23 letter, Truman, as one participant recorded, said "he guessed it was O.K., but he obviously had misgivings." At that point Clifford entered the fray. Speaking passionately against Ross and Clayton, he argued that to give White House permission to Wallace to allow publication of his letter implied presidential approval of the ideas it contained. Moreover it established a dangerous precedent that "any time a crook stole a secret paper . . . it had to be given out to the press."[43]

Clifford's arguments proved persuasive. Clayton changed his position, and Truman declared that he was now strongly opposed to the release of the letter. What Clifford, Clayton, and Truman did not know was that Ross had already told Wallace to publish it. Hoping he had not done so, Ross called the secretary of commerce in the presence of his colleagues, only to find that Wallace had already released the letter. A sheepish Ross conveyed that news to Truman and admitted that he had given Wallace permission to publish on his own authority. George Elsey wrote in his private notes: "Clifford and I are aghast at Ross's action— we are waiting and wondering what storm will come tomorrow."[44]

Rumor, gossip, and speculation were now rife. What were Wallace's motives? When push came to shove, would Truman back Byrnes or Wallace? Once again Corcoran's secretly taped phone conversations convey well the flavor of Washington at the moment. Talking with State Department official J. Anthony Panuch, Corcoran observed that Wallace wanted to leave the administration and that "he would like to go out under circumstances where he thinks he might be a hero. I think he's asking for it." Truman, Corcoran continued, did not have the courage to dismiss Wallace, and "the longer he defers that courage, the more Wallace can make . . . Truman his captive, instead of he being Truman's." Agreeing that Wallace was in a strong position, Panuch told Corcoran that Byrnes's advisers thought the episode showed that "Truman is absolutely sold on the power of the left-wing group over the Democratic Party."[45]

At 3:30 p.m. on Wednesday, September 18, Truman and Wallace talked in the White House for the first time since the Madison Square Garden speech. Before the meeting, Wallace had received both good and bad news. He learned that of the 1,150 communications received by the Commerce Department, 950 expressed their support for Wallace's speech. But he was also presented with accurate information that various officials had advised Truman during the day to obtain a pledge of silence from Wallace on foreign affairs, and, if he failed to get it, to fire him. Those advisers appear to have included Clayton and Bernard Baruch.[46]

The president opened the meeting by complaining that he had suffered from sleepless nights and threats from Byrnes to leave Paris unless Wallace stopped talking about foreign policy in public. According to Clifford, Truman had expected Wallace to submit his resignation that afternoon. But he was to be disappointed, for Wallace was in a resolute mood. Peace, he explained to Truman, would be an important issue in the congressional elections, and the American people were concerned by the administration's "get tough with Russia policy." "You, yourself, as Harry Truman," Wallace asserted, "really believed in my speech." "But Jimmie Byrnes," Truman responded, "says I am pulling the rug out from under him. I must ask you not to make any more speeches touching on foreign policy. We must present a united front abroad."[47]

Wallace then said the immediate problem was the speech he was scheduled to deliver in Providence, Rhode Island, on September 24. He proposed to issue a disclaimer making clear that his address did not represent the views of Truman or his administration but was part of a vital public debate on the direction of American foreign policy. After reading part of the statement, Truman interjected that it would not do: Wallace must stop talking about international affairs. As Wallace privately reflected, the subtext to Truman's instruction was clear: "the threat of forcing a resignation in case I refused to stop talking was definitely in the background of this conversation."[48]

Wallace countered that Truman was being too pessimistic. The controversy would serve to bring out the Democratic vote and might, therefore, prevent the election of a Republican Congress. Gloomily, Truman forecast that the Republicans would win anyway. Wallace went on to say that at Madison Square Garden he had attempted to cast the Democratic party as an agent of peace, and he cited the views of others who agreed that current U.S. policy would lead to war with the Soviet Union. In an attempt to placate Wallace, Truman claimed he had not got tough with Stalin, and that once the peace treaties being crafted in Paris were signed he would ask Congress to approve a loan to the Soviet Union.[49]

Wallace also tried to play on Truman's insecurity about his status as the guarantor of Roosevelt's legacy by suggesting that sections of the American public believed the New Deal had been abandoned. "The progressives of the country," Wallace contended, "did not realize that Truman is as progressive as he really is in his heart. They have a false impression of him and therefore it will be necessary in order for him to get the leftwing vote to demonstrate his attitude very decisively and wholeheartedly."[50]

Despite Wallace's various arguments, it was clear that Truman would not waver from his insistence that the secretary of commerce stop talking about foreign affairs in public. That being the case, Wallace asked for guidance: "What shall I tell the press when I go out? There are 100 or more hungry wolves out there." Charlie Ross was called into the room, and together the three men hammered out a statement. Ross wanted Wallace to avoid talking about foreign policy issues even after the Paris meeting had ended, but Truman was willing to allow the ban only for the duration of the conference. The question of Wallace's public discussion of international affairs would be reevaluated after the Paris meeting.[51]

At the end of their two-hour-and-twenty-minute discussion, a smiling Wallace emerged to tell a throng of reporters that he had no intention of resigning from the cabinet. He then read his statement, written in pencil, which said the meeting had been amicable, and, as a result, Wallace had decided "he would make no public statements or speeches until the Foreign Ministers' conference in Paris is concluded."[52]

Truman's meeting with Wallace that day, and Wallace's press statement, only postponed the problem. The question of whether Wallace would speak publicly about foreign affairs after the Paris Conference, and, if so, whether he would support the administration's policies, had not been answered. Byrnes, however, now entered the fray from Paris, and in the process forced Truman to resolve the issue.

There had been no direct contact between president and secretary of state since the controversy over Wallace's speech erupted. That situation changed on Thursday morning, September 19, when Truman received a personal message from Byrnes that reflected the anger he had felt since Wallace's New York remarks. Byrnes reminded the president that on medical advice he had tendered his resignation in April and had agreed to stay on only until the signing of the peace treaties. He then issued a clear ultimatum: "If it is not possible for you, for any reason, to keep Mr. Wallace as a member of your Cabinet, from speaking on foreign affairs, it would be a grave mistake from every point of view for me to continue in office, even temporarily." Should Truman be unwilling to ask Wallace to refrain from chastising the administration's foreign policy, "I must ask you to accept my resignation immediately."[53]

Byrnes went on to lay out the arrangements that would need to be made should he feel compelled to resign. He would wait in Paris until the new secretary of state arrived. If Truman did not wish to appoint Byrnes's successor on such short notice, an official other than the secretary of state could lead the American delegation at the conference.[54]

Byrnes's sudden resignation, the diplomatic vacuum that would be left in Paris, the criticism of presidential leadership that would inevitably follow—these were eventualities that Truman certainly wished to avoid. To calm Byrnes, he tried to set up a transatlantic phone conversation, but it could not be arranged. When Byrnes suggested a teletype conference instead, Truman agreed. To carry out this form of communication, Byrnes went to the message room of the American embassy in Paris while the president gathered with his advisers in the White House Map Room.[55]

In a conversation dominated by the secretary of state, Byrnes expressed his complete dissatisfaction. He argued that Wallace's statement the day before, indicating he would refrain from speaking publicly about international affairs until the close of the Paris meeting, had not improved the situation. The obvious implication of that pledge, Byrnes told Truman, was that "he will renew his criticism of your present foreign policy as soon as the Conference is over. We are promised only a moratorium from criticism of your policies by your own Administration."[56]

Truman, who was assisted in the crafting of his responses by Clifford and Ross, explained that his understanding with Wallace was *not* that he would be allowed to resume his public criticism of the administration after the Paris Conference. Rather, the situation would be "reexamined" and Wallace would then be informed "as to whether he may make, as a Cabinet member, any speeches or statements affecting our foreign policy." Truman also made clear that the approach to relations with Russia adopted by himself and Byrnes during recent months would not be reassessed at the end of the Paris Conference, only Wallace's right to comment on it in public.[57]

As in his earlier message to Truman, Byrnes suggested that the president's failure to restrain Wallace further would force him to resign. His comments during their teletype exchange were interspersed with references to the steps he might take if Wallace were not punished more severely. He said Truman might need to "let us [the American delegation in Paris] come home now." "If Wallace is influenced by any ill feeling toward me," he added, "it is possible that if you accept my resignation he might be willing to support your foreign policies or at least refrain from attacking such policies."[58]

Byrnes claimed not to be calling for Wallace's dismissal, but that was clearly the thrust of his arguments: "I do not want to ask you to do anything that would force Mr. Wallace out of the Cabinet, however, I do not think that any man who professes any loyalty to you would so seriously impair your prestige and the prestige of the Government with the nations of the world."[59]

The conversation ended amicably with talk of sharing a drink. "I'll be doing something I think you ought to be doing in an hour," Truman declared. "I still believe in liberty," Byrnes responded, "and am willing to strike a blow for it." Despite the badinage, Truman was left "uncharacteristically depressed by the situation," as Clifford recalled. When Clifford asked at the end of the day whether he would be taking his customary swim in the White House pool, Truman said he was not in the mood. He would instead retire to his family quarters to think things over.[60]

Truman's general approach to dealing with associates was to endorse their ideas even if he did not in fact agree with them. This was his strategy for creating a pleasant, cohesive administration—hence his undiluted support in private for Wallace's foreign policy ideas. It was in diametric opposition to Truman's popular image as the down-to-earth Midwesterner who always spoke his mind. As a result, in administration dealings Truman often did not express his true feelings. His frustrations became dangerously pent up, so when he did feel the need to express himself honestly he often did so with unrestrained fury.

To vent his anger, Truman tended to write hostile, occasionally unprintable letters. Sometimes, after he had calmed down, he would decide not to send them. George Elsey recalled that "He had an amusing habit of sometimes sort of stepping out of himself, and talking about the President as though the President were a third person, somebody else. And at times he sort of forgot he was President. Some of those letters that he would write that he shouldn't have written, he was sort of forgetting that he was President of the United States."[61]

On the evening of September 19 Truman took a number of newspaper articles about the Wallace affair with him to his quarters, and as he read them his anger began to boil over. Apparently he concluded that the secretary of commerce had deliberately set out to discredit him. Without consulting any of his advisers, he wrote an embarrassingly hostile letter to Wallace, demanding his resignation, and dispatched it by courier to Wallace's office. Wallace recalled that the message was "not abusive but it was on a low level . . . it didn't contain profanity—I just remember that it was on a low level."[62]

Wallace always claimed he had acted to spare Truman's blushes, calling him to suggest that he take the letter back as it would reflect poorly on the president should it be released. The version of events given by Ross at the time squares with Wallace's. But Clark Clifford later provided a plausible alternative account. At a meeting the next morning on Friday, September 20, Truman informed his staff of the previous night's activities. Worried that his letter to Wallace might enter the public domain, he asked Clifford to retrieve it. "It's not the sort of item we want in someone else's possession," Truman said, "especially Henry's." Clifford then called Wallace, requesting the return of the letter. As he wanted to ensure that Wallace complied, Clifford did not comment on the import of Truman's desire to have Wallace return the letter. In other words, Wallace was encouraged to return the letter because he may well have assumed that this meant his dismissal from the cabinet had been revoked. Wallace sent a messenger to return the letter, now resealed, and the president destroyed it. It seems that no one, apart from Truman or Wallace, ever read it.[63]

Truman had nonetheless resolved to send Wallace packing, even if his intemperate letter was not the best way to go about it. Calling Wallace at 10 a.m., he calmly stated: "Henry, I am sorry, but I have reached the conclusion that it will be the best that I ask for your resignation." "If that is the way you want it, Mr. President, I will be happy to comply." Shortly afterward, Truman received a short letter from Wallace. "Dear Harry: As you requested, here is my resignation. I shall continue to fight for peace. I am sure that you approve and will join me in that great endeavor."[64]

News of Wallace's dismissal still needed to be passed on to the American people, and Truman wasted no time in doing so. A White House press conference was set for 10:40 a.m., and Truman marched into a packed room sporting a blue serge suit and smiling. Before beginning, he bantered with some of the correspondents. When one reporter at the back asked another in front to move "a little to the left," everyone, including Truman, began to laugh as someone queried: "To the left?" The ironic political symbolism was lost on no one.[65]

When the "all in" signal was given, Truman stood up and announced that he wished to make a statement on foreign policy. Reading in a calm, steady manner, he argued that while the American public was free to disagree on any matter, it was essential that the government be united. "I have today asked Mr. Wallace to resign from the Cabinet," Truman continued, as his views clearly clashed with those held by the rest of the administration. As he read the line, there were audible gasps of astonishment among the assembled press, and a low whistle from one journalist. Truman went on to express his regret at Wallace's departure but said he felt certain that the Iowan "will be happier in the exercise of his right to present his views as a private citizen. I am confirmed in this belief by a very friendly conversation I had with Mr. Wallace on the telephone this morning." Truman added that all future foreign policy statements would be cleared by the State

Department, and that Secretary Byrnes enjoyed his "complete confidence." When he finished, the correspondents in the front row
shouted, "Thank you, Mr. President" in unison as they turned and
raced from the room. When the room was finally emptied, Truman
sat down, turned to Ross, and said, "Well, the die is cast."[66]

Wallace, for his part, spoke to the American people that evening in
a broadcast from his apartment at the Wardman Park Hotel. He argued that no task was more important than working for peace. And
that was what he intended to do, especially as his resignation had removed the constraints imposed on him by his September 18 pledge to
refrain from talking about foreign affairs for the duration of the Paris
Conference.[67]

Wallace then proceeded to clarify some of the confusion that had
arisen over his New York address. Despite his argument that Soviet
dominance in Eastern Europe was as inevitable as U.S. hegemony in
the Western Hemisphere, he was still committed to the concept of
"One World." He abhorred all forms of imperialism, whether Soviet,
British, or American. He realized that the sort of regionalism described
in his speech needed to be balanced with a proper concern for the sovereign rights of individual nations. Wallace ended his broadcast by
promising "to carry on the fight for peace."[68]

Wallace had known for some time that his opposition to Truman's
foreign policy meant his days in the administration were numbered.
Nevertheless his dismissal hurt. Eight thousand messages of support,
including communications from Albert Einstein and Hellen Keller,
helped relieve his anguish. A public opinion poll showing that 70 percent of those who had followed the controversy thought Truman was
right to sack Wallace, did not.[69]

With the Wallace situation now resolved, Truman wrote a breezy
letter to his mother and sister. "Well I had to fire Henry today," he reported,

> and of course I hated to do it. Henry Wallace is the best Secretary
> of Agriculture this country ever had unless Clint Anderson turns
> out as I think he will. If Henry had stayed Sec. of Agri. in 1940 as
> he should have, there'd never have been this controversy, and I

would not be here, and wouldn't that be nice? Charlie Ross said I'd shown I'd rather be right than President, and I told him I'd rather be anything than President. My good counselor, Clark Clifford, who took Sam Rosenman's place, said *"Please* don't say that." Of course Clark, Charlie and all the rest of my good friends are thinking in terms of 1948—and I'm not.

Henry is the most peculiar fellow I ever came in contact with. . . .

Well, now he's out, and the crackpots are having conniption fits. I'm glad they are. It convinces me I'm right. . . .[70]

The letter showed that Truman recognized the dismissal of Wallace as a political risk, one that could hurt him in the 1948 presidential election. He knew Wallace was still a hero to many on the left in the Democratic party. He knew Wallace would prove to be a vocal and persistent critic from outside the cabinet. He knew too that Wallace was the only remaining connection between himself and FDR's domestic and international New Deal. He had severed that link.

When Truman decided in 1946 to get tough with the Soviet Union, Wallace's days in his administration were inevitably numbered. But it was one thing to conclude that a harder line should be adopted, quite another to develop a coherent foreign policy that could be presented to the American people. That coherent policy was unveiled by the president the following year with the Truman Doctrine and the Marshall Plan. Aid to Greece and Turkey, and to Western Europe, laid the foundations of the containment policy that was to characterize American foreign policy until the end of the cold war—and in terms of the global role it defined for the United States, even beyond that.[71]

Wallace, however, came back to haunt Truman. Running as the presidential candidate of the Progressive party in 1948, he never appeared able to secure enough votes to reach the White House. But using his campaign to lambaste Truman for heightening tensions with the Russians and for undermining the United Nations, it seemed that Wallace might split the liberal vote to such an extent that Truman would lose the election to the Republican challenger, Thomas Dewey. That turned out not to be the case, as most liberal Americans concluded that

Wallace's view of the Soviet challenge and the appropriate U.S. response to it was implausible. Receiving just over 2 percent of the vote, Wallace was unable to prevent Truman from pulling off the greatest surprise, come-from-behind victory in the history of American presidential elections.[72]

While Wallace drifted into obscurity, wiling away his time on his farm in South Salem, New York, Truman forged ahead with the policy of containment. With the governments in Greece and Turkey bolstered, the Western European economy on the road to recovery, the Berlin crisis of 1948–1949 resolved to the West's liking, and the establishment of NATO, containment enjoyed notable successes in Europe.[73]

In Asia, however, the story was different. Mao Zedong achieved power in China; Communist North Korea invaded the South, dragging the United States into a war that lasted three years; and in Vietnam the Communists seemed close to defeating the French, achieving national independence, and giving Moscow one more ally in the cold war. How to contain communism in Asia turned out to be a thorny problem not only for Truman but for his successor in the White House, Dwight Eisenhower.[74]

PART III

Eisenhower, Wilson, and the Origins of the Vietnam War

CHAPTER 7

A New Wilsonianism

—

"He would often ask a question that would sort of
blow a proposition out of the water. . . . He had
the capacity for simplifying if not oversimplifying,
and he made a great contribution."
—DILLON ANDERSON, consultant to the
National Security Council, in an interview, 1969

ELECTION NIGHT, November 4, 1952. As the returns came in, it became clear that after twenty years in the wilderness the Republican party had recaptured the presidency with a war-hero general from Kansas at the top of the ticket. For Dwight D. Eisenhower, the elation could have been matched only by his emotions at the time of the VE-day celebrations, seven and a half years earlier.[1]

World War II had been the great event that had converted an anonymous figure into a national hero. Born in Texas, raised in Kansas, Eisenhower had spent the years before the war rising gradually up the ranks of the military. Having attended West Point, the Command and General Staff School at Fort Leavenworth, and the Army War College, he went on to serve under Douglas MacArthur in the Philippines. Eisenhower proved himself to be highly intelligent (he finished first in his class at Fort Leavenworth), astute, and diligent. When World War II broke out, he was able to give full expression to those qualities. His responsibilities increased exponentially—and he achieved great things.

He was appointed commander of American and Allied forces in Britain, planned the invasion of North Africa in late 1942, and, most notably, organized Operation Overlord, the Allied invasion of Nazi-occupied France in 1944. By war's end, Eisenhower was a national hero. He was viewed by many as the military architect of the defeat of Hitler. From this point on, high political office was always in the cards for Ike.[2]

After the war Eisenhower sustained his high public profile. He served as army chief of staff, became president of Columbia University, and was appointed supreme commander of NATO forces. After revealing that his sympathies lay with the GOP, Eisenhower soon emerged as a front-runner in the race for the 1952 Republican presidential nomination. It was clear that he had one great virtue: he could win. For a party that had not won a presidential election in almost a quarter-century, that was a crucial strength. Eisenhower's defeat of Adlai Stevenson in the 1952 election was comprehensive.[3]

The newly elected president's first obligation was to assemble his administration, including his foreign policy team. To that end he appointed the imperious John Foster Dulles secretary of state. Related to two earlier secretaries of state, experienced as a diplomat and an international lawyer, Dulles's credentials in foreign affairs were impeccable. Allen Dulles, John Foster's brother, was installed as the new director of the Central Intelligence Agency.[4]

For his secretary of defense, Eisenhower's thoughts turned to Charles E. Wilson, the portly, silver-haired president of General Motors. "I had met him several times since the war," Eisenhower recalled in explaining his interest in Wilson. "He had a reputation as one of the ablest of our executives in big corporations. I sought an experienced man of this kind because of the huge procurement, storage, transportation, distribution, and other logistical functions of the Defense Department which, in my opinion, needed to be directed by experts. It seemed to me that a man of such qualifications could team up with professional soldiers to the great advantage of the nation." Eisenhower's consideration of Wilson, in other words, reflected his conviction that business skills were transferable to governance. Ike's inclination to appoint Wilson was strengthened by the enthusiastic recommendations the General Motors president received from Gen. Lucius Clay, among others.[5]

Wilson had indeed enjoyed a distinguished career in industry. Born in Ohio in the same year as Eisenhower, 1890, he developed an early interest in engineering and graduated from the Carnegie Institute of Technology. He worked as an engineer for Westinghouse Electric in Pittsburgh before being hired by a General Motors subsidiary, the Remy Electric Company of Anderson, Indiana. By 1928 he was a vice president of GM, and in 1941 he became president of the company, acquiring the nickname "Engine Charlie." During World War II Wilson played a key role in ensuring that GM made a major contribution to military production, including a quarter of all the tanks and aircraft engines turned out in the United States.[6]

Despite what might seem a rather conventional biography for an industrial leader, aspects of Wilson's life indicated he was not quite that—and in retrospect make his dissent during Eisenhower's presidency less surprising than it would otherwise have been. His family had a socialist tradition, and his father Thomas Wilson, a Welsh immigrant, had apparently established a union local in Pittsburgh. As well as voting for Eugene V. Debs, the Socialist candidate for president, the young Charles Wilson was a business agent for a union local. Following a strike at General Motors in 1937, he played a leading role in the negotiations that led to the recognition of the United Automobile Workers. A number of Wilson's colleagues felt he had been too conciliatory. Along with his reputation for outspokenness, Wilson's background showed that he was not averse to the unconventional. That quality would become more apparent once he entered the political arena.[7]

When Eisenhower offered him the position of secretary of defense in a meeting at the Hotel Commodore in New York City on November 19, 1952, Wilson promptly accepted, telling Eisenhower he was the only man in the world from whom he would take the job. The next day the president-elect announced his selection of Wilson to replace Robert A. Lovett as secretary of defense, at the same time revealing his appointment of Dulles as the new secretary of state.[8]

Less than an hour after Eisenhower had announced his appointment, Wilson cut short a meeting with General Motors executives in

Detroit so that he could speak to reporters. He avoided questions about his policy ideas but predicted that he would have "no trouble" in working with Eisenhower. While acknowledging that heading up the Pentagon was "a very tough assignment," he approached the undertaking with panache. He would, Wilson told the journalists huddled in his office, give the job of secretary of defense the "darndest whirl it has ever had."[9]

The political reaction to Wilson's appointment was generally positive. Senator Guy M. Gillette of Iowa thought Wilson would "fill the post [at the Pentagon] with judgment and ability," while his colleague and fellow Democrat in the Senate, John J. Sparkman of Alabama, described Wilson as "one of our great industrial leaders." "I know of nothing to stand in the way of his confirmation," he added. Privately, however, some Republican leaders expressed doubts over Wilson's appointment. Henry Cabot Lodge, for example, who was to become Eisenhower's ambassador to the United Nations following the surprise loss of his Senate seat to John Kennedy, told the president-elect that Wilson lacked the skill needed to handle Congress and public opinion. That was not a problem, Eisenhower replied, as he intended to handle the Pentagon's public and congressional relations himself. A number of officials in the Eisenhower administration would soon come to share Lodge's view that in the political arena Wilson was a greenhorn.[10]

Wilson discharged his first official duty a little more than a week after his appointment when he accompanied Eisenhower on a promised trip to Korea, where American involvement in the war continued. It gave Wilson the chance to survey conditions in Asia firsthand. His mood during the trip was decidedly upbeat: he felt confident, as the president did, that the skills he had developed in the business world would ensure his success in Eisenhower's administration. He would run the Defense Department as he had General Motors, he explained to soon-to-be chairman of the Joint Chiefs of Staff Adm. Arthur Radford during the flight from Wake Island to Pearl Harbor. Radford told Wilson this was probably wishful thinking. "For instance," he asked, "would you not have trouble in General Motors if at the end of your fiscal year you did not know how much money you would have to run the company for the next year?" "Of course," Wilson replied. "You can't run any organization that way." "Well," Radford reflected, "you will find out how to do it in the Pentagon. The Secretary of Defense often faces that problem." Wilson had been speaking with the innocence of one unversed in the ways of Washington.[11]

The battle that broke out in January 1953 over the confirmation of Wilson's appointment as secretary of defense exposed that naiveté. At the Senate Armed Services Committee hearing on his nomination, Wilson ruffled feathers by revealing his intention to retain $2.5 million in General Motors stock as well as bonuses of more than $600,000. He did not wish to sell these securities because the tax penalty would be severe. To committee members Wilson's position created a clear conflict of interest, as GM received about 8 percent of the dollar total of all Pentagon contracts. When asked whether he would be capable of making a decision detrimental to the interests of GM and thus the value of his stock, Wilson replied: "Yes, sir, I could. I cannot conceive of one because for years I thought what was good for our country was good for General Motors and vice versa." It was a costly faux pas. Soon Wilson's remark was being reported as, "What's good for General Motors is good for the country."[12]

The controversy over his confirmation was defused only when Wilson agreed to sell his stock. But it was an inauspicious start for the industrialist. He had appeared to lack the savvy required to prosper in the political milieu. It was an image he would never shake. That was unfortunate because it caused his colleagues in the Eisenhower administration to equate his lack of political shrewdness with a lack of policy shrewdness, and that assumption was unsound. Wilson's policy formulations were in fact often creative and sensible.

After Eisenhower was sworn in as president on January 20, 1953, he sought, with the help of John Foster Dulles, to adapt the foreign policy he had inherited from Harry Truman. Along with the vast majority of Americans, Ike accepted the premise on which Truman's approach to international affairs had been based—that a Moscow-led Communist monolith represented a grave threat to American interests and those of the West in general, and that the United States was compelled to play a global role in order to counter this challenge. But Eisenhower differed from Truman over methods and stated objectives.

Truman had defined the containment of further Communist expansion as the central goal for American foreign policy. Eisenhower and his advisers, by contrast, spoke more ambitiously of the liberation of Soviet-dominated Eastern Europe, though Ike realized that this brash rhetoric scarcely constituted a feasible policy. Liberation could have been achieved only by war with the Soviet Union in a region where the geostrategic advantage would be Moscow's. Indeed, when the 1956 Hungarian uprising created the sort of instability that the liberation policy was in theory supposed to exploit, Eisenhower's response was conspicuously supine. Despite its distinctive rhetorical adornment, then, the basic objective behind Eisenhower's foreign policy, as with Truman's, was the containment of communism beyond the areas where it already held sway.[13]

While fundamental aims remained the same in practice, Eisenhower altered the means by which those objectives were to be achieved. Much of this reorientation related to the president's linkage of domestic and international goals. A fiscal conservative, Ike was determined to balance the budget. The huge increases in defense spending outlined in the Truman administration's seminal 1950 NSC-68 document, fleshing out the containment policy, seemed to Eisenhower to work against the achievement of his fiscal objectives. He sought therefore to cut military expenditures. The trick was to do that without reducing U.S. effectiveness in waging the cold war. This dilemma could be resolved, Eisenhower calculated, by a number of methods. First, America's nuclear arsenal should be developed. Spending on conventional weapons and forces would be curtailed, and as this comprised the largest element in defense expenditure, the overall military budget could still be trimmed. U.S. superiority in nuclear weaponry should be used to engage in "brinkmanship," threatening massive retaliation in order to keep the Soviet Union and its allies in line. Second, the Central Intelligence Agency would play a more active role. Rather than simply collecting intelligence, its original mission under Truman, the CIA would covertly carry out some American foreign policy. Third, the United States would build collective security pacts comparable to NATO in other regions of the world. This would ensure that America's allies, not the United States alone, expended resources in defending the Free World.[14]

In the end, the Eisenhower administration used all these methods. Nuclear weapons were developed, but overall defense spending was limited to $35 to $40 billion per year. (NSC-68 had recommended $50 billion.) Brinkmanship was used periodically. In Iran in 1953 and Guatemala a year later, the CIA overthrew governments deemed undesirable. New pacts, notably the Southeast Asia Treaty Organization (SEATO), were created with American leadership.[15]

Scholarly understanding of Eisenhower's presidency, including his record as a foreign policymaker, has been transformed since the 1980s. Historians' original assessment of Eisenhower was almost uniformly negative. The standard view was that John Foster Dulles dominated him; that his conceptualization of foreign affairs left the United States with the undesirable alternatives of responding to Communist initiatives by threatening nuclear war or doing nothing; and that his leadership style was lethargic and uninspiring. To an extent this unflattering view of Eisenhower was related to the cult of Kennedy that developed after the assassination in Dallas. To assert JFK's greatness was a relative judgment, and what Kennedy aficionados seemed to be saying was that Eisenhower's torpor highlighted Kennedy's dynamism while Lyndon Johnson's crudeness, both personal and political, demonstrated JFK's sophistication.[16]

A far more enthusiastic interpretation of Eisenhower emerged in the 1980s. As Stephen Ambrose and other historians examined the documentation that was becoming available, they came to appreciate that Eisenhower, contrary to appearances, was very much in control of policy and his subordinates. In foreign affairs these Eisenhower revisionists praised Ike for both his toughness and moderation. He had stood up to the Communists when necessary, in 1958–1959, for example, when Soviet premier Nikita Khrushchev challenged Western access rights to West Berlin. But at the same time he had kept the peace during a dangerous period in the cold war and had prevented the arms race from spiraling out of control by resisting considerable domestic pressure, particularly in his second term, to increase defense spending.

In this portrait Eisenhower appeared less impulsive than his successors, Kennedy and Johnson.[17]

One way to compare the soundness of these radically different interpretations of Eisenhower is to examine his record on Vietnam. It is a complex issue, one that can be used to support a positive or damning appraisal. Eisenhower can be commended for refusing to deploy troops in Vietnam at the siege of Dienbienphu, but criticized for the commitment he made to combat communism in Vietnam once the French began to disengage. That undertaking was one his successors felt obliged to continue, with devastating consequences. Eisenhower's course of action in Vietnam should be evaluated in relation to the policy options available to him. In this sense Charles Wilson played an important role, as he came to oppose the deepening of American involvement in Vietnam advocated by most of Eisenhower's advisers.

The situation facing Eisenhower and Wilson in Vietnam in January 1953 was one of crumbling French control of its colony. The policy they inherited from Truman was the furnishing of financial aid for French operations in Vietnam. The basic problem for France was that a nationalist movement led by the Vietminh, a Communist-dominated organization headed by Ho Chi Minh, had been gathering momentum; and Ho had used the opportunity created by Japan's surrender at the end of World War II to declare Vietnamese independence. France, however, was determined to maintain its empire, including control over Indochina, the valuable and prestigious possession that comprised Cambodia and Laos as well as Vietnam. The result was an eight-year war with the Vietminh that brought France a humiliating defeat.[18]

American diplomacy soon became closely aligned with French policy in Vietnam. Convinced that Stalin sought to expand beyond his Eastern European satellite states, the Truman administration sought to encourage the development of economically rejuvenated, politically stable, anti-Communist states in Western Europe, including France. A belief that acceptance of French objectives in Vietnam was needed to ensure Paris's acceptance of U.S. strategic objectives in Europe was one reason why Truman and his advisers decided against pressing for Vietnamese independence. Another was their concern that Ho Chi Minh was doing Stalin's bidding. The Truman team therefore responded to the outbreak of war between France and the Vietminh by adopting a position that was implicitly pro-French. To be sure, they dismissed French requests for military aid in the late 1940s. But considerable Marshall Plan funding to France, beginning in 1948, allowed French leaders to deploy more resources in Vietnam than they would have otherwise been able to.[19]

American support for the French in Vietnam became explicit in 1950. By this point the situation there and the general international context had changed. For one thing, the Vietminh had proved to be a military match for the French army. While French forces controlled urban areas, the Vietminh held sway in the countryside. By avoiding pitched battles, carrying out guerrilla raids, and constantly mobilizing support among the populace, the Vietminh had put themselves in a strong position. As Mao Zedong's army began to prevail over the government of Chiang Kai-shek in China in 1949, the prospect of Chinese Communist backing for the Vietminh seemed real. Accordingly, the French told the Truman administration they might have to concede defeat in Vietnam unless U.S. military aid was forthcoming.[20]

These warnings prompted the Truman administration in 1950 to give the French military aid for their war in Indochina. Yet despite infusions of American aid, the reshaping of political appearances with a Vietnamese head of state (Bao Dai) who supposedly enjoyed a high degree of independence from the French, and the appointment of a dynamic head of the French armed forces in Indochina, Jean de Lattre de Tassigny, things continued to go badly for France. Yet Truman and his advisers remained sympathetic to requests from Paris for additional military aid. Opposed to the deployment of American troops in Vietnam, especially once U.S. involvement in the Korean War was under way, they were concerned that the French would weary of the war against the Vietminh and so abandon it. That would leave Washington with the decision of whether to fight in Vietnam or concede defeat to the Communists. If U.S. military assistance sustained French resolve in Vietnam, that dilemma would not have to be confronted. Backing the French effort in Vietnam would also make Paris more sympathetic to the idea of a European Defense Community, involving the integration of French and German forces into a multinational army—a plan the United States had endorsed.[21]

This was the situation inherited by Eisenhower, Wilson, and other U.S. officials in 1953—growing American support for the French war against the Communists in Vietnam. Wilson's foreign policy ideology, administrative style, and personality shaped his response to this unfolding drama in Southeast Asia. It would prove to be markedly different from the reactions of Eisenhower and other senior officials.

Wilson "held to a fundamentally defensive conception of the use of American power," as one historian has written. He was "not a hard-liner." Of course, Wilson's views existed within a cold war framework. Regarding the Soviet Union and Communist movements worldwide as threats the United States had to meet, Wilson thought Asia would become the key theater in the cold war contest. But compared to most Republicans and Democrats, Wilson was a moderate. Absent from his statements was the shrill anti-communism so evident in John Foster Dulles's pronouncements. He neither approved of the secretary of state's penchant for atomic diplomacy nor cared for the adventurism inherent in the counterinsurgency and "Flexible Response" concepts that many military pundits and liberal anti-Communists began to develop in the 1950s.[22]

Wilson's commitment to a foreign policy of restraint was based on two considerations: his evaluation of the Russian challenge and his convictions on the resources the United States should devote to the cold war. Wilson was rather less fixated on the Soviet menace than many of his contemporaries. The Russians were not "10 feet tall," he once observed. He argued that insecurity, not a sense of powerful invulnerability, was prevalent among Russian leaders, insisting that they feared America's superiority in nuclear weaponry and industrial development. The Soviet experience in World War II, Wilson also believed, made Moscow wary of military conflict. "As long as you have militant communism, you have a threat to the free world," he explained. "[But] that doesn't mean that the Russians necessarily want war. They still have a very vivid recollection of what war means. The victors in a modern war lose—they don't lose as much as the vanquished, but they lose."[23]

Wilson's view of resource deployment for national defense mirrored Eisenhower's. While wanting to develop nuclear weapons, he was determined to keep overall military spending on a tight rein in order to achieve a balanced budget and a stable national economy. Because he did not regard the Soviet threat as horrifyingly ominous, and because he opposed constant increases in defense expenditure, Wilson recommended a prudent use of American power overseas. This conviction would shape his approach to the question of America's proper role in Vietnam.[24]

Wilson's administrative style also influenced his contribution to the debate in the Eisenhower administration over Vietnam: he liked to be the official who raised thorny issues. Consultant to the National Security Council Dillon Anderson recalled that Wilson played the role of devil's advocate—he had the ability to ask the really effective question that would expose shortcomings in the arguments of his colleagues. When the issue of Vietnam came to the fore, then, Wilson's definition of his role in the administration indicated that he was likely to challenge the assumptions of Eisenhower and other officials.[25]

Wilson's personality was also a factor. Thick-skinned and blunt, he was temperamentally suited to the role of dissenter. Anderson recalled one of the first National Security Council meetings at which the argument was made that instead of securing a settlement to the Korean War, Eisenhower ought to use nuclear weapons to defeat China. As Anderson relayed the story, Wilson

> sat there with a cigarette in his mouth, and he would sit and it would burn right down till it started burning his lips, and then he would put it away and light another one and it would burn right down there; and when the discussion was over he's supposed to have turned to the President and said, "Mr. President, I understand from what's been said that we could lick China. What I don't understand is what we would do with China after we got them licked."[26]

Standing alone, as he frequently did, Wilson often irritated his colleagues. Gen. Matthew B. Ridgway thought he was "fond of a large audience, and of lengthy, and often rambling discussion of topics having no direct relation to the subject for which we had been assembled." "I came away convinced," Ridgway added, "that either his mental processes operated on a level of genius so high I could not grasp his meaning, or that considerations beyond the soldier's comprehension were influencing his thinking." Wilson also managed to get under the skin of Eisenhower's chief of staff, Sherman Adams, who described the secretary of defense as "preposterously opinionated."[27]

All these factors—his general outlook on foreign policy, the way he defined his role in the administration, his personal traits—helped generate and shape the dissent that Wilson would come to express on Vietnam. His relationships with colleagues, especially Eisenhower and John Foster Dulles, would help determine the effectiveness of that dissent. For his part, Eisenhower developed an ambivalence toward Wilson. He admired his organizational skills and his eye for talent evident in the quality of his appointments at the Pentagon. He enjoyed Wilson's sense of humor. And he found his nonalarmist view of the Soviet Union agreeable: "I never thought the Russians were doing anything but bluffing, and neither did Charlie Wilson."[28]

At the same time Eisenhower was vexed by Wilson's habit of bringing what he regarded as routine Pentagon matters to his attention. "Charlie, you run defense," Eisenhower instructed. "We both can't do it, and I won't do it. I was elected to worry about a lot of other things than the day-to-day operations of a department." Wilson's lack of political acumen and tendency to digress also dismayed Eisenhower at times, causing him on one occasion to blurt out, "How in hell did a man as shallow as Charlie Wilson ever get to be head of General Motors?"[29]

Wilson's prospects for success were further diminished by Eisenhower's view of Wilson's proper responsibilities. Ike defined Wilson's role as managerial rather than as policymaking. He expected his secretary of defense to effect the kinds of economies in the military budget to which he had committed his administration. But Eisenhower did not encourage or expect Wilson to influence the conceptualization of either foreign or defense policy. That was to be the concern of Eisenhower and John Foster Dulles. This arrangement, which Wilson understood, appears to have discouraged him from developing his dissent further. It also meant that his views were greeted with less respect than they merited.[30]

Wilson and Dulles, as Eisenhower's third secretary of defense, Thomas S. Gates, recalls, "were not close." There was a politeness to their relationship, an exchange of New Year's and birthday greetings, and get-well messages at times of illness. But that civility was not matched by a meeting of minds or a blending of personalities. Wilson did not embrace Dulles's view of the cold war as an urgent, moralistic crusade, and his folksiness did not interact easily with Dulles's rather austere formality. The nature of Wilson's relationships with Eisenhower and Dulles reduced the likelihood that his dissent on Vietnam would be favorably regarded and thus effective.[31]

Wilson had not thought much about Vietnam before January 1953. During the early days of the Eisenhower administration he was noncommittal when the issue arose, indeed almost entirely taciturn. On March 24, 1953, for instance, he contributed nothing to a discussion with Eisenhower, Dulles, Secretary of the Treasury George M. Humphrey, and Director of Mutual Security Harold E. Stassen about increasing aid to the French in Vietnam, a performance he repeated two days later at a meeting between American officials and a French delegation headed by Prime Minister René Mayer and Minister of Foreign Affairs Georges Bidault. Wilson was still familiarizing himself with the Indochina issue.[32]

On other matters, however, Wilson was beginning to show a capacity for independent and innovative thinking. When Stalin died on March 5, he urged Eisenhower to seize the moment by offering the new Soviet leadership "a plan for peace," though he failed to provide the specifics of this initiative. He proposed a similarly bold course of action when it came to China policy. During a cabinet discussion on bringing the Korean War to a close, Wilson stunned his colleagues by asking the president: "Is there any possibility for a package deal? Maybe we could recognize Red China and get the Far East issues settled." Trying to conceal his dismay at what he considered to be an outlandish proposition, Eisenhower called the idea unsound. Another two decades would elapse before the United States, under the presidency of Richard M. Nixon, began a dialogue with the Chinese that would culminate in recognition by the end of the 1970s. In retrospect, Wilson's advice can be said to have been prescient.[33]

Beginning in the spring of 1953, Wilson became more involved in discussions on Vietnam. He asked the Joint Chiefs of Staff for an evaluation of the plan for victory presented by French officials during their visit to Washington in late March. During talks in Paris in April, he joined Dulles in pressing the French to strengthen the Vietnamese National Army by adopting U.S. methods used to train South Koreans. Wilson's greater immersion in the Vietnam issue forced him to begin defining his views. As he did so, he developed a number of reservations about American involvement in that part of the world.[34]

Eisenhower, meanwhile, was reaching some preliminary conclusions about his secretary of defense. While generally satisfied with Wilson, he was concerned by his lack of political skills, especially in dealing with Congress. On May 14 the president evaluated his leading advisers in his diary. "In his field," he said of Wilson,

> he is a really competent man. He is careful and positive, and I have no slightest doubt that, assisted by the team of civilian and military men he has selected, he will produce the maximum of security for this country at minimum or near minimum cost. If he fails, it will be because of his inability to sell himself and his programs to Congress. . . . Mr. Wilson is prone to lecture, rather than to answer, when asked a specific question. This not only annoys many members of Congress, but it gives them unlooked for opportunities to discover flaws in reasoning and argument.
>
> It is the one direction in which I feel that Charlie Wilson has a definite weakness.[35]

During Eisenhower's first summer in the White House the French began to take the kinds of initiatives in Southeast Asia that U.S. officials had been urging. In May 1953 Gen. Henri Navarre was appointed the new head of French forces in Indochina. By July the French government had declared its intention to "perfect" the independence of Vietnam, Cambodia, and Laos, an announcement designed to appeal to nationalist sentiment. Next, Paris presented to the Eisenhower administration the Navarre Plan, which sought to gain the upper hand in Vietnam by enlarging the Vietnamese National Army and deploying an additional nine French battalions. The troops dispersed throughout Vietnam would combine with these new forces in mounting a major attack on Ho's forces in the Red River Delta, the Vietminh stronghold in the north. Implementing this plan, the French informed Eisenhower, would require another $400 million in U.S. aid.[36]

With other administration officials, Wilson came to support the Navarre Plan, believing it offered the best chance for victory over the Vietminh. But he developed concerns too, and by January 1954 he was moving toward a position that down the road American troops should probably not be deployed in Vietnam. This represented an evolution in his thinking. In response to a query in June 1953 from Maine's Republican senator Margaret Chase Smith, about whether Eisenhower should fight in Indochina as his predecessor had in Korea, Wilson said it would depend on "the circumstances prevailing at the time." In other words, he did not rule out the possibility of sending U.S. troops to Vietnam.[37]

Seven months later his views had changed. By this time Eisenhower had granted the French $385 million for the Navarre Plan. But the actions of the Vietminh jeopardized that operation. They invaded central and southern Laos, which bordered Vietnam to the west, prepared to attack northern Laos, and heightened guerrilla activity in northern Vietnam. These various thrusts compelled Navarre to disperse his forces, whose consolidation had been a prerequisite for the Navarre Plan. By the start of 1954 both sides had sent forces to Dienbienphu, a village in the north of Vietnam, for what would be the decisive battle in the Franco-Vietminh conflict.[38]

The Joint Chiefs, meanwhile, were asked in January 1954 to evaluate a Planning Board Study for Indochina, NSC-177, and an annex to that document which raised the issue of whether the United States should intervene in the event of a French withdrawal. Along with Deputy Secretary of Defense Roger Kyes, Wilson took the view on January 7 that the annex was no longer worth consideration—a decision upheld by Eisenhower the following day. By 1954, then, Wilson was showing signs of concern that America might be dragged into a war in Vietnam. Later in the year he came to regard any deepening of the U.S. commitment with suspicion. Where earlier he had only scratched the surface of the Vietnam issue, approaching it with the tentativeness of one coming to grips with a new subject, in 1954 Wilson would express himself with greater force and precision, spelling out to Eisenhower and his advisers the implications of their efforts to combat communism in Southeast Asia.[39]

CHAPTER 8

"Nothing But Grief":
Contesting a Commitment

===

"I would like to ask you men a question. Do you
think the American people think we ought to
intervene over there [in Indochina] and send
ground troops in and take over the war? What do
you think about it? Anyone want to tell me?"
—CHARLES WILSON, comments to the press,
May 4, 1954

WILSON'S CONCERN over American involvement in Vietnam intensified during the course of 1954. Before the French surrender at Dienbienphu in early May, he felt ambivalent. He was disturbed by the
possibility that the United States might end up bailing out or replacing
the French in Indochina, but sometimes he did contemplate those
courses of action. It was after the fall of Dienbienphu that Wilson became an unequivocal opponent of U.S. escalation in Vietnam. He had
reservations about backing Ngo Dinh Diem, the man the Eisenhower
administration came to endorse as the leader of a non-Communist
South Vietnam; objected to the creation of the South East Asia Treaty
Organization; protested the plan to pour military aid into South Vietnam; and warned generally of the perils for America in placing itself

under obligations in that part of the world. In taking these positions, Wilson identified a variety of factors he saw as drawbacks in selecting Vietnam as a battleground to meet the Communist challenge.

The background to the development of Wilson's views in early 1954 was the rapidly approaching French defeat in Vietnam. Vietminh forces had surrounded the French in the garrison at Dienbienphu, launching an intense assault in mid-March and seizing the fire bases where the French had stored artillery. Moreover the Vietminh destroyed the airfield, rendering the resupply of French forces at Dienbienphu even more difficult. Reflecting these setbacks on the battlefield was the French decision to permit Indochina to be placed on the agenda of an international conference on Asian issues set for Geneva. With the Soviet leadership in a seemingly conciliatory mood after Stalin's death, Paris hoped that the Russians might press the Vietminh to accept a Geneva settlement that was charitable toward French interests.[1]

These developments compelled the Eisenhower administration to consider its response. Regarding the plan to discuss Indochina at Geneva, Ike and his advisers had no alternative but to go along with it. Still, they worried that the negotiations might result in a general acceptance of Communist rule in at least a substantial part of Vietnam; and they considered stepping into the breach if the French decided to cut their losses in Indochina. By the spring of 1954, in other words, U.S. military intervention in Vietnam was being considered. When French Chief of Staff Gen. Paul Ely visited Washington in late March, the use of American force was discussed not as an option following a French defeat but as a way of preventing such a defeat in the first place. Chairman of the Joint Chiefs Radford was interested in aiding the French with an air strike on Vietminh forces at Dienbienphu.[2]

Eisenhower, however, came to feel this sort of action depended on developments on three other fronts: among the allies, in Congress, and with the French themselves. As he believed the French could have been doing much more to win in Vietnam, he was unwilling to provide greater military support until they promised to change their ways. Specifically, he wanted greater U.S. involvement in shaping military strategy, a pledge to keep French troops in Indochina, and a commitment to eventual independence for the Vietnamese in order to generate grassroots support for French actions.[3]

Eisenhower regarded congressional approval as another prerequisite for U.S. military action in Indochina. When the president asked Dulles to see if that support would be forthcoming, a meeting with congressional leaders was convened on April 3 at the State Department. Dulles's request that the administration be granted the authority to use American air and naval power if deemed necessary met with a chilly response. Warning that there must be "no more Koreas," the congressional delegation predicted that the deployment of U.S. ground troops would inevitably follow the dispatch of air and naval forces. Only if allies such as Britain backed the proposed enterprise, and if France accelerated the process leading to independence, would Congress approve the use of American military power in Indochina. In a sense these congressional stipulations coincided with the Eisenhower administration's own views. Although relating more to his long-term plans than his ideas for saving Dienbienphu, Dulles had been thinking in terms of "United Action," a security pact for Southeast Asia involving the United States, Britain, France, Australia, and other states. This coalition, he calculated, would encourage the French to push for victory in Indochina and ensure that any U.S. military involvement was part of a collaborative effort.[4]

On April 5 the French requested an immediate U.S. air strike to save Dienbienphu. Eisenhower refused, but at a National Security Council meeting the following day it was decided to draw up a contingency plan for military intervention and to promote United Action. The administration's attempts to lay the diplomatic foundations for military action foundered, however, on the rocks of British recalcitrance. Winston Churchill's government simply did not attach the same importance to Indochina as did the Eisenhower administration. London did not believe that defeat in Indochina would lead to the loss of that entire region, and it thought France might secure a favorable settlement at Geneva. Churchill was especially determined to prevent Britain from being drawn into a costly war in the jungles of Southeast Asia. He would contemplate entering a collective security pact after the Geneva conference, but not before. When Dulles made a last-ditch request in late April for a promise of support from the British, which would facilitate congressional approval of an air strike to save the French, the Churchill government turned it down. Under constant attack from the Vietminh, and with no relief from their allies, the French surrendered at Dienbienphu on May 7, a day before the Geneva Conference was scheduled to begin discussions on a settlement for Indochina.[5]

Before the fall of Dienbienphu, Wilson's feelings about American military involvement were mixed. He did not discount the possibility that Eisenhower might need to use force to deter the Communists in Vietnam, though he hoped the French could do the job themselves. On March 23, for instance, Wilson sent Dulles a letter in which he endorsed two recent memoranda on Indochina—one by the Joint Chiefs of Staff, the other by Gen. G. B. Erskine, the chairman of a special subcommittee of representatives from Defense, State, the CIA, and the Joint Chiefs—neither of which opposed U.S. military intervention. The Joint Chiefs in fact argued against a variety of compromises that could be made with the Vietminh, suggesting that the United States might need to fight alone if the French withdrew. Erskine reported that his subcommittee was opposed to such options as a cease-fire, partition, coalition government, and elections, and recommended instead that Eisenhower consider ways of continuing the struggle against the Communists in Indochina should the French withdraw.[6]

As Wilson contemplated U.S. escalation, his concerns about that course of action deepened. In particular he was troubled by political conditions in Vietnam, grasping that fundamentally this was a civil war rather than a case of blatant aggression by a Communist nation against a defenseless neighbor. He also wondered whether the American people would back a decision to send troops to Vietnam. Wilson began to believe that these realities made it difficult for the United States to achieve its optimal military objective, namely the destruction of communism in Vietnam. Emphasis on political factors would become the key theme in Wilson's dissent in 1954.

The secretary of defense indicated that these issues were on his mind at a National Security Council meeting on February 4 which discussed whether to dispatch John O'Daniel to Indochina. "There was no doubt whatsoever of General O'Daniel's capacity to judge the military situation," he remarked, "but some skepticism existed in the Pentagon as to General O'Daniel's qualifications in the political and psychological field." Five days later Wilson reflected on the domestic political context in the United States. Asked by reporters whether the Eisenhower "New Look" defense program could be applied to Indochina, he said he thought not: "most Americans are not very keen for us to engage in the fighting down there, see." Indochina was not "the kind of place" where the United States could use its nuclear weapons.[7]

Wilson's nagging doubts about the situation in Vietnam prompted him to contest openly the administration's view that the outcome of this struggle was vital to American interests. At an NSC meeting on March 25 he boldly asked "whether it would be sensible to forget about Indochina for a while and concentrate on the effort to get the remaining free nations of Southeast Asia in some sort of condition to resist communist aggression against themselves." An unimpressed Eisenhower expressed "great doubt as to the feasibility of such a proposal, since he believed that the collapse of Indochina would produce a chain reaction which would result in the fall of all of Southeast Asia to the Communists." Plainly, Eisenhower subscribed to the domino theory in private as well as in public.[8]

As the fall of Dienbienphu neared, Wilson continued to emphasize the political dimension of the crisis in Vietnam. At a press conference in early May he explained: "One of the things that complicates the Indochina situation is that to some degree it was a civil war or revolution. We think of it as completely Communist aggression, but all the peoples of the world don't look at it that way and that is the difficulty with many things. You just can't simplify them and say they are this or that. They have different facets and complications and you have to take a look at each one of them on its own and weigh its pro and con." Questioned about the likelihood of direct U.S. intervention in Indochina, Wilson reiterated his belief that the American people would have no sympathy for such a policy.[9]

After the French surrender at Dienbienphu, Wilson's fears about U.S. involvement in Vietnam increased. With French extrication from Indochina via the Geneva talks a likelihood, the question of whether

Washington would replace Paris in fighting the Vietminh was now paramount. Wilson worried that the United States would end up in a quagmire, fighting a losing cause.

At a May 10 White House meeting involving Eisenhower, Dulles, and other officials, Wilson adopted the position that he would essentially maintain for the rest of 1954: Eisenhower should be wary about placing himself under any obligations in Indochina. When the president sent Wilson on a fact-finding trip to the Far East in mid-May, it only strengthened his conviction. Before departing Washington, Wilson told the press that a Communist victory in Indochina would not jeopardize America's overall policy in the Far East, a view that Secretary of State Dulles had also expressed publicly earlier in the day. Wilson went on to define the objectives of his mission: "Familiarize myself with the situation over there and get firsthand information from our folks there."[10]

Wilson's three-week travels included stops in Alaska, Japan, Korea, Formosa, Hong Kong, and the Philippines, among others—but not Indochina. Nevertheless a good many of his conversations related to the situation there. In talks with Chiang Kai-shek, the Formosa-based former leader of China and close American ally told Wilson, as the secretary of defense later reported, that the United States "was wasting its time and money in Indochina. American aid had better be channelled elsewhere, since the great issues in Asia would not be settled in Indochina." This was blunt and sobering advice. A meeting in the Philippines also touched on Vietnam. There Chargé William S. B. Lacy conveyed to Wilson concerns from the U.S. embassy in Saigon: "It is important [to] remember certain factors which make us view [the] picture occasionally with less optimism. There [is a] time when political deterioration becomes disintegration. We believe that time [has been] reached and passed in Vietnam. Vacuum of political authority exists [in] Vietnam." For his part, Wilson observed that "it [was] most important [to] realize [the] differences[,] attitudes[,] and cultural histories of [the] Indochinese." His trip to the Pacific thus confirmed his belief that political factors made a defeat of the Vietminh unlikely, and that Eisenhower should not make a deep commitment to combating communism in Indochina.[11]

On his return from the Far East on June 2, an exhausted secretary of defense fielded questions from reporters who had gathered at Washington National Airport to greet him. Wilson stressed that Indochina was not a simple case of Communist belligerence. "The problem actually is a little confused over starting as a civil war," he said, "and while the Communists have regularly exploited any trouble that they could find anywhere in the world, it is not so clear to everyone that it's a Communist aggression." "I happen to think that most of the problems [in Indochina] are on a political level," Wilson added, not on a military level.[12]

The Geneva Conference now became a focus of attention. From the outset of talks it was understood that one possible modus vivendi was a partition of Vietnam. With the Communists in control of much of the north, and France dominant in the south, a division of the country was feasible, at least in the short term. In the end, a number of factors helped to produce a settlement on this basis, not least political developments in France. Prime Minister Joseph Laniel had promised Bao Dai that he would permit no partition at Geneva. But on June 12 his government fell, replaced by one under the leadership of Pierre Mendès-France, who was not only prepared to permit the division of Vietnam but promised to resign if no agreement were reached at Geneva by July 20. Increasing the momentum toward peace were the Russians and Chinese, both of whom encouraged the Vietminh to accept a settlement they considered less than ideal.[13]

Wilson, meanwhile, remained doubtful about American involvement in Indochina. At a National Security Council meeting on June 17 he argued against sending to Vietnam substantial amounts of U.S. military equipment that might well end up in the hands of the Vietminh. Two weeks later he displayed the same sort of caution when telling John Foster Dulles in a phone conversation that the United States should not "get too far in it [Indochina] until we do know [more about French intentions]. Without Indochina or a part of it, we should consider how much obligation we want to take—maybe it is a British-Indian problem more than ours."[14]

In mid-July the Geneva talks finally bore fruit. The agreements, signed on the 21st, called for a cease-fire; a temporary division of Vietnam along the seventeenth parallel, with the Communists controlling the north; and nationwide elections two years hence—supervised by a commission comprising officials from Poland, Canada, and India—to reunite the country. Neither north nor south Vietnam could permit foreign bases on their soil or receive additional military equipment, nor could they enter into military alliances. The Eisenhower administration did not sign but, in a statement, merely "took note" of the Geneva Accords. That way Ike protected himself to some extent from domestic criticism (forthcoming nonetheless from the right) that he had given away a sizable chunk of Vietnam to the Communists; and he maintained his maneuverability in terms of future U.S. policy in Indochina.[15]

It was during this period that Eisenhower reached some important conclusions. While not eager to deploy ground troops in Vietnam, in effect he made a major commitment to maintain a non-Communist government in the south. Further, he was prepared to demonstrate that commitment by pouring military aid into the south, building up the anti-Communist armed forces there, and creating a defense pact for the region akin to NATO—the Southeast Asia Treaty Organization. These decisions represented a milestone on the road to full American involvement in the war.[16]

In response to these undertakings to bolster South Vietnam, Wilson's dissent became more strident. After Geneva, the ambivalence he had displayed about American involvement in Vietnam before the fall of Dienbienphu developed into an unambiguous opposition. In challenging Eisenhower's policies, he emphasized a number of considerations, in addition to the political factor he had already pointed out, that indicated the dangers of staying the course.

Much of Wilson's dissent in the summer and early fall of 1954 was directed at SEATO, whose formation was being energetically promoted by Dulles. At a July 24 meeting attended by various officials but not the president, Wilson raised the issue of elections in Vietnam. Dulles explained that as the Vietminh would probably win, "we would have to take the position in 1956 that conditions were not favorable for the free expression of the will of the population." Wilson went on to assert that "we should back away from the idea of a military pact and go ahead with the economic aspects" in forging an alliance with Southeast Asian countries. Dulles strongly disagreed. Abandoning SEATO, he insisted, would be an "unmitigated disaster."[17]

At a meeting of the NSC on August 12, Wilson made another attempt to change Eisenhower's policies. During a discussion of the terms for SEATO, he declared that "we should not back into a war over Laos, Cambodia or Vietnam," to which Dulles responded that SEATO meant these three states would be "the beneficiaries of united action against an aggressor." Wilson also objected to a provision that would give the president authority to take prompt military action in an emergency. Eisenhower conceded that any president who used this authority would subsequently need to bring the matter before Congress.[18]

Wilson, though, continued to make his case. "It was necessary to make a distinction among various countries in the Far East," he said. "For example, we might support a military action in the Philippines when we would not support such action in Laos, Cambodia or Vietnam. . . . we never had a vital interest in the latter countries." "We should not trap ourselves into going to war in Southeast Asia," he made clear, "to save South Vietnam." For Wilson, SEATO's chief drawback was that it might ensnare the United States in a war with the Vietminh.[19]

The secretary of defense seemed concerned too by the determination of Eisenhower and Dulles to cancel the nationwide elections set for 1956 in Vietnam. When Dulles argued that a Communist victory in these elections was inevitable, and that "our real objective should be to avoid having any such elections," Wilson asked whether the administration was prepared therefore to undermine the Geneva Accords. Dulles suggested that the issue did not arise as the United States had not actually signed those agreements, while Eisenhower shared the view that preventing Ho's victory via the ballot box was an important U.S. objective.[20]

The meeting closed with Wilson, Dulles, and Eisenhower again locking horns. When one official stated that the administration should decide exactly where it would confront Communist aggression, Dulles said the plan was for SEATO "to draw the line to include Laos, Cambodia, and South Vietnam on our side." "The theory of the treaty," he added, "was that if the Communists breached the line we would attack Communist China." Wilson interjected that it would be difficult to commit to defending Laos, Cambodia, and South Vietnam, as "their loss would not be a loss to us, inasmuch as they had never belonged to us." The observation provoked a bitter reaction from his colleagues. Dulles said he had already made clear that the United States would respond to Chinese aggression. Harold Stassen, director of the Foreign Operations Administration, declared that "a gain by the Communists was a loss to us, no matter where it occurred." "Some time we must face up to it," concurred Eisenhower. "We can't go on losing areas of the free world forever."[21]

Wilson had not only made his opposition to a deeper U.S. involvement in Vietnam more explicit in this NSC meeting than in earlier policy discussions, he had also broadened the basis for that dissent. No longer were his views anchored exclusively in an appreciation of political realities in Vietnam—the civil-war dimension to the instability there, the force of nationalism, the popularity of Ho. Also of concern, he now suggested, was the questionability of key U.S. interests in Vietnam. Significant too was the need to present a positive image of the United States overseas—an objective that would be compromised by a U.S. refusal to uphold the Geneva Accords.[22]

In the days after this meeting, Wilson continued to worry about SEATO, though he appears increasingly to have recognized the inevitability of its formation. On August 17 he provided Dulles with a memorandum outlining the official, generally supportive Pentagon view of SEATO. But the same day he sent Dulles a frank letter stating his personal reservations:

> I have the minimum amount of optimism about what really can be accomplished at this stage, and I cannot get away from the feeling that the British and India have a great responsibility in the matter if not the primary responsibility.
>
> After the initial organization of the matter, I would think it would be very helpful if we could lie back a bit and be the people

that the rest of them had to get to go along rather than for us to take the initiative and have the British and the Hindus and everyone else involved in the matter throw roadblocks in our way.

Disingenuously perhaps, given his enthusiasm for SEATO, Dulles replied on August 25 that he too had "very little optimism about this. However, I think we have to proceed at least to the point of making the treaty. Otherwise, we seem to abandon the entire area without a struggle."[23]

Wilson's concerns about Vietnam persisted through September. Toward the end of an animated NSC meeting on the 24th, Allen Dulles suggested that the United States and France needed "to unite firmly in support of one local leader" in order to stabilize South Vietnam. In response, the secretary of defense declared that "an even more desirable course of action was for the United States to get completely out of the area. The chances of saving any part of Southeast Asia were, in his opinion, nothing."[24]

By this time it was clear that Wilson's reservations about SEATO had made no impact. Dulles had spent much of August lining up allies for the new organization, and by September 8 his work was done. The United States, Britain, France, Australia, New Zealand, Thailand, Pakistan, and the Philippines signed on to this security pact for Southeast Asia. Dulles believed that SEATO represented a major accomplishment—an effective bulwark against the Communists in the region. But SEATO had glaring deficiencies. Several key countries—India, Indonesia, and Burma—refused to join, and SEATO contravened the Geneva Accords, thereby tarnishing America's image abroad. The new organization did not formally include Laos, Cambodia, or southern Vietnam, but its protocol did commit the treaty signatories to the defense of these countries—even though the Geneva agreements had prohibited either North or South Vietnam from entering an alliance. Eisenhower could claim that the United States had been merely a bystander, not a signatory, at Geneva. Still, it didn't look good.[25]

Besides questioning the establishment of SEATO, Wilson also seems to have queried the decision to back Ngo Dinh Diem as the leader of South Vietnam. Eisenhower had good reason to support Diem, who had an appealing dual image as nationalist and anti-Communist.

Trained to serve in the French bureaucracy, this ardent Catholic un-
covered a Communist-led rebellion in 1929, punished the ringleaders
severely, and was rewarded by the French with a senior government
position. He resigned when the French decided against introducing
the reforms he had recommended. His reputation for independent
thinking was enhanced by his refusal in later years to work with the
Japanese, Bao Dai, or the Vietminh. When Diem left Vietnam, settling
in New Jersey, he developed cordial relations with prominent Catholic
Americans, including Democratic senators John Kennedy and Mike
Mansfield. But Diem had shortcomings too. An elitist, he found it difficult to connect empathetically with the Vietnamese populace—a
weakness magnified by his Catholic faith, given that most of the people were Buddhist. He also lacked a political base. His only strong supporters seemed to be his own family, which, as one historian puts it,
had "a well-earned reputation for clannish self-interest." In time these
weaknesses would become conspicuous.[26]

Bao Dai made Diem prime minister of what became South Vietnam in the summer of 1954. The circumstances surrounding the appointment are still murky, but the Eisenhower administration may
have influenced the decision. As the French soon questioned the
soundness of Diem's selection as leader, this issue became the source of
acrimonious Franco-American debate in late 1954.[27]

Wilson hinted at his dissatisfaction with Diem's appointment at an
October 6 NSC meeting in which Allen Dulles reported that talks between American and French officials had resulted in a joint decision in
favor of the Diem government. The CIA director added that "not
everybody in Vietnam would like this decision, and it was therefore too
early to say that this Government's position had become any stronger."
Wilson interjected that "he didn't like what was going on in Vietnam
either." He may have been thinking that Eisenhower's support for
Diem implied a long-term American commitment to the protection of
his government, thereby producing the sort of U.S. entanglement in
Vietnam that he was so anxious to avoid. Later in the same meeting,
during a discussion of the dispute over the Chinese Nationalist off-
shore islands, Wilson declared that "the moment was certainly at hand
for a complete new look at our policies in the Far East."[28]

As Wilson continued to contest his colleagues' commitment to South Vietnam during October, he challenged the idea that Eisenhower should pour military aid into the South. On the 18th he clashed with John Foster Dulles over the financial implications of American backing for Diem in an Oval Office meeting with Eisenhower and Robert Cutler, special assistant to the president. Wilson, Cutler noted, "seemed to be of the opinion that it would be hopeless to try to save South Vietnam, and that further expenditures were wasted money." In both a conciliatory and confrontational vein, Dulles said he had just written Wilson acknowledging that a plan to provide South Vietnam with $500 million was "silly." On the other hand, furnishing a lesser sum "for the purpose of building up a sufficient local force to insure internal stability and counteract subversion was reasonable and wise." The secretary of state thought it should cost no more than $100 million. Nation building in Southeast Asia would cost money. Having been charged by Eisenhower with making economies in the military budget, Wilson could not view these developments with equanimity.[29]

By late October most of Eisenhower's advisers had agreed on the need for a crash military program in South Vietnam: dollars would be sent for the training of Vietnamese military units in order to bolster Diem's position. But at a National Security Council meeting on October 26, Wilson took great exception to the idea. With his colleagues speculating on the reasons for French opposition to the planned U.S. scheme, a frustrated secretary of defense spoke straight from the shoulder: "In his view the only sensible course of action was for the U.S. to get out of Indochina completely and as soon as possible. The situation there was utterly hopeless, and these people should be left to stew in their own juice." "What we were doing in Indochina was being done for our own purposes and not for the French," Eisenhower retorted. "If we continued to retreat in this area the process would lead to a grave situation from the point of view of our national security." He added that "we should try to get the French out of the Indochina area." Wilson was not yet prepared to defer to the president. "If we had ever been in control of Indochina, as we had once been in the Philippines," he countered, "he would feel differently about it. As matters stood, however, he could see nothing but grief in store for us if we remained in this area."[30]

With tempers rising, Cutler asked Wilson whether he was calling upon the National Security Council to reverse its recommendation to the president five days earlier for a crash military program in South Vietnam. Isolated and under pressure, Wilson, lamely, said he was not. But that was precisely what he had been calling for. He went on to say that the NSC's decision on military aid had been based on the assumption that the British and French would support it, but it now appeared this backing would not be forthcoming.[31]

The intensity and candor of Wilson's initial remarks made this NSC meeting the zenith of his dissent on Vietnam. His backtracking when pressed, however, was the first indication of how impossible he thought it would be to crack the consensus that had crystallized in the Eisenhower administration in favor of nation building in South Vietnam. His sense of resignation would become still more apparent in 1955.

As fall turned to winter, Wilson's determination to avoid situations that might lead to American participation in another war remained apparent. At a press conference on November 30 he was peppered with questions about the likely U.S. response to Russian or Chinese aggression. He replied that the decision to go to war would have to be resolved prudently, case by case—unless there was a direct Soviet attack on the United States, which would obviously require an immediate response. With the reporters continuing to press him, Wilson launched into an impassioned exposition:

> I don't approve of another world war. . . . I don't think that wars solve problems. I think they create a whole new bunch of them, and after a third world war we would wind up with a whole lot of problems at the end of it just like we had at the end of World War I and World War II, and I am getting so old I remember those problems; I remember the wars, and I don't think we have made much progress in the world with those wars, so while I am very much sold, with no reservation, that we must be militarily strong to protect our freedom and our type of government in the Free

World, I would just like to go on the record with all of you that I
don't approve of a third world war, and I like to keep remembering
all the time that the purpose of our country is peace.[32]

In early 1955 Wilson apparently accepted the idea that he could not
alter Eisenhower's policies in Vietnam. Gradually he climbed aboard
the administration bandwagon that was moving toward a greater
American involvement in Southeast Asia. With the United States replacing the French during the course of 1955 as the chief guarantor of
a non-Communist South Vietnam, the secretary of defense participated in administration discussions on how best to bolster Diem. In
early February Wilson endorsed Harold Stassen's recommendations
for additional aid to Indochina.[33]

Wilson's new willingness to be a team player was evident on several
other occasions in 1955. On May 4 he offered the secretary of state his
views on the attributes needed by the person who would be appointed
chief of the U.S. Military Assistance Advisory Group (MAAG) in South
Vietnam. At a National Security Council meeting a month later, Wilson advised that his department agreed with Dulles's view that the administration should postpone discussion on the holding of all-Vietnam
elections. In December 1955 he sent Dulles a letter in which he argued
that MAAG should be allowed to increase its personnel beyond the previously established ceiling of 342 in order to maintain internal security
in South Vietnam. By the end of 1955, signs of Wilson's earlier dissent
had evaporated.[34]

Part of the reason for Wilson's increasing compliance after early
1955 was the simple recognition on his part that his colleagues would
not yield. Another contributory factor was probably his sense of isolation within the administration. In the run-up to the 1954 congressional
elections, Wilson had once again put his foot in his mouth publicly,
this time at a press conference in Detroit. In discussing unemployment, he had argued that those without work should move to find a
job: "I've got a lot of sympathy for people where a sudden change
catches 'em—but I've always liked bird dogs better than kennel-fed
dogs myself. You know, one who'll get out and hunt for food rather

than sit on his fanny and yell." Not surprisingly, comparing the unemployed with dogs produced a wave of protests.[35]

Wilson's proclivity for clumsy remarks came to a head in the early spring of 1955, following statements he had made suggesting there existed a weapon more destructive than the hydrogen bomb, and that the loss of the Quemoy-Matsu islands to Communist China would be insignificant. After a National Security Council meeting on March 10, Eisenhower asked Wilson into the Oval Office to administer something more stern than a slap on the wrist. The president used this meeting to caution Wilson "as to the casual statements he was constantly making in press conferences and elsewhere—which sometimes cause very definite embarrassment to the administration"—especially in matters of foreign policy. Two days later Eisenhower reflected in his diary on this aspect of Wilson's conduct: "While I think that he considers himself a master of public relations, he seems to have no comprehension at all of what embarrassment such remarks can cause the secretary of state and me in our efforts to keep the tangled international situation from becoming completely impossible."[36]

With his "bird dogs" remark perceived as responsible for the loss of GOP votes in the 1954 congressional elections, and with the rebuke from Eisenhower a few months later, Wilson felt chastened—and, consequently, a need to demonstrate his willingness to subordinate his personal views to the administration's broader interests. From this point of view, continuing to challenge Eisenhower's policies in Vietnam seemed undesirable, as any controversial remarks on this subject would probably be interpreted as further examples of his erraticism. His confidence thus dented, Wilson became a dutiful supporter of the president's nation building in South Vietnam. He remained one until he left the Eisenhower administration in October 1957.[37]

George Ball has received great credit over the years for his role in anticipating the pitfalls awaiting Lyndon Johnson's policy of escalation in Vietnam. How much more prescient, then, was Charles Wilson's identification a decade earlier of the troubling long-term implications of Eisenhower's handling of events in Indochina. Wilson understood that the Vietnam crisis was more a case of a nationalist uprising than

Communist aggression, that greater American involvement in this conflict would ultimately alienate the American people, that there were no vital U.S. interests at stake, and that the fiscal implications of staying the course in Vietnam were serious. That Eisenhower paid little attention to the generally cogent analysis provided by Wilson after the fall of Dienbienphu reflects poorly on his leadership. It undercuts the argument of those revisionists who praise the general for his shrewdness in foreign policy matters. A more astute president would have taken Wilson's dissent on board.

PART IV

Kennedy, Stevenson, and Cuba

CHAPTER 9

The Rivals

———

"Why, that's impossible. Adlai Stevenson is a bitter
man. He's a bitter, deeply disillusioned, deeply
hurt man."—JOHN F. KENNEDY, 1960, on the
possibility of Stevenson's nomination as the
Democratic presidential candidate

"How could I ever go to work for such an
arrogant young man!"—ADLAI STEVENSON,
summer 1960, referring to JFK

As THE United States continued in the 1960s to grapple with the
demands of world leadership, two issues obsessed the nation's leaders.
Vietnam—the decision to enter that war, and then the attempt to win
it—dominated their thoughts in the middle and latter part of the
decade. But at the start of the sixties it was Cuba that took precedence
over the cluster of other concerns, such as Berlin and the space race,
that competed for the attention of John Fitzgerald Kennedy and his
administration.

Kennedy was elected to the White House in 1960 having pledged
to energize the nation after what he regarded as the sluggish, uninspiring presidency of Dwight Eisenhower. As a young, dynamic leader
he would, Kennedy told the American people, get the country moving
again. What that rather vague promise meant when it came to foreign

policy, at least for the first two years of his presidency, was the adoption of a generally hard line approach toward the Soviet Union and its Communist allies. Nowhere would this truculent policy be more in evidence than in Kennedy's handling of Fidel Castro, the Cuban revolutionary who had seized power in 1959, establishing a left-wing government and a potential Russian ally only ninety miles off the coast of Florida. In the end, the issue of Cuba would provide the most embarrassing event of Kennedy's administration—the Bay of Pigs fiasco—and the most dangerous episode not only of his presidency but of the entire cold war era, the Cuban missile crisis of 1962, when America and Russia teetered on the brink of the nuclear war that all rational people had feared since the destruction of Hiroshima and Nagasaki in 1945.

As Kennedy pondered the thorny problem of how best to handle Castro, he was challenged at every turn about the soundness of his thinking and his policies by the man who, apart from JFK himself, was the most famous Democrat in America, Adlai E. Stevenson, his party's candidate for president in 1952 and 1956. Stevenson had gone down to heavy defeats to Eisenhower on both occasions but had emerged with his credibility intact. He had run stylish campaigns and had shown an erudition that had inspired liberal Democrats, if not the nation as a whole; and besides, Eisenhower's heroic status as the military architect behind the defeat of Hitler in World War II would have enabled him to trounce any Democrat, including Kennedy—and everybody knew it. Hence Kennedy had no alternative but to appoint Stevenson somewhere in his administration. He made the man from Illinois his ambassador to the United Nations.

Kennedy and Stevenson would clash over the Bay of Pigs invasion, the Cuban missile crisis, and much else besides. To understand their dispute in its fullest context, an examination of their relationship before the Kennedy presidency, and especially during the 1960 political season, is essential. The battle for the Democratic presidential nomination that year created a rift between Kennedy and Stevenson that would make it difficult for them to forge a solid working relationship when Kennedy was president. In addition, his contacts with Soviet leader Nikita Khrushchev in 1960 enhanced Stevenson's belief that, more than Kennedy, he understood Khrushchev's thinking. This would bear on the subsequent Kennedy-Stevenson dialogue on how the United States should meet the challenges of the cold war, including the one presented by Cuba.

Before 1960 Kennedy and Stevenson had got on well, though there were occasional tensions. Their relationship developed in the 1950s, by which point both men had established political careers of note. Backed by the millions of his father, Joseph P. Kennedy, JFK's rise had been meteoric. Dogged by ill health, including a weak back and (as diagnosed later) Addison's disease, he nonetheless served in the navy in World War II before being elected in 1946 to the House of Representatives from Massachusetts. He married Jacqueline Bouvier in 1953, a year after winning a seat in the Senate. Kennedy combined a political career with an infamously racy personal life—his promiscuity remained unaffected by his marriage—and claims to a literary talent. He had published two books, *Why England Slept* in 1940 and the Pulitzer Prize–winning *Profiles in Courage* sixteen years later. He had put in the bulk of the work for the first book, a rewriting of his undergraduate thesis at Harvard. His claims to the authorship of *Profiles in Courage* were far slighter. An aide, Theodore Sorensen, had in fact written most of it.[1]

Where Kennedy came from the East Coast and was new money, Stevenson hailed from the Midwestern state of Illinois and was very much old money. He was born with politics in his blood. His maternal great-grandfather was a close friend of Abraham Lincoln, and his paternal grandfather, Adlai E. Stevenson, had been vice president of the United States from 1893 to 1897. Educated at the Choate School, Princeton, Harvard, and Northwestern University Law School, Stevenson worked as a newspaper editor and a lawyer before entering the political arena in the 1930s. He served in the administration of Franklin Delano Roosevelt during the early days of the New Deal, was elected president of the Chicago Council on Foreign Relations, and worked for much of World War II in the Navy Department. His focus at the end of the war and after was on America's role in the newly formed United Nations. Stevenson was elected governor of Illinois in 1948, defeating his Republican opponent in a landslide. As a candidate, he had promised to clean up government and to address a number of pressing issues, including educational and welfare reform. As governor, Stevenson by and large made good on those promises.[2]

Thus by 1952 Stevenson was in a strong position to win reelection as governor, which was very much his intention. That was why when President Harry Truman, no less, asked him to seek the Democratic presidential nomination instead, he demurred. But the pressure on Stevenson to run for the White House in 1952 proved irresistible, especially after his dazzling keynote address at the Democratic National Convention in Chicago. On the third ballot he was drafted as the party's nominee for president. The inevitable defeat at the hands of Eisenhower followed, a result repeated four years later.[3]

Early relations between Stevenson and John Kennedy were friendly enough. Joseph Kennedy contributed financially to Stevenson's campaigns for governor in 1948 and for the presidency in 1952, though privately Stevenson remained suspicious of the Kennedy patriarch's brazen ambition. But JFK respected Stevenson, as Robert Kennedy later confirmed: "My brother liked him a lot or admired him a good deal. We tried on his behalf in 1952 [in Massachusetts]." Four years later JFK still backed Stevenson. At a March 1956 press conference he announced his support for Stevenson in the race for that year's Democratic presidential nomination. Ultimately, however, the 1956 campaign sowed the first seeds of discord between the two men. Before the Democratic convention in Chicago that year, Kennedy and his advisers tried to persuade Stevenson to name JFK as his vice-presidential running mate. Rather than choose Kennedy, however, Stevenson threw the selection open to the delegates at the convention. Kennedy was thus drawn into a contest he wished to avoid, as it put his burgeoning reputation on the line. He lost the battle to Tennessee senator Estes Kefauver.[4]

Kennedy's disappointment at Stevenson's lack of support for him in 1956 was magnified a year later when the Illinoisan criticized JFK's proposal that the French grant Algeria its independence. Stevenson thought it would jeopardize NATO unity. Kennedy was again irritated by Stevenson when, in 1958, he was quoted in *U.S. News and World Report* as having said that JFK had "three strikes against him: religion [no Catholic had ever been elected president], too young, too rich." "To

Kennedy," one historian has written, "such comments were petulant and ungenerous."[5]

The campaign for the Democratic presidential nomination in 1960 multiplied the tensions that had developed between Kennedy and Stevenson in the 1950s. Kennedy's attitude toward the nomination of his party was unequivocal: he wanted it. On January 2, 1960, in a statement read before a crowd of effusive supporters packed into the Senate Caucus Room, he made public what every informed citizen already knew to be the case: he was a candidate for president. Stevenson felt more ambivalent. In light of his defeats in 1952 and 1956, he thought it unseemly to campaign through the primary season for the delegates he would need to secure the nomination at the Democratic convention in Los Angeles. But, like many of his ardent admirers, he clung to the idea that the White House was his destiny. So if his supporters wished to organize on his behalf throughout the country, he would not hinder that effort. If a deadlocked convention turned to him once again as his party's nominee, he would accept the challenge. Helping his prospects was the fact that his reluctance to fight openly for the nomination did not halt the development of a pro-Stevenson nationwide organization.[6]

The possibility that Stevenson might once again win his party's nomination haunted Kennedy throughout the spring and summer of 1960. Behind those fears lay a peculiar mixture of contempt and envy. On the one hand, JFK thought of Stevenson as prissy, effeminate, naive, and ineffective. On the other, he coveted Stevenson's oratorical skills, wit, sense of style, and above all the fanatical support he enjoyed from the liberal wing of the Democratic party. While Kennedy's contempt for Stevenson made him think he deserved to win, his envy of the man caused him to doubt his ability to do so.

To block a last-minute drive for Stevenson in Los Angeles, JFK tried to persuade, cajole, even intimidate him into endorsing the Kennedy campaign. His broader objective was to increase liberal support for his own candidacy. Kennedy's chief problem during the primary season, apart from the need to deal deftly with the religious issue created by his Catholic faith, was to assure liberals that he shared their ideals despite his image as a hawk on foreign policy and his failure to take a stand against Senator Joseph McCarthy. A vote of confidence from Stevenson would help immeasurably with the liberal community.

The quid pro quo offered to Stevenson was the promise of an appointment as secretary of state, an appealing proposition given his deep interest in foreign affairs, in exchange for his public support of Kennedy. But Stevenson refused to throw in his lot.

In early February Stevenson had left for a two-month tour of Latin America. On his return he met in Illinois with his good friend, the distinguished economist Barbara Ward, around the time of the Wisconsin primary in which Kennedy secured a handy victory over Minnesota senator Hubert Humphrey. Ward was also on good terms with JFK, and though it is unclear whether she did this on her own initiative or was conveying an offer from the Kennedy camp, she suggested Stevenson come out for JFK in return for a promise that he could run the State Department. "Look," Stevenson responded, "my difficulty is that I don't think he'd be a good president. I do not feel that he's the right man for the job; I think he's too young; I don't think he fully understands the dimensions of the foreign dilemma that are coming up; and I cannot in conscience throw my support to someone whom I do not really think is up to it." "I admire him," he assured Ward. "I think he's a fine young man; I don't see him as a president. I can't in conscience suddenly say, because I want to be secretary of state, 'Okay, I have changed my mind.'" Stevenson told Ward that he did not want the Democratic nomination but might well accept it if drafted because he was confident he could defeat Nixon, the likely Republican candidate.[7]

Even after Kennedy's decisive victory over Humphrey in the West Virginia primary, Stevenson still refused to back him. During May, in fact, he appeared to be building his own credentials for the nomination. When the Soviet shooting down of American pilot Gary Powers's U-2 plane aborted the Paris summit between Eisenhower and Khrushchev, the sudden deterioration in Soviet-American relations caused some Democrats to turn to Stevenson, who seemed to offer a more experienced brand of leadership than Kennedy. This was why, as Arthur Schlesinger has confirmed, JFK continued to make gains among Democrats after West Virginia until the end of May, when there was "a convulsive movement" toward Stevenson.[8]

This left Kennedy in a state of indignation, as the journalist Arthur Krock discovered when calling him on May 24. Stevenson was working for the nomination, observed Krock. "And how!" JFK responded. Even though Kennedy had a week earlier indicated that Stevenson could be the next secretary of state, he was now less inclined. "The tone," Krock wrote in a private memorandum, "clearly reflected Kennedy's irritation that Stevenson is encouraging support for his nomination among Democrats whom Kennedy felt would otherwise be for him, and, especially in California, were impeding his prospect."[9]

Relations between Kennedy and Stevenson deteriorated further after the Oregon primary. When JFK triumphed again, as he did in all the primaries he entered in 1960, he journeyed to Stevenson's home in Libertyville, Illinois, for a meeting. Flying into Chicago, Kennedy intended to take advantage of an earlier indication from Stevenson that he would come out for the winner of the Oregon primary. William McCormick Blair, Jr., and Newton Minow, who had both urged Stevenson to support Kennedy, met JFK at the airport. During the drive to Libertyville, Kennedy asked whether he should offer the position of secretary of state to Stevenson directly. Minow warned against it. Stevenson would resent it, he said, and furthermore "you don't want to tie your own hands."[10]

In the meeting with Stevenson, Kennedy vented his frustration in no uncertain terms. "Look, I have the votes for the nomination and if you don't give me your support, I'll have to shit all over you. I don't want to do that but I can, and I will if I have to." Stevenson claimed he could not come out for Kennedy because he wanted to be in a position to act as a conciliator between Kennedy and Senate Majority Leader Lyndon Johnson, who was delaying his campaign for the nomination until the convention. The discussion between Kennedy and Stevenson concluded with no meeting of minds.[11]

Stevenson was stunned by Kennedy's aggression. "I should have told the son-of-a-bitch off," he said later, "but, frankly, I was shocked and confused by that Irish gutter talk. That's pretty cheap stuff." After this conversation there was no chance that Stevenson would declare his support for Kennedy.[12]

JFK was no more satisfied with the discussion than Stevenson. "Guess who the next person I see will be," Kennedy asked Blair after the meeting, "the person who will say about Adlai, 'I told you that son-of-a-bitch has been running for President every moment since 1956'?" "Daddy," Blair replied shrewdly. On returning to the airport, Kennedy told a friend: "I learned one thing today and that is that Adlai Stevenson will never be my secretary of state." Recalling Stevenson's comment that he might serve as an intermediary between JFK and Johnson, Kennedy laughed. "I don't think Adlai realizes that Lyndon Johnson thinks that he's a fruit. The idea of Adlai Stevenson as a bridge between me and Lyndon Johnson is a joke. If he were a great diplomat, he would have been able to come up with a better one than that."[13]

Bad feelings between JFK and Stevenson continued to simmer during the pre-convention period that summer. When Kennedy asked at a dinner in Georgetown in mid-June what Stevenson was playing at, William Attwood explained that Stevenson's main concern was the defeat of Nixon. He wished to remain available for a draft should the convention deadlock. An unimpressed Kennedy claimed he had the nomination sewn up, that he would never take the second spot on a Stevenson-Kennedy ticket as the venerable journalist Walter Lippmann had suggested, and that Stevenson's political judgment was atrocious. On learning of JFK's comments from Attwood, Stevenson remarked that he could never work for Kennedy.[14]

The most intriguing feature of the primary season for Stevenson was the encouragement he received from the most unlikely of sources: the leader of the Soviet Union. Curious though it was, Nikita Khrushchev had good reasons for wanting Stevenson as president. He had a rapport with the Democrat and regarded him, as did many liberals in the United States, as America's new Franklin Roosevelt, the president who had so improved Soviet-American relations. Khrushchev's intervention in U.S. politics in 1960 enlarged the sense of intimacy between Stevenson and the Soviet premier. So when Stevenson advised Kennedy after his election as president, he did so believing he had a keener sense than JFK of the Soviet leadership's mind-set.

When Khrushchev established contact with Stevenson in 1960, he was building on a relationship of some trust. Surveying the American scene during the 1950s, the Russian premier had concluded that of all the leading American politicians, Stevenson was the one most interested in better relations with Moscow. His positive view of Stevenson was reinforced by two personal meetings, the first in 1958 during Stevenson's tour of the Soviet Union, and the second in Des Moines, Iowa, during Khrushchev's 1959 visit to the United States. Both discussions were cordial and constructive; each man came away with the belief that the other had a genuine interest in reducing Soviet-American tensions.[15]

Khrushchev's decision to interject himself into the 1960 presidential election was grounded in his policy objectives as well as his liking for Stevenson. During the late 1950s Khrushchev had reduced military expenditures so that he could spend more on the civilian economy. He believed that in the nuclear era troops and conventional weapons were less important, and he also realized that most of his military spending went on conventional rather than nuclear forces. That being the case, he could modernize his nuclear arsenal and at the same time reduce overall military expenditures by cutting spending on troops and conventional weapons. This would allow additional resources to be invested in the civilian economy, thereby raising the standard of living for the Russian people.[16]

Khrushchev introduced sweeping reforms in pursuit of that objective. From 1955 to 1960 he reduced the number of Soviet troops from 5,763,000 to 3,623,000. Defense spending as a share of gross national product fell too during the second half of the 1950s. Then, in January 1960, Khrushchev announced his most sweeping cuts yet: Russian military manpower would be reduced by one-third.[17]

From Khrushchev's perspective, these latest cuts would make sense only if the United States pursued a friendlier policy toward Moscow. The Eisenhower administration, with its ideas about the "liberation" of Soviet satellite states in Eastern Europe and the use of nuclear "brinkmanship" to restrain Russian ambitions, did not appear to be very interested in better relations with the Soviet Union. But with 1960 a presidential election year, and with Eisenhower constitutionally prohibited from running for a third term, Khrushchev knew that in January 1961 there would be a new administration in Washington, one, he hoped, that would try to get along with the Soviet Union.

As Khrushchev examined the field of presidential candidates in 1960, he believed that Stevenson was the most eager to forge close ties with Russia. "We had confidence in his intention to improve relations between our two countries," Khrushchev recalled, "so his would have been the most acceptable candidacy as far as we were concerned." Khrushchev's analysis of the situation was accurate. Of all the likely presidential candidates—Stevenson, Kennedy, Humphrey, Johnson, Nixon, and Nelson Rockefeller—Stevenson was the most determined to reduce cold war tensions. Astonishingly, Khrushchev decided to help his favorite candidate become president.[18]

In early January 1960, the same month Khrushchev announced he was slashing the Soviet military by a third, Ambassador Mikhail Menshikov telephoned Stevenson to request a meeting so that he could pass on some birthday gifts and messages from Khrushchev. Hence on January 16 Stevenson visited the Soviet embassy in Washington for private talks with Menshikov. Their meeting had the drama and suspense of a John le Carré novel. The two men spoke sotto voce throughout, and when on two occasions a waitress entered the third-floor parlor in which they were talking, Menshikov halted the conversation.[19]

The Russian ambassador began by presenting Stevenson with gifts from Khrushchev, including caviar, wine, and fruits. Menshikov then conveyed a message from the Soviet premier, which revealed that he was concerned about the U.S. presidential election, believed Stevenson to be the most likely of all the candidates to improve Soviet-American relations, and wanted to help his campaign by having the Soviet press either praise or criticize Stevenson—whichever the Illinoisan thought would do him the most good.[20]

If Stevenson was shocked by this offer of Soviet support, he did not show it. He calmly thanked Menshikov for both "this expression of Khrushchev's confidence" and the actual offer of assistance, but he made it clear that he would not be a presidential candidate in 1960. Moreover he emphasized his misgivings about foreign interference in an American election. "Even if I was a candidate I could not accept the assistance proffered," Stevenson recalled saying. "I made it clear to him that I considered the offer of such assistance highly improper, indiscreet and dangerous to all concerned." Stevenson reiterated those points in a letter to Menshikov six days later.[21]

Despite being rebuffed by Stevenson, Khrushchev nonetheless planned to back the Democratic presidential candidate in 1960, even if, as it now appeared, it was not to be Stevenson. Not only did Khrushchev despise the likely GOP nominee, Nixon, he also thought the Democrats were in general more conciliatory toward Moscow than their Republican counterparts. Whoever the candidates were, in Khrushchev's view the Democrat would be friendlier than the Republican. With that in mind, he decided to abort the Paris summit with Eisenhower in May 1960 not only because of the American refusal to apologize for the entry of Gary Powers's U-2 plane into Soviet airspace, but probably also because he did not wish the Republican party to reap the political benefits of a successful summit.

Although refusing to declare his candidacy for president, despite pressure from Khrushchev and backers within the United States, Stevenson found himself the recipient of growing support in the spring of 1960. In addition to organizational and financial preparations for a push on Stevenson's behalf at the Democratic convention in Los Angeles, a spontaneous pro-Stevenson movement gathered momentum at the grass roots. Abandoning their vacations, driving cars and riding buses, embarking on what they regarded as a crusade as much as a political campaign, the Stevenson legions set out for Los Angeles from myriad points across the continent. The hope of his backers was a deadlocked convention, out of which a consensus could crystallize in favor of Stevenson as a compromise candidate.[22]

Furthering that hope was the decision by Stevenson to enter the Sports Arena, the convention site, to join the Illinois delegation on the night of July 12. Customarily candidates stayed away from the convention hall until the nominee had been selected, but as Stevenson was not technically in the race he felt able to break with protocol. As he walked onto the floor, the galleries—packed with his supporters—broke into ecstatic cheers. With emotions running high and the demonstration on his behalf showing no sign of abating, Stevenson was unable to seat himself. After being directed toward the rostrum, he spoke briefly: "I know who's going to be the nominee of this convention," he declared, "the last man to survive."[23]

Nominating speeches and the roll call of the states were scheduled for the following day. Speaking for Stevenson, Senator Eugene McCarthy of Minnesota delivered one of the finest, most profoundly moving nominating speeches ever made at a party convention. "Do not reject this man," McCarthy exhorted his fellow Democrats. "Do not reject this man who has made us all proud to be Democrats. Do not leave this prophet without honor in his own party."[24]

After McCarthy's address, described by Stevenson as probably "the most eloquent utterance I have ever heard," the convention erupted. Thousands of Stevenson supporters who had been marching outside the Sports Arena poured into the convention hall. Paper banners were lifted high. A massive papier-mâché ball, composed of petitions with signatures calling for Stevenson's nomination, bounced above the demonstrators. And all the time a crescendo of voices demanded "WE WANT STEVENSON." For at least a moment this frenzy must surely have struck fear in the heart of John Kennedy.[25]

Nothing like it had occurred at a Democratic convention in living memory. But the Stevenson campaign had flattered to deceive. Very few of those standing, cheering, and clapping were delegates who would actually vote. When the roll call began, Kennedy secured victory on the first ballot, winning 806 votes. Johnson received 409; Stevenson only 79-1/2. Stevenson's almost decade-long journey for the White House was at an end.[26]

Two days later he introduced Kennedy for his "New Frontier" speech, in which he accepted his party's nomination. "I have come to say goodbye," Stevenson began, "but not farewell." He went on to describe his party's nominee as a man "who embodies the hopes of the generation which is rising to power in the world." But Kennedy and his advisers had been appalled by Stevenson's performance at the convention. He had refused Robert Kennedy's offer to make the nominating speech for JFK; and he had tried at the last moment to steal the nomination himself, despite his previous defeats and Kennedy's success in the primaries.[27]

Robert Kennedy said later that Stevenson's posturing in Los Angeles "irritated [JFK] and frustrated all of us. They're just . . . different types and kinds of people." His performance at the convention "seemed to us to be the actions of an old woman." Garry Wills, a perceptive observer of the American scene, writes that what annoyed the Kennedys most was the manifest depth of support for Stevenson among liberals. The Kennedys "took all the praise of Stevenson as an attack on John Kennedy, on the fake liberal." The historian Richard Walton has concluded that "The men around Kennedy . . . and maybe Kennedy himself never forgave Stevenson for that act of sacrilege [in seeking the nomination at the last moment], for having had the presumption to stand, even so briefly, in the path of the anointed."[28]

Two key questions about Kennedy and Stevenson emerged after the Democratic convention. First, what role would Stevenson play in the Kennedy campaign against Nixon in the autumn? Second, would JFK ask Stevenson to be his secretary of state, assuming a Kennedy victory in November? The first issue was resolved on July 31 when Stevenson journeyed to Hyannisport for a meeting with JFK and the rest of the Kennedy clan. After five hours "in the bosom—or the shark's teeth—of the Kennedy family," as he put it in a letter to a friend, he agreed to campaign energetically for the Democratic ticket in the autumn. JFK was pleased to receive the commitment as he thought Stevenson would help turn out the liberal vote. It was decided that Stevenson would focus his efforts on California and New York, the states where his influence was greatest.[29]

Kennedy kept under wraps his feelings about his likely secretary of state. Nor did Stevenson raise the issue. But both men were preoccupied with it. Stevenson was keenly interested in the post. His expertise lay in foreign affairs, and with the presidency now beyond his grasp, heading the State Department seemed the next best thing. Kennedy was less enthusiastic. Stevenson's unwillingness to back his candidacy during the primaries and his last-minute grab for the Democratic nomination had angered him. Despite pressure from Eleanor Roosevelt, Chester Bowles, and other liberal Democrats to install Stevenson at State, Kennedy already had another idea in mind: appoint Stevenson United Nations ambassador. That would appear to make use of

Stevenson's foreign policy expertise while denying him the power and status that went with the job at State. This issue of how Kennedy would use Stevenson's talents in his administration would come into sharper focus after the November election.[30]

Even as Kennedy enlisted Stevenson's services for the autumn campaign, the tension between the two men that had been so evident before and during the convention continued. Driving in Kennedy's Cadillac, after introducing the candidate at a rally in California, Stevenson commented on JFK's tan: "You look wonderfully well, Jack." Kennedy explained that it came from campaigning in open-top cars. "I never would do that," Stevenson declared prissily. "It's awful, the sun in your eyes, and dust. You can't see for hours afterward."[31]

Although he remained convinced of Kennedy's vanity and arrogance, Stevenson campaigned hard for the Democratic ticket that autumn, making no less than eighty-four speeches. He played an important role in allaying liberal doubts about JFK. While providing a ringing endorsement of Kennedy in public, Stevenson was privately troubled by JFK's campaign statements, particularly on Cuba. Having moved somewhat to the left to secure the Democratic nomination, Kennedy had turned back to the right in taking on Republican nominee Richard Nixon. Determined to appeal to the political center of the American electorate, JFK was anxious to undercut anticipated charges from Nixon that he was soft on communism. Accordingly, Kennedy took a very hard line on Cuba, blasting Nixon for his failure as Eisenhower's vice president to prevent the rise to power of Fidel Castro. On October 20 Kennedy proposed a plan that sounded very much like the Bay of Pigs operation he would carry out as president in the spring of 1961. The United States, he argued, should "strengthen the non-Batista democratic anti-Castro forces in exile, and in Cuba itself, who offer eventual hope of overthrowing Castro." Stevenson regarded Kennedy's belligerent proposal as an "appalling blunder." His concerns were not assuaged until JFK assured him that he would handle Cuba diplomatically through the Organization of American States. This JFK-Stevenson exchange on Cuba during the 1960 campaign foreshadowed their later differences on this key cold war issue during Kennedy's time in the White House.[32]

In his own, subtle way, Nikita Khrushchev remained a player in the presidential election in the autumn of 1960. Knowing that the next American leader would be Kennedy or Nixon, Khrushchev had no hesitation in favoring the Democrat. The Soviet leader did not rate Kennedy as highly as Stevenson, but he thought of him as a rising political star. He had spoken to JFK during his 1959 trip to the United States when he met with a group of senators. Although Kennedy arrived late, Khrushchev was impressed by him. He liked JFK's affable demeanor, and he greeted the young senator cordially: "I've heard a lot about you. People say you have a great future before you."[33]

The Russians courted Kennedy, as they had Stevenson, before the 1960 political campaign. Both Khrushchev and Menshikov recognized that Kennedy would be a strong contender for the Democratic nomination. JFK, however, probably feared that either the right in America or perhaps Khrushchev himself would use evidence of close contacts between himself and Soviet officials to damage him politically at a later date. When Menshikov came to his Senate office in early 1959, Kennedy, as one of his assistants recalls, gave the Russian ambassador "very short shrift." The same aide explained that "Kennedy wasn't very interested in having any significant conversation. I think he was just very wary. He didn't know what Menshikov would say or try to—he didn't like the politics of it." A few weeks later, when Menshikov invited Kennedy to spend a weekend at the Soviet estate in Maryland, he refused.[34]

Despite this iciness, Khrushchev found Kennedy more acceptable in the autumn of 1960 than Nixon, whose anti-Communist diatribes over the years had irritated him. Hence the Soviet leader took action behind the scenes to damage Nixon's candidacy, even though in public he remained neutral. In particular he prevented the return of captured pilot Gary Powers to the United States before the November election, fearing that Powers's release might aid Nixon. Discussing the matter with his advisers, he argued that "The United States government has asked us to release Powers. Now is *not* the time to do it because the two presidential candidates are both trying to cash in on an improvement in relations. If we release Powers now it will be to Nixon's advantage."[35]

"You know, Mr. Kennedy, we voted for you," Khrushchev revealed when meeting the new president at the Vienna summit in June 1961. "How?" JFK inquired. "By waiting until after the election to return the pilots." Kennedy laughed and declared, "You're right. I admit you played a role in the election and cast your vote for me."[36]

Despite rooting for Kennedy over Nixon, Khrushchev remained more attached to Stevenson in a personal sense and to his potential contribution to reducing cold war tensions. He had not enjoyed the sort of dialogue with Kennedy that he had with Stevenson before and during 1960. This led Khrushchev to conclude that Stevenson had an important role to play in any postelection dialogue between the superpowers.

On Tuesday, November 8, Election Day, as Kennedy waited with his family at Hyannisport for the results, Stevenson was home in Libertyville. He voted at midday, took a phone call from Marlene Dietrich, had dinner with his son, and then went to close friend Bill Blair's apartment to watch the election returns on television. Kennedy won by a whisker—34,221,463 votes to Nixon's 34,108,582—though he prevailed more comfortably in the electoral college. For Stevenson there was now one question of paramount importance: would Kennedy make him secretary of state?[37]

Stevenson's hopes were dashed precisely one month later when he was called to Kennedy's Georgetown home. In that December 8 meeting the president-elect offered Stevenson the UN ambassadorship. Candidly, Stevenson told Kennedy he preferred to be secretary of state, and that he could not accept the UN post until knowing who would head the State Department. Stevenson was alarmed, he said, by rumors that Kennedy might appoint Harvard dean McGeorge Bundy. "I won't work for that young Republican," he told JFK.[38]

For both Kennedy and Stevenson, the meeting was a major disappointment. "The President[-elect]," Robert Kennedy recalled, "was shocked. Of all the conversations he ever had with major figures over a period of five years, one of the most unsatisfactory was when he invited Stevenson to become Ambassador to the UN. He was absolutely furious. He said, 'He should say he wants it or he doesn't want it—but to act petulant, to say he was going to think it over, and again raising the question of he couldn't make up his mind.'"[39]

While Kennedy was more convinced than ever that Stevenson was a vacillating Hamlet, Stevenson regarded JFK as a sort of Macbeth—the man who had seized a crown that was not rightfully his. The Illinoisan was crestfallen. "Of course I expected to be Secretary [of State]," he later explained, "and it was a great blow." Despite his concerns, Stevenson accepted the UN ambassadorship after being informed by Kennedy that Dean Rusk, who had served in the Truman administration, would be the next secretary of state.[40]

Stevenson's procrastination over the UN was only one episode in December that increased Kennedy's distaste for him. The second was the report on Stevenson submitted by the FBI to JFK on December 29, 1960. FBI Director J. Edgar Hoover, who despised liberal Democrats, had collected information in the 1950s that could tarnish Stevenson's reputation, including the false allegation that he was homosexual—ironic given Hoover's own alleged sexual inclinations. Various canards, such as the claim that Stevenson was part of a gay group in New York City in which he was known as "Adelaide," were passed on to JFK in the FBI report. Since Kennedy had earlier said of Stevenson, "He must be a switcher," the FBI report strengthened a view that JFK already held. Kennedy would continue to dwell on the idea that Stevenson was effeminate. Florida senator George Smathers recalled discussions with Kennedy in which "We sometimes talked about the fact that he [Stevenson] just wasn't masculine enough for Jack Kennedy."[41]

On January 20, 1961, Stevenson joined other Cabinet appointees on the platform behind Kennedy as he took the oath of office and delivered an inaugural address in which he made clear the vigorous role he intended America to play in world affairs during his presidency:

Let the word go forth from this time and place, to friend and foe alike, that the torch has been passed to a new generation of Americans—born in this century, tempered by war, disciplined by a hard and bitter peace, proud of our ancient heritage—and unwilling to witness or permit the slow undoing of those human rights to which this nation has always been committed, and to which we are committed today at home and around the world.

Let every nation know, whether it wishes us well or ill, that we shall pay any price, bear any burden, meet any hardship, support any friend, oppose any foe to assure the survival and the success of liberty.[42]

When the ceremony ended, administration officials jumped into limousines for the trip to the White House reviewing stand. Alone among those of Cabinet rank, Stevenson had not been provided with a car. On that freezing afternoon he began the walk to the White House knowing that this oversight was almost certainly a conscious snub by the "Irish Mafia," the long-serving aides who took care of Kennedy's arrangements. Hence Stevenson began his service in the Kennedy administration in a manner that would continue right up to the day when a president was assassinated in Dallas: he was out in the cold.[43]

CHAPTER 10

Operation Castration

———

"The top priority in the United States
Government—all else is secondary—no time,
money, effort, or manpower is to be spared."
—ROBERT KENNEDY, January 1962, on the
importance of overthrowing Fidel Castro

Hᴵˢ APPOINTMENT as John Kennedy's UN ambassador in New
York was a homecoming for Stevenson. His early political career had
been fashioned in the crucible of the United Nations. He had attended
the San Francisco Conference that launched the new international organization in the spring of 1945, and had participated in the UN General Assemblies of 1946–1947. In these familiar surroundings the dutiful Stevenson explained and defended policies in the Kennedy years
that privately he often questioned.[1]

These differences between JFK's policies and those promoted in
private by Stevenson were inevitable. Simply put, Stevenson and
Kennedy *did* hold different views on what America's role in the world
should be. Although both had a common frame of reference, namely
the cold war, and so shared a number of general ideas—such as the belief that the United States must meet the Soviet challenge—there were
divergences, some subtle and some wide, between their approaches.

Kennedy's core conviction was that the United States must increase military spending and adopt a generally hard-line approach to

adversaries such as the Soviet Union and Cuba. The errors of 1930s appeasement must not be duplicated in the 1960s. Appreciating that nationalism rather than Communist expansion emanating from Moscow was often the cause of instability in developing nations, fashioning an economic aid program to meet the aspirations of those peoples for a higher standard of living, and a willingness to use negotiations in order to reduce cold war tensions, were all to some degree rhetorically embraced by JFK in the late 1950s and in his presidential campaign. For Stevenson, however, these were the central components of his foreign policy philosophy.[2]

The personal differences evident in their pre-1961 rivalry continued to hamper the Kennedy-Stevenson relationship after JFK's inauguration as president, and they served to accentuate their policy differences. From Kennedy's point of view, Stevenson was a stuffed shirt. He liked advisers to be pithy, not expansive, humorous rather than philosophical. Stevenson made no attempt to fall in line with the new administration's stylistic ethos. He was also an incorrigible grumbler. Throughout his time as UN ambassador, and virtually every week during the early part of Kennedy's presidency, Stevenson talked of resigning. That worried the likes of Assistant Secretary for International Organizations Harlan Cleveland, and his concern over a possible Stevenson break with the New Frontier was relayed to JFK. Administration officials soon realized that Stevenson was a whiner and that his threats were to be ignored. Kennedy, however, regarded them as an annoying distraction.[3]

Stevenson, for his part, believed, as he always had, that JFK was arrogant, calculating, and dangerously overconfident in his own abilities. He was unhappy with the harsh treatment he often received at the hands of the president. John Bartlow Martin writes that "Stevenson seems to have thought of Kennedy as cold-blooded, even heartless. . . . He sometimes said that President Kennedy treated him with a cruel wit." Stevenson's dissatisfaction with Kennedy, including his unflattering view of JFK's leadership abilities, was often expressed in conversations with friends and colleagues. These comments were sometimes passed on to JFK, damaging relations between the two men.[4]

The personal and policy differences between Kennedy and Stevenson were part of a larger story—the thorny relationship between the new president and many of the liberals he appointed to his administration. Those Democrats, such as Stevenson, Undersecretary of State Chester Bowles, Assistant Secretary of State for African Affairs G. Mennen Williams, and Harlan Cleveland, were designed to give a progressive veneer to the New Frontier and to satisfy the left wing of the party. But Kennedy distanced himself from that wing when crafting foreign policy, convinced that their recommendations were impractical. Stevenson's ostracism within the Kennedy administration was thus emblematic of the general isolation in which liberal Democrats found themselves as JFK began to implement his foreign policy.[5]

A dilemma faced Kennedy on entering the White House. He had run for president by emphasizing the threat posed by Khrushchev and Castro, yet both those enigmatic leaders viewed the Kennedy presidency as an opportunity to improve relations with the United States. Castro knew that Eisenhower and members of the Cuban exile community in Florida had developed a plan for military action to overthrow him. Simply because he wished to stay in power, Castro hoped that Kennedy would cancel the operation he had inherited. Khrushchev's interest in reducing superpower tensions was linked to the cuts he had made in defense spending in order to invest more in the civilian economy. The Soviet premier recognized that his policy could be implemented without damaging Russian security only if Kennedy were prepared to modify what Khrushchev regarded as Eisenhower's hard-line approach to Moscow.[6]

Castro and Khrushchev conveyed their interest in improved relations with Washington in different ways. Castro and his advisers made various public statements expressing the hope that JFK would rescind Eisenhower's plan for military action against Cuba. Khrushchev communicated his desire for a thaw in the cold war to Kennedy privately, through intermediaries such as Stevenson and the veteran Democrat Averell Harriman.

Although it was JFK who had been elected president, Khrushchev continued to enjoy a greater rapport with Stevenson. He had a history with Stevenson that his one brief introduction to JFK in 1959 did not match. So it was not surprising that only days after Kennedy's election,

Khrushchev generated an extensive dialogue with Stevenson on the future of Soviet-American relations.

On November 16 Menshikov brought Stevenson a message from Khrushchev saying, "Your activities toward better relations, lessening tensions, are very much appreciated and will always have support in Moscow." He implied that Kennedy's election heralded exciting possibilities for a Soviet-American rapprochement. There was a chance for "fruitful action now, especially in relation to disarmament. He had high hopes that we can reach understandings. *War must be avoided.* He does not wish to argue about who is stronger, but to reach understandings and cooperate." Khrushchev also emphasized the importance of reaching agreement on a nuclear test ban. Hinting perhaps at a special role for Stevenson, he said the discussion on disarmament could take place between government representatives off the record.[7]

Menshikov wasted no time in arranging another meeting with Stevenson. On November 28 in New York he told Stevenson he had relayed the contents of their previous conversation to Khrushchev, who had sent a reply. Translating from extensive notes in Russian, Menshikov read his leader's latest message to Stevenson: "Mr. Khrushchev says he has read with great interest and special satisfaction about Stevenson's hope that pressing problems can be settled and relations improved between the U.S. and the U.S.S.R." Khrushchev went on to discuss disarmament, Germany and Berlin, and colonialism. Asked by Menshikov for his response, Stevenson said Khrushchev's comments on disarmament were encouraging, but his remarks on Berlin were unhelpful and those about colonialism mere propaganda.[8]

Resuming their discussion the next day, Menshikov and Stevenson concentrated on disarmament. Stevenson found this talk less productive but nevertheless agreed to see Menshikov again, on December 15. This discussion reinforced Stevenson's earlier impression that the Russians were eager to explore the possibilities for disarmament. He also learned from a meeting that same day between Menshikov and Harrison Salisbury of the *New York Times* that the ambassador—and so presumably the Soviet leader as well—was interested in arranging a summit meeting between Kennedy and Khrushchev.[9]

Realizing that his dialogue with Khrushchev via Menshikov was relevant to Kennedy's postelection assessment of the Communist challenge, Stevenson decided to transmit the substance of his conversations to JFK and his close aides, revealing Khrushchev's interest in better relations. Stevenson did not naively believe that Khrushchev's initiative represented a chance to end the cold war, but he did consider it important to explore this opportunity.[10]

He put that argument to Kennedy in a telephone conversation on January 13, 1961, explaining that he had

> talked to Rusk and Chester [Bowles] several weeks ago urging them to suggest to you or discuss with you sometime what seems to me the most important first thing that this administration has to do— and that is to discover what is in K[hrushchev]'s mind, if possible. There's only one way I know of and this would be by direct talks in Moscow without formality by somebody who is not the diplomatic agent but someone who corresponds to Khrushchev's concept of power. That is, a political figure rather than a diplomatic one; someone who would go there after the inauguration as your emissary to review the situation and exploit what opportunities there may be. I think it is important to find out what his troubles are—as well as to explore with him ours. I am told one trouble of his may be his health—which we don't know anything about. Extremists in the Presidium and China—and what he has to deal with. I think we will not find anyone easier to deal with than K is. I think it is important to find out whether he wants to expand the cold war—if we make proposals on general and complete disarmament—how are we going to proceed—does he want an effective U.N., or is he determined to destroy it?—I know how he reveals himself in conversation—and it could be this could determine quite a good deal, especially if he wants to do business—What we want to do is to discover some means of creating a favorable world order and we must explore the kind of thing we could do . . . we could with grace make a gesture in their direction.[11]

Kennedy responded that they should discuss the merits of ordering home Llewellyn Thompson, their ambassador in Moscow, to advise how best to handle Khrushchev. Reflecting on Stevenson's plan, he asked: "Who would be the best one to talk to K?" "I think the unhappy thing," Stevenson replied, "is the best one is me. But I haven't wanted to suggest this and it would come at an awkward time—but I would do this if it were deemed wise and helpful—and I would put other things aside." He added that another possibility was Averell Harriman, though the problem with Harriman was that "he always insists on talking—and has difficulty in hearing." Stevenson volunteered his services not solely out of vanity but because of the rapport he had developed with Khrushchev. Alluding to his past relationship with the Soviet leader as well as his own stature, he told the president that "it would be best to send someone K knows and with whom he has had dealings before—someone he would be quite sure would represent you—someone influential—not just a personal diplomat." "Good," Kennedy declared as a way of concluding their conversation on the subject. "We will have a chance to talk before we come to a final judgment on this."[12]

Stevenson's advice was more subtle than the assessments by most of Kennedy's advisers. Rather than thinking in terms of a monolithic Communist bloc, Stevenson noted the tensions between Russia and China. Instead of assuming Khrushchev was an omnipotent dictator, he realized that the Soviet leader faced a variety of domestic political forces. Most important, Stevenson made a strong case for a frank Soviet-American dialogue. He was certain that Kennedy should respond positively to the feelers put out by Khrushchev since the election.

Reflecting on international issues in the weeks leading up to JFK's inauguration, Stevenson focused on relations with the Soviet Union. To the extent that he did consider Cuba, he again highlighted the importance of diplomacy. On December 30 he urged Ted Sorensen to include in Kennedy's inaugural address a section expressing "Eagerness to reduce tensions by negotiation in the hot spot areas (Germany, the Taiwan Strait, the Middle East, Congo, Cuba, Laos)."[13]

In between Kennedy's election and inauguration, Stevenson thus promoted a dialogue with Moscow and Havana designed to reduce cold war tensions. Although he may not have been entirely aware of it, his were dissenting arguments: the president-elect had come to the op-

posite conclusion. The initiatives from Khrushchev and Castro, he decided, should be ignored. Convinced that Cuba provided the Soviet
Union with an unacceptable bridgehead in the Western Hemisphere
and that Havana would encourage revolutions throughout Latin
America, and influenced almost certainly by his promise during the
presidential campaign to overthrow Castro, Kennedy decided it was
best not to parley with the Cuban leader but to oust him.

As for relations with the Russians, JFK wanted to put himself in a
position of strength by bolstering America's military power. Kennedy
must have known what was in fact the case, that Khrushchev would interpret this military buildup as a rejection of the accommodation he
had sought. Nonetheless the new president forged ahead with plans for
substantial increases in defense spending.

If Stevenson's call for a dialogue with Castro and his main ally,
Khrushchev, was the first instance of his dissent from Kennedy's Cuban
policy, the Bay of Pigs invasion was the second. In the early days of the
new administration, the Kennedy team considered a cluster of strategies to weaken Castro's grip on power, such as economic sanctions and
the use of the Organization of American States (OAS) to pressure
Cuba diplomatically. But in the end they pinned their hopes on the Bay
of Pigs operation in an attempt to dispose of the Castro problem
quickly and decisively. One official dubbed the plan "Operation Cas-
tration." The term summed up rather neatly the entire thrust of
Kennedy's policies toward Cuba before the missile crisis.[14]

Eisenhower bequeathed the plan to Kennedy, who had probably
first learned of it in July or September 1960 from national security
briefings he had received from CIA director Allen Dulles. The original plan was for the CIA to train Cuban émigrés in Guatemala for an
invasion of their homeland at Trinidad on Cuba's southern coast. On
becoming president, Kennedy resolved to carry out the operation provided that U.S. involvement could be kept secret. For that reason the
CIA changed the location for the invasion from Trinidad to the more
sparsely populated Bay of Pigs.[15]

Stevenson was kept in the dark about the operation until a week before it was launched. Rather than generating a wide-ranging debate on
the merits of the CIA plan, Kennedy tried to avoid any opposition. In

practice this meant ensuring that those liberal Democrats whose opposition could be predicted, including Bowles, Sorensen, and Stevenson, were not informed. As it turned out, both Bowles and Sorensen
got wind of the plan. Bowles thereupon produced for Dean Rusk a
memorandum outlining his objections, which Rusk handed on to an
unimpressed Kennedy. When Sorensen confronted him with the information he had received about the invasion, Kennedy terminated the
conversation abruptly. "I know everybody is grabbing their nuts on
this," he told Sorensen, implying that there was a measure of timidity
on the part of those who found fault with the operation.[16]

Stevenson received no official information on the invasion plan until April 8. In *A Thousand Days*, his memoir-cum-history of the
Kennedy years, Arthur Schlesinger claimed that Kennedy was eager to
include Stevenson in the discussions on the Bay of Pigs. The president,
he has written, believed that what Stevenson said at the UN should be
the truth even if it were not the whole truth. "The integrity and credibility of Adlai Stevenson," he apparently told Schlesinger, "constitute
one of our great national assets. I don't want anything to be done which
might jeopardize that." Accordingly Kennedy sent CIA official Tracy
Barnes with Schlesinger to brief Stevenson.[17]

Press Secretary Pierre Salinger, however, revealed that Kennedy's
hand had been forced; his gesture was less generous than it appeared.
On April 7 Tad Szulc had written in the *New York Times* that several
thousand men, trained in Guatemala, Florida, and Louisiana, had been
recruited to overthrow Castro. Reading the article, Stevenson's public
relations adviser Clayton Fritchey thought the story seemed to have
the ring of truth. Over cocktails he asked his boss whether he had been
"holding out" on him. Stevenson insisted he knew nothing and inquired about the facts Fritchey had at his disposal. Fritchey replied that
he knew only what he had read in the *Times*. After their conversation,
Stevenson and Fritchey contacted Schlesinger, who then accompanied
Barnes to New York for a meeting with Stevenson. Schlesinger must
have told Kennedy about Stevenson's inquiry, hence JFK could have
arranged the briefing for Stevenson only after receiving that information. Otherwise Stevenson would have been left totally out of the loop
on the Bay of Pigs.[18]

The briefing that Barnes gave Stevenson on April 8 was partial and misleading. According to Schlesinger, Stevenson was informed of

> the exile group. We told him we were training them, supplying weapons, I'm not sure that we told him that there would be U.S. planes, but we told him there would be no U.S. combat troops involved. We told him that the Cubans were armed by us and the money had come from the United States, and it was going to take place. But there was a failure of communication. I fear we inadvertently left him with the impression that it would not take place until the General Assembly adjourned. It was set up so it could be called back. . . . We gave Stevenson no date. We knew it would go ahead in the next week or ten days, but no date had yet been set.[19]

Cleveland and Stevenson deputy Francis Plimpton, both of whom attended the meeting, recall that the briefing was neither accurate nor complete. "They made it look as if it was essentially a non-American operation that we were helping with," Cleveland recalled, adding that Barnes failed to divulge the extent of American involvement in the training of the Cuban refugees. According to Plimpton, Barnes merely stated that a venture financed by émigrés might take place on Cuban shores, and that no U.S. facilities had been used in the training for this operation apart from an abandoned army post in Louisiana. Stevenson was justified in grousing later to Salinger that he was "never told the full extent of the plan."[20]

Even though he had been permitted only a partial glimpse of the Bay of Pigs scheme, one which prevented him from appreciating the truly central role played by the U.S. government in shaping it, Stevenson nonetheless opposed it. Both at the meeting with Barnes and later that same day over lunch with Schlesinger, Cleveland, and Fritchey, he explained his reservations. Schlesinger wrote in his journal that "AES made it clear that he wholly disapproves of the project, objects to the fact that he was given no opportunity to comment on it, and believes it will cause infinite trouble. However, he is substantially a good soldier about it and is prepared to try and make the best possible US case." Cleveland too recalled Stevenson being "quite negative" about the plan.[21]

After Kennedy gave the go-ahead, the Bay of Pigs operation got under way on Saturday, April 15, only a week after Stevenson's conversation with Schlesinger and Barnes. The initial phase of the plan involved a B-26 bombing attack on Castro's main airfields. The assault proved to be only partially successful, leaving a number of Cuban T-33 jet trainers undamaged.[22]

Given the recent deterioration of U.S.-Cuban relations, it could be anticipated that many observers would suspect the Kennedy administration's involvement in the attack. The CIA therefore devised a cover story. As the main squadron of B-26s set out for Cuba from Nicaragua, other planes headed for Florida where the pilots claimed they had been members of Castro's air force and had carried out the attack before defecting to the United States. To corroborate the story, the insignia of the Cuban air force was painted on their planes.[23]

Castro knew immediately that the story about defecting pilots was nonsense and that a plan had been developed to attack Cuba. In fact Cuba had already complained to the United Nations that the United States was preparing just such an assault, a soon-to-be-discussed charge that Stevenson was prepared to refute.[24]

On the same morning as the attack at the Bay of Pigs, Cuba lodged another complaint with the UN. In the General Assembly, Foreign Minister Raúl Roa raised the issue of American air strikes on Cuba. It was decided to refer the matter to an emergency meeting of the Assembly's First Committee in the afternoon.[25]

That Saturday Stevenson lunched with his good friend, Alicia Patterson. Meanwhile the State Department drafted for Stevenson a speech advancing the cover story of defecting Cuban pilots in order to refute Roa's charges. An unaware Harlan Cleveland checked with the Bureau of Inter-American Affairs to determine whether the account of defecting pilots was accurate. The Bureau spoke to CIA officials who, having fashioned the cover story in the first place, naturally validated it. Cleveland assured Stevenson that the attack on Castro's airfields had indeed been carried out by defecting pilots.[26]

Hence Stevenson came before the First Committee prepared to present a largely fictitious narrative of events. Roa began the proceedings by denouncing the attack on Cuba, adding that the air strike was "undoubtedly the prelude to a large-scale invasion organized, equipped and financed by the United States Government" with the help of Cuban refugees "being trained in United States territory and in Guatemala by experts of the Pentagon and the Central Intelligence Agency." The story about defecting pilots, Roa added, was a cynical distortion of the truth.[27]

Stevenson replied that the attack had been made by defecting Cuban pilots who were currently seeking political asylum in the United States. Without denying the possibility of a CIA-organized invasion by Cuban exiles, he asserted that "there would not under any conditions be an intervention in Cuba by United States armed forces, and the United States would do everything in its power to ensure that no Americans participated in any actions against Cuba." Stevenson went on to show a photograph of one of the planes, used by the defectors, which bore Cuban air force tail markings. He concluded by reiterating Kennedy's claim that the issue was between opposing groups of Cubans, not between Washington and Havana.[28]

Watching on television, CIA propaganda chief Dave Phillips marveled at Stevenson's ability to present such a catalogue of lies so convincingly. Then he realized that Stevenson could not have been told that the defecting pilots story was a fabrication.[29]

Much to Stevenson's chagrin, the CIA cover story soon began to unravel. The Kennedy administration provoked suspicion by refusing to reveal the identity of the defecting pilots. Castro claimed to have recovered rocket fragments with the marking "U.S.A." after the air strike. Auxiliary fuel tanks were recovered just a few miles off the coast, close to Havana, indicating that the defecting planes had flown from a more distant location than the Cuban mainland. One other problem for the CIA was that by sheer coincidence a genuine defector *had* landed in Florida. Newsmen soon noticed differences between that plane and the two that had supposedly flown from Cuba.[30]

By Sunday, April 16, Stevenson began to realize that he had been deceived by his own government—and ultimately by Kennedy himself. His suspicion was confirmed Monday morning when McGeorge Bundy came to New York to brief Stevenson. The two men ate breakfast in the ambassador's living quarters at the U.S. embassy, an apartment at the

Waldorf. Framed letters written by Jefferson and Lafayette and superb objets d'art adorned Stevenson's residence which, set high above Manhattan, provided a glorious view of the city. This uplifting setting contrasted sharply with the grubby business at hand.[31]

Bundy told Stevenson what had actually happened and what was about to. Given his fatigue (he had been at a party the night before) and his dismay at knowing that he had lied in the United Nations, Stevenson listened to the national security adviser stoically. Bundy recalls that Stevenson was "very decent about it. He did not fuss about the box he was in. All he wanted was more information so he would not dig deeper holes."[32]

Bundy's briefing came not a moment too soon. The brigade of Cuban émigrés, attempting a landing at the Bay of Pigs that very morning, had been engaged by Castro's forces. Stevenson's next appearance in the United Nations took place against the background of this raging battle on the shores of Cuba. In the UN that morning, Raúl Roa issued a complaint: his government wished to state formally that it had been invaded by "a mercenary force organized, financed and armed by the Government of the United States and coming from Guatemala and Florida." He proceeded to flesh out that claim.[33]

In a vigorous but flawed defense of American policy, Stevenson categorically denied Roa's allegations. "The United States had committed no aggression against Cuba," he claimed, "and no attack had been launched from any part of the United States." He assured his colleagues that U.S. troops would not be sent to Cuba. As the brigade comprised Cuban exiles rather than American forces, and had set out from Guatemala and not the United States, Stevenson's statement was, strictly speaking, accurate. But he had plainly and conveniently avoided the question of whether the CIA had trained the Cuban émigrés and planned that morning's invasion.[34]

Stevenson had unwittingly deceived the UN two days earlier. This time he had misled, if not actually lied, quite knowingly. Paradoxically, he had done so out of a sense of honor and loyalty. Despite his opposition to the Bay of Pigs and his public humiliation on April 15, he believed his first duty as UN ambassador was to defend his government's policies, whatever their merits.

Distorting the truth on April 17 was nonetheless galling. Its effect on his credibility concerned him deeply. After the UN meeting, Stevenson entered an elevator in the Waldorf Towers as his close friend Jane Warner Dick left it. Dick recalled being "shocked by his appearance. He looked dazedly right through me, apparently not seeing me. I was sure that either he was desperately ill or that something frightful had happened." Worried, she followed Stevenson back to his apartment in the Towers and asked why he was so upset. He replied quietly:

> You heard my speech today? Well, I did not tell the whole truth; I did not know the whole truth. I took this job at the President's request on the understanding that I would be consulted and kept fully informed on everything. I spoke in the U.N. in good faith on that understanding. Now, my credibility has been compromised, and therefore my usefulness. Yet how can I resign at this moment and make things still worse for the President?[35]

Stevenson's doubts about the Bay of Pigs operation were magnified when the invasion began to falter disastrously. Castro had been well prepared, calling up his militia of 200,000 the day before the invasion. On the day of the landing he rounded up 100,000 Cubans who allegedly opposed his government and hence might lend support to the exile force. When the invasion took place, coral reefs smashed many of the brigade's boats before the exiles were able to reach the shore. Worried that American participation was becoming public knowledge, Kennedy canceled an air strike on Cuba's main airfields that was set for the morning of the invasion. The inevitable surrender of the exile force began on Wednesday, April 19.[36]

Kennedy was inconsolable. He had never suffered a comparable failure in his political career. Crying in his wife's arms, phone call after phone call to his father, walking alone in the White House garden at four in the morning that Wednesday—those few days in mid-April were perhaps the most depressing in his entire life. "Let me tell you something," said Kennedy to the wily Democrat Clark Clifford. "I have had two full days of hell—I haven't slept—this has been the most excruciating period of my life. I doubt my Presidency could survive another catastrophe like this."[37]

Once he realized the Bay of Pigs invasion would fail, Kennedy was determined to seem no weaker to Khrushchev than he already appeared. In this, he was supported by Robert Kennedy, who had taken personally his brother's defeat at the hands of Castro. "That's the most meaningless, worthless thing I've ever heard," he thundered on hearing one administration official argue that Washington should simply accept Castro as leader of Cuba. "You people are so anxious to protect your own asses that you're afraid to do anything. All you want to do is dump the whole thing on the president." As attorney general, Robert Kennedy's charge did not include foreign affairs. But once the disaster at the Bay of Pigs took place, JFK—believing that when the chips are down one should turn to family—gave his brother a voice on international affairs, especially Cuba. Robert Kennedy would exercise it for the rest of his brother's presidency.[38]

The most direct way of exacting revenge on Castro, one which Robert Kennedy might well have found agreeable, was to send in American troops to overthrow the Cuban leader. The inevitable outrage this would have provoked in the United Nations, and especially among Latin American countries with unpleasant memories of U.S. gunboat diplomacy in the Western Hemisphere, was probably one reason John Kennedy rejected that military alternative. Another, more important factor was the link, as the president saw it, between Cuba and Berlin. If he attacked Cuba, Kennedy calculated, Khrushchev would surely move on West Berlin.[39]

Although the option of invading Cuba was thus impractical, JFK agreed with his brother that the United States must appear tough rather than conciliatory at this critical juncture. Accordingly, he replied unapologetically to an indignant letter from Khrushchev about American involvement in events at the Bay of Pigs. He warned that the Soviet premier should neither intervene militarily in Cuba, unless he wished to provoke a U.S. attack on the island, nor use the Bay of Pigs as a pretext to stir up trouble in other parts of the world.[40]

Kennedy delivered an equally uncompromising message two days later, in a speech in Washington before the American Society of Newspaper Editors. The Bay of Pigs, he told them, showed the dangers of underestimating the threat posed by international communism. "Let me then make clear as President of the United States," he concluded, "that I am determined upon our system's survival and success, regardless of the cost and regardless of the peril." An adviser meeting with JFK in the Oval Office shortly after this speech said he thought Kennedy's belligerence was unhelpful. "I didn't want us to look like a paper tiger," said Kennedy. "We should scare people a little, and I did it to make us appear still tough and powerful."[41]

Stevenson, meanwhile, continued to fight for Kennedy at the United Nations, delivering a robust statement on Cuba on Tuesday, April 18. He read out the message just sent by JFK to Khrushchev, emphasized that the Bay of Pigs invasion had not been launched from U.S. territory, and castigated Castro for the policies he had implemented since taking power. In another speech, on Thursday, April 20, Stevenson continued to claim that his government had not been involved in the Bay of Pigs. He made clear, however, the administration's sympathy for the cause of the Cuban exiles, whom he described as "the real Cuban patriots."[42]

As well as providing a rhetorical defense of American policy, Stevenson tried to protect Kennedy from further embarrassment by preventing the passage of resolutions condemning the United States. Four were introduced in the UN during this period. A seven-power Latin American resolution was the mildest and most acceptable to Kennedy and Stevenson. The Romanian and especially the Soviet resolutions were the least desirable. A Mexican resolution was the most problematic. Less appealingly bland than the seven-power version, it had a chance of gaining widespread support from UN delegates. Stevenson exerted himself, both in his speech on April 20 and in behind-the-scenes discussions, to ensure that only the seven-power resolution was adopted. It called upon member states "to take such peaceful action as is open to them to remove existing tension." Stevenson's effort at damage control had worked.[43]

Despite his success in helping Kennedy salvage his reputation, the Bay of Pigs fiasco had been a painful experience for the UN ambassador. Stevenson, who prized his image as a man of principle above all, had been forced to mislead and even lie in the most public of forums, in front of the American people and the world. In the days that followed, he reflected on the impact of this episode on his credibility. "I find my halo isn't sitting quite as comfortably since they played that Cuba trick on me," Stevenson confided to Eugene McCarthy. He told another friend, "The Cuba absurdity made me sick for a week while I had to indignantly defend the U.S. (and got finally a harmless resolution) but I've been surprised how little it seems to have affected my personal regard."[44]

The whole business diminished Stevenson's respect for Kennedy. Before the 1960 election Stevenson had thought of him in a slightly contradictory way, as both a callow youth and a cold operator, but a man with potential nonetheless. The development of that potential was what Stevenson hoped to observe during the early days of the new administration. Instead the Bay of Pigs reinforced Stevenson's view of JFK. Kennedy's decision to authorize the invasion suggested that he was dangerously inexperienced. His willingness to compromise Stevenson's credibility at the UN revealed his lack of scruples. In the days after the Bay of Pigs, Stevenson vented his frustration privately. "That young man," he said to the journalist Mary McGrory after leaving a White House meeting, "he never says 'please' and he never says 'I'm sorry.'" Despite his dismay, Stevenson did not resign.[45]

The situation facing Kennedy after the Bay of Pigs was that Castro still held power. Hence the crucial question: how should JFK now handle the Cuban leader? In the debate among administration officials over this issue, Stevenson was part of a fairly solid phalanx of liberals who encouraged Kennedy to adopt a patient approach. Richard Goodwin told the president he should concentrate on the Alliance for Progress, JFK's aid program for Latin America; that was the surest way to immunize the Western Hemisphere against Castro's influence. Chester Bowles urged Kennedy "to get the Cuban situation in perspective." If action against Cuba were required, he argued, it should be taken diplomatically through the OAS.[46]

Stevenson, more than anyone else after the Bay of Pigs, mustered his intellectual resources and appealed to Kennedy's in calling for more kid glove and less iron fist in dealings with Castro. On April 23, 1961, he furnished the president with a memorandum entitled "Some Lessons from Cuba," which asserted that the end of colonialism had created a vacuum which would be filled by either "independent states" or "Communist-type regimes." To ensure that it was usually the former would not be easy because the Soviet Union enjoyed several advantages in former colonial areas: the fact that the Western nations used to be colonial rulers, the Soviet state's trumpeting of Lenin's anti-colonial philosophy, and the ideological appeal of communism to the poor.[47]

In countering the Russian appeal in these places, Stevenson impressed upon Kennedy the need to accept with equanimity that communism would gain footholds. "Some countries probably cannot be saved from Communism," he wrote. "The West should not be too upset by this. They will continue to be problem countries, and probably no better advertisement for Communism than, say, Hungary. We must avoid a sort of hysterical panic of the John Birch sort whenever some hopeless area tries a more drastic way out of its problems." Stevenson argued against the idea that any country going Communist was dangerous because it would trigger revolutions in adjoining nations. The domino theory, he explained to JFK, did not necessarily work in practice.[48]

Kennedy should resist the temptation to overthrow leftist governments by force, Stevenson continued, as that would make him look like a neocolonialist and, moreover, galvanize support within those countries for the existing regimes. Instead, "We should make long term sustained economic assistance the central tool for dealing with the post-colonial world." That approach would build up the middle class in those areas, providing the social and economic basis for stable democratic governments. It would also demonstrate that the West was no longer interested in exploiting lesser powers.[49]

As for Cuba, Stevenson's message for Kennedy was clear—don't use force again to overthrow Castro. "We are not going to be destroyed in our beds," he assured the president,

> even if Castro does continue to mismanage Cuba for another decade. If by that time other parts of Latin America are forging ahead and the Cuban worker is still pretty miserable and the peasant collectivized, the genuine tides of popular opinion may move

the other way. Of one thing we may be sure—the 19th century system of gunboat diplomacy or landing the Marines is highly unpopular.

This may tax our patience, but we did not get through the agonies of the Industrial Revolution by relying wholly on the police force. We had great reforms, as well. In the developing world, these are the decisive instruments. Premature and heavy handed police work is more likely to switch loyalty to the extremists and revive 300 years of painful history.[50]

In pointing out the advantages of an aid package for Latin America over military action against the likes of Cuba, Stevenson closed his memorandum by attempting to disabuse Kennedy of the notion that he was proposing a predictably "soft" liberal alternative: "It is not a weak policy in the developing world. It is simply a national choice of instruments. The tools of aid are expensive. But they are also strong."[51]

A little more than a month later, on May 27, Stevenson provided Kennedy with another memorandum. Devoted to UN and disarmament issues rather than Cuba, it fleshed out the historical background to "East-West" relations that he had touched upon in his April memorandum. Stevenson reflected on the reasons for Soviet suspicion of the West. Marx, he wrote, had predicted that capitalist powers would trigger imperialist wars among themselves and would seek to crush any socialist governments that came to power through revolution. "During the adult life of the men now ruling the Kremlin," Stevenson boldly observed, "the democracies of Western Europe have done all too much to prove him right." The two world wars could be construed as imperialist in origin, and during Woodrow Wilson's presidency the United States had indeed intervened during the Russian civil war in an attempt to oust the Bolshevik government.[52]

He did not exonerate Stalin's excesses, Stevenson explained, but the pre–World War II background did help account for Moscow's suspicion of the West. Events during the cold war—such as "the Western volte face in 1955 from their own disarmament proposals, after Russia had accepted them; Suez, 1956; Lebanon, 1958 . . . ; the U-2 episode; and Cuba, 1961"—had magnified those concerns. Stevenson speculated that Khrushchev was genuinely interested in bringing about a measure of disarmament, and he touched on the emerging split between Russia and China, Khrushchev's "inferiority-superiority complex," and the Soviet leader's desire to redirect resources from defense to the civilian economy.[53]

Stevenson's memorandum was one of the most remarkable documents produced by a senior American official during the cold war. He had relied on none of the staples of post-1945 U.S. thinking on international affairs—Communist monolithism, falling dominoes, the lessons of the 1930s—which had been repeated by American policymakers ad nauseam for fifteen years and would be again for years to come. In discussing Sino-Soviet tensions, Western mistakes, and Khrushchev's military cuts, he explored issues that did not fit neatly into traditional U.S. policy formulations on the Russian challenge. For its evenhandedness, sense of nuance, and appreciation of the historical context of contemporary problems, Stevenson's memorandum represented a considerable intellectual achievement.

In his post–Bay of Pigs memoranda, Stevenson had urged JFK to change his Cuban policies as part of a general reappraisal of his approach to the cold war. Kennedy, he argued, should be less obsessed with overthrowing Castro, more concerned with implementing the Alliance for Progress, and more committed to reducing tensions with the Soviet Union. It was the third time Stevenson had offered an alternative to the president's policies—the first being his call for a postelection dialogue with Moscow and Havana, the second his opposition to the Bay of Pigs invasion. As it turned out, this was the third time Kennedy rejected his advice.

Rather than adopting the patient approach suggested by Stevenson, JFK decided to continue the drive to overthrow Castro. A National Security Council meeting on May 5 affirmed that "U.S. policy toward Cuba should aim at the downfall of Castro." Direct military intervention, though not feasible in the short term, would be regarded as an option, and American capabilities for intervention should "be maintained at an adequate level." As well as pursuing the Alliance for Progress, the Kennedy administration would collaborate militarily with its Latin American partners in meeting the Cuban challenge, and would increase the activities of the U.S. Information Agency in Latin America. It became clear over the course of the next year that Kennedy had decided to emasculate Castro through a multifaceted approach. Economic, diplomatic, and covert pressure would be applied, and plans for military action against Cuba prepared.[54]

The one element that Stevenson endorsed in this anti-Castro campaign was the use of diplomatic channels, especially the OAS. He viewed this approach as preferable to the sort of crude display of force evident at the Bay of Pigs. Reliance on international organizations such as the OAS appealed to Stevenson's Wilsonian values, and the collaboration between the United States and Latin American countries this would entail was consistent with his call for greater emphasis in American foreign policy on relations with the developing nations. In addition to the Alliance for Progress, Stevenson regarded OAS pressure as the most valuable weapon in Kennedy's anti-Castro arsenal.

Knowing of Stevenson's interest in the OAS as a forum for handling Cuba, and wishing to placate him after his humiliation at the UN, JFK sent Stevenson on a tour of South America to restore the goodwill lost by the April invasion. Later in his presidency, Kennedy would treat Stevenson with contempt. But at this time he seemed worried that Stevenson would resign his post in a blaze of negative publicity for Kennedy. Given the context of his wafer-thin margin of victory over Nixon the previous autumn and the disaster at the Bay of Pigs, the last thing Kennedy needed was the loss of the man who, apart from himself, had the highest public profile in his administration.

Before Stevenson set out for South America, Kennedy convinced him that the White House now understood that a developmental program for Latin America was the best way to isolate Castro. "We have things pretty well turned around now," Stevenson told the economist Barbara Ward in a chirpy letter at the end of May, "so that the objective [of my trip] is groundwork for the 'Alliance for Progress' conference in Montevideo in July, and economic and social cooperation with the political reprisals against Castro muted." Consequently he felt "better about the whole project now that we have our philosophical approach on sound ground."[55]

During his trip, which lasted from June 4 to 22, Stevenson sent regular reports on his conversations with Latin American leaders to the State Department and the White House. Aware of Kennedy's interest in using the OAS to pressure Cuba, Stevenson kept Washington informed of the views of the officials he met on possible OAS action against Castro. On his return to the United States he furnished Kennedy with an extensive report on his trip. He discussed Cuba's growing influence throughout the region, especially among educators, unions, and the poor; and he suggested ways to counter Castro's appeal, such as asking Cuban students and intellectuals in exile who had originally supported Castro to liaise with their counterparts in Latin America. He mapped out a plan for isolating Cuba diplomatically from other OAS countries. On July 6 Kennedy wrote to Stevenson, thanking him for his "excellent report." "It was most helpful," he added. "We continue to get good reports on your trip, which came at a most important time."[56]

Cuba was ultimately ejected from the OAS in early 1962 after a meeting in Punta del Este, Uruguay. But OAS pressure proved to be only one thread in the anti-Castro tapestry woven by Kennedy after the Bay of Pigs. The central strand in that effort was a determination to weaken Castro through covert action. In this sense JFK's approach followed from his thinking during the buildup to the Bay of Pigs. That invasion attempt was designed to oust Castro while concealing U.S. involvement. Now Kennedy sought the same objective—Castro's overthrow—to be achieved with what this time would hopefully be the successful cloaking of America's role.

Kennedy was intrigued by the world of espionage and saw it as exciting rather than ethically dubious. Belying his carefully crafted reputation as an intellectual—he had won the Pulitzer Prize for *Profiles in Courage*—his favorite novels were Ian Fleming's James Bond stories. He had even met Fleming, asking the author's advice on how to deal with Castro. When told on another occasion that America had its own James Bond, William Harvey, a man who had made his name in intelligence circles in the 1950s by overseeing the building of a six-hundred-yard tunnel under Communist East Berlin, Kennedy insisted on meeting him. As one Kennedy aide tells the story, this "pistol-carrying, martini-drinking adventurer was found and sent over to the White House."[57]

Kennedy's penchant for cloak-and-dagger tactics was more than an instinctive fascination. It was also a matter of policy conviction. In studying the British appeasement of Hitler for his undergraduate thesis at Harvard, the young JFK had become interested in the relationship between policymaking elites and the public. British leaders had been unable to meet the Nazi challenge by readying the nation for war at an early enough stage, Kennedy believed, because of the public's determination to stay out of any future conflict in Europe. Hitler, as a dictator rather than a democratic leader, had no need to consider public opinion when formulating military policy. He could do what he liked. Sending the level of German military spending skyrocketing, as he did, was a decision he could make without a second thought as to how his policy would play with the public. The conclusion drawn by Kennedy from this analysis of the origins of World War II was that at times it was necessary for democratic leaders to pursue their international objectives surreptitiously, to make sure that national security would not be compromised by public whim. It was an elitist outlook, to be sure, but for Kennedy the only way, paradoxically, to protect the public interest.[58]

After World War II Kennedy shifted this line of thinking into a cold war context. In order to meet the threat posed by communism in general and the Soviet Union in particular, the United States should not be hesitant about resorting to cloak-and-dagger tactics. When Kennedy became president, therefore, he was determined to find covert solutions to some foreign policy problems.

The Bay of Pigs left that resolve unaffected. The president wasted no time in the wake of that disaster in establishing a special task force to "contain the spread of Castroism and unseat the communist government in Cuba." This group soon received numerous proposals for anti-Castro covert initiatives, supplied by the Pentagon and the CIA. By late summer 1961 Kennedy had approved a CIA program that included an improved collection of intelligence on potential opposition to Castro within Cuba, the use of propaganda against Castro, and the development of a resistance movement that would carry out acts of sabotage on the island. Kennedy funded this covert program with more than $5 million.[59]

In November 1961 this plan of action was formalized and expanded into what would stand, until the Cuban missile crisis in October 1962, as the centerpiece of JFK's drive to depose Castro: Operation Mongoose. Robert Kennedy was a key influence on his brother's decision to authorize Mongoose, and indeed would play a major role in the shaping of that operation. Robert's desire for revenge on Castro may be seen in the notes he scribbled on November 3, 1961, after a White House meeting on the situation in Cuba: "My idea is to stir things up on island with espionage, sabotage, general disorder, run & operated by Cubans themselves with every group but Batistaites [followers of Batista, Castro's predecessor as Cuban leader] & Communists." In the weeks and months that followed, Robert Kennedy's obsession with Castro did not dim. In January 1962 he told government officials that getting rid of Castro was the single most important objective of the Kennedy administration.[60]

So it was that in late November 1961 John Kennedy, determined to make amends for the Bay of Pigs, and influenced by his brother's zeal, established Operation Mongoose in order "to help Cuba overthrow the communist regime." The aim was to use covert pressure to keep Castro off his stride, and ultimately to oust him by triggering within Cuba a revolt to which American military forces could lend their support. JFK spared no resources in ensuring that Operation Mongoose was equipped to achieve its objectives. An annual budget of around $50 million, four hundred CIA officials, and hundreds of motorboats were at the disposal of Mongoose planners, making it larger than all previous CIA operations worldwide. The initial focus of the operation was confined to the collection of intelligence on Cuba. But this was followed by a more ambitious second phase in the late summer of 1962.[61]

A key component of Mongoose was the development of contingency plans for military action against Cuba. These were in fact long-standing by the time Kennedy became president. Hence Pentagon officials were well prepared when only a day after the failure of the Bay of Pigs invasion Kennedy asked them to plan for an assault on Cuba, as they were during Operation Mongoose when requested, as they often were, to update these contingency plans.[62]

As well as putting down on paper their thoughts on how to attack Cuba, Pentagon officials were also able to test out their ideas with a series of large-scale military maneuvers in the spring of 1962. The first of these, Lantphibex-1-62, in which forty thousand military personnel participated, ended with a landing on Vieques, an island close to Puerto Rico. Kennedy kept a close eye on the maneuver; he observed it from the deck of the USS Enterprise. Lantphibex was soon followed by other practice operations in the Caribbean, including Quick Kick and Whip Lash.[63]

The desperation of U.S. officials to get rid of Castro also resulted in an effort to assassinate the Cuban leader. Beginning in the final months of the Eisenhower presidency with a plan to contaminate some of Castro's cigars with botulinum toxin, the CIA in the early 1960s hatched various plots to kill Castro. As this drive to assassinate Castro continued, a bizarre alliance between the mob and the U.S. government was established. The CIA recruited a former FBI agent, who hired underworld figure John Rosselli, who in turn brought on board head of the Chicago Mafia Sam Giancana and Cosa Nostra chief Santos Trafficante.[64]

It is known that at least one and probably two attempts to assassinate Castro were made just before the Bay of Pigs invasion. The first involved passing a poison pill to an official in the Cuban government to put in Castro's drink. In the second plot, a Cuban exile was to give poison pills to a friend who worked in a restaurant frequented by Castro; he would put the pills in Castro's food. Clearly, neither plan succeeded. But new assassination schemes were developed thereafter.[65]

A number of Kennedy associates have claimed that his sense of morality made it unthinkable that he would have endorsed the effort to eliminate Castro, thereby implying that the CIA was attempting this on its own initiative. But the evidence, including Kennedy's comments at the time, the recollections of a friend, and the clear interest expressed by some of the president's advisers in killing Castro, indicates that JFK almost certainly knew about and supported the assassination plots.[66]

Kennedy's almost certain endorsement of the assassination plots, along with Operation Mongoose and the updated plans for military action against Cuba, made for an elaborate post–Bay of Pigs effort at the covert level to overthrow Castro. Kennedy complemented these clandestine initiatives with policies in the public arena also designed to undermine Castro's position. Diplomatic pressure was brought to bear in early 1962 when Kennedy's delegation at a Punta del Este conference engineered the expulsion of Cuba from the Organization of American States, thereby isolating Castro within the Western Hemisphere. Within days of that development, it was announced that JFK had decided to extend the economic sanctions imposed by Eisenhower so that all trade between the United States and Cuba, apart from the export of key foodstuffs and medical supplies to Cuba, was prohibited. Damaging the Cuban economy, calculated Kennedy, would erode Castro's popularity at home and so hasten the fall of his government.[67]

Stevenson was obviously aware of some of Kennedy's post–Bay of Pigs policies toward Cuba, such as the economic embargo and OAS action. He appears to have been kept out of the loop, however, on JFK's covert drive to topple Castro. There is no evidence of his knowing of Operation Mongoose (before the Cuban missile crisis), the contingency plans to attack Cuba, or the assassination attempts. He may have been confronted with information on these policies in October 1961, when a Cuban delegate at the United Nations accused the Kennedy administration of planning to kill Cuban officials. Not privy to the CIA plots, Stevenson had no reason to believe the allegation. "In reply to that repulsive accusation," he declared indignantly, "I would only say that it is ridiculous and that, little as the United States likes Fidel Castro and his associates, it abhors assassination as a means of accomplishing political objectives."[68]

Stevenson would have been shocked to learn of Kennedy's clandestine efforts. It was the antithesis of the more patient approach, centered on the Alliance for Progress, he had advocated. Even to the limited extent of his own knowledge, though, he remained dissatisfied not only with Kennedy's handling of Castro but his foreign policy in general. On the afternoon of November 11, 1961, the economist John Kenneth Galbraith rode the air shuttle with Stevenson to Washington.

Recording Stevenson's comments in his journal a few days later, Galbraith noted that "Adlai is only moderately happy about his job. Too many detailed instructions from Washington—the State Department advises him, more or less, at what hour to see [Soviet Foreign Minister Andrei] Gromyko, when to interrupt to go to the men's room and how long to stay there. He thinks the New Frontier is too much like the old one."[69]

In the spring of 1962 Khrushchev decided to dispatch nuclear missiles to Cuba. His motives for doing so remain a subject of debate among historians. Fear that Kennedy would use force to remove Castro and concern over the gap between America's strong and Russia's relatively weak nuclear arsenal appear to have been important considerations. In what may have been a complex decision, Khrushchev perhaps had other ideas in mind, such as responding to the Chinese charge that Moscow was failing to bolster revolutionary states such as Cuba, and trying to acquire another card to play in the ongoing dispute over Berlin.[70]

If the desire to defend Cuba from an anticipated American invasion and to respond to the U.S. lead in the nuclear arms race were key motives behind Khrushchev's decision to place missiles in Cuba, Kennedy played a major role in bringing about that decision. The Bay of Pigs invasion, the exclusion of Cuba from the OAS, the imposition of economic sanctions, Mongoose (Khrushchev appears to have known of the operation's existence, if not its name), and the threatening U.S. military maneuvers in the Caribbean in the spring of 1962 must have convinced Khrushchev that an American attack on Cuba was imminent. Likewise the huge military buildup initiated by Kennedy, the largest in U.S. peacetime history before the Reagan years, as well as the young president's lack of restraint in revealing publicly the extent of America's nuclear lead over the Russians (Eisenhower had been much more discreet) can only have heightened Khrushchev's determination to even things up somewhat by increasing the number of Soviet missiles capable of reaching American soil. In other words, had JFK not resolved to oust Castro and to bolster military spending at a time when Washington enjoyed a huge advantage over Moscow in nuclear weaponry, Khrushchev may well not have sent missiles to Cuba, and there might have been no Cuban missile crisis. That, however, is not to justify Khrushchev's ploy. He could have protected Cuba by providing troops and conventional but not nuclear weapons, and could have moved to close the missile gap by accelerating the production of intercontinental ballistic missiles to be based in the Soviet Union. Neither of these initiatives would have resulted in the nuclear standoff that in October 1962 so nearly brought about war.

After seeking and receiving Castro's blessing for missile deployment in Cuba, Khrushchev authorized a Soviet military buildup on the island, which began in the summer of 1962. By September that buildup included not only Russian troops, of which there were nearly 42,000 by the time of the October crisis, and conventional weapons, but nuclear missiles as well. By this point the Soviet military presence in Cuba had become a focus for partisan politics in Washington. As the press, along with U.S. intelligence services, kept tabs on Russian activities in Cuba, the American public was aware in August and September that a serious challenge was being mounted by Khrushchev only ninety miles off the coast of Florida (though they and the press did not know that nuclear weapons were being deployed). Republicans in both houses of Congress wasted no time in responding to these press reports on the escalating Russian threat. Far better than Kennedy's cautious response would be a decision to blockade, even to invade, the island—so argued many Republicans in the autumn of 1962, and it intensified the heat on JFK.[71]

Kennedy decided that a low-key approach would undercut his GOP critics most effectively. Accordingly, he told the American people in press statements on September 4 and 13 that, contrary to what his adversaries were saying, there was little to worry about. As the Russian buildup in Cuba included no offensive, surface-to-surface nuclear missiles, it was not a threat to American security. In order to provide the American people with a firm assurance on the matter, Kennedy promised to act decisively should Khrushchev put nuclear weapons on the island. If Cuba were to become "an offensive military base of significant capacity for the Soviet Union," JFK stated at his press conference on September 13, "then this country will do whatever must be done to protect its own security and that of its allies." This commitment proved to be important. Once the missile crisis began, Kennedy felt compelled to take vigorous action to remove the nuclear weapons from Cuba rather than accept their deployment as a fait accompli, in part because of his public pledge to do so.[72]

Kennedy's private reaction to the Soviet military buildup could scarcely have been more different from the moderation he generally displayed in public. Whereas he had urged the American people to pay no heed to what he characterized as the irresponsible belligerence of his Republican critics, behind closed doors he too favored a hard-line approach to Cuba and its Soviet benefactors. He stepped up Operation Mongoose and approved the further development of contingency plans for an attack on Cuba. Nor was it a case of just updating plans on paper. Ammunition was delivered to Florida bases, for example, and a squadron of fighters was stationed at Key West. A navy official would later claim that the Kennedy administration had been "getting ready to invade Cuba."[73]

Another sign that the patience of Kennedy and his advisers over Castro was wearing thin was PHIBRIGLEX-62, an amphibious training exercise set to take place on October 15. Akin to the military maneuvers that had been staged in the spring, PHIBRIGLEX-62 would see 24,000 marines and navy personnel carry out an assault on the Caribbean island of Vieques to overthrow—as the Pentagon informed the press—a hypothetical dictator named Ortsac. Read that name backward and it becomes clear for whom this training exercise was designed.[74]

All of Kennedy's pre-missile-crisis initiatives lead to an unavoidable question: had he decided to attack Cuba, even before finding out about the missiles on the island? The evidence does not support that claim, but it is clear that he was putting himself in a position to authorize such an assault on very short notice. Perhaps these military preparations would not have been advanced had the Soviet buildup in Cuba not taken place. On the other hand, the updating of contingency plans preceded that buildup, so it is possible that the readying of the U.S. military for an attack on Cuba would have occurred even if Khrushchev had not dispatched troops and weapons to the Caribbean.

The whole equation changed for Kennedy when a U-2 surveillance mission over Cuba produced photographs which, when analyzed by

CIA officials, revealed that Russian missiles were on the island. National Security Adviser McGeorge Bundy passed this news to the president on the morning of October 16 as he was eating breakfast in a wing chair in the family quarters of the White House. Khrushchev "can't do this to me" was, Bundy recalled, the thrust of Kennedy's response. In moments of reverie, JFK liked to see himself as his generation's Winston Churchill, the man he had idolized since his student days when researching the British reaction to the growing threat posed by Hitler's Germany in the 1930s. He liked to see himself as the man who could heroically stand up to the Russians in a time of crisis, just as Churchill had with the Nazis. In mid-October 1962 he would get the chance to show his mettle in just this way. For Adlai Stevenson, meanwhile, the strangest period in his political life was about to unfold, one that would bring both unprecedented acclaim and demoralizing criticism.[75]

CHAPTER 11

War or Peace

▬

"I tell you now that I will never fear to negotiate
in good faith with the Soviet Union, for to close
the door to the conference rooms is to open a
door to war. Man's tragedy has all too often been
that he has grown weary in the search for an
honorable alternative to war and, in desperate
impatience, has turned to violence."
—ADLAI STEVENSON, 1952

"So, we may have the war in the next 24 hours."
—JOHN KENNEDY, in a meeting with
congressional leaders, October 22, 1962

"Reputation, reputation, reputation! O, I have lost
my reputation! I have lost the immortal part of
myself. . . ."—CASSIO, in Shakespeare's *Othello*

NINETEEN SIXTY-FOUR saw the release of the finest black comedy
ever filmed, *Dr. Strangelove: Or, How I Learned to Stop Worrying and
Love the Bomb*. Directed by Stanley Kubrick, it presented moviegoers
with an apocalyptic tale in which the United States and the Soviet
Union stumble toward nuclear war. It was a piece of fiction, of course,
but it was not fantastical. Just two years earlier John Kennedy and
Nikita Khrushchev had found themselves on the nuclear precipice in

the most dangerous confrontation of the cold war, the Cuban missile crisis. The difference was that in *Dr. Strangelove* the superpowers failed to prevent a nuclear attack; in October 1962 peace was achieved.

As the stakes could not have been higher, the Cuban missile crisis was the great transcendental challenge of the Kennedy presidency. Although of a much different duration, it was to JFK what the Civil War was to Abraham Lincoln, and what the Great Depression had been to Franklin Roosevelt. In some ways it was even more critical. Had Lincoln failed, America would have been divided. Had Roosevelt failed, the capitalist system in the United States might have collapsed. Had Kennedy failed, a nuclear holocaust could have ensued. In October 1962, therefore, Kennedy had to get it right.

As he compelled Khrushchev to withdraw nuclear weapons from Cuba without having to make intolerable concessions, JFK has often—though by no means always—been praised by historians for his handling of the situation. Any evaluation of his decisions during the missile crisis, however, must take account of the range of options that Kennedy received from his advisers. Once again, it was Adlai Stevenson who played the role of dissenter—challenging assumptions, formulating alternative proposals, and incurring the wrath of Kennedy and those hawkish officials who took umbrage at Stevenson's insistence that the president should offer concessions to the Russians in order to end the confrontation. The clash between Kennedy and Stevenson is an important part of the history of the Cuban missile crisis.

It was on Tuesday, October 16, 1962, that Kennedy had to come to terms with the news that, contrary to almost all his advisers' expectations and Khrushchev's earlier assurances, Russian nuclear weapons were in Cuba. The president was stunned by the Soviets' duplicity and aggression. The key question he faced was: how should the United States respond to the missiles in Cuba? Recalling the limited and manifestly ineffective discussions that had preceded the botched Bay of Pigs invasion, Kennedy was determined this time to generate a wider-ranging debate, one the CIA and the military would not necessarily dominate. Accordingly he set up a special group of advisers—the Executive Committee of the National Security Council, or ExComm as it became known—which would meet regularly during the crisis in order to advise the president.[1]

In the first of these ExComm meetings, which began just before noon on Tuesday, October 16, Kennedy took a position he would maintain throughout the day: the United States would have to respond with force to the missile deployment in Cuba. "We're certainly going to do number one. We're going to take out these missiles. The questions will be whether, what I would describe as number two, which would be a general air strike. That we're not ready to say, but we should be in preparation for it. The third is the general invasion." In other words, Kennedy was considering three options: an air strike on the missile sites, a broader strike on those sites and on other Russian military installations in Cuba, and an invasion of the island.[2]

In his first discussion with Adlai Stevenson, Kennedy again made the case for military action. It just so happened that Stevenson had that morning departed by shuttle from New York for Washington so that he could attend a State Department press conference and a White House luncheon for the crown prince of Libya. After that luncheon Kennedy briefed Stevenson about the missiles in Cuba. "We'll have to do something quickly," he told his UN ambassador. "I suppose the alternatives are to go in by air and wipe them out, or to take other steps to render the weapons inoperable." As he would throughout the crisis, Stevenson urged Kennedy to adopt a more cautious approach: "Let's not go to an air strike until we have explored the possibilities of a peaceful solution." "I was a little alarmed," Stevenson later revealed, "that Kennedy's first consideration should have been the air strike. I told him that sooner or later we would have to go to the U.N. and it was vitally important we go there with a reasonable case."[3]

Despite Stevenson's call for restraint, Kennedy continued to focus on the military alternatives. In the second ExComm session, which convened early Tuesday evening, he enumerated the same three options he had outlined in the earlier meeting: a limited air strike, a more general strike, and invasion. Of the three, he preferred the general air strike. He still showed no interest in nonmilitary alternatives such as the establishment of a naval blockade around Cuba to prevent further shipments of Soviet missiles to the island, or a diplomatic settlement

such as the removal of America's Jupiter missiles in Turkey in exchange
for the withdrawal of Russian nuclear weapons from Cuba. So out of
mind were the Jupiters as a potential mechanism for defusing the crisis, in fact, that at one point Kennedy even forgot they were in Turkey.
Grousing about the Russian decision to put missiles in Cuba, he declared, "It's just as if we suddenly began to put a major number of
MRBMs [medium-range ballistic missiles] in Turkey. Now that'd be
goddamn dangerous, I would think." "Well," McGeorge Bundy interjected, "we did, Mr. President." It was a scene that would not have
looked out of place in Kubrick's *Dr. Strangelove*.[4]

This picture of a president bent on bombing Cuba is at odds with
the popular image of a commendably restrained JFK who handled the
missile crisis with the sort of cool aplomb that Björn Borg would display during five-set Wimbledon finals. It is worth considering why he
was so determined to use force. One factor was the commitment he
had made to the American people, in his statements of September 4
and 13, to take strong action should Khrushchev install missiles in
Cuba. Those statements were clearly on Kennedy's mind on October
16 as he discussed them with ExComm colleagues.[5]

Another influence was the administration's pre-crisis preparations
for military action against Cuba. Contingency plans for such action
had long existed, but in the autumn of 1962, as the Russian military
buildup in Cuba gathered pace along with criticism of his apparent in-
action by his political foes, Kennedy had secretly ordered the acceler-
ation of planning for a possible attack on Cuba. When Kennedy and
his advisers met on October 16 to discuss the situation, they did so in
the knowledge that the U.S. military was ready to strike the Caribbean
island. "How long did it take to get in a position where we can invade
Cuba? Almost a month? Two months?" asked Kennedy in the first Ex-
Comm meeting. To JFK, therefore, a forceful response to the missiles
in Cuba made sense given the extent to which his military was ready
to act.[6]

As Kennedy was so certain on October 16 that military action was
required, it is fortunate that he did not feel obliged to make a snap decision. Had he done so, the evidence indicates that he would have ordered an air strike on the missile sites in Cuba. Inevitably this would

have resulted in the deaths of Russian military personnel. To preserve Soviet credibility, Khrushchev would probably have responded in kind, against West Berlin or the Jupiter missiles on the Russian border in Turkey or elsewhere. Unless cooler heads had suddenly prevailed, World War III might have been the result. In retrospect, therefore, Kennedy's initial handling of the Cuban missile crisis was not one of his finest moments.

During the first forty-eight hours of the crisis it was left to other U.S. officials to consider the dangers of a military response and to define alternative strategies. Many advisers supported Kennedy's call to arms. But not all of them. In the second ExComm meeting it was Secretary of Defense Robert S. McNamara who hatched the plan to blockade Cuba. Undersecretary of State George Ball was another adviser who differed from Kennedy in his reading of the situation. "This coming in there, a Pearl Harbor, just frightens the hell out of me as to what goes beyond," an impassioned Ball declared in the second ExComm meeting (foreshadowing his later, more famous role as a critic of U.S. escalation in Vietnam during Lyndon Johnson's presidency). "You go in there with a surprise attack," he continued. "You put out all the missiles. This isn't the end. This is the *beginning.*"[7]

The observations of McNamara, Ball, and others converted a consensus in favor of the use of force into a debate over the respective merits of military action and a blockade. The one Kennedy adviser to articulate in a sustained way an alternative to these two approaches, though his proposals contained elements present in both of them, was Adlai Stevenson. Historians have usually misrepresented Stevenson's role during the missile crisis. They often fail to mention that he did come to endorse the blockade, and that his support for negotiations was based on the assumption that a military strike on Cuba should be carried out if all other methods designed to bring about the withdrawal of the missiles failed.[8]

JFK did not invite Stevenson to participate in the evening ExComm session on October 16, an early sign perhaps that during the crisis the president wished to keep at arm's length this adviser who had consistently opposed his handling of the Cuban situation. But Stevenson was determined to have an impact on Kennedy's thinking, and by

Wednesday, October 17, he was ready to provide the president with a memorandum detailing his suggestions. Before composing it, he scribbled down for his own use a series of notes about the situation. The gist of what he wrote was that Kennedy should send personal emissaries to Khrushchev and Castro to issue them an ultimatum: failure to remove the missiles from Cuba would result in American military action to ensure their destruction. Stevenson also discussed how best to consult NATO and Latin American allies, and the need for Kennedy to make two speeches to the American people, the first informing them of the Russian missile deployment in Cuba, and the second—Stevenson seemed to suggest—announcing an imminent military strike (if necessary).[9]

These notes revealed Stevenson's concurrent fears about the use of force, and his ability to see things from the perspective of Moscow and Havana as well as of Washington. If Kennedy attacked Cuba, he wrote, would Khrushchev "retaliate against Turkey etc? Against Berlin? Laos? South Vietnam? Do we say all bases are negotiable but not while he has IRBMs [intermediate-range ballistic missiles] in Cuba?" Stevenson also considered why Castro is "a danger to US, if US which has far more missiles is not a danger to him?" and the need for Kennedy to prepare himself "for the argument that if we have base in Turkey, etc, they have right to have base in Cuba."[10]

The more Stevenson mulled things over, the more these concerns—the imperative to avoid a military engagement, and the accompanying need to participate in give-and-take negotiations—came to dominate his thinking. This was evident in the memorandum he gave Kennedy later the same day. In it Stevenson accepted that a U.S. attack on Cuba might be required should Khrushchev refuse to withdraw the missiles; but he underlined the importance of negotiations as a way of preventing such a scenario. "If war comes," he told Kennedy,

> in the long run our case must rest on stopping while there was still time the Soviet drive to world domination, our obligations under the Inter-American system, etc. We must be prepared for the widespread reaction that if we have a missile base in Turkey and other places around the Soviet Union surely they have a right to one in

Cuba. If we attack Cuba, an ally of the USSR, isn't an attack on NATO bases equally justified. One could go on and on. While the explanation of our action may be clear to us it won't be clear to many others. Moreover, if war is the consequence, the Latin-American republics may well divide and some say that the U.S. is not acting with their approval and consent. Likewise unless the issue is very clear there may be sharp differences with our Western allies who have lived so long under the same threat of Soviet attack from bases in the satellite countries by the same IRBMs.

But all these considerations and obstacles to clear and universal understanding that we are neither rash, impetuous or indifferent to the fate of others are, I realize only too familiar to you.

I know our dilemma is to strike before the Cuban sites are operational or to risk waiting until a proper groundwork of justification can be prepared. The national security must come first. *But the means adopted have such incalculable consequences that I feel you should have made it clear that the existence of nuclear missile bases is NEGOTIABLE before we start anything.*

Our position, then, is that we can't negotiate with a gun at our head, a gun that imperils the innocent, helpless Cuban people as much as it does the US, and that if they won't remove the missiles and restore the status quo ante we will have to do it ourselves—and then we will be ready to discuss bases in the context of a disarmament treaty or anything else with them. In short, it is they, not the US, that have upset the balance and created this situation of such peril to the whole world.

I confess I have many misgivings about the proposed course of action, but to discuss them further would add little to what you already have in mind. So I will only repeat that it should be clear as a pikestaff that the US was, is and will be ready to negotiate the elimination of bases and anything else; that it is they who have upset the precarious balance in the world in arrogant disregard of your warnings—by threats against Berlin and now from Cuba—and that we have no choice except to restore that balance, i.e. blackmail and intimidation *never*, negotiation and sanity *always*.[11]

This was no lily-livered letter: Stevenson condemned Soviet actions and acknowledged that an attack might be needed to remove the missile threat from Cuba. But he did want Kennedy to try diplomacy before resorting to force.

Heartfelt they may have been, but Stevenson's proposals fell on deaf ears. While Stevenson conceded that military action against Cuba might be required, on October 17 Kennedy was convinced that it *was* required. It was no surprise, then, that Stevenson's memorandum, as Ted Sorensen reveals, "annoyed" JFK. NATO would be weakened as a result, Kennedy believed, as Stevenson's implied solution of taking the Jupiters out of Turkey to induce the Russians to do the same with their missiles in Cuba would be interpreted by America's partners as a case of JFK selling out a trusted ally. Kennedy also thought Stevenson's suggestions too timid: rather than making concessions, the United States should indict Russia for its endangerment of world peace.[12]

Late Wednesday afternoon Stevenson went to New York for the following day's debate at the United Nations. He would return two days later to reiterate and refine the proposals he had made in his memorandum to Kennedy. In the intervening period the key development was the conversion of JFK from an air-strike supporter to a backer of the blockade. The president was away from Washington for part of this time, keeping to his planned schedule of speeches on behalf of Democrats running in the congressional elections in November. The ongoing discussions in ExComm influenced JFK's thinking; even if he was absent for a meeting, Robert Kennedy relayed the substance of the discussion to him. Mostly it supported either the sort of military action the president had initially preferred or a blockade, with support for the latter growing as the crisis unfolded.[13]

By Thursday, October 18, JFK gave the first indication that he was shifting from his initial position of military action against Cuba. In the ExComm meeting that morning he did not show his hand, discussing various options without indicating his preference. He considered the merits of the military approach but did the same with the blockade; and he even mentioned the possibility of the kind of trade (involving the Jupiter missiles in Turkey) favored by Stevenson. Kennedy also concentrated on what he saw as the link between Cuba and Berlin. Time and again he warned that Khrushchev's response to U.S. action had to be considered, and that with either a blockade or an attack on the island the Soviet leader would most likely respond by moving on Berlin. That troubled the president.[14]

In a private meeting with Dean Acheson that afternoon, JFK gave a clear indication that he was leaning toward the blockade. Emphasizing his concern about attacking Cuba, he used the Pearl Harbor metaphor introduced by George Ball and echoed by Robert Kennedy. An unimpressed Acheson insisted that Kennedy's best bet was still the air strike.[15]

As he retired that evening, Kennedy had made the provisional decision to blockade (or quarantine) Cuba. Worried that a military strike on Cuba would appear to the world as an immoral, Pearl Harbor–type attack, triggering a military response from Khrushchev (most likely in Berlin, in the first instance), and aware that a quarantine was the more flexible option in that it did not preclude the subsequent adoption of either a diplomatic or a military approach to the crisis, the blockade seemed to JFK the most prudent and potentially effective plan of action.[16]

The following day Kennedy flew to Ohio and Illinois on another already-scheduled campaign trip for the upcoming congressional elections. Before leaving, though, he instructed Robert Kennedy to secure a consensus in ExComm in support of the blockade. That proved to be no easy matter when, at the ExComm meeting held in the State Department the following morning, McGeorge Bundy spoke forcefully in favor of an air strike, as did Acheson, CIA Director John McCone, Chairman of the Joint Chiefs Maxwell Taylor, and Secretary of the Treasury Douglas Dillon. McNamara and Robert Kennedy countered by again declaring their support for the blockade. To move things along, Rusk said ExComm should split into two groups, one comprising the officials who backed the blockade, the other those advisers advocating the air strike. Each group was charged with producing a draft explaining in full its preferred policy option. When the two groups reassembled it was apparent that the blockade supporters had done a better job of drawing up a complete, cogent draft than the hawks. As the discussion continued, McNamara and other military representatives suggested that an air strike could be carried out sometime after the blockade had been instituted. Robert Kennedy took "particular note of this shift," realizing that it represented the military's recognition that a quarantine was in the cards. "It was now pretty clear," he told his Ex-Comm colleagues, "what the decision should be."[17]

Just as the meeting was winding down, Stevenson, who had returned that afternoon from New York, entered the room. When a few minutes later Rusk asked if he had any views on how the administration should proceed, he answered, "Yes, most emphatic views." Invited to elaborate, Stevenson declined, saying he did not think it helpful in view of the direction of the discussion, a reference to the consensus for a quarantine that had apparently been reached. "But you are in favor of blockade, aren't you?" he was asked. He said he was, but that "we must look beyond the particular immediate action of blockade; we need to develop a plan for solution of the problem—elements for negotiation designed to settle the current crisis in a stable and satisfactory way and enable us to move forward on wider problems." He was working on ideas for a settlement and would present them the following day.[18]

After a call from Robert Kennedy, who asked him to cut short his campaign trip to the Midwest, JFK left Chicago on the morning of Saturday, October 20, arriving at the White House at 1:30 p.m. That afternoon the president again met with his ExComm advisers, including his UN ambassador. For Stevenson it turned out to be a bruising encounter. This was the meeting when the president, after hearing restatements of the pro-quarantine and pro–air strike positions, announced that he was "ready to go ahead with the blockade" and to authorize military preparations to carry out an air strike should the quarantine prove ineffective. Fleshing out the recommendations he had made that same day in a memorandum to Kennedy, Stevenson argued that in addition to the announcement of the blockade, the president in his speech, and Stevenson at the United Nations, should propose a diplomatic settlement. It would be based on the idea of a militarily neutral Cuba, involving a withdrawal from Guantanamo and a promise not to invade the island, along with the removal of the Jupiter missiles from Turkey and Italy by the United States, and the withdrawal of all missiles (and perhaps all Russian military personnel too) from Cuba by the

Soviet Union. Kennedy was unimpressed: he "rejected the thought of surrendering our base at Guantanamo in the present situation. He felt that such action would convey to the world that we had been frightened into abandoning our position. He was not opposed to discussing withdrawal of our missiles from Turkey and Greece [Italy is what Kennedy or the drafter of these minutes presumably meant], but he was firm in saying we should only make such a proposal in the future." "Though the president was courteous but firm," other officials—McCone, Dillon, and former Secretary of Defense Robert Lovett—"intemperately upbraided Stevenson," as George Ball recalled. Stevenson soldiered on, insisting that the United States "must be more forthcoming about giving up our missile bases in Turkey and Italy. He stated again his belief that the present situation required that we offer to give up such bases in order to induce the Russians to remove the strategic missiles from Cuba." It was Pentagon official Paul Nitze who took his turn to cudgel Stevenson, saying he "flatly opposed making any such offer, but said he would not object to discussing this question in the event that negotiations developed from our institution of a blockade."[19]

Why had Stevenson received a tongue-lashing so severe that, according to one writer who later interviewed him, "The bitter aftertaste of that Saturday afternoon . . . stayed with him until his death"? After all, earlier in that same meeting McNamara had said that following the blockade the Kennedy administration, in order to persuade the Russians to remove the missiles from Cuba, would need to participate in negotiations in which "we would have to be prepared to accept the withdrawal of United States strategic missiles from Turkey and Italy and possibly agreement to limit our use of Guantanamo to a specified limited time." Even Kennedy himself declared in this meeting that "at an appropriate time we would have to acknowledge that we were willing to take strategic missiles out of Turkey and Italy if this issue was raised by the Russians."[20]

In a sense, the differences between Stevenson and Kennedy at this juncture were related to what had separated them over the issue of Cuba before the missile crisis: Stevenson's more urgent insistence on the value of diplomacy. But the missile crisis had changed Kennedy, and this would become more apparent by the end of the confrontation.

Faced with the prospect of a third world war, possibly a nuclear conflict, he resolved to make the cold war less hazardous, to ameliorate Soviet-American relations. It was one thing to understand nuclear war as an abstraction; it was quite another to *experience* events that made this theoretical scenario a distinct possibility. This had the effect of narrowing the gap between Kennedy's thinking and that of Stevenson, so that like his UN ambassador, JFK viewed a settlement negotiated after the establishment of a blockade as the best way to end the crisis. Now the differences between the two men were over the scope of the concessions and the timing of their offer. Kennedy rightly saw the ceding of Guantanamo as a concession incompatible with the nation's credibility on the world stage and with American public opinion. Ultimately he was happier for the withdrawal of the Jupiters from Turkey to remain a secret rather than become a public component of the settlement that ended the crisis. And he indicated no willingness at this time to promise not to invade Cuba in the future.

As for timing, Kennedy believed it would be inappropriate to offer to remove missiles from Turkey and Italy. The United States should discuss the issue only after the Russians had raised it. Kennedy probably thought that arranging a diplomatic settlement in this way would smack less of appeasement and more of a statesmanlike act to preserve the peace. The implicit point made by Stevenson, however, was that it was essential to minimize the time between the announcement of the blockade and the commencement of serious negotiations with a concrete agenda for ending the crisis. That way the chances of the crisis leading to war because of escalation or accident would be reduced. For all the anger they aroused in the ExComm meeting, Stevenson's proposals—and his alone among Kennedy's advisers—contained all the elements present in the final settlement of the missile crisis. The fact that Stevenson had not fully presented his ideas in ExComm until after a consensus in favor of the blockade had been forged contributed to the hostility he encountered. Weary men with frayed nerves suddenly had to consider a new approach just when they thought the issue they had been grappling with for days and nights had been resolved. Stevenson's proposals nevertheless merited more attention from his colleagues than the short shrift they received.

Although the shift in JFK's thinking in the midst of the missile crisis brought him closer to Stevenson on policy, his personal regard—and that of his brother—for the UN ambassador reached a new low. When the Saturday afternoon ExComm meeting ended, the Kennedy brothers and close aide Kenneth O'Donnell walked out onto the Truman Balcony. Robert Kennedy was "furious," as O'Donnell recalled. "He's not strong enough or tough enough to be representing us at the UN at a time like this," the attorney general told his brother. "Why not get him out of there, and put somebody like John McCloy in his place." JFK did dispatch McCloy to New York to assist Stevenson; he also sent Arthur Schlesinger to help write the speeches Stevenson would make at the UN during the crisis. As Schlesinger was about to leave for New York, Robert Kennedy had a word: "We're counting on you to watch things in New York. That fellow is ready to give everything away." JFK's own disgust at Stevenson's performance in ExComm would become apparent in a grubby episode after the missile crisis when he planted in the press a story that compared Stevenson's proposals in ExComm to the appeasement of Hitler.[21]

A presumably dazed Stevenson headed off that Saturday evening to a Washington party. Spotting O'Donnell among those present, he walked over for a chat. O'Donnell told him that the president thought no less of him for his dissent that afternoon—though Kennedy's later actions showed this was not the case. "I know that most of those fellows will probably consider me a coward for the rest of my life for what I said today," said Stevenson. "But perhaps we need a coward in the room when we are talking about a nuclear war."[22]

The next day, Sunday, October 21, Stevenson modified his views in a memorandum on the "political program" he thought Kennedy should propose. As in ExComm the day before, Stevenson discussed the importance of Kennedy introducing the terms for a negotiated settlement to the crisis at the same time he announced the blockade. And once again he argued that the president should be willing to evacuate Guantanamo and promise not to invade Cuba. With the Soviet Union being required to remove all its missiles, military equipment, and personnel from the island, the principle underpinning the settlement would be the neutralization—in other words, the demilitarization—of

Cuba. Stung by his colleagues' criticism the previous day, Stevenson no longer recommended the withdrawal of the Jupiters from Turkey and Italy. This, he said, "would divert attention from the Cuban threat to the general problem of foreign bases." He even expressed his belief that the settlement he proposed, because it would deprive Castro of Russian military backing, could lead to the overthrow of his government.[23]

These private revisions of his plan for ending the crisis did not prevent Stevenson from clashing again with Kennedy in the ExComm meeting that afternoon. Indicating once more that he was not averse to taking the Jupiters out of Turkey and Italy at a later point in the crisis, the president asked Paul Nitze to study the Jupiter issue. But he remained opposed to the idea that he should offer Khrushchev concessions at the same time he announced the blockade. Inviting Khrushchev to a summit meeting to discuss the crisis was part of an early Ted Sorensen draft of the speech to be given by Kennedy, and this created a bone of contention between Stevenson and JFK, who decided to drop the proposal from his speech. "The United States," Stevenson argued, "would be forced into a summit meeting and [so he] preferred to propose such a meeting." Kennedy disagreed, adding:

> we could not accept a neutral Cuba and the withdrawal from Guantanamo without indicating to Khrushchev that we were in a state of panic. An offer to accept Castro and give up Guantanamo must not be made because it would appear to be completely defensive. He said we should be clear that we would accept nothing less than the ending of the missile capability now in Cuba, no reinforcement of that capability, and no further construction of missile sites.[24]

Outside of ExComm the most important meeting for Kennedy that Sunday was one he held with a group of officials that included Gen. Walter Sweeney. Sweeney told JFK that the United States had probably identified no more than 60 percent of all the Russian missiles in Cuba, and that even in a best-case scenario an air strike would destroy just 90 percent of those missiles. In other words, according to Sweeney, even if Kennedy decided to authorize an air strike, he should expect to destroy no more than 54 percent of the Soviet missiles on the island. This meant that Khrushchev would still be able to carry out a retaliatory nuclear strike on the United States from Cuba, whether JFK opted for the blockade or the air strike. The Joint Chiefs of Staff on October 19, and McNamara the day after, had told Kennedy essentially the same thing. To hear it from the commander-in-chief of the Tactical Air Command, though, added weight to the claim. For Kennedy it confirmed that his decision to choose the blockade was the right one. Next he needed to explain this decision to the American people and to the world. That he would do the next day. Stevenson, meanwhile, returned to New York late on Sunday evening to ready himself for the defense in the United Nations of Kennedy's stance on Cuba.[25]

On Monday, October 22, Kennedy continued to consult his Ex-Comm advisers. His comments that day revealed a commendable caution and common sense. Asking about the status of his request the previous day that the Joint Chiefs issue instructions to U.S. military commanders in Turkey not to fire the Jupiters without first securing presidential approval, Kennedy was told that the Chiefs had considered it unnecessary as these orders were already in place. Unimpressed, Kennedy insisted that fresh orders be sent reminding commanders in Turkey of the restrictions on their authority. "We don't want these nuclear warheads firing without our knowing about it," the president told his advisers. He was determined to make sure that a trigger-happy military officer would not take the kind of rash action that could convert a confrontation into a nuclear exchange. For the remainder of the crisis Kennedy would show the same prudence—and that helped prevent a third world war.[26]

In the evening, after a tense meeting with congressional leaders, Kennedy began his televised address to the American people:

> Good evening, my fellow citizens. This Government, as promised, has maintained the closest surveillance of the Soviet military buildup on the island of Cuba. Within the past week unmistakable evidence has established the fact that a series of offensive missile sites is now in preparation on that imprisoned island. The purpose

of these bases can be none other than to provide a nuclear strike capability against the Western Hemisphere.

From this point on, the missile crisis was no longer a matter of concern only for Kennedy and his advisers. It sparked fear in peoples and their leaders throughout the world. "The 1930's taught us a clear lesson," Kennedy continued: "Aggressive conduct, if allowed to grow unchecked and unchallenged, ultimately leads to war. This nation is opposed to war. We are also true to our word. Our unswerving objective, therefore, must be to prevent the use of these missiles against this or any other country and to secure their withdrawal or elimination from the Western Hemisphere." In seeking to achieve this objective, JFK explained, he would establish a quarantine around Cuba, increase surveillance of the island, reinforce Guantanamo, and call meetings of the Organization of American States and the United Nations Security Council.[27]

On Tuesday, October 23, JFK was busy on a number of fronts. He continued discussions with ExComm advisers. He sent a reply to the uncompromising letter he had received that day, in which Khrushchev had described the U.S. plan to blockade Cuba as "a serious threat to peace" and the missiles sent to Cuba as necessary for the defense of the island. He also dispatched Robert Kennedy to Soviet ambassador Anatoly Dobrynin, thereby establishing an important channel of communication with the Russians that he would again use later in the crisis. What Dobrynin said to Robert Kennedy, however, could have served only to heighten the tension JFK must have felt. The last he had heard, Dobrynin told the attorney general, Russian ships were under orders to proceed to Cuba. That seemed to indicate that a Soviet-American clash on the seas was unavoidable.[28]

There is no record as to whether the president slept well that night, but it would have been surprising if he had. With Soviet ships hours away from confronting the American blockade, war might begin the next day. If Kennedy had heard the extraordinary comments of a Soviet press officer to a U.S. official at the UN that evening, his equanimity would have been even more disturbed: "This could well be our last conversation. . . . New York will be blown up tomorrow by Soviet nuclear weapons."[29]

On Wednesday morning, October 24, Kennedy sat with his Ex-Comm advisers in the Cabinet Room, listening to periodic reports from naval intelligence on the situation on the seas. Of immediate concern were two Soviet ships, the *Gagarin* and the *Komiles*, and a submarine that were approaching the blockade line, five hundred miles from Cuba. Other Russian ships were also en route for the island. Would they try to continue past the quarantine line, thereby making military conflict inevitable? The pressure was immense. "These few minutes were the time of greatest worry by the President," wrote Robert Kennedy later that day in notes on the meeting. "His hand went up to his face & covered his mouth and he closed his fist. His eyes were tense, almost gray, and we just stared at each other across the table." This was the eye of the storm.[30]

"Mr. President, I have a note just handed to me," interjected McCone. "It says that we've just received information through ONI [Office of Naval Intelligence] that all six Soviet ships that are currently identified in Cuban waters . . . have either stopped or reversed course." Subsequent reports confirmed this news. Kennedy moved quickly to reciprocate Khrushchev's restraint: he ordered the navy not to intercept any Russian vessel for an hour so as to give the ships time to carry out any orders they had received to reverse course. War had been averted—for the time being at least.[31]

On the following day, Thursday, October 25, Kennedy considered the action to be taken beyond the enforcement of the quarantine. He spoke most about intensifying the blockade to prohibit not only weapons but petroleum, oil, and lubricants (POL). Other ExComm officials considered various post-blockade options: an air strike, a negotiated settlement involving the Jupiters in Turkey, an extension of the quarantine to POL. Kennedy had to deal with another truculent letter from Khrushchev, which had been sent the previous day. "I regret very much," he replied to the Soviet premier, "that you still do not appear to understand what it is that has moved us in this matter." Khrushchev's decision to send missiles to Cuba—and to lie about it—was the root cause of the crisis, Kennedy reiterated.[32]

On October 25 probably the most famous episode of the missile crisis occurred: Adlai Stevenson's fiery, televised confrontation in the

United Nations Security Council with Valerian Zorin, Russian ambassador to the UN. In the days preceding this exchange Stevenson had been busy on Kennedy's behalf. Despite his disagreements with the president behind closed doors, Stevenson dutifully defended Kennedy's policies in public. On the afternoon of October 22 he went to the office of UN Secretary General U Thant to inform him that Kennedy's speech that evening would be on Cuba and would be tough. After JFK's address, Stevenson called for an emergency session of the Security Council to discuss the crisis, a request soon duplicated by Soviet and Cuban officials.[33]

In that Security Council meeting on the afternoon of October 23, Stevenson defended America's stance with vigor in a speech composed by Schlesinger and other aides. Communist aggression had been the root cause of international instability since World War II, Stevenson argued, and by aligning itself with the Soviet Union, Castro had allowed Moscow to penetrate and threaten the Western Hemisphere. That was intolerable. The need to avoid the mistakes of appeasement in the 1930s, and to show resolve to America's adversaries, demanded that the missiles be removed from Cuba. Stevenson's address provoked hostile responses from Ambassador Zorin and Cuban representative Mario Garcia-Inchaustegui. After the Security Council session, Stevenson spoke to the press to continue to build the public case for Kennedy's handling of the crisis and against the Soviet missile deployment in Cuba. As Zorin had not denied there were missiles in Cuba, he told the assembled journalists, it was clear that the blockade of the island was required. He urged the Security Council and the international community to treat with disdain the "protestations of innocence which we may expect to hear [from Russian officials] in the next few days."[34]

On October 24 Stevenson, along with John McCloy, met with delegates at the UN, seeking to reassure those African and Asian representatives who doubted Kennedy's approach, fearing it would prompt a Soviet-American clash on the seas. Stevenson asked them to convey those fears to the Russians, as that might help persuade Khrushchev that it would be too dangerous to challenge the blockade.[35]

On Thursday, October 25, round two of the contest between Stevenson and Zorin in the UN Security Council got under way. The mental sharpness of Zorin, described by one of Stevenson's aides as a "heavy, tough Communist hatchet man, with a face like a battle-ax," was not what it once had been. By 1962 he was suffering from seizures and poor memory. Hence he was not in the best state of mind to deal with the relentless attack launched by Stevenson on the Soviets.[36]

Stevenson began by asserting that the Russian deployment of missiles in Cuba—of which, he said, he had photographic evidence—threatened the peace and necessitated the American blockade of the island. Tentative, was how Zorin described Stevenson's statement. If the United States had unambiguous evidence showing the missiles in Cuba, he added, why did Kennedy not present it to Gromyko in their meeting on October 18? The United States did have hard evidence, Stevenson retorted. He proceeded to ask Zorin to clarify his position, as he was now denying the presence of missiles in Cuba, something he had not done two days earlier.

> STEVENSON: Do you, Ambassador Zorin, deny that the U.S.S.R. has placed, and is placing medium and intermediate-range missiles and sites in Cuba? Yes or no? Don't wait for the translation, yes or no?

> ZORIN: I am not in an American courtroom, sir, and therefore I do not wish to answer a question that is put to me in the fashion in which a prosecutor puts questions. In due course, sir, you will have your answer.

> STEVENSON: You are in the courtroom of world opinion right now, and you can answer yes or no. You have denied that they exist, and I want to know whether I have understood you correctly.

> ZORIN: Continue with your statement. You will have your answer in due course.

> STEVENSON: I am prepared to wait for my answer until hell freezes over, if that's your decision. And I am also prepared to present the evidence in this room.[37]

Stevenson, who had taken pains beforehand to convince himself of the authenticity of the CIA photographs of the missile sites, now presented them to the Council. Zorin responded by observing that during the Bay of Pigs episode Stevenson had shown fake photographs of a Cuban aircraft, whose pilot had allegedly defected from Castro's air force. "As to the authenticity of the photographs, about which Mr. Zorin has spoken with such scorn," Stevenson responded,

> I wonder if the Soviet Union would ask their Cuban colleagues to permit a United Nations team to go to these sites. If so, Mr. Zorin, I can assure you that we can direct them to the proper places very quickly.
>
> And now I hope that we can get down to business, that we can stop this sparring. We know the facts, Mr. Zorin, and so do you, and we are ready to talk about them. Our job here is not to score debating points: our job, Mr. Zorin, is to save the peace. If you are ready to try, we are.[38]

Impassioned, lucid, and persuasive, Stevenson was in top form. His performance did much good for the United States in winning over world opinion. It also provided what for many people would be the most memorable moment of the missile crisis. Not surprisingly, Stevenson's stock rose with the public. Letters singing his praises poured into his office. Even some Republicans who had regarded him as too soft and liberal admired the guts he had shown in his encounter with Zorin. The press, too, thought Stevenson had covered himself in glory. The *Chicago Tribune* editorialized: "We have had our differences with Adlai Stevenson in the past . . . but we must salute him now. His eloquent, fiery, and effective presentation of the case of the United States concerning the treachery and deadliness of the soviet missile and bomber buildup in Cuba was wholly admirable."[39]

Stevenson's style and cerebral qualities had long given him what JFK had referred to as a cult following among sections of the American public. But the image created by his performance at the United Nations was more complete than ever before: this was a Stevenson with balls as well as brains. The fear of a revitalized rival is what prompted Kennedy to take steps after the missile crisis to tarnish Stevenson's newly burnished reputation.[40]

On Friday, October 26, the morning after his triumph over Zorin, Stevenson flew from New York to Washington to rejoin the ExComm

debate in which he had not participated for five days. In a sense this
ExComm meeting was a replay of the heated exchange of October 20
when Stevenson had spoken of concessions and been scolded for doing
so. But this time the role played by Kennedy was quite different. Com-
mencing in the Cabinet Room at 10 a.m., this ExComm discussion followed good news some three hours earlier: the navy had intercepted
and boarded the *Marucla*, a Lebanese ship sailing for Cuba under Soviet charter (with no weapons on board). This enforcement of the
quarantine would not give Khrushchev reason to retaliate, but because
it was the first vessel to be inspected it made the blockade of Cuba appear credible. Hence the feeling pervaded the morning's ExComm
meeting that the first stage of the second week of the crisis was complete. The blockade had been successfully implemented. Now the second stage, devising a plan for the action that should be taken next, had
begun.[41]

Air strike, invasion, extension of the blockade to POL, and various
diplomatic options were discussed. Praised by Rusk for his performance at the UN the preceding day, Stevenson reviewed the agenda
for talks at the United Nations involving U Thant, whom he was due
to meet later that day. He would try to bring about an immediate de-
escalation of tension through an interim agreement: Khrushchev
would halt work on the missile sites in Cuba, and send no more offensive weapons to the island, in return for a suspension of the blockade.
This would provide a two- or three-week period in which a root-and-
branch settlement of the crisis could be negotiated. Considering the
likely elements of such a settlement, Stevenson predicted that the Russians would request "a new guarantee of the territorial integrity of
Cuba. They need that; that's what they said these weapons were for."
"It is possible," he added, "that the price that might be asked of us . . .
might include dismantling bases of ours, such as Italy and Turkey."
Within a day, Khrushchev would indeed seek commitments from
Kennedy not to attack Cuba and to remove the Jupiters from Turkey
(though not Italy). Better than his ExComm colleagues, Stevenson was
able to anticipate Khrushchev's next move.[42]

As in the ExComm meeting on October 20, CIA Director McCone
wasted no time in expressing his disgust for Stevenson's line of thinking.

This time, however, Kennedy did not add his weight to the attack on Stevenson. "Our quarantine itself won't remove the weapons," he observed. "So we've only got two ways of removing the weapons. One is to negotiate them out. . . . And the other is to go over and just take them out [by force]. I don't see any other way we're going to get the weapons out." Kennedy implied that by outlining a diplomatic settlement, Stevenson was considering one of only two approaches that could actually get the missiles out of Cuba. Hence Stevenson was being realistic, not naive. In a sense, the contrast between Kennedy's reaction to Stevenson's arguments on October 20 and 26 was to be expected, given that JFK had said on the 20th that he was not opposed to making concessions, only to doing so as part of his initial policy response to the missiles in Cuba. But the contrast also reflected the impact which the experience of leading America and the Free World during the most dangerous crisis of the cold war had made on Kennedy. His fear of war, especially nuclear war, was greater, thus his heightened interest in using diplomacy to end the crisis. In effect his views had moved closer to Stevenson's. This would become more apparent the following day.[43]

On the evening of October 26 the entire equation changed for Kennedy, Stevenson, and other American officials with the arrival of a long letter from Khrushchev. It was one of the most remarkable documents of the cold war. Free of the formalities that usually characterize diplomatic correspondence, it was emotional and direct—so much so that some have wondered, uncharitably and unconvincingly, if the Soviet leader had not downed one vodka too many before writing it.[44]

Khrushchev's letter was slightly vague, but the gist of what he seemed to offer was the removal of the missiles from Cuba in return for a no-invasion pledge from Kennedy. What suggested this is what Khrushchev had in mind is that the same proposal was made that day by Aleksandr Feklisov, a KGB officer in Washington, to ABC reporter John Scali over lunch. Scali then informed the State Department of the offer. Administration officials were encouraged, assuming that Feklisov was acting on orders from Khrushchev. He was not: he had made the proposal on his own initiative. It was a fortuitous coincidence, reinforcing the inclination of the Kennedy administration to view the offer in Khrushchev's October 26 letter as serious.[45]

Before Kennedy and his advisers were able to draft a response to Khrushchev's offer, another letter from the capricious Soviet leader arrived the following morning, Saturday, October 27. More formal than his correspondence the night before, and broadcast publicly by Radio Moscow, this letter to Kennedy altered the proposed settlement. Khrushchev now demanded the withdrawal of the Jupiters from Turkey in addition to a promise not to invade Cuba, in exchange for the removal of the missiles. A more sober mood thus permeated the ExComm meeting that convened at 10 a.m. in the Cabinet Room.[46]

It was a dilemma for Kennedy: how to respond to two different sets of Khrushchev proposals made within a matter of hours. In the end, JFK decided with no little shrewdness to accept the quid pro quo offered in Khrushchev's October 26 letter, essentially ignoring his public message of the 27th. The traditional explanation of how ExComm devised this clever strategy—that it was Robert Kennedy who came up with the idea—was provided by Robert Kennedy himself in his *Thirteen Days*. But the transcript from the tape of the ExComm meeting makes clear that this was a notable example of the proclivity of memoirists to inflate their own importance. Robert Kennedy, with Llewellyn Thompson, did help persuade a wavering JFK to use this ploy, but a number of other advisers urged the president to try this approach before Robert Kennedy did so. These included Paul Nitze, McGeorge Bundy, Ted Sorensen—and Adlai Stevenson. Back in New York and thus absent from the ExComm meeting, Stevenson nonetheless sent Kennedy a draft for a public statement, which read:

> The United States never had any territorial designs against Cuba, but of course we cannot tolerate Soviet Cuban aggression against us or our sister republics. The Soviet offer to withdraw weapons in Cuba is welcome, and we give assurance of our peaceful intentions towards Cuba. In the meantime, it is imperative that further developments of Soviet bases stop and discussions proceed with the Secretary General of the United Nations in New York.

Stevenson also advised against considering the withdrawal of the Jupiters from Turkey. In other words, he was saying Kennedy should embrace Khrushchev's letter of October 26 but ignore the one sent the following morning.[47]

Not only did Stevenson help forge the consensus in ExComm in favor of this ploy, he also played a role in the actual writing of the letter that Kennedy sent to Khrushchev that evening. Robert Kennedy and Sorensen produced the final version of that message but based it on two drafts, one from Stevenson and one from the State Department. The opening paragraphs of the Robert Kennedy–Sorensen message were in fact almost identical to the introductory section in Stevenson's draft. It is another example of how his contribution during the missile crisis has been undervalued.[48]

For his part, Kennedy was superb on October 27. He marshaled the discussions in ExComm with great skill. He remained cool under unimaginable pressure. In stark contrast to his performance on the opening day of the missile crisis, he was an advocate for diplomacy, not force. What concerned Kennedy was the likelihood, as he saw it, of Khrushchev rejecting his ploy and once again demanding the withdrawal of the Jupiters from Turkey. What, then, should be his next step? His military advisers were unequivocal: they wanted a massive air strike on Cuba on Monday morning, October 29, to be followed a week later by an invasion of the island. But Kennedy was not so sure. There were two nonmilitary options he wished to try first. One was the intensification of the blockade by intercepting POL. The other, which he dwelt on most, was a deal on the Jupiters. He pointed out to Ex-Comm officials that removing the technologically antiquated Jupiters from Turkey was something his administration had considered even before the missile crisis, and that to most people trading the Jupiters in Turkey for the missiles in Cuba would seem fair.[49]

The bottom line for Kennedy was that forfeiting the Jupiters was preferable to war in the Caribbean. "I'm just thinking about what we're going to have to do in a day or so," he said to his advisers,

> which is 500 sorties, and 7 days, and possibly an invasion, all because we wouldn't take the missiles out of Turkey.
>
> We all know how quickly everybody's courage goes when the blood starts to flow, and that's what's going to happen to NATO.

When we start these things and they [the Russians] grab Berlin,
everybody's going to say: "Well, that was a pretty good proposition."
Let's not kid ourselves. . . . Today it sounds great to reject it,
but it's not going to, after we do something.

"We can't very well invade Cuba," he added, "with all the toil and
blood it's going to be, when we could have gotten them [the Soviet
missiles] out by making a deal on the same missiles in Turkey. If that's
part of the record, then I don't see how we'll have a very good war."[50]
The trouble with giving up the Jupiters was that Khrushchev had
demanded this concession in a publicly broadcast message. To cede
those missiles, therefore, would give the impression of the United
States caving in under pressure from the Russians. To avoid that, JFK
asked Robert Kennedy to invite Ambassador Dobrynin to his office in
the Justice Department that evening to inform him off the record that
the president planned to remove the missiles from Turkey a few
months after the Cuban crisis had ended. Robert Kennedy carried out
those instructions.[51]
In the event Khrushchev rejected that offer and insisted that any
agreement on the Jupiters be incorporated into the formal public settlement to the crisis, JFK developed a plan to make such a deal more
palatable: Turkey and other NATO governments would be encouraged
to call for a Jupiter trade, by making clear to them that an American
strike on Cuba might well cause Khrushchev to retaliate in Turkey and
in Berlin, and that the withdrawal of the Jupiters from Turkey would
be followed by the deployment of Polaris submarines in the Mediterranean. That way, agreeing to a Jupiter trade would come across as a
statesmanlike response to the concerns of his NATO partners rather
than a case of Kennedy appeasing the Russians and selling out his allies. Some evidence indicates that JFK may have fashioned yet another
Jupiter-centered strategy for ending the crisis. In 1987 Dean Rusk
claimed that the president had instructed him on October 27 to ask
Andrew Cordier of Columbia University to arrange on a moment's notice for U Thant to call publicly for the removal of missiles from both
Cuba and Turkey. Evidence also suggests that Stevenson played a role
in the formulation of this plan.[52]

In the final analysis, it seems, Kennedy would have agreed to a public deal on the Jupiters if that is what it took to get Russian nuclear
weapons out of Cuba without the use of force. No one saw it this way,
but by promoting a diplomatic rather than a military solution with
greater insistence as the crisis unfolded, JFK had in effect moved closer
to the outlook of Stevenson, his great rival.

Kennedy had served his country well that day, but he found it difficult to sleep. So he stayed up late with his long-serving, fiercely loyal
aide Dave Powers, watching one of his favorite films, *Roman Holiday*.
Not even the grace, beauty, and charm of Audrey Hepburn, one sus-
pects, could have deflected his attention from the day's events. He had
responded wisely to the problem created by Khrushchev's different sets
of proposals. Nevertheless the sickening sense remained that the momentum toward war was irresistible. An early-morning CIA report had
revealed that a number of the Russian missile sites in Cuba appeared to
be fully operational. The shooting down of an American U-2 plane
over Cuba had resulted in the death of the pilot, Maj. Rudolf Anderson. The U.S. military, meanwhile, continued its preparations in case
Kennedy ordered an attack on Cuba. Military aircraft were taking off
from an airport in Miami at a rate of one a minute, and British sources
compared the massing of troops in Florida to the south coast of England before D-day. Had Kennedy known what Fidel Castro recommended on the night of October 26–27 in a message to Khrushchev,
his outlook would have been even gloomier. Castro told the Soviet
leader that the United States was about to attack Cuba, probably with
an air strike but possibly by invasion. If it were the latter, Castro advised, Khrushchev should respond with a nuclear strike on the United
States.[53]

Disturbed by the intensification of the crisis, troubled in particular
by intelligence information indicating that a U.S. attack on Cuba was
at hand, Khrushchev decided on Sunday, October 28, to end the crisis
by accepting the offer made by Kennedy the previous day. He composed a letter along those lines to JFK. Fearful that any delay might
mean war, he ordered an official to speed through the city to deliver it
in person to Radio Moscow for immediate broadcast. Received in
Washington around 9 a.m., Khrushchev's message expressed gratitude

for "the sense of proportion you have displayed and for realization of the responsibility which now devolves on you for the preservation of the peace of the world." The Soviet premier revealed that he had issued "a new order to dismantle the arms which you described as offensive, and to crate and return them to the Soviet Union." He went on to say he regarded "with respect and trust the statement you made in your message of October 27, 1962, that there would be no attack, no invasion of Cuba." Khrushchev made no mention of the Jupiters in Turkey.[54]

At the ExComm meeting that convened two hours later, there was a palpable sense of relief. The president was "in great form," an aide noticed. "He was smiling and he was full of humor and he, too, had obviously felt a great burden lift." Kennedy agreed to a public statement, and later in the day a reply to Khrushchev, welcoming his message. It was, said Kennedy, "an important contribution to peace." A meeting between Robert Kennedy and Dobrynin that morning provided informal confirmation of the settlement described in the correspondence between Khrushchev and JFK, but with the secret addendum that the Jupiters in Turkey would be withdrawn. It was more than a month before Russian missiles (and IL-28 bombers) were withdrawn from Cuba and the American blockade of the island was lifted. But for all intents and purposes the Cuban missile crisis ended on Sunday, October 28.[55]

Despite the differences and tensions between himself and the president in the first week of the crisis, Stevenson had served Kennedy well. His defense in the United Nations of JFK's stance over Cuba had been nothing less than brilliant. At the height of the crisis he was able to anticipate Khrushchev's next moves and to help the president formulate an effective response to Khrushchev's different sets of proposals. Yet after the crisis ended Kennedy was seething with anger toward Stevenson. At a dinner on November 15 he spoke of Stevenson in a way, according to one journalist present, that "did nothing to dispel the rumors that he was less than 100 percent behind his UN ambassador."[56]

Three weeks later Charles Bartlett, a very close friend of Kennedy, and Stewart Alsop wrote an article, "In Time of Crisis," for the *Saturday Evening Post*. An account of the missile crisis based on interviews with administration officials, it was also a vicious attack on Stevenson.

Included was a headline which proclaimed: "An opponent charges, 'Adlai wanted a Munich. He wanted to trade U.S. bases for Cuban bases.'" In the text of the article, Alsop and Bartlett quoted "a nonadmiring official" who said that "Adlai wanted a Munich. He wanted to trade the Turkish, Italian and British missile bases for the Cuban bases." To provide a visual illustration of the point, the article included a photograph of an unimposing, nervous-looking Stevenson.[57]

In an act stunning for its cold malice, it was John Kennedy himself who planted this hostile account of Stevenson's role during the crisis. The president's appointment book shows that Kennedy spent at least seventy minutes on November 11 with Bartlett, who had already informed the president of his intention to write the article with Alsop. So JFK had the opportunity to knife Stevenson, and that is exactly what he did. Stewart Alsop has acknowledged that Kennedy read the article before publication, editing the section on Stevenson to make the UN ambassador's position seem less rational. Before publication, Alsop also revealed to the executive and managing editors of the *Post* that the president himself was the "nonadmiring official" who alleged that Stevenson "wanted a Munich." The editors instructed Alsop and Bartlett to ask Kennedy whether he really wanted to include such a damning quote. "I want it in," Kennedy insisted.[58]

The article caused enormous controversy. Stevenson was stunned and his many supporters denounced the way he had been treated. Kennedy tried to pour oil on troubled waters: statements were issued making clear his support for Stevenson (ironic given what is now known about his role as a source for Alsop and Bartlett) and his regret over the episode. The Washington rumor mill rumbled on, however, when at a press conference Kennedy declined the opportunity to put on record his belief that the description by Alsop and Bartlett of Stevenson's views was inaccurate. Publicly Stevenson said he was content with Kennedy's defense of him. Privately he was less diplomatic: John or Robert Kennedy, he believed, had been a source for the article.[59]

No record exists to explain Kennedy's motives, but what seems most likely is that he feared Stevenson, so boosted by his confrontation with Zorin at the UN, might pose a threat to either himself in 1964 or Robert Kennedy in the 1968 race for the Democratic presidential

nomination. This is precisely what some of Stevenson's supporters suspected. One State Department official who worked closely with
Stevenson also wondered about Robert Kennedy's role in this affair,
saying he could imagine the attorney general "having an instinct for
the jugular on the political jealousy. It was, 'Hey, now. We've got to
watch this guy. He's going to become a national hero, coming out
against the Communists this way. When the only real chink in his ar-
mor has been that he's a liberal and soft and so forth. He might be a
real alternative to Kennedy in 1964. And we better cut him down to
size, fellas.'" That interpretation makes sense. Decoded, the Alsop-
Bartlett article suggested that the new image of Stevenson as a tough
cold warrior, created by his showdown with Zorin, was an illusion, that
behind closed doors he was as woolly-minded and soft on communism
as ever. Via the *Saturday Evening Post* article, JFK sought, within a matter of weeks of the missile crisis, to deprive Stevenson of his newly acquired political asset, namely that he now appeared to be a resolute
anti-Communist as well as a stylish progressive.[60]

The paradox of this final clash between Kennedy and Stevenson
over Cuba was that it occurred at a time when JFK was moving closer
to Stevenson's way of looking at American foreign policy—attaching
more importance to diplomatic than to military approaches to the cold
war, and seeking to reduce tensions between Washington and Moscow.
True, it was not Stevenson who had brought about that change; it was
Kennedy's experience of managing the most dangerous crisis of the
cold war. It sobered him, tempering some of his more belligerent im-
pulses. In an interview with the press a week before Christmas 1962, a
reflective president showed the extent to which the fear of a superpower war now preoccupied his thoughts:

> I think, looking back on Cuba, what is of concern is the fact that
> both governments were so far out of contact, really. I don't think
> that we expected that he [Khrushchev] would put the missiles in
> Cuba, because it would have seemed such an imprudent action for
> him to take, as it was later proved. Now, he obviously must have
> thought that he could do it in secret and that the United States
> would accept it. So that he did not judge our intentions accurately.

Well, now, if you look at the history of this century, where World War I really came through a series of misjudgments of the intentions of others, certainly World War II, where Hitler thought that he could seize Poland, that the British might not fight, and if they fought after the defeat of Poland they might not continue to fight, Korea, where obviously the North Koreans did not think we were going to come in, and Korea, when we did not think the Chinese were going to come in, when you look at all these misjudgments which brought on war, and then you see the Soviet Union and the United States so far separated in their beliefs, we believing in a world of independent sovereign and different diverse nations, they believing in a monolithic Communist world, and you put the nuclear equation into that struggle, that is what makes this . . . such a dangerous time, and that we must proceed with firmness and also with the best information we can get, and also with care.

It is difficult to imagine Kennedy articulating these sentiments earlier in his presidency. Before the missile crisis he certainly could not have empathized with them in the same way.[61]

Thus in the final year of his life Kennedy charted a different course in foreign policy, one that drew him closer to Stevenson's thinking. In the summer of 1963 he approved the establishment of a "hot line" between Moscow and Washington, which would provide instant communication between the superpower leaders in the event of another major crisis. He delivered what would become a famous speech at American University, in which he called on Americans to reconsider their attitude toward the Soviet Union. And he endorsed the Nuclear Test Ban Treaty, an agreement without cold war precedent. In the autumn that year he talked with Foreign Minister Gromyko about ways to increase cooperation between the superpowers, such as a Soviet-American moon project. While Kennedy authorized new acts of covert sabotage against Cuba in 1963 in a program reminiscent of Operation Mongoose, in the final weeks of his life he showed strong signs of interest in reaching some sort of accommodation with Castro.[62]

Kennedy had not gone from being a cold warrior to a pacifist. He still regarded the Communist challenge as a serious matter. In Vietnam, for example, he continued to deepen America's involvement in a struggle that, for his successor Lyndon Johnson, would turn out to be a nightmare. Nevertheless, in the final months of his life Kennedy was more determined than ever before to use diplomacy to make the world a safer place. That made the tragedy of his assassination in Dallas on November 22, 1963, all the greater.[63]

Adlai Stevenson also died suddenly—from a heart attack on a London street in the summer of 1965. That too was a loss for all those who yearned for a sensible definition of America's role in the world. Stevenson had worked his entire political life to that end.[64]

PART V

Johnson, Ball,
and the Vietnam War

CHAPTER 12

The Accidental President
and the Tardy Rebel

＝

"Within five years we'll have three hundred
thousand men in the paddies and jungles [of
Vietnam] and never find them again."
—GEORGE BALL, November 7, 1961,
in conversation with John F. Kennedy

ON THE morning of Friday, November 22, 1963, Vice President
Lyndon Baines Johnson boarded Air Force Two with his wife, Lady
Bird, for a flight from Fort Worth to Dallas. Five minutes after Johnson's plane touched down at Love Field, John and Jackie Kennedy
landed in Air Force One. On the ride from Love Field to the Trade
Mart, where he was scheduled to speak, President Kennedy was struck
down by an assassin's bullets. Johnson was two cars behind in the mo-
torcade when the shots rang out. The Secret Service agent in the vice
president's car reacted instantaneously: he pushed Johnson down,
vaulted the seat, and then sat on his shoulder to protect him and keep
him down. The driver then accelerated away, heading toward Parkland
Hospital where an attempt would be made to save Kennedy's life. At
1:20 p.m., Central Standard Time, Kennedy aide Kenneth O'Donnell
broke the terrible news pithily to Johnson: "He's gone." From that

moment, Johnson was faced with a dilemma he could never resolve: how to succeed an icon and yet appear credible. It was as if a soprano played Tosca after Maria Callas had just finished a performance in the role; or an actor appeared as Richard III the night after Laurence Olivier had played the same part in the same theater. In truth, it was an impossible challenge for Johnson. Only Harry Truman could have understood how he felt.[1]

In the whirl of events that followed, Johnson and his entourage headed for Love Field to take Air Force One back to Washington. He was sworn in as president before takeoff. After emerging from the plane at Andrews Air Force Base, Johnson made a brief statement, saying "I will do my best. That is all I can do." He was then met by three senior officials, Secretary of Defense Robert McNamara, National Security Adviser McGeorge Bundy, and Undersecretary of State George Ball. As Secretary of State Dean Rusk was on a plane bound for Tokyo at the time of the assassination, Ball had served as acting secretary of state that afternoon. It had been a frenetic few hours, in which Ball dispatched messages to the nation's governors and drafted various proclamations, including the one Johnson would need to declare Kennedy's funeral a day of national mourning. With McNamara and Bundy, Ball joined Johnson on the short helicopter ride to the White House. He noted the emotional state of the new president, who "seemed near a state of shock. He moved erratically, and I saw twitches in his face." Johnson used the flight to highlight his determination to retain the services of these three senior Kennedy advisers. "You're men I trust the most," he told them. "You must stay with me. I'll need you. President Kennedy gathered about him extraordinary people I could never have reached for. You're the ablest men I've ever seen. . . . I want you to stand with me."[2]

Able men were precisely what Johnson would need as he assumed control of the presidency. Healing the wounds of a traumatized nation would not be easy, and with the power and prestige he inherited from Kennedy came problems of policy and politics. The civil rights bill, designed to end segregation in the South, was stalled in Congress. Tax cuts prepared by JFK had likewise been stymied on Capitol Hill. And in the final months of the Kennedy presidency, the Communist challenge in Vietnam had moved to center stage. The bloody repression of the Buddhists in the summer of 1963 by Ngo Dinh Diem, America's ally in South Vietnam for nearly a decade, had been shocking; and his overthrow and assassination three weeks before Kennedy's own murder raised questions about the stability of the new government in Saigon and its capacity to resist pressure from the Communists.

Two days after becoming president, Johnson reviewed the situation in Vietnam in a meeting with his advisers. Henry Cabot Lodge, the American ambassador in Saigon, began the discussion by offering his colleagues an optimistic assessment of developments since the coup against Diem. John McCone countered by gloomily observing that there had been "a continuing increase in Viet Cong activity" since Diem's removal, "as evidenced by a larger number of Viet Cong attacks." Johnson suggested that American support for the coup against Diem had been a mistake. But his overthrow was a fait accompli, the president added, hence the United States would have to pursue its objectives in Vietnam in the context of these changed circumstances. He called for greater unity of outlook among American officials in South Vietnam, agreed that his administration should be generous in dispensing economic aid to Saigon, and revealed his determination to win the war. "I will not lose in Vietnam," he declared.[3]

Three days later, on November 27, Johnson addressed a joint session of Congress—and a nation still in shock. The salient theme of his speech was the need for America to pay homage to its fallen leader by continuing his policies and achieving his objectives. By connecting the endeavors of his administration to what had become—because of the events of November 22—the sacred work of the Kennedy presidency, Johnson believed he could secure for himself a sense of political legitimacy. "The greatest leader of our time," he stated,

> has been struck down by the foulest deed of our time. Today John Fitzgerald Kennedy lives on in the immortal words and works that he left behind. He lives on in the hearts of his countrymen.
>
> No words are sad enough to express our sense of loss. No words are strong enough to express our determination to continue the forward thrust of America that he began. . . .

And now the ideas and ideals which he so nobly represented
must and will be translated into effective action. . . .

This Nation will keep its commitments from South Viet-Nam
to West Berlin.[4]

Thus within a few days of Kennedy's assassination, Johnson had
promised privately and publicly to stay the course in Vietnam. He did
so in part because he shared the core beliefs on foreign policy embraced by most Americans since World War II: remember the lessons
of the 1930s; always confront belligerent dictators; and assume that
Moscow's influence with Communist movements anywhere in the
world is substantial, and that the conversion of any country to communism will likely result in the "loss" of neighboring nations to the
Communist camp. But Johnson's address before Congress revealed another impulse behind his initial determination to prevent a Communist
victory in South Vietnam: a recognition that reversing Kennedy's policy in that part of the world was unthinkable, for it would implicitly
cast doubt on the sagacity of a leader whose wisdom could not now be
questioned. Cold war assumptions and the ghost of Kennedy had tied
Johnson's hands in Vietnam. It would require an extraordinary man
even to begin to untie them.

Untie Johnson's hands, however, was exactly what George Ball
would attempt to do. As is now widely known, Ball came to oppose
American escalation in Vietnam and ultimately Johnson's decision to go
to war. Not surprisingly, Ball became a hero to many after the war in
Vietnam turned into a catastrophe and his dissent became public knowledge. Here was the savvy soothsayer who had the guts to stand alone and
tell Johnson, McNamara, and the rest that they were wrong. If only
Johnson had listened to him, so much that came to pass would have been
different: there would have been no defeat in Vietnam; Johnson would
have enjoyed another term as president; the kinds of liberal reforms that
had begun with Franklin Roosevelt's New Deal would have continued;
and the shift to a harsher America that began with the election of
Richard Nixon in 1968 might have been prevented or delayed.[5]

Ball deserves his place in history. He did articulate a well-reasoned
case against the war in Vietnam. If Johnson had heeded his advice, the

consequences would have been profound and beneficial. But in the case of Ball one must approach the past rather like Irwin, the teacher in Alan Bennett's play *The History Boys*—with a determination to debunk myths. Ball was certainly the leading dissenter on Vietnam in the Johnson administration, and in July 1965 he fought hard to change the minds of Johnson and other officials about going to war. But at most of the key junctures to that point, the moments when America's commitment to the struggle in Vietnam deepened significantly, Ball voiced no opposition to the changes in Johnson's policies. He was a rebel when it came to Vietnam, but a tardy and inconsistent one.[6]

In retrospect, this pattern was discernible from that first meeting on Vietnam held by Johnson on November 24. In addition to the president, only Ball and five other officials attended. In the memorandum on that discussion produced by McCone, there is no record of Ball uttering a single word. It would have been difficult on that occasion to question the entire validity of American involvement in Vietnam. But Ball might have challenged some of the assumptions underpinning the policies inherited by Johnson, perhaps sowing seeds of doubt in the president's mind. He missed an important opportunity, and it would not be the last time he would do so.[7]

Lyndon Johnson brought to the White House greater political experience than any president in the twentieth century. He had been born in Gillispie County, Texas, in 1908, not with a silver spoon in his mouth like John Kennedy but with politics in his blood, indeed in every corpuscle. Although the farming and real estate ventures of his father, Sam Ealy Johnson, Jr., brought only meager returns, his passion for politics provided young Lyndon with a valuable education. A member of the state legislature for six terms, Sam Johnson would take his son onto the floor of the Texas House of Representatives and on the campaign trail. And Lyndon loved it. For him, politics became not a hobby but an obsession. Like his hero Franklin Roosevelt, Johnson was one of the most consummate American politicians of the twentieth century. In part that was because his interest in politics had begun when he was so young.[8]

In Johnson's youth, teaching was viewed as a solid platform on which to build a political career. Accordingly Johnson enrolled at

Southwest Texas State Teachers College. His pedagogical experience included a stint at an all-Mexican school in Cotulla, Texas. After that his rise in the 1930s was meteoric: he served in Washington as secretary to Texas congressman Richard Kleberg before being appointed Texas director of the National Youth Administration, Roosevelt's program for unemployed youth. In 1937 he was elected to the House of Representatives on a strongly pro–New Deal platform.[9]

Despite defeat in a 1941 campaign for the Senate—spurious vote reporting thwarted him—he won election to that chamber seven years later by a margin of eighty-seven votes, using the same sort of unsavory tactics himself. Nicknamed "Landslide Lyndon" thereafter, he came to be seen as representing the seamier side of politics, an image he could never altogether shake.[10]

Johnson's career in the Senate might have begun dubiously, but he went on to dazzle and dominate that body. He became the Democratic Minority Leader in 1953, and, after the 1954 elections, the Senate Majority Leader. His ability to get done what he wanted to get done was legendary. He could be viewed as either brilliant or a cynical operator, but his effectiveness could not be questioned. "The Treatment" was the phrase used to describe the range of emotional and physical tactics employed by Johnson to persuade others to think along his lines. Towering over a colleague, with his face less than an inch away, he used flattery, cajolery, intimidation, and coercion to persuade. It was a style that gave Johnson's personality the sort of heightened quality that made him seem at times like a character out of a Tennessee Williams play.[11]

To remain politically viable in a Texas that became increasingly conservative in the 1940s and 1950s, Johnson shifted to the right on issues such as union power and civil rights. But he gave signs of becoming a truly national figure rather than a sectional leader devoted only to the interests of the South when he promoted the Civil Rights Act of 1957 and took a highly visible stance on the national security challenge posed by the Soviet Union's successful launching of the satellite *Sputnik*. Johnson appeared to be readying himself for a presidential campaign in 1960.[12]

He did aspire to the White House, but the tactics he used to realize that ambition proved manifestly ineffective. Rather than enter the

1960 Democratic primaries as Kennedy did, he bided his time, hoping that a deadlocked convention would turn to his brand of experienced leadership. Once Kennedy wrapped up the nomination, though, he asked Johnson to be his vice-presidential running mate. Johnson accepted, and two months after JFK's victory in November 1960 he became vice president.[13]

The Kennedy years were lonely for the big and often uncouth Texan, who did not fit at all with the elegant stylistic ethos of the new administration. For Johnson, power was oxygen; and unlike the position of Senate Majority Leader, which had given him real clout, the vice presidency was a largely ceremonial post. Moreover JFK was respectful toward him but not warm, while Robert Kennedy's hatred of him knew no bounds. He was therefore an outsider, looking in wistfully on the court of Camelot.[14]

Johnson struggled as vice president to define a role for himself, and Kennedy struggled to find one for him. In the end, Johnson spent a significant amount of time serving as JFK's goodwill ambassador, visiting thirty-three countries on eleven trips. One of the most important of these was a mission to Asia in May 1961. Included on his itinerary was Saigon, where Johnson was to have talks with Diem and reassure the president of South Vietnam of Kennedy's support against the Communist insurgency. That support was much needed as Diem's position had grown increasingly precarious. Eisenhower's aid to Diem in the 1950s had not prevented the Viet Cong from stepping up its resistance to his regime at the end of the decade. Adding to the sense that the Communists were on the march in Southeast Asia at the start of the Kennedy years was the civil war in neighboring Laos. There too the Communists exerted considerable influence. Kennedy helped arrange a cease-fire in Laos in 1961, but the situation remained troubling.[15]

In his talks in Saigon, Johnson secured Diem's agreement to a series of proposals from Kennedy aimed at bolstering American support for the South Vietnamese government. Reporting to JFK on his discussions with Diem, Johnson emphasized the need for Washington to continue to bear the burden in opposing Communist expansion in Southeast Asia, and predicted that the moment might well come when the United States would need to consider the deployment of substantial forces in South Vietnam. Johnson thus knew that Vietnam was a serious issue, but in the spring of 1961 he could not have imagined the extent to which it would come to define his life in politics.[16]

Johnson looked on as Kennedy ratcheted up the U.S. presence in South Vietnam, so that by the time of his assassination there were 16,700 U.S. military officials there, compared with 685 at the end of Eisenhower's presidency. Johnson observed with a critical eye the encouragement offered by some officials in the Kennedy administration, beginning in the late summer of 1963, to a coup against Diem. They hoped his removal would usher in a less repressive government, one more able to win popular support. The overthrow of Diem, Johnson believed at the time and later, was an egregious error, one that destabilized South Vietnam and played into the Communists' hands. Diem had not been perfect, but as a long-established leader he provided at least a measure of stability. As things turned out, it was Johnson who would have to grapple with the troubling ramifications of Diem's demise.[17]

Where Johnson was a son of the South, George Ball's path to political prominence began in the Midwest. Born in Iowa in 1909, Ball moved with his family to Illinois thirteen years later. He was precociously bright and, even at a young age, independently minded: while his parents and brothers remained ardent Republicans, the teenage George developed a distaste for the Harding and Coolidge presidencies, and switched his allegiance to the Democratic party. As one authority on Ball has put it, "He became an iconoclast within his own family."[18]

After graduating from Northwestern with a degree in English literature and near the top of his class from Northwestern Law School, Ball headed off to Washington during the exciting early days of the New Deal. He worked initially in the Farm Credit Administration and then in the Treasury Department, but by 1935 he was on his way back to Illinois to practice law. It was while working in the law that Ball met the man whose political career would be so entwined with his own over the next quarter-century: Adlai Stevenson. As Democrats in a law firm replete with Republicans, they were naturally drawn to each other. The two men began a dialogue on policy issues, including international affairs, that would continue through the years.[19]

With the help of Stevenson, Ball made his return to government in Washington in 1942. His wartime service included a stint as a director of the U.S. Strategic Bombing Survey, charged with assessing the impact of air attacks on Germany. The conclusions reached by Ball, based in part on interviews of Germany's war-production chief Albert Speer, were not as clear-cut as might have been expected. Even as late as June 1944, according to Speer, German war production was approximately three times as great as it had been at the start of the war, a statistic that called into question the efficacy of earlier Allied bombing raids. This finding, that air attacks were of limited effectiveness in vanquishing a people, influenced Ball's attitude—some two decades later—to Lyndon Johnson's authorization of air strikes against the Communist enemy in Vietnam.[20]

After the war, Ball helped establish a law firm, Cleary, Gottlieb, Friendly and Cox, that would become one of the most prominent in America. Crucially for the development of his career, Ball brought to the firm as a client the French government. Over the course of the next decade, traveling to Paris once a month, Ball came to know well the movers and shakers in postwar France, in particular that great advocate of European integration, Jean Monnet. No one exerted more influence on Ball's thinking in his adult life than Monnet. The promotion of European unity, particularly in the economic sphere, would remain Ball's abiding concern. Relations with developing nations were important for the United States, he acknowledged, but unlike such liberal thinkers as Chester Bowles, Ball believed America's focus should be on Europe, not Asia and Africa. As with the conclusions he drew on the use of airpower during World War II, his geographic priorities shaped his view of the Vietnam War. Dissipating U.S. power and prestige in a Southeast Asian country that was not of central importance to American interests was, in Ball's opinion, clearly unwise.[21]

Ball's dealings with the French not only fueled his interest in European integration, they also familiarized him with their painful experiences in Indochina. Just as America fought a long war in Vietnam and lost, so earlier had the French. The same factors that accounted for the

French defeat made an American victory in Vietnam unlikely, and
many of the arguments advanced by French officials who supported
their war in Indochina would be repeated a decade or more later by
Lyndon Johnson's advisers. Thus when the Johnson administration
moved America toward a land war in Vietnam in 1964–1965, Ball could
see dangerous parallels with the French experience in Indochina. As he
explained in his memoirs, the French officials he met made clear their
frustrations over the war.

> Not only was the terrain of Indochina clearly unfit for the type of
> warfare France's seasoned overseas troops had been trained to fight,
> but the irrational willingness of the Viet Minh to take staggering
> losses made them an unconquerable adversary. I was to think of this
> often nine years later, when America compulsively repeated all of
> France's mistakes on the same hostile terrain and against essentially
> the same enemy. The French disclosed the same propensity for
> self-deception, seduced by the same self-serving arguments that
> were later to lead my countrymen astray; they even comforted
> themselves with the same statistics of kill ratios and body counts
> that Americans were to recite with such macabre assurance during
> the middle 1960s. Just as the American civilian and military leaders
> were later to concoct new surefire ways to win the war, so the
> French periodically announced new tactical schemes . . . that would
> magically assure victory in a short period.[22]

As he had in 1952 and 1956, Ball supported Stevenson for the Democratic presidential nomination in 1960. With friends such as Arthur
Schlesinger and John Kenneth Galbraith working for JFK, however, Ball
had at least a toe, if not a foot, in the Kennedy camp. Thus in the new
administration he received an appointment as undersecretary of state for
economic affairs. In November 1961 he was promoted to undersecretary
of state, replacing Bowles, the liberal idealist with whom neither Rusk
nor JFK had found it easy to work.[23]

Ball was never part of the Kennedys' inner circle of advisers. He had
been too closely identified with Stevenson, and that created limits as to
how close Ball could hope to get to the president. But Ball's competence

was clear to everyone. He developed a close rapport with Rusk; and even if JFK was not especially fond of Ball, at least he respected him.[24]

For his part, Ball did not look at Kennedy and his close associates through the rose-tinted spectacles worn by the president's most ardent admirers. "He regarded much of the Kennedy style and dash with considerable skepticism," one journalist wrote—"those snappy young men running around the White House did not necessarily strike him as brilliant." He did not care for the palpable disdain for Stevenson shared by the president and those closest to him. Although he found JFK "intellectually alert and quick to understand a given problem, he was not," in Ball's opinion, "profound in either his analyses or his judgment." He seemed prone to superficial examinations of issues, rarely pondering their long-term dimensions.[25]

Ball, however, kept these misgivings under wraps, thereby retaining, as the number two man in the State Department, an influential position in the administration. Therein lay a significant difference between Ball and other cold war dissenters such as Wallace and Stevenson: Ball was a very canny politician. Although he held strong views on American foreign policy, he was wary about articulating them boldly in public in a way that would expose embarrassing differences between himself and the president or other senior officials. For Ball, loyalty to superiors was a greater obligation than declaring unceasingly an ardently held point of view at odds with prevailing opinion. Thus he did not become politically isolated.

If Ball were to make a stand, as he would on Vietnam, he would do so with extreme care. He would pay attention to timing. Rather than opposing presidential policy at every juncture, he would be selective— dissenting intermittently, endorsing the administration line on other occasions. Moreover he would deliberately set out to cultivate an image as a pragmatist rather than as a defender of high-minded principle. "George has a certain moral framework to his ideas," remarked a friend, "but he would be absolutely appalled if someone ever said that he did. George is very careful to camouflage his moral concerns—so he can be a better and more realistic player." In part this approach derived from Ball's observations of Stevenson during his presidential campaigns. He adored Stevenson—the tears he shed for him at his memorial service in 1965 prompting a consoling Lyndon Johnson to say, "George, I never trust a man who can't cry for a friend," were heartfelt—but he could not help feel that Stevenson's overt support for moralistic causes (such as the unilateral suspension of U.S. nuclear testing) reduced his effectiveness. It left him open to criticism that he was a naive liberal. Ball was determined that no such charge could be leveled at him.[26]

Yet he did begin work in the State Department in 1961 with some of the same reservations Stevenson had about the tendency toward gung-ho, excessively militaristic approaches to cold war issues. This would be evident not only in Ball's opposition to the Vietnam War but in his resistance in October 1962 to recommendations that the president respond by force to the Russian deployment of nuclear missiles in Cuba. Like Stevenson, Ball believed that if a country in Africa or Asia was about to go Communist, generally speaking it was best for the United States not to overreact. If Moscow sought to bolster that country, it would probably end up damaging its own credibility. So it was nothing for American policymakers to get worked up about. In Ball's view, power was a real and priceless commodity in international affairs, and the erosion of power was due principally to its inappropriate application.[27]

In addition, Ball had no time for the liberal fad du jour: nation building, the belief that an infusion of U.S. aid and know-how could convert poverty-stricken Third World countries into prosperous, Western-style democracies. "*Hubris,*" was Ball's characterization of such thinking.[28]

This set of convictions represented the prism through which Ball viewed the international issues that arose during the Kennedy years, including the situation in South Vietnam. Initially finance, foreign aid, and trade were the matters that absorbed Ball's attentions. Vietnam seemed more of a sideshow than a major drama on the world stage. But like Kennedy and his other advisers, Ball devoted more time to Vietnam as the New Frontier unfolded.[29]

The occasion when Ball articulated with vigor his objections to the increase in American support for the Saigon government during Kennedy's presidency came in the autumn of 1961. Worried by Communist activity in South Vietnam, the president had sent his close military aide Gen. Maxwell Taylor and Deputy Special Assistant for National Security Affairs Walt Rostow there to appraise the situation. Taylor and Rostow called on Kennedy to send over an eight-thousand-man task force, including combat troops. Before a meeting with Taylor and other officials on November 4, Ball revealed his reservations about the Taylor-Rostow proposals in a conversation with McNamara and his deputy, Roswell Gilpatric. He was, he declared,

> appalled at the report's recommendations; we must not commit forces to South Vietnam or we would find ourselves in a protracted conflict far more serious than Korea. The Viet Cong were mean and tough, as the French had learned to their sorrow, and there was always danger of provoking Chinese intervention as we had in Korea. Moreover, . . . unlike Korea, the Vietnam problem was not one of repelling overt invasion but of mixing ourselves up in a revolutionary situation with strong anticolonialist overtones.

To Ball's chagrin, McNamara and Gilpatric responded frostily. How to prevent a Communist takeover of South Vietnam was for them, Ball noted, the pertinent question, not—and this was Ball's point—whether it was worth the effort in the first place.[30]

Three days later Ball decided to make his arguments directly to Kennedy. In a private conversation he told the president that he regarded the Taylor-Rostow recommendations as dangerous, entailing as they did the deployment of U.S. forces in South Vietnam. In less than five years, he predicted to Kennedy, the United States would find itself with 300,000 troops bogged down in Vietnam. "That was the French experience. Vietnam is the worst possible terrain both from a physical and political point of view." Rather than asking Ball to elaborate, JFK gave him short shrift: "George, you're just crazier than Hell. I always thought you were one of the brightest guys in town, but you're crazy. That just isn't going to happen."[31]

Returning to his office in the State Department, a somber Ball vented his frustration. "We're heading hell-bent into a mess, and there's not a Goddamn thing I can do about it," he told his chief of staff, Bob Schaetzel. "Either everybody else is crazy or I am." As it turned out,

Kennedy agreed to augment U.S. assistance to South Vietnam, but without deploying combat troops, at least not for the time being.[32]

That was the end of Ball's overt dissent on Vietnam during the Kennedy years. From the president's dismissive response, it was clear to Ball that he would welcome no more grumbling about Vietnam. Ball had no desire to become ostracized, and a few weeks later, when he replaced Chester Bowles as undersecretary of state, he was reminded of the importance placed by the Kennedys on loyalty: Bowles's opposition to the Bay of Pigs operation was thought to be the main reason for his departure.[33]

Ball continued to keep tabs on the situation in Vietnam. He paid close attention to relevant reports from the State Department's Bureau of Intelligence and Research. He gave a major speech on Vietnam in April 1962, in which he both stressed the importance of America's commitment to combating communism there and warned that "this is not a type of struggle congenial to the American temperament." In private he periodically expressed concern over developments in Saigon. "The Viet-Nam business was getting out of hand rapidly," he groused to one official on July 1, 1963, before repeating the complaint in a phone conversation with Dean Rusk that same morning. He also developed an informal alliance with those individuals in the administration who shared some of his concerns: State Department officials Roger Hilsman and Averell Harriman, and NSC staff aide Michael Forrestal. But despite participating in twenty-five meetings with the president on Vietnam, and speaking on the phone to him on the same subject no fewer than a dozen times, not once did he call for a fundamental reappraisal of American policy, as he had in November 1961. Given Kennedy's acerbic reaction on that occasion, it was for Ball a case of once bitten, twice shy.[34]

Not only did Ball provide no consistent opposition to Kennedy's policies, he played a major role in binding America yet more tightly to South Vietnam. A watershed moment followed the decision by the Saigon government in late August 1963 to raid Buddhist pagodas and jail hundreds of monks who opposed the Diem government's anti-Buddhist policies. It was thought this repression was the insidious handiwork of Diem's brother, Ngo Dinh Nhu, and his wife. Already a number of Buddhists had been killed, and several Buddhist monks had burned themselves to death in protest. Ball was deeply troubled by the Nhus. Diem's inability to extricate himself from them caused Ball to side with Hilsman, Harriman, and others who believed that the only way to create a government in Saigon with enough popular appeal to block the Communists was to oust Diem.[35]

The opportunity to do just that presented itself on the weekend of Saturday, August 24. Kennedy's new ambassador in Saigon, Henry Cabot Lodge, reported by telegram that some generals in South Vietnam were discussing the feasibility of a coup against Diem. For the only time during the entire Kennedy presidency, all of the principal foreign policy officials—the president, McNamara, Rusk, Bundy, and McCone—were away from Washington. That Saturday afternoon, Ball played golf with State Department official U. Alexis Johnson. As he putted the ninth hole, Ball saw Hilsman and Harriman waiting for him. They drove with Ball to his house, where they showed him the message they wished to send Lodge in response to his telegram. The proposed message to Lodge declared that the Kennedy administration could no longer tolerate a government in Saigon in which Nhu exerted influence, and that if Diem did not get rid of Nhu, Washington would not stand in the way of those South Vietnamese military leaders who wished to overthrow Diem. With minor modifications, Ball endorsed the telegram. He also agreed to seek Kennedy's approval. Calling him at Hyannis Port, Ball informed the president about the proposed cable to be sent to Lodge. Kennedy said he agreed to its transmission providing Rusk and Gilpatric did likewise. Their approval was secured, and the message was sent.[36]

When the president and his advisers convened on Monday, August 26, to review the weekend's events, the general feeling was that Ball, Hilsman, and Harriman had acted too hastily. Maxwell Taylor pointed out the divisions within the South Vietnamese military, McNamara wondered whether any new leader would be more effective than Diem, and McCone too disapproved of the encouragement given to the generals.[37]

This debate over the overthrow of Diem continued to rage over the next few days. Ball fought his corner robustly. In a meeting on August 28 he asserted that "it would be difficult if not impossible for us to live with a situation in which Nhu was ascendant in Vietnam. . . . We had no option but to back a coup. We are already beyond the point of no return. The question is how do we make this coup effort successful." When both McNamara and Kennedy argued that the United States should not support the coup simply because the momentum behind it seemed irresistible, Ball did not back down. "We can't win the war against the Communists with Diem in control," he insisted. "The U.S. position in the eyes of the world is being badly damaged. Hence, we can't back off from our all-out opposition to Diem and Nhu. . . . We [must] decide to do the job right. There is no other acceptable alternative. We must decide now to go through to a successful overthrow of Diem."[38]

As it turned out, the generals decided not to move against Diem at that time. But two months later they did carry out a coup in which Diem was killed. A series of ephemeral, ineffective governments followed in South Vietnam. For all of Diem's failings, it seems clear that he would have proved a more stable, reliable partner for the United States in the struggle against communism than the leaders who succeeded him. Moreover it can be cogently argued that the overthrow of Diem tied the United States more closely to the governments that followed in Saigon. Given the Kennedy administration's considerable involvement in the August discussions about an overthrow of Diem, there was a definite sense in the administration after Kennedy's death that the United States had an obligation to defend the succeeding governments in Saigon because American officials had helped create them. As the historian Robert Dallek has written, "Once the U.S. government played a part in determining who ruled in South Vietnam, it assumed an additional responsibility for the life of that nation." In this way the coup against Diem was a major milestone for the United States on the road to war in Vietnam. George Ball had played no small part in setting it up.[39]

It was not during the Kennedy years, therefore, that Ball provided strong opposition to U.S. escalation in Vietnam. Nor did he seize the opportunity presented by the assassination of Kennedy to try to convince the new president to change course in that part of the world. Not until later did Ball challenge Lyndon Johnson over the war that would ultimately destroy him.

CHAPTER 13

Devil's Advocate

"[Johnson] was always a very reluctant fellow, but
he always got kind of dragged along, kicking and
screaming. The impetus toward escalation [in
Vietnam] never came from Lyndon Johnson,
I can assure you of that."—GEORGE BALL, 1971

"[Johnson said,] 'George Ball was very helpful. I
really miss old George.' Then he told me for two
or three minutes . . . about how he had asked
George to be the devil's advocate on various
things and how well he's done on it. . . ."
—HARLAN CLEVELAND, recalling comments
by Lyndon Johnson in February 1968

I N Lyndon Johnson's early days in the White House, almost all the
news coming out of Vietnam was bleak. Intelligence experts in the State
Department informed him that the military effort against the Communists in the South had been on the wane for months. The strategic hamlet program, on which hopes had been pinned as a way to separate vil-
lagers from Communist influence, had fallen far short of expectations.
In early December an official from the U.S. mission in Long An
Province, supposedly a showcase of the program, reported that "the
only progress made . . . during the month of November 1963 has been

by the Communist Vietcong." Adding to the sense of gloom was the mission to Saigon on which Johnson sent McNamara a week before Christmas. On his return, the secretary of defense pulled no punches in presenting his impressions to the president. "The situation is very disturbing," he asserted. "Current trends, unless reversed in the next two or three months, will lead to neutralization at best and more likely to a Communist-controlled state."[1]

A little over a month later, things went from bad to worse. A group of young officers led by Gen. Nguyen Khanh overthrew the military junta that had ruled South Vietnam since the fall of Diem. This indicated that the hopes that lay behind American backing for the coup against Diem—that it would usher in a period of stable and progressive government and thereby reduce the appeal of the Communists—were chimerical. In 1964 coups became commonplace as government replaced government in Saigon at a rate that could have suggested to an observer that he was in postwar Italy rather than Southeast Asia.[2]

This sobering trend in the first months of Johnson's presidency impressed upon him the gravity of the situation. He had come to the White House with a keen sense of the importance of upholding Kennedy's commitment to prevent South Vietnam from going Communist; now he had a fuller sense of exactly how difficult that would be.

As Johnson considered his options in Vietnam, a number of factors in addition to the Kennedy legacy and standard cold war assumptions influenced his thinking. One was the need he felt to prove his credentials in the international arena. He had neither the military background that had helped immunize Eisenhower from criticism, nor a striking foreign policy success such as the Cuban missile crisis that had buoyed Kennedy. Johnson surely was aware of the image he projected as a whiz in domestic policy but a greenhorn in foreign affairs. He was also dogged by insecurity, which coexisted with his ego and bravado. He suspected that Establishment types looked down their noses at him as an uncouth Texas hick. All this left Johnson with a determination to prove himself as a statesman. A foreign policy success would be ideal, but at the very least a foreign policy failure had to be avoided.

Besides shoring up his personal credibility, Johnson wanted to preserve America's credibility on the international stage. Cold war adversaries would have to be disabused of any notion that America could be pushed around with a new president at the helm. "They'll think with Kennedy dead we've lost heart," Johnson told his aide Bill Moyers. "So they'll think we're yellow and don't mean what we say." "Who?" asked Moyers. "The Chinese," replied Johnson. "The fellas in the Kremlin. They'll be taking the measure of us. They'll be wondering just how far they can go."[3]

Johnson also considered how Vietnam might influence domestic politics in America. He vividly recalled the impact that the "loss" of China to the Communists had made on Truman's presidency. Should he lose in Vietnam, LBJ concluded, he could expect a similar buffeting. As he explained to a journalist in February 1964, "There's one of three things you can do [about Vietnam]. One is run and let the dominoes start fallin' over, and God Almighty what they said about us leaving China would just be warmin' up compared to what they'd say now. I see Nixon is writin' about it today and Goldwater, too. You can run or you can fight, as we are doin', or you can sit down and agree to neutralize all of it." A Communist triumph in Vietnam, Johnson believed, would strengthen the hand of the right in America, weaken the Democratic party, and imperil his own presidency.[4]

Johnson saw another connection between the foreign and the domestic: he believed staying the course in Vietnam was a long-term necessity if he were to retain support on Capitol Hill for his cherished Great Society programs which he hoped would transform America. The consensus for liberal reform, he was certain, would evaporate if things went badly in Vietnam. "If I don't go in now and they show later I should have gone," he said on one occasion, "then they'll be all over me in Congress. They won't be talking about my civil rights bill or education or beautification. No, sir. They'll be pushing Vietnam up my ass every time. Vietnam. Vietnam. Vietnam." Johnson's short-term view of the link between Vietnam and the Great Society could be different. In 1964, for example, he was wary about enlarging America's commitment to South Vietnam because it might distract from the need to pass the civil rights bill he had inherited from Kennedy. But his general sense was that he must prevail in Vietnam in order to maintain the momentum behind Great Society reform.[5]

All these factors—his personal credibility, America's credibility overseas, the fear that Vietnam would become another China, and the connection between the war and the Great Society—encouraged LBJ to adopt a hard-line stance toward Vietnam. Other considerations, however, made Johnson more cautious. One of these was the concern that a tougher U.S. approach in Vietnam might bring China or even Russia into the conflict. Chinese intervention in the Korean War suggested this was not far-fetched; and Johnson knew that this scenario carried with it the frightening possibility of a nuclear exchange between the great powers.[6]

Johnson also worried about the effect of events in Vietnam on the 1964 presidential election. He was anxious that the South not go Communist before the election, but neither did he wish to damage his electoral chances by expanding U.S. involvement in a way that would invite closer scrutiny of his policies there. He said as much to Maxwell Taylor in March 1964.[7]

Beyond his concerns about the 1964 election and possible Chinese and Russian entry into the Vietnam War, Johnson displayed a general caution about the situation that made him skeptical of escalating U.S. involvement. This image of a prudent LBJ runs counter to the traditional view, rooted to some extent in Camelot mythology, that a belligerent and (in foreign affairs) ignorant Johnson pushed America into a war that the more sophisticated Kennedy would have avoided. But this line of thinking pays insufficient attention to the fact that the coup against Diem occurred during Kennedy's presidency, and that JFK authorized a huge increase in U.S. military personnel in South Vietnam. Yet this interpretation still permeates some of the literature on Johnson and the Vietnam War.

In the spectrum of opinion on Vietnam in his administration, the president's views were not particularly hard-line. When Johnson met Walter Lippmann in the late spring of 1964, for example, he did not dismiss out of hand the venerable journalist's arguments for neutralizing Vietnam (championed by French president Charles de Gaulle) which many observers thought would lead to a Communist Vietnam. After Lippmann left, Johnson explained his concerns to McNamara,

Ball, and McGeorge Bundy, all of whom had participated in the discussion with Lippmann: "How could he [the president] maintain his
posture as a man of peace in the face of the Southeast Asia crisis? How
could he carry a united country with him if we were to embark on a
course of action that might escalate under conditions where the rest of
the world would regard us as wrong-headed?" Johnson was never much
taken with the notion of neutralization, but his discussion of the subject on this occasion revealed his fears about what lay ahead for the
United States in Vietnam.[8]

That said, Johnson *did* take steps that increased U.S. involvement.
They were often incremental so as not to appear significant, but their
cumulative effect was considerable, culminating in the deployment of
large numbers of U.S. combat troops in the summer of 1965. One such
incremental step was the application of covert pressure against North
Vietnam. In February 1964 Johnson authorized Operation Plan 34-A,
as it became known, for a four-month trial period. Its objective, as Mc-
Namara recalls, was "to convince the North Vietnamese that it was in
their self-interest to desist from aggression in South Vietnam." Although it accomplished little, the operation was extended in May for
an additional four months.[9]

As well as seeking to undermine Ho Chi Minh's position through
clandestine pressure, Johnson began to consider the feasibility of air
strikes against North Vietnam—though again he showed a good deal
of caution when pressed on the matter. The impetus for the bombing
of the North came from the Joint Chiefs of Staff, who believed that
more needed to be done to defeat the Communists. On January 22,
1964, they sent McNamara a memorandum calling for a U.S. air assault on the North as well as the use of American combat troops to
fight the war. When McNamara passed these proposals on to the president, Johnson responded by asking the Joint Chiefs to formulate more
specific recommendations. This they did, emphasizing the importance
of U.S. air attacks on the Ho Chi Minh trail, used by North Vietnam
to supply Communists in the South by way of Laos and Cambodia, and
on military and industrial centers in the North. In late February Johnson informed Ambassador Lodge that he had directed McNamara and

Rusk to plan for the application of military and diplomatic pressure against North Vietnam. He added that McNamara would visit Saigon in March to obtain Lodge's views on the matter.[10]

Before heading off with Maxwell Taylor to South Vietnam, McNamara received his final instructions from Johnson: "Bob, I want to see about a thousand pictures of you with General Khanh, smiling and waving your arms and showing the people out there that this country is behind Khanh the whole way." McNamara dutifully obliged, but it highlighted one of the flaws in Johnson's thinking: his failure to appreciate fully the nationalist dimension of the struggle in Vietnam. Making Khanh and McNamara do their double-act made the former seem less an authentically independent representative of the South Vietnamese people, more of an American puppet. That did not help in the battle with the Communists for "hearts and minds."[11]

Returning to Washington, McNamara reported that the Saigon government's position was precarious. He recommended an increase in U.S. assistance so that, among other things, the South Vietnamese could augment their armed forces by fifty thousand men. The United States should not initiate air attacks on North Vietnam, he argued, but planning for such an assault should be advanced. Johnson endorsed McNamara's proposals at a National Security Council meeting on March 17. "Putting in more U.S. forces, pulling out of the area, or neutralizing the area" constituted the available options, he said. "The course we are following is the only realistic alternative. It will have the maximum effectiveness with the minimum loss." He also liked the flexibility of McNamara's proposals: they "did not foreclose action later if the situation did not improve as we expected." That was a clear reference to the contingency planning for air strikes against North Vietnam, but Johnson rejected the demands of the Joint Chiefs, who wanted to go further than McNamara by taking immediate action against the North. The president thought the South was not yet strong enough to survive the inevitable retaliatory attacks from the North, and the dangers of triggering Chinese or even Soviet intervention were too great.[12]

Despite the greater assistance for Khanh authorized by Johnson at this NSC meeting, the Communists remained on the offensive in the spring and summer of 1964. Leadership in Saigon continued to be ineffectual. The Viet Cong continued to increase recruitment, and Ho backed the Viet Cong with ever more zeal. Communists in Cambodia and Laos were also in a belligerent mood. A CIA intelligence assessment, submitted to Johnson on May 15, added to the sense of dismalness. "The over-all situation in South Vietnam remains extremely fragile," it stated. "If the tide of deterioration has not been arrested by the end of the year, the anti-Communist position in South Vietnam is likely to become untenable." Reporting to the National Security Council that same day on yet another trip to Saigon, McNamara said much the same thing. A despondent Johnson reacted to McNamara's news by saying that "the situation in South Vietnam was deteriorating and caused us to be extremely alarmed. The religious situation is explosive. A great effort will be necessary to turn the tide back to our side."[13]

As Johnson considered this "great effort," he concentrated on two approaches: one was the bombing campaign against North Vietnam promoted by the Joint Chiefs; the second was the introduction of a congressional resolution to obtain backing on Capitol Hill for presidential actions in Vietnam. Johnson's key advisers on Vietnam convened in Honolulu in early June to mull over these options. With the Saigon government in a serious but not a critical state, and with U.S. public opinion not yet decisively in favor of U.S. escalation in Vietnam (a spring 1964 Gallup poll revealed that 63 percent of Americans paid little or no attention to the struggle against the Communists in Southeast Asia), Johnson's advisers procrastinated: they reached no decision on bombing campaigns or congressional resolutions.[14]

That outcome mirrored Johnson's own outlook in the early summer of 1964, for he too wished to defer the decision on his next step. He wanted to secure passage of the civil rights bill before introducing a congressional resolution on Vietnam, and he was wary of taking any action before the presidential election that would throw the spotlight on his Vietnam policies. Rather than a resolution or air strikes, LBJ settled in June on a more modest alternative: a public relations campaign to explain more effectively to the American people "what we are doing and why" in that part of the world.[15]

Johnson was not moving with haste toward an irrevocable commitment to a full-scale land war in Southeast Asia, but he *was* moving in that direction. Only one man, it seemed, might be able to stop him.

For the first six months of Johnson's presidency, George Ball was not a vocal opponent of U.S. escalation in Vietnam. Perhaps Ball felt a need to crystallize his views before explaining them to Johnson and other officials. Or perhaps Ball was thinking strategically, identifying a moment or a series of moments when his dissent would be most effective. Certainly other issues were occupying his attention, including policy toward Cyprus, Panama, and Brazil, and trade.[16]

Ball's biographer James Bill makes the perceptive point that he wanted to bide his time before taking a bold stand on a key issue because of his concern over Johnson's attitude toward the role he had played in the August 24, 1963, cable that signaled American backing for a coup against Diem. Because Johnson strongly believed that removing Diem was a mistake, by implication the cable for which Ball was partly responsible was an error too. If LBJ concluded from this episode that Ball was an irresponsible operator, perfectly capable of the sort of independent action that could embarrass a president, his days in the State Department would be numbered. Indeed, as the early months of Johnson's presidency passed, Ball watched as one by one the other officials behind the August cable—Hilsman, Harriman, and Forrestal—were either moved sideways into less influential positions in the administration or sacked. Keeping his head down, being efficient, showing his loyalty to Johnson—these mattered more to Ball in the winter of 1963–1964 than disparaging U.S. policy in Vietnam in a way that might have confirmed for Johnson that Ball was a dangerous and expendable maverick rather than a reliable team player.[17]

Ball's approach paid off. He suffered on one occasion, in March 1964, when Johnson read him the riot act for failing to notify him that he had responded in the middle of the night to a coup in Brazil by endorsing the new government there: "I don't care a fuck that it was three in the morning: I want to know what's being done whatever time of night it might be." Apart from that, relations between Johnson and Ball were cordial, so much so that Ball was able to say two years after Johnson had left the White House, "He treated me with great consideration and courtesy all the time. . . . He knew that I was honest with him and that I wouldn't double-cross him, and loyalty was very big in his vocabulary."[18]

To the extent that he participated in the Johnson administration's early discussions on Vietnam, Ball's concerns were largely presentational: how to put the most favorable gloss on Johnson's policies for the press. In considering this matter, Ball did not criticize American policy in Vietnam. In a phone conversation with McGeorge Bundy in mid-December 1963, for example, he argued that press reports saying the military situation in Vietnam had deteriorated since the coup against Diem should be dampened. When the coup bringing Khanh to power took place in late January, Ball did not use the opportunity to make the case that the manifest instability of the South Vietnamese government showed that Johnson was backing a losing horse. Instead he busied himself by answering queries from Johnson and McNamara about how best to respond to press interest in the Khanh coup and by dispatching a perfunctory telegram to Lodge, stating "We have so little info on motivations and other factors involved in current crisis that we leave to your judgment how to handle."[19]

By mid-May 1964 Ball was still giving no clear sign that he opposed U.S. policy in Vietnam. In a telephone discussion in which Johnson spoke of securing additional funding from Congress for the effort in Vietnam, Ball raised no objections. Dean Rusk was being candid when he recalled that "George Ball didn't come into my office every other day saying, 'Look, we've got to do something radically different in Viet Nam.'"[20]

Vocal he may not have been, but Ball was becoming increasingly worried about the state of affairs in Vietnam. "This is even more serious than Cuba," he said to Alexis Johnson on April 21, 1964, reiterating the point three weeks later with McNamara: "The picture . . . although not hopeless, is certainly not too good." Ball was troubled not only by developments in South Vietnam but by the way his colleagues examined the situation without challenging fundamental assumptions: "I felt as though an accelerating current were propelling us faster and faster toward a gigantic waterfall. Yet no one was questioning the navigation, only how to rev up the engines to make the ship run faster:

'How?' was the obsessive question. How could we apply the vast power at our command to impose our will on the North Vietnamese and the Viet Cong?"—not whether the effort should be made in the first place.[21]

The one glimmer of hope for Ball was the president himself, who seemed in a less belligerent mood than his advisers. "Among all the top command," Ball would later say, "I found President Johnson the most reluctant to expand America's involvement. He was wary, among other things, of repeating MacArthur's error of attacking too close to the Chinese border; he did not want American boys to have to fight the Chinese hordes again."[22]

This impression was reinforced by Ball's attendance at the president's meeting on May 27 with Walter Lippmann. For two weeks Ball had been concentrating more on the issue of Vietnam, and as he did so he was buoyed by Johnson's reaction to Lippmann's arguments. In a letter to Rusk on May 31, Ball described the comments made by LBJ to McGeorge Bundy, McNamara, and himself in a discussion that followed the meeting with Lippmann, before proceeding to give his own considered opinion on Vietnam. This letter to Rusk marked the beginning of what one writer has called Ball's "dissent by memorandum." In developing his alternative view of American policy in Vietnam, Ball's preferred modus operandi was the memorandum. His letter of May 31 proved to be the first of many on the subject.[23]

In this letter to Rusk, Ball suggested that while Johnson had not been persuaded by the argument that Vietnam should be neutralized, he was "quite clearly impressed by Lippmann's contention that the United States was presenting itself in a bad light to the world by refusing to negotiate and entertaining the possibility of enlarged military action." Ball therefore felt confident that "the President would not act hastily." This comforted him, for he had been troubled by the tendency among Johnson's advisers to press ahead in Vietnam without sufficient prudence:

> When I first moved back into the Vietnamese situation a fortnight ago, I had the feeling that plans were going forward too precipitously and that there was an inarticulate wish to sweep the difficult

issues under the bed. It seemed to me that much of our planning was proceeding on the assumption that, since we were in danger of losing by pursuing the present course, we should promptly undertake a more decisive plan of action even though (a) no one could be sure that the new plan of action would have the desired effect and (b) the risks of a major catastrophe might be vastly enlarged.[24]

Given this concern, and aware of the president's evident caution about escalation, Ball had, he explained to Rusk, worked with Alexis Johnson in the last few days to slow the momentum that was building in the administration in favor of air strikes against North Vietnam. Both men had been finding it "personally difficult to advocate a course of action that could result in the loss of many American lives, the further disruption of Western solidarity, and grave dangers of escalation—at a time when we feel unprepared to do all that we know to be possible to reverse the downward trend (if it exists) in South Viet-Nam."[25]

With Alexis Johnson's help, Ball appended to the letter a number of questions that Rusk might ask other U.S. officials in the talks on Vietnam that were about to commence in Honolulu. These questions reveal much about the nature of Ball's concerns over American involvement in Vietnam, and introduced some of the salient themes of his dissent as it would develop over the next fourteen months. Did the Johnson administration believe air strikes against the North would be effective, asked Ball, or were they being recommended merely because the current action against the Communists was not working? Had sufficient attention been paid to the impact on morale in the South of the threats that might be expected from North Vietnam, China, and possibly the Soviet Union in response to a U.S. air attack on the North? Would the bombing of the North really disrupt Viet Cong activity in the South? Could the protection provided by Washington to the Saigon government lead to the deployment of U.S. troops in the South, and if so, had consideration been given to how this would cast the United States in the role of an old colonial power and weaken support for the Johnson administration from the American public and the nation's allies? Why was the administration considering air strikes against the North when a recent war-game exercise, in which McGeorge Bundy, Maxwell Taylor, and others had participated, had indicated that such strikes would be ineffective? How would the United Nations react to a U.S. assault on North Vietnam? By articulating these kinds of questions, Ball presented the skeletal framework of his dissent over Vietnam. He would flesh it out in the months to come.[26]

If Ball's response to administration discussions on air strikes against the North and to the president's reaction to Lippmann's arguments provided the first spark for Ball's dissent on Vietnam in the Johnson years, his meeting with Charles de Gaulle in Paris on June 5 supplied the second. Given his emerging opposition to U.S. policy, Ball seemed an incongruous choice for a diplomatic mission in which de Gaulle's support would be sought for any expansion of America's role in Vietnam. But one of Ball's traits that LBJ came to admire most was his ability to argue privately against administration policy while dutifully defending that same policy in diplomatic and public arenas. "George," Johnson said to Ball on one occasion, "you're like the school teacher looking for a job with a small school district in Texas. When asked by the school board whether he believed that the world was flat or round, he replied: 'Oh, I can teach it either way.' That's you. You can argue like hell with me against a position, but I know outside the room you're going to support me. You can teach it flat or round." Knowing, then, that Ball would follow his instructions to the letter, Johnson asked Ball to assure de Gaulle of America's commitment to peace in Southeast Asia, but also to determine whether de Gaulle would be supportive should Johnson decide that the fragility of the Saigon government and the increasing threat posed by North Vietnam and China made further U.S. action in Vietnam essential. Although he would not say it explicitly to the French president, Ball was being asked to find out whether de Gaulle would back LBJ if he bombed North Vietnam.[27]

After a warm greeting from de Gaulle, Ball began their talks in the opulent surroundings of the Elysée Palace on the afternoon of June 5 by handing over a letter from Johnson. De Gaulle read it, said he would reply soon, and then turned to Ball and declared, "I am ready to listen." Ball proceeded to explain that if the Communist insurgency in South Vietnam continued to threaten the Saigon government, President Johnson would be compelled to take military action against the

North, even though this might draw China into the conflict. Ball assured de Gaulle that Johnson ultimately desired a political settlement, but believed that such a settlement would work only if negotiated by a strong South Vietnamese government backed by American power.[28]

De Gaulle's response was candid: whether it maintained its military involvement in Vietnam at its present level or increased it, the United States would lose. Despite its military superiority, it would fail because the political and psychological dimensions of this conflict were paramount. The Vietnamese, de Gaulle asserted, "regard the US as a foreign power and a very powerful foreign power. The more the US becomes involved in the actual conduct of military operations the more the Vietnamese will turn against [the] US."[29]

As for France's participation, Johnson could forget about it: the French, he made clear, regarded Southeast Asia as "rotten" fighting territory for a Western power. "Even if the US were involved France would not get into a war in Asia, as an ally or otherwise." Rather than adopting a military approach, argued de Gaulle, the United States should follow the path of diplomacy. A multilateral negotiation, involving not only the United States and North and South Vietnam but France, India, China, Japan, and other nations would be particularly effective, as it would be difficult for Ho to continue killing people in South Vietnam once such international pressure had been brought to bear.[30]

As de Gaulle was not privy to Ball's private opinions on Southeast Asia, he could not have known that on Vietnam he and Ball were singing from the same hymn sheet. Ball, of course, did realize this; and though he was anxious to show his loyalty to Johnson by carrying out his diplomatic assignment without even hinting at his sympathy for the Frenchman's views, he did spot a small window of opportunity to use de Gaulle's arguments, at least by implication, to endorse his own emerging dissent. In a telegram to Johnson and Rusk shortly after his meeting with de Gaulle, Ball stated: "I had the feeling throughout our conference that the General was speaking honestly and with no apparent animous [sic] toward the United States. I felt that he was stating his convictions. I did not feel that he was trying to persuade us or to put pressure on the United States but rather that he was deeply convinced that, sooner or later, events would lead us to his point of view." De-coded, Ball was saying that this was not a crank but a sincere man whose ideas should be taken seriously.[31]

Ball's hope that his talks with de Gaulle would nudge the adminis-tration debate in his direction proved to be unfounded. "Since de Gaulle's views supported what I had been arguing to my colleagues," Ball recalled, "I hoped they would reinforce my position, but when I returned from Europe, I found Lyndon Johnson unimpressed, or at least unwilling to listen, as he was then preoccupied with strengthen-ing his domestic flanks." Specifically the president was continuing to think about introducing a resolution in Congress to gain backing for any escalation in Vietnam that he might authorize. In this endeavor Ball would play a central role.[32]

The famous occasion for the passage in Congress of the resolution on Vietnam was an episode (or episodes, allegedly) that occurred in the Gulf of Tonkin, off the coast of North Vietnam, in early August 1964. On the morning of Sunday the 2nd, the U.S. destroyer *Maddox* re-ported that it was under attack from North Vietnamese patrol craft and was returning fire. Johnson, who received the news while still in his bedroom, must have been surprised by such Communist aggression. The *Maddox* was not part of the relatively threatening covert operation 34-A in which the United States organized naval attacks on North Vietnam in boats manned by the South Vietnamese (and sometimes by Americans as well). Rather the *Maddox* was in the Gulf of Tonkin as part of another clandestine initiative approved by Johnson, the De Soto patrols, which conducted surveillance by steaming close to the North Vietnamese coast to cause the activation of Communist radar installations. The radar locations could then be electronically estab-lished by the American ship involved.[33]

It must have been clear to Johnson that the North Vietnamese may have mistaken the *Maddox* as an attack vessel, for a 34-A-type attack had been carried out against the North on July 30–31. This consider-ation accounts in part for the president's moderation in the White House meeting with senior advisers, including Ball, in the late morn-ing of August 2. "We concluded that an overeager North Vietnamese boat commander might have been at fault or that a shore station had miscalculated," recalled Johnson. "So we decided against retaliation." As Dean Rusk recorded in his memoirs, Johnson's reaction to the attack on the *Maddox* on August 2 gives the lie to those who claim the president was from the outset hellbent on using events in the Gulf of Tonkin to escalate the war. As he announced at a press conference on August 3, Johnson did decide to show resolve by ordering an additional destroyer to join the *Maddox* in continuing patrols off the North Vietnamese coast, instructing them to retaliate if attacked. But LBJ's overall response to the incident on August 2 was restrained.[34]

That restraint evaporated on August 4 when he received a report that North Vietnamese ships had now fired at the *Maddox* and the *C. Turner Joy*. Such provocation required a retaliatory U.S. strike, Johnson believed, and it created an opportunity to seek congressional backing for his actions in Vietnam. The problem that soon emerged, though, was the authenticity of this second attack. By the early afternoon the on-scene U.S. naval commander in the Gulf had warned that unusual weather effects on radar and other factors might account for the impression that U.S. vessels were under attack when in fact they were not.[35]

For more than four decades the events of August 4 in the Gulf of Tonkin have been disputed. Did the alleged attack take place or not? That has been the question. In the last decade or so a consensus has begun to form that there was no such assault. According to Edwin Moise in his 1996 study on the subject, evidence suggests that no attack occurred, a view echoed three years later by Fredrik Logevall in *Choosing War*. Robert Schulzinger has also argued that there probably was no attack, and John Prados, who in 2003 secured the declassification of U.S. naval intercepts of North Vietnamese radio communications, upon which McNamara ultimately rested his contention that there had been a Communist attack on the American ships, categorically concludes that no assault took place on August 4. For one thing, the North Vietnamese radio messages actually refer to the attack on U.S. shipping on August 2.[36]

Only decades after the event, however, has all this become clear. It does not follow that Johnson deliberately set out to manufacture a crisis in August 1964. At the time, he was presented with reports that the attack might not have occurred, but also reports that it had. His not unreasonable assessment of the balance of evidence was that it probably had taken place. The fact that the *Maddox* had already been attacked on August 2 no doubt led him to that conclusion.

Johnson's error was in making that judgment too hastily. When he spoke with his advisers in the early evening of August 4, with congressional leaders immediately after that, and to the American people shortly before midnight, he did so believing that the attack had definitely occurred, hence U.S. reprisals were justified. Johnson brings to mind Henry V in the court scene in Shakespeare's play: from his advisers he wanted good arguments for taking military action against an enemy, but he was not concerned whether they were watertight.[37]

That leaves the question as to why the president was in such a hurry to order a retaliatory strike and to enlist congressional support for his policies. A desire to send a signal to Ho Chi Minh that the United States would not be pushed around was one motivation. But Johnson's calculations included domestic as well as international considerations. In a conversation on the morning of August 4 with Kenneth O'Donnell, Johnson agreed with JFK's old acolyte that unless he responded forcefully to the Communist challenge in the Gulf of Tonkin he would leave himself vulnerable to accusations of weakness from the right and its representative who had just won the Republican presidential nomination, Barry Goldwater.[38]

In addition to the campaign against Goldwater that lay ahead in the autumn, Johnson was concerned about Congress. Uppermost in his mind was the trouble Harry Truman had encountered by going to war in Korea without seeking congressional approval. "If we stay in South Vietnam much longer or have to take firmer action," he told his advisers shortly after taking over the presidency, "we've got to go to Congress." Getting Congress on board would nullify its ability to challenge Johnson's policies in Vietnam, at least for a time, and legitimize the president's actions.[39]

Once Johnson had decided how to react to perceived events in the Gulf of Tonkin, the implementation of his policy choices was straightforward. A retaliatory strike successfully destroyed a number of North Vietnamese boats and oil storage tanks. After its introduction in Congress, the Tonkin Gulf Resolution passed quickly and decisively—by 88 to 2 in the Senate, and unanimously in the House. The resolution authorized Johnson to "take all necessary measures to repel any armed attack against the forces of the United States and to prevent further aggression," and declared that the United States was "prepared, as the President determines, to take all necessary steps, including the use of armed force, to assist any member or protocol state of the Southeast Asia Collective Defense Treaty requesting assistance in defense of its freedom." It was the blank check from Congress that Johnson had sought.[40]

Three days after passage of the resolution, the president met with his advisers in the Cabinet Room. He wanted to express, he told them, "his basic satisfaction with what had been accomplished in the last week. . . . The reaction from Congress was good, and also from the people, judging by the polls." He went on to say that further U.S. military action might be required. He "did not wish to escalate just because the public liked what happened last week. We would have to pick our own ground; nonetheless, instead of letting the other side have the ball, we should be prepared to take it. He asked for prompt study and recommendations as to ways this might be done with maximum results and minimum danger. He did not believe that the existing situation would last very long." The president's comments were ambiguous. While he indicated that the United States might soon have to seize the initiative in Vietnam, he wanted to do so in a way that incurred few risks—"minimum danger," as he put it.[41]

This ambivalence was no doubt a true expression of Johnson's feelings at this juncture. He continued to display caution. On August 4 he stated clearly in his address to the American people that U.S. retaliation to the Gulf of Tonkin incident was to be limited: "We still seek no wider war." As he had told congressional leaders earlier that same evening, "We want them to know we are not going to take it lying down, but [also that] we are not going to destroy their cities." Johnson probably also wished to assure the Chinese that he had no desire to draw them into the conflict. In deciding on the precise nature of the retaliation, moreover, he rejected advice to bomb ships in Haiphong harbor or to mine it.[42]

Despite elements of prudence in his decision-making, Johnson's use of events in the Gulf of Tonkin to secure a congressional resolution sanctioning greater U.S. involvement in Vietnam took him a step closer to war. Rather than opposing Johnson's actions in August 1964—if opposed was how he felt—George Ball remained silent. Given the letter he had sent Dean Rusk at the end of May, explaining his reservations about escalation in Vietnam, his dissent could have been anticipated. But it was not forthcoming.

At key meetings on dealing with the Tonkin incident, Ball often said nothing—at the National Security Council sessions with the president on the afternoon of August 4, and in the postmortem meeting on August 10. Surprisingly, Ball opposed neither the retaliatory strike on North Vietnam after the presumed attack on the 4th, nor the introduction of the Tonkin Gulf Resolution. Years later Ball explained his decision to back the resolution by saying he "just felt . . . 'Let's go get this authority.' It didn't seem to me that implied in this was much more than that. 'Let's get some authority from Congress,' rather than act entirely—again, this was perhaps a lawyer's instinct—on the basis of the implied powers of the President, war powers of the President. I just thought we ought to tidy up. That was really what it was."[43]

At the time, though, Ball could not have viewed the resolution as such a trivial matter. Its language was sweeping, the authority handed to Johnson considerable. Congressional hearings on the resolution made this clear. Asked by Senator John Sherman Cooper of Kentucky whether he believed the resolution permitted Johnson to take the nation to war in Vietnam, Senator William Fulbright replied, "That's the way I would interpret it." The Tonkin Gulf Resolution entrenched vast authority in Johnson's hands, the exercise of which could lead America into war. And Ball knew it.[44]

Ball's phone conversations after the attack on the *Maddox* revealed his own preoccupation with domestic politics. On the morning of August 3 he told McNamara that the Republican leader in the Senate, Everett Dirksen, was "starting to stir this thing up. . . . Once the Senate cranks up today they will blow this up a little." A few minutes later he warned McGeorge Bundy that "the Republicans might want to take off on this in some speeches this afternoon and it could get touchy."

Clearly Ball feared that the Republicans would exploit Communist aggression in the Gulf in order to embarrass the president. Given that
concern, a resolution—demonstrating Johnson's resolve—would help
thwart the president's opponents on Capitol Hill.[45]

Ball not only supported the resolution but was active in its drafting.
In later years he would try to distance himself from his role in producing the text. He claimed to have had only "a slight hand in tinkering
with the language," and in his memoirs he neglected to mention that
he had played any part in its drafting. One has the impression of a man
embarrassed at his involvement in a measure that authorized U.S. escalation in Vietnam, his opposition to which had brought him so much
praise.[46]

Ball's fingerprints, however, were all over the resolution. Johnson
recalled that it was Ball and Rusk who did the bulk of the work on it.
William Bundy said it was Ball and State Department legal adviser
Abram Chayes who "did the principal drafting." Rusk told William
Bundy on August 5 that Ball and McGeorge Bundy were "going over
the final touches" to the resolution. Ball thus provided much of the language that legitimized the president's right to wage war in Vietnam.[47]

In his memoirs Johnson wrote, "My first major decision on Vietnam had been to reaffirm President Kennedy's policies. This was my
second major decision: to order retaliation against the Tonkin Gulf attacks and to seek a congressional resolution in support of our Southeast Asia policy." On neither decision did Ball dissent.[48]

It was after the Tonkin resolution that Ball began to provide the sort
of vigorous opposition to U.S. policy in Vietnam on which his historical reputation rests. Even then he was neither as bold nor as consistent
as might be assumed. Nevertheless, that fall represented a watershed for
Ball: previously halting and hesitant, he became more willing to explain
at length his unease over the administration's policies.

The turning point was a long memorandum entitled "How Valid
Are the Assumptions Underlying Our Vietnam Policies?" that Ball sent
to Rusk, McNamara, and McGeorge Bundy on October 5. It was a
thorough, wide-ranging, intellectually credible, and—to anyone convinced of the need to respond forcefully to the Communist challenge
in Vietnam—shocking piece of work.[49]

Of significance is not only Ball's analysis but the document's origins: there is strong evidence that it was written in response to encouragement from the president that Ball play the role of devil's advocate. Was Ball, then, to some extent an artificial opponent of the war? Without Johnson's nudging, would Ball's dissent have moved beyond his sporadic resistance to American policy represented by his exchange with Kennedy in the autumn of 1961 and his letter to Rusk in the spring of 1964? Ball detested subsequent accusations that his opposition to the war was contrived, insisting it was heartfelt. To be sure, there was a chicken-and-egg dimension here. Johnson encouraged Ball to articulate alternatives to American policy, but he did so in part because he knew of Ball's misgivings over U.S. escalation in Vietnam. Nonetheless, unlike the other episodes of dissent examined in this book, Ball's was to some degree dissent by presidential invitation.[50]

The key meeting in defining Ball's role as the Cassandra of the Johnson administration took place on September 19. Ten days earlier the president had agreed to resume naval patrols in the Tonkin Gulf, which had been halted after the August episode. He was prepared to retaliate if the Communists attacked American forces, or if a large-scale North Vietnamese–Viet Cong assault on South Vietnam were mounted. When on September 18 the White House received reports that the U.S. destroyers *Morton* and *Edwards* had been attacked in the Gulf of Tonkin while on a De Soto patrol, the issue of reprisals arose. Johnson displayed commendable caution. McGeorge Bundy noted at the time that the president was "very skeptical about the evidence to date. . . . [He] made it clear that he was not interested in rapid escalation on so frail evidence and with a very fragile government in South Vietnam." Johnson was right to be wary: later reports cast doubt on whether an attack had taken place.[51]

Mulling the matter over with his advisers on September 19, Johnson "continued to make clear his very grave doubt that there had been any hostile vessels, let alone an intent to attack." McNamara, however, thought it important for Johnson to demonstrate American resolve by sending another De Soto patrol into the Gulf of Tonkin. That recommendation horrified Ball:

Mr. President, I urge you not to make that decision. Suppose one of those destroyers is sunk with several hundred men aboard. Inevitably, there'll be a Congressional investigation. What would your defense be? Everyone knows the De Soto Patrols have no intelligence mission that couldn't be accomplished just as well by planes or small boats at far less risk. The evidence will strongly suggest that you sent those ships up the Gulf only to provoke attack so we could retaliate. Just think what Congress and the press would do with that! They'd say you deliberately used American boys as decoy ducks and that you threw away lives just so you'd have an excuse to bomb. Mr. President, you couldn't live with that.[52]

Johnson said he found Ball's argument convincing. But when Gen. Earle Wheeler and Rusk argued that the patrols should be continued in order to show North Vietnam that the United States would not allow itself to be driven from the area, the president saw merit in that approach too. He then indicated that he liked the idea of Ball dissecting the proposition that had been advanced. "At some time in the future," he observed,

> a brutal prosecutor like Tom Dewey might be asking how we got into these troubles [in Vietnam], and he wanted to be sure that the answers would be good. He reminded the group of the Pearl Harbor hearing, and said that he did not wish to have his people playing tennis or riding horseback when they should be available for crucial decisions. . . . [He] then instructed Secretary McNamara and General Wheeler to prepare a general argument showing the justification for further de Soto patrols, and including both military arguments and political arguments like those of Secretary Rusk. He asked that Secretary Ball serve as critic of the argument thus developed so that he could make a judgment on the matter.[53]

Johnson's approach to this question spurred Ball to action, for he now began to compose his first major memorandum opposing U.S. escalation in Vietnam. Working into the night over a two-week period, Ball—realizing the sensitivity of a document that would challenge the

premises of American policy in Vietnam—dictated most of the memorandum into a tape recorder in the library of his home, away from the
State Department. Only his principal assistant and two or three secretaries were aware of his undertaking. On October 5 Ball sent copies of
the sixty-seven-page memorandum to Rusk, McNamara, and McGeorge
Bundy, and placed two copies in his safe. He decided against sending the
memorandum to Johnson.[54]

What Rusk, McNamara, and Bundy read was a bravura critique of
U.S. policy. Ball began by describing four options for the Johnson administration: (a) continue its current approach; (b) deploy troops in
South Vietnam; (c) bomb North Vietnam; or (d) work toward a negotiated settlement. The first option would fail, he predicted, resulting in
the ejection of U.S. forces by a neutralist coup in Saigon, or the adoption of one of the other three options. The second option of sending
American ground forces to South Vietnam was unappealing too, as it
would increase opposition in Vietnam to the United States and lead to
substantial American casualties. Only the third and fourth strategies,
therefore, merited attention; and it was to an evaluation of air strikes
versus diplomacy that Ball devoted the remainder of his paper.[55]

Bombing North Vietnam, Ball asserted, would fail. It would neither
bring about a more stable South Vietnamese government nor discour-
age Hanoi from assisting the Viet Cong. Moreover, air strikes against
North Vietnam would cause Hanoi to retaliate by sending large numbers of troops into the South. This, in turn, would compel Johnson to
send ground forces into the South to prop up the Saigon government.[56]

It was a mistake, therefore, for the Johnson administration to assume that it could calibrate the conflict in Vietnam with sufficient precision to ensure that the Communist response to American intensification of the war would be acceptable or desirable. On the contrary,
escalation would be inevitable:

> It is in the nature of escalation that each move passes the option to
> the other side, while at the same time the party which seems to be
> losing will be tempted to keep raising the ante. To the extent that
> the response to a move can be controlled, that move is probably in-

effective. If the move is effective, it may not be possible to control— or accurately anticipate—the response.

Once on the tiger's back we cannot be sure of picking the place to dismount.[57]

These words would turn out to be prescient. Ball also grasped the salient motive behind the determination of many administration officials to prevail in Vietnam: credibility. "In spite of the strategic importance of the real estate involved," he wrote, "our primary motive in supporting the Government of South Viet Nam is unquestionably political. It is to make clear to the whole Free World that we will assist any nation that asks us our help in defending itself against Communist aggression." Ball cited Robert Kennedy's comment—that if the United States did not deter communism in Vietnam no one would believe its promise to defend West Berlin—as an example of how U.S. officials had spread the idea that Vietnam was a key test of America's role as protector of freedom throughout the world. Ball's reference to Robert Kennedy was an astute piece of psychology, for he was well aware of Johnson's antipathy for Bobby. What better way to discredit a position in Johnson's eyes than by associating it with Robert Kennedy.[58]

Rather than believing that escalation in Vietnam would prove that America was true to its word, Ball claimed, many of the nation's allies thought it was being drawn into

a fruitless struggle in South Viet-Nam—a struggle we are bound to lose. They fear that, as we become too deeply involved in a war on the land mass of Asia, we will tend to lose interest in their problems. They believe that we would be foolish to risk bogging ourselves down in the Indo-China jungle. They fear a general loss of confidence in American judgment that could result if we pursued a course which many regarded as neither prudent nor necessary.

What we might gain by establishing the steadfastness of our commitments we could lose by an erosion of confidence in our judgment.[59]

Ball now sketched the outlines of a diplomatic settlement that could extricate the United States from Vietnam at minimum cost. Realistically he acknowledged that any settlement would require the removal of American forces, though such a withdrawal might be phased. The Saigon government would have to become a coalition that would include the Viet Cong. An international commission could be established to ensure that such a settlement was enforced. Ball concluded by asserting that a root-and-branch review of U.S. policy in Vietnam was vital: "It is essential that this be done before we commit military forces to a line of action that could put events in the saddle and destroy our freedom to choose the policies that are at once the most effective and the most prudent."[60]

McNamara, Bundy, and Rusk responded frostily to Ball's memorandum. They seemed more concerned that the paper might be leaked than in debating the arguments it contained. McNamara, in particular, viewed it with repugnance. Ball recalled that the secretary of defense was "absolutely horrified. He treated it like a poisonous snake. . . . He really just regarded it as next to treason, that this had been put down on paper." Nevertheless McNamara, with Rusk and Bundy, agreed to devote two Saturdays to a discussion of the memorandum with Ball. His three colleagues were so dismissive of his paper in the first of those scheduled sessions, on November 7, that Ball decided to cancel the second. They made clear that they were "dead set against the views I presented and uninterested in the point-by-point discussion I had hoped to provoke."[61]

Three decades later McNamara revealed that he and the others had been skeptical because Ball was seen as a Europeanist and hence an adviser who did not regard Asian matters as important for American foreign policy. But McNamara acknowledged that they should have been more receptive to Ball's ideas: "George's memo represented the effort of an honest man pushing a series of propositions that deserved thorough debate at the highest levels. He had our respect—but he deserved more than that." The memorandum should have been discussed with Ball, McNamara reflected, and passed on to the State Department, the Pentagon, the CIA, and the NSC for their assessment.[62]

McNamara, Bundy, and Rusk may have wanted to keep Ball's memorandum under wraps, but news of it apparently reached the press with great alacrity. James Reston of the *New York Times* had called Michael Forrestal, as Forrestal revealed to Ball the next day, to ask "when the high-level review of Viet-Nam policy was going to be held." When Forrestal pleaded ignorance, Reston insisted "there was something going on; that he has it from the highest authority that there is a 'devil's advocate'; that work was being done on contingency plans in this situation." Reston had neither Ball's name nor knowledge of his October 5 memorandum, but he knew of an official with the role that Ball was now playing. The reference to the "highest authority" indicates that Johnson himself, who presumably knew of Ball's memorandum even if he had not read it by this point, had tipped off Reston. Shrewdly the president must have calculated that by making clear he was in favor of a devil's advocate, the press would be less likely to think Ball's dissent represented a lack of unity within the administration. Later in the year Joseph Alsop learned that it was Ball who had challenged American policy in Vietnam. He chose the occasion to write a column deriding Ball's knowledge of Asian affairs.[63]

Ball's memorandum thus caused a few ripples but failed in its basic objective—to generate an extensive review of the U.S. position in Vietnam. Ball's analysis was perceptive, prescient, and important. His tactics in presenting it, however, were flawed. He should have sent it not only to McNamara, Rusk, and Bundy but to the president as well. He claimed that he did not wish to burden Johnson in the midst of a presidential campaign, only a month before the election. But by not doing so he made it easier for his colleagues to disregard his paper, for among all those senior officials it was Johnson who might have been most sympathetic to his views. Despite the Tonkin Gulf Resolution, Johnson had exhibited a good deal of wariness on Vietnam. As things turned out, the president would not see Ball's memorandum until February 1965.

The silver lining for Ball in late 1964 was the prudence the president continued to display as tensions mounted in Vietnam. In the wake of a Viet Cong assault on the American air base at Bien Hoa, north of Saigon, Johnson resisted pressure from the Joint Chiefs in early November to retaliate against the North. When a number of Americans were killed in an attack on a U.S. officers' billet in Saigon on Christmas

Eve, he remained immune to the arguments of those advisers who insisted he respond with force.[64]

Despite Johnson's caution, the pressure for escalation mounted. Most troubling was the fact that by the end of the year the administration had learned that organized battalions of uniformed North Vietnamese troops were being deployed in the South. This made the position of the Saigon government more precarious than ever. As 1965 dawned, there was a palpable sense in Washington that concrete decisions by the president could not be postponed much longer, that the fork in the road had almost been reached. A reluctant Johnson would soon be forced to make the decision he had been dreading—to fight a full-scale land war in Vietnam. Ball's dissent would intensify in the early months of 1965 as that moment approached.[65]

CHAPTER 14

Crossing the Rubicon

"In our anxiety to build up support for the
struggle in South Viet-Nam, we have tended to
exaggerate the consequences for US power and
prestige of a tactical withdrawal from South
Viet-Nam. . . . By and large, the world knows that
the government in Saigon is a joke, and if our
withdrawal resulted from an effort to face this
problem squarely, friendly nations would not
interpret it as a US failure to keep its
commitments. More likely most nations would
consider that we had more than kept our
commitments to Viet-Nam—and that our decision
to force the issue of stability was a mark of
prudence and maturity."—GEORGE BALL,
memorandum, "Cutting Our Losses in
South Viet-Nam," June 28, 1965

By 1965 the pressure on Johnson for decisive action in Vietnam had
intensified. In early January Maxwell Taylor, now ambassador in Saigon,
pulled no punches in telling the president that "we are presently on a
losing track and must risk a change. . . . To take no positive action is to
accept defeat in the fairly near future." On the 27th McGeorge Bundy
provided the president with a memorandum explaining that he and Mc-
Namara had reached an important conclusion: it was time for Johnson

to abandon the middle course (between withdrawal and war) he had been pursuing, and step up the military pressure on the Communists. In large measure, Bundy said, this had to be done to shore up the confidence of the tottering South Vietnamese government. After reading this memorandum, Johnson sent Bundy to Saigon to report on the situation there and to consider U.S. strikes on North Vietnam. While Bundy was there, the Viet Cong attacked the American base at Pleiku, killing eight Americans and wounding more than a hundred. Johnson's administration now went into crisis mode, and the president himself moved toward the decision that would make an American war in Vietnam unavoidable: he would authorize the bombing of North Vietnam.[1]

When the news from Pleiku arrived, Johnson called a meeting of the National Security Council on the evening of February 6. The favored retaliatory measure was for U.S. planes to strike three targets in North Vietnam, and for the South Vietnamese to attack a fourth. The idea received almost unanimous backing from the sixteen officials present, with Johnson himself making clear his own belief that this action was essential.[2]

As he had at the onset of Johnson's presidency and during the Gulf of Tonkin episode, Ball did not flag his opposition to U.S. escalation at this important meeting. "We are all in accord," he said to his colleagues,

> that action must be taken. We need to decide how we shall handle the air strikes publicly. The Soviets may call for a conference. We must make clear that the North Vietnamese and the Viet Cong are the same. We retaliate against North Vietnam because Hanoi directs the Viet Cong, supplies arms, and infiltrates men. We need to answer the question as to why we are striking North Vietnam when the Americans were attacked by Viet Cong in South Vietnam.

The diplomatic fallout from U.S. air strikes on North Vietnam and matters of policy presentation appeared to preoccupy Ball, not whether the strikes should be authorized in the first place.[3]

Ball later explained that he supported the air strikes against North Vietnam for tactical reasons, not out of conviction: "The demand for prompt retaliation was overwhelming and I realized that further frontal opposition would be not only futile but tactically unwise. I could gain nothing by antagonizing my colleagues if the President could no longer be deterred." Ball may have been right: opposition to a retaliatory measure that seemed so justified given the provocation at Pleiku might have eroded his credibility and reduced his future effectiveness. Yet this was an occasion when dissent from Ball would have received support from a notable figure, Senator Mike Mansfield, whom Johnson had asked to attend the meeting. "The North Vietnamese attack has opened many eyes," Mansfield declared. "We are not now in a penny ante game. It appears that the local populous in South Vietnam is not behind us, else the Viet Cong could not have carried out their surprise attack." That came as a jarring note after the unanimity that had preceded it. But it fell on deaf ears, as Johnson responded by simply announcing, "The strike on the four targets was authorized." If Ball had backed Mansfield, he would not have prevented Johnson from proceeding with the air strikes. But it might have generated a discussion of the pros and cons of such an approach. That, in turn, might have prompted Johnson to move with less haste to his next step, a sustained bombing campaign against North Vietnam.[4]

Because of fog, only one of the four planned retaliatory strikes took place. At a meeting between the president and his advisers on the morning of February 7, it was agreed that, apart from the attack to be made by the South Vietnamese air force, the strikes that had not yet been carried out should be canceled. "We all felt that a second-day strike by U.S. planes might give Hanoi and Moscow the impression that we had begun a sustained air offensive," Johnson later wrote. "That decision had not been made." Here was a vestige of the prudence that had earlier been the hallmark of Johnson's handling of the situation in Vietnam.[5]

That commendable caution evaporated in a meeting the following morning, called by the president to weigh the report submitted by Mc-George Bundy on his return from Vietnam. Bundy's report urged Johnson to authorize a prolonged bombing campaign against North Vietnam on the grounds that it would immediately boost morale in the South and might dent Hanoi's confidence for the long run. At the meeting on the 8th there were differences of opinion about the speed with which the bombing campaign—Rolling Thunder, as it became known—should be implemented, but there was general agreement on the necessity of the operation. Johnson summed up the discussion by saying "we face a choice of going forward or running. We have chosen the first alternative."[6]

As Johnson concluded, a group of congressional leaders, invited to bring about bipartisan support, joined the meeting. The president explained that in December a plan to pressure North Vietnam had been postponed to provide time for strengthening the Saigon government. "We are now ready to return to our program of pushing forward in an effort to defeat North Vietnamese aggression without escalating the war." After Bundy's report was summarized for the congressional leadership, Johnson went on to assert that the Tonkin Gulf Resolution "plus the legal power of the Presidency made it possible for him to carry out on a manageable level an effort to deter, destroy and diminish the strength of the North Vietnamese aggressors and to try to convince them to leave South Vietnam alone."[7]

Worried that the South was about to fall to the Communists; no longer discouraged by an upcoming presidential election from upping the ante in Vietnam; surrounded by advisers who exhorted him to escalate, Johnson's views hardened in early 1965. The decision to launch Operation Rolling Thunder was the clearest sign of that.

It is easy to think of Rolling Thunder as another milestone, like the Tonkin Gulf Resolution, on the road to Johnson's war in Vietnam. But it was much more than that. It made war inevitable, as it meant that Johnson would have to dispatch U.S. troops to Vietnam. As the veteran Democrat Clark Clifford wrote in his memoirs:

> No connection between bombing the North and sending American ground troops was recognized and discussed *before* the bombing began. . . . Here was the greatest failure in the entire decision-making process. History sometimes turns not on what was considered, but on what was *ignored*. Such was the case in February 1965.
>
> In none of the discussions leading up to Rolling Thunder was the President told, either by the Joint Chiefs of Staff or his Sec-

retary of Defense, that once bombing of the North began, the military would require, and demand, American combat troops, first to protect the American air bases from which the bombing was launched, and then, inevitably, to begin offensive operations against the enemy.[8]

Johnson was under the dangerous illusion that he could bomb North Vietnam without going to war. One official, however, had considered carefully the likelihood that a U.S. bombing campaign would lead to the deployment of American troops, and that official was George Ball. That observation had been a salient point in his October 1964 memorandum, which Rusk, Bundy, McNamara, but not Johnson had read. If anyone was capable of telling the president on that morning in early February that bombing would lead to troops and thus war, it was Ball. But he failed to do so. He reported to his colleagues about discussions on Vietnam with Russian officials, and a letter that had been sent to the UN secretary general explaining American actions in that part of the world. But he did not speak against Rolling Thunder.[9]

Perhaps Ball was again thinking tactically. It is clear from the stand he took during the remainder of February that he viewed U.S. escalation in Vietnam with increasing skepticism. But with Johnson and his advisers so determined to proceed with Rolling Thunder, he may have felt that dissent on this occasion would leave him dangerously isolated. That may have been a misjudgment. As the stakes were so high—war or peace, the credibility of American foreign policy, the future of Johnson's presidency—this was not a time for reticence. Ball should probably have been less cautious. Had he told Johnson that the bombing of North Vietnam would lead inevitably to U.S. troop deployments in the South, and asked the president whether he was therefore ready to go to war, Johnson would have had a keener sense of the consequences of his decision. After February 8 Ball would articulate his dissent on Vietnam more openly and with greater vigor. But by then the die had been cast. Johnson confirmed on February 13 that Rolling Thunder would proceed, and on March 2 a hundred aircraft bombed an ammunition depot in the North. But it was on February 8 that Johnson made the crucial decision, and Ball, for all his foresight and acuity, did nothing to give him pause.[10]

In the days that followed, however, he became increasingly vocal in his opposition. The first instance of this came on February 10 when news arrived that a Viet Cong attack on enlisted men's barracks at Qui Nhon had killed some Americans and injured others. In a discussion between administration officials before Johnson joined the meeting, McNamara demanded U.S. strikes on three targets in North Vietnam. Supported by Ambassador Thompson, Ball urged caution: he suggested postponing these retaliatory strikes until Soviet Premier Alexei Kosygin, who was visiting North Korea and about to head to China, had left the Far East. A U.S. counterattack while Kosygin was in the region, Ball feared, would put pressure on the Russians to lend a helping hand to North Vietnam. And any retaliation to the attack at Qui Nhon should be carried out by the South Vietnamese, not by U.S. forces. When the president arrived, Ball continued to make these points but succeeded only in persuading Johnson, McNamara, and the others that the strikes be confined to two, not three, targets.[11]

Three days later Ball again advocated a moderate approach, in a memorandum to Johnson after discussions with McNamara, McGeorge Bundy, and Ambassador-at-Large Llewellyn Thompson. Ball drew the president's attention to the differences between his and Thompson's position and that of McNamara and Bundy. While all agreed on the need to bomb North Vietnam in order to press the Communists toward a political solution, Ball and Thompson did not believe it would compel Hanoi to halt the insurgency in the South. Ball also highlighted the risks involved in increased bombing of the North, particularly the provocation of the Chinese, and recommended the use of the UN Security Council and an international conference as forums in which an overall settlement to the conflict in Vietnam could be sought. A diplomatic strategy was essential, Ball argued, to "make clear to the world that our objectives are peace and freedom," and to "pre-empt a probable peace offensive by the Communists."[12]

Johnson reacted oddly and, from Ball's point of view, disappointingly to this memorandum. At a meeting with Ball, Thompson, and Bundy, LBJ read the memorandum with alacrity before asking Ball to explain the logic behind his arguments. Without further comment, Johnson thanked Ball and returned his paper to him. "Why he followed that uncharacteristic course," Ball later wrote, "I do not know."[13]

In a phone conversation two days later, Johnson's dismissive attitude toward Ball's recommendations was again apparent. Negotiations to end the crisis in Vietnam did not appeal, the president explained. He was "not happy with the thought of our saying, 'pop, pop, pop, sending up three airplanes,['] and then saying, [']come on into my living room and let's talk.'" This would be "a great indication of weakness." Ball disagreed: "It is a matter of whether it is better for us to take the [diplomatic] initiative. In the Cuban missile crisis we went into the UN first and at the time we were showing strength."[14]

Given that he had earlier encouraged Ball to play the role of devil's advocate, Johnson's frosty response to Ball's February 13 memorandum is difficult to fathom. Perhaps the most plausible explanation is that the president was troubled by Ball's decision to collaborate with Thompson on this occasion in articulating his opposition. Having Ball as a lone dissenting voice in his administration squared with Johnson's belief that all views on Vietnam should be expressed. But that did not mean he wanted his undersecretary seeking allies, building a constituency for his views, and forcing other officials (such as McNamara and Bundy) to define their position in relation to Ball's. That, Johnson might have feared, could cause deep divisions within his administration. Despite the encouragement he had given to Ball's nonconformism, Johnson—like Shakespeare's Lear—was obsessed with the unity and loyalty of those close to him.

It was better that Johnson had authorized the dissent of one official than of none. But it would have been better still if he had given Ball free rein to generate a continuous discussion with other senior officials on the merits of his arguments, and perhaps win converts. This would have given Ball the opportunity (albeit a slight one) to prevail in the administration debate on Vietnam, and at the very least to subject the assumptions of Johnson, McNamara, and others to the sort of rigorous scrutiny that could only have been salutary.

Johnson's reaction to his memorandum only increased Ball's determination to pressure the president to change course in Vietnam. Using

his October 1964 memorandum—which Johnson still had not read—
was, he decided, the way to do it. On February 24, therefore, he handed
close Johnson aide Bill Moyers the October document at lunch. Moyers read it and was, Ball recalled, "struck by it and insisted—as I had assumed he would—on giving it to the President that afternoon." The
next morning Moyers called Ball to report that Johnson had read the
memorandum twice, "found it fascinating and wanted to know why he
had not read it before."[15]

LBJ convened a meeting on February 26 to consider Ball's views. It
became clear that he had read the paper with great care. "He challenged specific points I had made," noted Ball, "and even remembered
the page numbers where those arguments occurred." But it was Mc-
Namara who took the lead in confronting Ball: he insisted that the undersecretary had exaggerated the difficulties facing the United States in
Vietnam. McNamara presented a plethora of statistics to prove his
case. The meeting was long; Ball's arguments received the sort of close
attention that had been conspicuously lacking from the discussion of
his February paper. But all of this was to no avail. As Ball himself put
it, "My hope to force a systematic reexamination of our total situation
had manifestly failed."[16]

By early March Ball's fears about the inevitable consequences of
Rolling Thunder were becoming justified: Johnson had authorized the
deployment of two Marine battalions to protect the U.S. air base at
Danang. These forces were only to defend the perimeter of the base,
but it was an important step nonetheless: the first time American
ground troops had been used in the war in Vietnam. The principle
guiding Johnson's policies had been to use all means possible to bolster
the Saigon government—money, military advisers, and, since the in-
ception of Rolling Thunder, a bombing campaign, but not troops.
With the deployment at Danang, LBJ had crossed the Rubicon.[17]

After that Johnson accepted a series of recommendations from
senior advisers to intensify the pressure on the Communists. On March
15 he not only urged the Joint Chiefs to devise methods to "kill more
VC [Viet Cong]," he also endorsed most of the proposals made by Gen.
Howard K. Johnson, army chief of staff, upon his return from a mission
to Vietnam earlier in the month, including expanded bombing of the

North. After key National Security Council meetings on April 1 and 2, which Ball missed as he was in Paris on NATO business, Johnson sent two additional Marine battalions to Danang and Phu Bai, changed the mission of these troops from defensive to offensive, stepped up Operation Rolling Thunder, and agreed to an increase of between eighteen and twenty thousand U.S. logistical troops.[18]

Despite public backing for the bombing of the North that formed the centerpiece of Johnson's Vietnam strategy in 1965—February polls indicated 83 percent support—signs of discontent grew, both at home and abroad. Grumblings in Congress and the press could be heard, while India, France, and Sweden soon echoed the inevitable criticisms from the Communist bloc. In early April seventeen nonaligned nations issued an appeal for negotiations "as soon as possible, without . . . any preconditions," to end the turmoil in Vietnam.[19]

This pressure moved the president to deliver a conciliatory speech on April 7 at Johns Hopkins University. He pledged to participate in unconditional negotiations and spoke of his willingness to alleviate the poverty of the region by backing a billion-dollar New Deal–style development agency for the peoples along the Mekong River. He also made clear, however, that the sine qua non of any settlement (thus contradicting his promise for unconditional negotiations) was an independent—in other words, non-Communist—South Vietnam. Johnson's vision of peace and economic regeneration for Vietnam may have seemed like a glossy package, but there were strings attached. Not surprisingly, Ho Chi Minh's spokesmen dismissed the president's proposal.[20]

Despite his Johns Hopkins offer, the thrust of Johnson's policies in Vietnam was continued escalation. In mid-April he asked McNamara to chair a meeting of U.S. officials in Honolulu to formulate new strategic proposals. The consensus of the meeting was that bombing alone would not suffice. U.S. personnel would be needed to fight a ground war in the South. American forces should be increased, it was argued, to 82,000.[21]

Throughout the spring Ball had continued to despair at the U.S. course in Vietnam. "The options [there] are lousy," he groused to Senator Fulbright on March 4, "and . . . it has to be put on the political track." A month later he gave further expression to his desire for a

diplomatic approach in his draft—written at the president's request—
for the Johns Hopkins address. After the Honolulu proposals, Ball
again felt compelled to confront the president directly.[22]

Ball pleaded with the president to show prudence. "There might be
a chance of tranferring the contest," he argued, "from the battlefield to
the ballot." Johnson responded by asking Ball for a memorandum outlining a diplomatic settlement. "If you can pull a rabbit out of the hat,"
he said, "I'm all for it!"[23]

The result was Ball's paper of April 21, "Should We Try to Move
Toward a Vietnamese Settlement Now?" In this memorandum Ball
warned of the repercussions of an increase in U.S. military personnel
in South Vietnam. The war would become Americanized; there would
be more U.S. casualties; infiltration from the North would grow. Ball
also argued that Rolling Thunder had been ineffective. While morale
might have improved somewhat in Saigon and declined somewhat
among the Viet Cong, there was no evidence that the infiltration of the
North Vietnamese into the South had been impaired.[24]

It was important, Ball went on, for Johnson to work speedily for a
diplomatic settlement. "We cannot continue to bomb the North and
use napalm against South Vietnamese villages without a progressive
erosion of our world position," he asserted:

> This erosion will be limited if we appear to be moving toward some
> kind of political solution. But that will take more than words. . . .
>
> I doubt that the American people will be willing to accept sub-
> stantially increased casualties if the war continues over a substantial
> period of time and there are no signs of active diplomacy. Distaste-
> ful as it is, we must face the hard fact that large and articulate ele-
> ments in the intellectual community and other segments of United
> States opinion do not believe in our South Vietnamese policy. In
> fact, to many Americans our position appears far more ambiguous—
> and hence far more dubious—than in the Korean War.
>
> Until now, the American people have gone along out of their
> great confidence in you and because United States casualties have
> been less than a weekend's traffic accidents.
>
> But even a doubling of the casualties would begin to make a
> difference.[25]

The settlement that Ball proceeded to propose called for the Viet Cong to suspend its guerrilla warfare and for Hanoi to stop infiltrating men and military equipment into the South. This was to be reciprocated: U.S. bombing would be halted, as would American and South Vietnamese attacks on the Viet Cong. An international commission would be established to supervise this cease-fire. The Saigon government, meanwhile, would announce an amnesty, permitting all Viet Cong who wished to do so to return to the North. A date would be set for elections in which the Viet Cong would be allowed to participate. Once those elections in South Vietnam had produced a new government, the United States would withdraw. The reunification of Vietnam could take place if the South Vietnamese people and their government favored it. The outcome of the political process described by Ball, therefore, might be the very thing that Johnson was so desperate to avoid: a united Vietnam under Communist rule. But this would be preferable, Ball implied, to a protracted war that sapped American credibility.[26]

Ball's lucid and provocative memorandum merited serious consideration, but it was clear when he next met with the president that his arguments had failed to convince. LBJ would endorse a number of the recommendations flowing from the Honolulu talks, so that by the end of May U.S. forces in South Vietnam exceeded fifty thousand. Things looked gloomy to Ball, yet Johnson continued to give him just enough encouragement to allow him to believe his dissent could prove effective. Although rejecting the main thrust of Ball's April 21 memorandum, LBJ asked Moyers to convey to his undersecretary of state that he was still "very interested" in what he had been saying. On April 24 Moyers phoned Ball to report that Johnson had spoken with him that morning "about the necessity of getting people doing nothing for 3-4 days but thinking about political and peaceful alternatives" in Southeast Asia.[27]

Spurred on by this news, Ball invited Dean Acheson and Lloyd Cutler for discussions that produced a detailed memorandum fleshing out the program promoted by Ball on April 21. Seeking support for this program, Ball sent a close aide to Saigon to speak to Ambassador Taylor and his deputy, Alexis Johnson. These were the men who would have to persuade the South Vietnamese government to accept this plan of action if it were to have any chance of succeeding, so their backing was essential. But Taylor and Alexis Johnson "threw cold water all over it," as Ball bitterly recalled. His attempts in the spring of 1965 to find a route toward a diplomatic settlement in Vietnam had reached a dead end.[28]

By mid-June 1965 the situation in Vietnam had gone from bad to worse for Johnson. Infiltration of North Vietnamese forces into the South was growing, as was the success of the Viet Cong against the South Vietnamese Army. Not surprisingly, the clamor from Johnson's military advisers for more U.S. troops was deafening.

Ball's opposition now reached a fever pitch: he began to pepper the president with papers pleading for restraint. Despite the escalation authorized thus far in 1965, Ball still had reason to believe that LBJ might be receptive to his arguments. On June 14 the president had told him over the phone that "he particularly liked what Ball has been doing—raising the red flag and saying we ought to give thought to different approaches." Ball may have been less encouraged had he known of Johnson's reaction in May to a letter in which Clark Clifford had in effect endorsed what Ball was saying. "This could be a quagmire," Clifford wrote. "It could turn into an open ended commitment on our part that would take more and more ground troops, without a realistic hope of ultimate victory. . . . I continue to believe that the constant probing of every avenue leading to a possible settlement will ultimately be fruitful. It won't be what we want, but we can learn to live with it."[29]

Johnson did not even bother replying to Clifford—another indication that he could live with Ball's dissent but had no desire to see a more widespread skepticism among his advisers. His cold-shouldering of Vice President Hubert Humphrey for also casting doubt on the wisdom of U.S. escalation in Vietnam was a further example of Johnson's concern that a truly wide-ranging debate might threaten the basic unity of his administration.[30]

Ball had a good sense of Johnson's attitude, but with the situation in South Vietnam crumbling and the president professing his interest in hearing more from his undersecretary of state, Ball stepped up his campaign to bring LBJ and his advisers, as he saw it, to their senses. On June 18 he furnished Johnson with another memorandum, "Keeping the Power of Decision in the South Viet-Nam Crisis," in which he appeared to bow to the inevitable by suggesting the president permit an increase in American forces to 100,000 for a three-month period to see if this would make a difference in terms of winning the war. If at the end of those three months it seemed that the United States could prevail without unacceptably high casualties, the military effort against the Communists could be sustained. If, however, it appeared the United States could not win "without a vast protracted effort, you [Johnson] should seek means of limiting the American commitment and finding a political solution at a level below the total achievement of our declared objectives." Reducing U.S. political and military backing for the Saigon government and promoting elections in the South were methods that could be used to extricate America from the war in Vietnam.[31]

Although Ball defined alternative approaches for Johnson, it must have been clear to LBJ, reading between the lines of Ball's memorandum, that his undersecretary expected the war to continue to go badly, and that his essential suggestion was withdrawal. The French experience in the 1950s, Ball maintained, indicated that Johnson would fail if he took the nation into a full-scale land war:

> The French fought a war in Viet-Nam, and were finally defeated—after seven years of bloody struggle and when they still had 250,000 combat-hardened veterans in the field, supported by an army of 205,000 South Vietnamese.
>
> To be sure, the French were fighting a colonial war while we are fighting to stop aggression. But when we have put enough Americans on the ground in South Viet-Nam to give the appearance of a white man's war, the distinction as to our ultimate purpose will have less and less practical effect. . . .
>
> Ever since 1961—the beginning of our deep involvement in South Viet-Nam—we have met successive disappointments. We have tended to underestimate the strength and staying-power of the enemy. We have tended to overestimate the effectiveness of our sophisticated weapons under jungle conditions. We have watched the progressive loss of territory to Viet Cong control. We have

been unable to bring about the creation of a stable political base in Saigon.

This is no one's fault. It is in the nature of the struggle.

The French had much the same experience.

They quoted the same kind of statistics that guide our opinions—statistics as to the number of Viet Minh killed, the number of enemy defectors, the rate of enemy desertions, etc.[32]

Ball's reference to statistics was a clear dig at McNamara, who had a penchant for framing foreign-policy issues in quantitative terms. Ball knew he had to discredit the arguments of the imperious secretary of defense, whom Johnson much admired, if he were to win over the president to his way of thinking.

Johnson's reaction to this memorandum, conveyed by Bill Moyers to Ball, gave him hope that winning him over was still a possibility. Moyers said Johnson had agreed with much of the memorandum, and had added:

I don't think I should go over 100,000 [U.S. military personnel in South Vietnam] but think I should go to that number and explain it. I want George to work for the next 90 days—to work up what is going to happen after the monsoon season. I am not worried about riding off in the wrong direction. I agree that it might build-up bit by bit. I told McNamara that I would not make a decision on this and not to assume that I am willing to go overboard on this—I ain't. If there is no alternative, the fellow here with the program is the way I will probably go.[33]

That Johnson did not appear to reject outright Ball's June 18 arguments encouraged the undersecretary to continue the fight. Accordingly he reiterated the point at a meeting on the 23rd that U.S. forces should not exceed 100,000, and that if this did not work the United States should begin to withdraw. McNamara was appalled by such a notion, arguing that the sizable increase in U.S. troop deployment requested by Gen. William Westmoreland was the better approach. With Ball and McNamara at loggerheads, the president instructed both men to elaborate on their proposals in memoranda for his consideration.[34]

Predictably, McNamara's paper endorsed Westmoreland's request for 175,000 American troops in 1965 and more thereafter. No less predictably, Ball's memorandum, completed on June 28 and titled "Cutting Our Losses in South Viet-Nam," was diametrically opposed to McNamara's. Bombing North Vietnam would not achieve America's political objectives, he asserted, and there was no guarantee that sending many more American troops would be effective. Hence "we should undertake either to extricate ourselves or to reduce our defense perimeters in South Viet-Nam to accord with the capabilities of a limited US deployment." Infusing Ball's paper was a marked sense of urgency: "This is our last chance to make this decision."[35]

Ball went on to enumerate the means by which Johnson could get out of Vietnam. He should state that he would not send U.S. troops into combat in the South. He should make clear that as American support for the South was based on the idea that its government was effective and genuinely representative of the South Vietnamese people, he would consider reducing his commitment unless a more representative government, favoring broad socioeconomic and political reforms, was established within a month. Such a stance, Ball predicted, would prompt the Saigon government either to adopt a more nationalist position by declaring it would make do without U.S. backing, or to fall in favor of a new government willing to negotiate a settlement with the Viet Cong.[36]

Ball rejected the idea that cutting its losses in Vietnam in this fashion would dismay America's allies. On the contrary, they would regard it as a prudent measure. Moreover Johnson should not believe that such a step would besmirch his reputation as the leader of a great power: "any prudent military commander carefully selects the terrain on which to stand and fight, and no great captain has ever been blamed for a successful tactical withdrawal." As the jungles and rice paddies of South Vietnam nullified America's greater technological sophistication, as the Viet Cong were highly motivated, as the Saigon government was a shambles and the Hanoi government was not, "a deep commitment of United States forces in a land war in South Viet-Nam would be a catastrophic effort. If ever there was an occasion for a tactical withdrawal, this is it."[37]

Ball's June 28 memorandum represented a more strident declaration of his views. Ten days earlier, probably as a sop to hard-line sentiment, Ball had said U.S. forces could be augmented to 100,000 under trial conditions. Now he was more emphatic: the United States should simply get out of the mess that the conflict in South Vietnam had become.

Ball's paper was considered the following day at a meeting attended by key foreign policy officials, but not the president. The problem with his memorandum, said McNamara, was that it did not offer Johnson a credible way out of Vietnam. For his part, Ball highlighted the irrevocability of the decision that the administration was now contemplating: "if we commit U.S. troops to substantial combat, we pass a breaking-point."[38]

With the bit now securely between his teeth, Ball continued his campaign by memoranda on July 1 when he sent Johnson yet another paper, "A Compromise Solution for South Viet-Nam." As candid with LBJ as he had ever been, Ball argued that the administration was left with a choice between negotiating a settlement for a U.S. withdrawal from Vietnam, or fighting a guerrilla-style war in unfamiliar terrain that would result in defeat and humiliation. The former approach was plainly preferable. Johnson should therefore bypass the Saigon government and initiate talks with Hanoi, with a view to convening an international conference that would devise a settlement to the conflict. This diplomatic solution might include elections in South Vietnam. Ball rejected the idea that a U.S. withdrawal would damage America's status as a world leader and the credibility of its international commitments, such as to the defense of West Berlin.[39]

On July 1 McGeorge Bundy passed on to the president this memorandum from Ball, along with those from McNamara calling for a huge increase in the number of American troops sent to South Vietnam; from the State Department's William Bundy saying that U.S. troop levels should not exceed 85,000; and from Dean Rusk who argued that abandoning the South Vietnamese would encourage Communist aggression throughout the world. In transmitting these memoranda, McGeorge Bundy sought to persuade Johnson to dismiss Ball's arguments: "My hunch is that you will want to listen hard to George

Ball and then reject his proposal. Discussion could then move to the narrower choice between my brother's course and McNamara's."[40]

Ball's potential influence over the administration debate on Vietnam worried Bundy as well as the secretaries of state and defense. A few hours before Bundy gave Johnson this note, he had sent the president another in which he reported that "both Rusk and McNamara feel strongly that the George Ball paper should not be argued with you in front of any audience larger than yourself, Rusk, McNamara, Ball, and me. They feel that it is exceedingly dangerous to have this possibility reported in a wider circle." Like Johnson, his leading advisers were prepared to tolerate Ball's dissent but determined to limit his opportunity to proselytize his cause.[41]

Before deciding whether to commit America to a full-scale land war in Vietnam, Johnson dispatched McNamara to Saigon in mid-July to consult with both U.S. and South Vietnamese officials. On his return the secretary of defense gave the president clear advice: Johnson must go to war to save South Vietnam from falling to the Communists. U.S. forces should be increased to at least 175,000; another 100,000 might well need to be sent in 1966. Congressional approval should be sought for calling up the reserves and the National Guard. In essence, McNamara urged Johnson to go to war.[42]

LBJ now convened a series of meetings with advisers, reminiscent of the fraught ExComm sessions during the Cuban missile crisis. As in October 1962, tensions were high, the stakes were great. For George Ball, these meetings represented his final opportunity to dissuade Johnson from a course of action that in the end would destroy his presidency, divide America, damage U.S. credibility in the world, and contribute to the unraveling of the liberal consensus that Franklin Roosevelt had forged in the 1930s.

In the first of these crisis meetings, which took place in the Cabinet Room of the White House on the morning of July 21, Johnson urged prudence: "We must make no snap judgments. We must consider carefully all our options." McNamara proceeded to explain the extent of Viet Cong influence in South Vietnam, and—with General Wheeler, chairman of the Joint Chiefs—how U.S. forces would fight the VC. "Isn't it possible," Ball interjected, "that the VC will do what they did against the French—stay away from confrontation and not accommodate us?" Wheeler replied that the Viet Cong would not be able to avoid American troops. McNamara claimed that the South Vietnamese Army would be able to regain control of areas held by the Communists if the VC did not fight in large units.[43]

When Johnson asked whether anyone opposed the escalation proposed by McNamara, a somber Ball responded: "I can foresee a perilous voyage—very dangerous—[I have] great apprehensions that we can win under these conditions. But, let me be clear, if the decision is to go ahead, I'm committed."

"But is there another course in the national interest that is better than the McNamara course?" Johnson asked. "We know its [sic] dangerous and perilous. But can it be avoided?"

"There is no course that will allow us to cut our losses," answered Ball. "If we get bogged down, our cost might be substantially greater. The pressures to create a larger war would be irresistible. Qualifications I have are not due to the fact that I think we are in a bad moral position."[44]

When LBJ asked, "What other road can I go?," Ball advised: "Take what precautions we can—take losses—let their government [in Saigon] fall apart—negotiate—[knowing there will be a] probable take over by [the] Communists. This is disagreeable, I know."

"Can we make a case for this," a seemingly sympathetic Johnson queried, "discuss it fully?"

"We have discussed it," said Ball. "I have had my day in court."

Johnson then assured his devil's advocate that he had not yet "made a full commitment. You have pointed out the danger, but you haven't proposed an alternative course." Another meeting between LBJ and his advisers was called for the afternoon.[45]

When this first session ended, Ball spoke a few words with Rusk before dashing from the White House to the State Department. There he spent a frenetic hour in his conference room drafting and redrafting a presentation to the president. He knew that McNamara, Rusk, and Bundy could not be dissuaded from escalation. His comments, therefore, would concentrate on winning over LBJ.[46]

Realizing that this was probably his last chance to prevent Johnson from going to war, Ball was blunt during the afternoon session in the

Cabinet Room. "We can't win," he declared. The war would be long, the Chinese Communists might intervene, and a "messy conclusion" was the best-case scenario. The Korean War experience, he argued, showed that American popular support for a war in Vietnam would decline once U.S. casualties mounted. If the United States could not win in Vietnam within a year, world opinion would also move decisively against Johnson's policies. Hence LBJ should not be reluctant to pull out: "Every great captain in history is not afraid to make a tactical withdrawal if condition[s] are unfavorable to him." Ball added that he doubted "an army of westerners can fight orientals in [an] Asian jungle and succeed."[47]

That argument seemed to strike a chord with Johnson. "This is important," he said, "can westerners, in [the] absence of intelligence, successfully fight orientals in jungle rice-paddies? I want McNamara and Wheeler to seriously ponder this question." Alluding to the weakness of the South Vietnamese government, Ball continued by asserting that U.S. backing for Saigon was akin to "giving cobalt treatment to a terminal cancer case." A long war, he added, "will disclose our weakness, not our strength."[48]

What Ball could not offer Johnson was a path to withdrawal while ensuring that South Vietnam did not go Communist. "The least harmful way to cut losses in SVN [South Vietnam] is to let the government decide it doesn't want us to stay there," he explained. "Therefore, put such proposals to [the] SVN government that they can't accept, then it would move into a neutralist position—and I have no illusions that after we were asked to leave, SVN would be under Hanoi control." This was the crux of the matter. Johnson remained determined that any settlement in Vietnam would not result in a Communist takeover of the South. Ball's unpalatable point was that this optimal objective could not be achieved if a disastrous war in Vietnam were to be avoided.[49]

Johnson found all of this sobering. "Wouldn't all these countries say Uncle Sam is a paper tiger—wouldn't we lose credibility breaking the word of three presidents" if South Vietnam were allowed to go Communist? "It would seem to be an irreparable blow. But, I gather you don't think so."

"The worse blow," Ball responded, "would be that the mightiest power in the world is unable to defeat guerrillas."

"Then you are not basically troubled by what the world would say about pulling out?"

"If we were actively helping a country with a stable, viable government," Ball replied, "it would be a vastly different story."[50]

After this exchange, Johnson said he had two concerns: whether Westerners could win a war in Asia, and how to fight in collaboration with a fundamentally unstable government. Invited by the president to continue his analysis, Ball suggested that America's allies in Western Europe would be untroubled by a U.S. withdrawal from Vietnam, and that the disadvantages of such a withdrawal would be only short term in comparison with the long-term catastrophe that McNamara's proposed escalation would entail.[51]

McGeorge Bundy disagreed: there was no evidence to support a policy of withdrawal, he claimed, and it would be contrary to "all we have said and done." Ball reiterated that his chief concern was that "we get bogged down and don't win." Rusk made clear that he backed Bundy and McNamara, not Ball: "If the Communist world finds out we will not pursue our commitment to the end, I don't know where they will stay their hand." Henry Cabot Lodge, newly reappointed ambassador to South Vietnam, argued that Ball was inordinately pessimistic. The United States could prevail militarily in Vietnam, he insisted. To fail to meet the Communist challenge at this juncture would be comparable to appeasement at Munich.[52]

Ball had failed to persuade his colleagues to support the diplomatic course of action he had outlined. Although it was not altogether clear from his remarks in the meeting, Johnson too remained unconvinced. That would become apparent in the days that followed.

Given the calamity that the Vietnam War turned out to be for Lyndon Johnson, it is hard to recount Ball's performance on July 21, 1965, without being struck by his insight and his foresight. The bottom line is that he was right, and everyone else in that room that day, including the president, was wrong. But Ball was like Cassandra: he was blessed with the gift of prophecy—he could see clearly how the war would turn into a catastrophe—but not with the ability to be believed.

For Ball, it seemed that his quest to prevent Johnson from taking America into war was all but over. But at the eleventh hour an ally and potential savior emerged: Clark Clifford, Johnson's close friend. After a meeting on July 22, Ball asked Clifford if his impression was correct, that Clifford was opposed to escalation. Clifford said it was, mentioning his cautionary letter to Johnson back in May. "Then you and I are in total agreement," stated Ball. "I have been looking for support for a long time. I think your influence with the President is tremendously important. I want to put into your hands a series of memoranda which I have sent to the President." Clifford agreed to receive them.[53]

After his conversation with Ball, Clifford was about to leave the White House when he was asked to speak to Johnson and McGeorge Bundy. Invited by the president to give his opinion about the plan to escalate in Vietnam, Clifford questioned the soundness of the recommendations the president had received from his chief advisers. It was not clear, he said, that the United States could win in Vietnam.[54]

Soon after Clifford returned to his office, an aide arrived from Ball with the memoranda he had been writing against U.S. involvement in Vietnam since October 1964. Clifford stayed up until 2 a.m. reading them. "They were," he recalled, "everything that I would have expected—forceful, fearless, and, to my mind, convincing." On the evening of July 23 Clifford told Ball over the phone that he had found his memoranda on Vietnam "impressive and persuasive." Although Ball spoke enthusiastically about Clifford's role in the administration debate on Vietnam, Clifford cautioned Ball not to get his hopes up. He had heard from a source, Clifford said, that Johnson had as good as made up his mind to accept McNamara's proposals. That source, Clifford later revealed, was Bill Moyers.[55]

Clifford's information proved to be well founded. At a meeting at Camp David on July 25 he reprised Ball's role by warning Johnson he could see nothing but disaster for America if the decision were to be to go to war. But Clifford's efforts, like Ball's, were to no avail. After the meeting an uncharacteristically introspective Johnson drove around Camp David by himself for an hour, then spent another hour walking alone through the grounds. He understood the enormity of the decision he had already essentially made. He understood that even if things were to go well, the United States would endure a long, painful struggle in

Vietnam. Nevertheless he believed it was a war he could not and should not avoid.[56]

At an NSC meeting on July 27 Johnson explained to his advisers why he believed this to be so. "We could get out on the grounds that we don't belong there," he stated, alluding to Ball's position. "Not very many people feel this way about Vietnam. Most feel that our national honor is at stake and that we must keep our commitments there." America's credibility as leader of the Free World was, in other words, the key factor. The president was concerned too by the possibility of a right-wing backlash if he were to walk away from Vietnam. On one occasion he warned Ball: "George, don't pay any attention to what those little shits on the campuses do. The great beast is the reactionary elements in this country. Those are the people we have to fear."[57]

At a televised White House press conference in the early afternoon of July 28, 1965, Johnson revealed to the American people that he was substantially increasing the number of U.S. forces in Vietnam. He did not say so, but in effect he was taking America to war. Ball's dissent had failed. He would remain in Johnson's administration until 1966 and would return in 1968 as LBJ's ambassador to the United Nations—the personification of the road Johnson should have taken in Vietnam but did not.[58]

The consequences of Johnson's failure to heed Ball's advice were profound: mounting grassroots opposition to the war, especially after the Tet Offensive; division within the Democratic party over the war; and reduced momentum behind Great Society reform. Exhausted and forlorn, Johnson announced at the end of March 1968 that he would not seek his party's presidential nomination for the election later in the year. He was walking away from the White House and from politics. His legacy was a presidency replete with paradox: a domestic policy record that by itself could have placed him on Mount Rushmore, alongside a war that became a catastrophe.[59]

PART VI

Conclusion

CHAPTER 15

Decision-Making in the
White House

===

"Two roads diverged in a wood, and I—I took the
one less traveled by, And that has made all the
difference."—ROBERT FROST, *The Road Not Taken*

IN THE early years of the cold war, dissenting officials sometimes made persuasive arguments and sometimes did not. The assessments by Henry Wallace and Joseph Davies of the Soviet challenge at the end of World War II were flawed. They failed to attach sufficient importance to Stalin's belligerent policies in Eastern Europe and in Iran. They failed to consider how these policies made it necessary for Washington to change its conciliatory wartime attitude toward Moscow. Harry Hopkins, though interested in the spring of 1945 in sustaining a cooperative relationship with Russia, was less naive: he could see postwar problems ahead, but he felt the United States had no alternative but to accept a Soviet sphere of influence in Eastern Europe in the short term. Charles Wilson, Adlai Stevenson, and George Ball, however, offered convincing criticisms of the foreign policies of the presidents under whom they worked. Had the advice of Wilson and Ball been heeded, the calamity of the Vietnam War would have been avoided. Had John Kennedy listened to Stevenson (and other dissenting officials), the Bay

of Pigs disaster would have been averted and—assuming that
Khrushchev's decision to deploy missiles in Cuba was in part a response
to JFK's hostile approach to Castro—the October 1962 missile crisis
avoided. The facile assumption cannot be made that every critique of
U.S. policy developed by administration officials in these years was cogent; the roles played by Davies and Wallace make that clear. But in
several instances dissenting officials succeeded in providing sound alternatives to presidential policies.

The experience of history sheds light on the White House
decision-making process and has implications for policymakers today.
Too often presidents, when identifying a consensus of opinion in their
administration in favor of a policy option they themselves find attrac-
tive, have sought to stifle the kind of wide-ranging debate that might
result in that consensus being challenged. Too often they have appeared
concerned that the development of strong internal criticism of a preferred approach to a foreign-policy problem would cast doubt on the
legitimacy of that approach. In other words, they have seen a correlation between the degree of support for a policy option and the value of
that option.

The history of U.S. decision-making during the cold war shows
manifestly that such a correlation has not always existed. Consider, for
example, Kennedy's handling of Castro. Before the Bay of Pigs invasion, he set out to limit debate among his advisers on the soundness of
that enterprise. Men such as Chester Bowles, Adlai Stevenson, and Ted
Sorensen were deliberately kept on the periphery of the administration's discussion of the operation, precisely because Kennedy anticipated their opposition. Yet it was the dissenters, not the majority of the
Kennedy team that backed the Bay of Pigs, who provided the president
with sounder advice.

JFK has received much praise for his management of the missile
crisis, and on the whole that praise is merited. His leadership became
increasingly effective as the crisis unfolded, and by the end of that confrontation he was determined to end it through diplomacy and not by
force. But he could have generated a more wide-ranging and probably
more effective debate in ExComm had he allowed men such as Arthur
Schlesinger, Richard Goodwin, and Chester Bowles to participate in

the group's discussions. This may well have resulted in more support for the general approach favored by Stevenson, of backing both diplomacy and the blockade, thereby making it less likely that administration hawks would prevail, as at the start of the crisis it appeared they would.

The story of Johnson, Ball, and Vietnam is similar, though not identical. At least LBJ actively encouraged Ball's dissent. He read Ball's memoranda carefully and showed signs in meetings of taking his warnings seriously. Johnson's own caution over escalation in Vietnam before Operation Rolling Thunder suggests that he did not simply use Ball for appearance's sake. But at the same time he did not want Ball to win allies in the debate on Vietnam. He did not mind having one devil's advocate in the administration, but he did not want several. When Clark Clifford declared his opposition to escalation in Vietnam, it took Johnson a long time before he allowed his friend to elaborate. Similarly LBJ showed no inclination to allow his vice president, Hubert Humphrey, who was also skeptical about the war policy, to exercise influence in the debate in the upper echelons of the administration.

Johnson himself had doubts about deepening U.S. involvement in Vietnam. Listening to Ball allowed him to explore those doubts. Obsessed with the loyalty and the unity of his advisers, however, he sought to ensure that Ball would not be able to work in tandem with other dissenters. It might have created a serious division within his administration, even though it would have given Ball a better chance to prevail in the debate over going to war.

What these episodes demonstrate is that when policy options are being discussed, presidents should resist the impulse to strengthen consensus and nullify opposition within their administrations. Paradoxically, they need to encourage opposition, to allow dissenters to articulate their views in an unrestrained fashion and win converts to their point of view. The history of American foreign policy since World War II makes it clear that the policy alternative backed by the majority, even when the support is overwhelming, has been the wrong option on several occasions: Stevenson and Cuba (before the missile crisis) and Ball and Vietnam show that to be the case. Wilson and Vietnam, arguably, shows that to be the case. Colin Powell and the war in Iraq certainly does.

The value of encouraging dissent is not only verifiable historically, it also makes intellectual sense. A policy decision is always a relative judgment in that it is based on the assumption that it is the strongest of available choices. Any sensible discussion on whether to adopt a particular approach to an international issue should therefore include a rigorous analysis of all reasonable options. Considering the ideas of dissenting officials may not only prevent the implementation of a misguided policy (as it could have done, for instance, had Johnson accepted Ball's sage counsel), it may also serve to confirm the value of a preferred option.

While generating wide-ranging debates increases the likelihood that presidents will make better choices, this does not mean that they should begin policy discussions without any idea of the approach they wish to adopt. A presidential tabula rasa would result in an administration without direction in foreign policy, leading to confusion among the American people over the nation's role in the world. A leader needs to enter the White House with a good understanding of the world situation, having pondered U.S. foreign policy in both its historical and contemporary settings, and having reached conclusions about the new administration's approach to international affairs. This is necessary if a president is to provide sufficient conceptual unity to the nation's foreign policy. The administration of Jimmy Carter, in which the two leading advisers—Secretary of State Cyrus Vance and National Security Adviser Zbigniew Brzezinski—tugged the president's foreign policy in what seemed at times to be diametrically opposed directions, is a case in point of a leader failing to impose himself with sufficient clarity and vigor. The result was uncertainty and vacillation. A president must decide upon the general direction of American foreign policy while remaining receptive to dissenting points of view on any particular issue.

The history of dissent in the White House in the early cold war years not only highlights the need for open, fluid discussions between presidents and their advisers, it also exposes some of the fundamental flaws in thinking about U.S. foreign policy. In particular, it reveals an inability to examine *assumptions* thoroughly. After the defeat of the French, Eisenhower and his advisers in 1954 concentrated on ways to back the government of South Vietnam, not on whether it was worth making the attempt to do so in the first place. Kennedy was fixated by the idea of getting rid of Castro; he did not even consider whether it was sensible to set that as a policy objective. Johnson (and most of his aides) focused on how to prevent the Communists from winning in South Vietnam, not on whether they should try to do so. Once the questions they considered had been framed in those ways, their attention was inevitably on the methods that should be used to achieve their objectives, not whether those objectives were sound.

Wilson, Stevenson, and Ball reached more sensible conclusions than their colleagues largely because they were willing to analyze assumptions. Wilson wondered whether the United States should be involved in Vietnam at all. Stevenson wondered whether it made sense to invest so much time and effort in trying to oust Castro. Ball wondered whether the fall of South Vietnam to communism would inflict irreparable damage on America's reputation as a superpower, as other advisers and Johnson himself believed. The major failures of American foreign policy since World War II have often been due to the tendency of various presidents and their advisers to select a strategy before evaluating assumptions.

One aspect of the intermittent failure of policymakers to get the fundamentals right has been an inability to think about the *long-term consequences* of their decisions. The dissenters have often been less myopic. Eisenhower, for instance, committed the United States to the defense of South Vietnam without much considering how that might tie his hands or those of future presidents should the situation there deteriorate. Wilson did reflect on that eventuality. In his energetic pursuit of the overthrow of Castro (and his bolstering of U.S. defense spending at a time when Khrushchev was cutting the Soviet military), Kennedy never thought about how the Russians might respond. In the end, of course, they did so by deploying missiles in Cuba. Stevenson at least paid some attention to the potentially negative impact of JFK's anti-Castro policies. George W. Bush, to give the latest, most conspicuous example, was obsessed with the removal of Saddam Hussein but did not reflect carefully enough on how difficult a U.S. occupation of Iraq might prove to be after Hussein had been overthrown. Winning the war in the sense of defeating Saddam was a short-term objective Bush could see was achievable; the long-term consequences of that action, however, did not significantly influence his thinking.

Dissent among U.S. officials also sheds light on the political geography of American foreign policymaking. It is striking that all of these dissenters—Davies, Hopkins, Wallace, Wilson, Stevenson, and Ball—came from the Midwest. Other examples come to mind as well: Clark Clifford and Hubert Humphrey opposing escalation in Vietnam during the Johnson years; Secretary of Defense Melvin Laird urging Richard Nixon, at the start of his presidency, to withdraw immediately from Vietnam; and Budget Director David Stockman opposing Ronald Reagan's military buildup in the 1980s on fiscal grounds. Of course the cold war consensus was shared by the vast majority of Americans and American officials, including those from the Midwest. But it does seem to have been the case that compared to, say, their East Coast counterparts, a number of Midwesterners were able to look with a more critical eye at U.S. foreign policy. That approach could produce someone like Senator Joseph McCarthy. It could also produce individuals who articulated more reasonable and cogent criticisms of America's role in the world.

The debate on the merits of American foreign policy during the cold war era should be ongoing. With the end of the cold war, the collapse of the Soviet empire in Eastern Europe, and indeed the collapse of the Soviet Union itself, it is understandable that a self-congratulatory tone has pervaded recent thinking on U.S. foreign policy, at a grassroots level and to some extent in the academic debate. Reflecting on the roles played by some dissenters in presidential administrations reveals the limits of such triumphalism. A succession of American presidents were right in taking the Communist challenge seriously and in resolving to play a global role in protecting and promoting freedom. But Wilson, Ball, and Stevenson, for example, allow one to envisage a cold war in which the United States prevailed over the Soviet Union but without suffering credibility-sapping defeats at the Bay of Pigs and in Vietnam, without helping trigger a confrontation as dangerous as the Cuban missile crisis, and without piling up colossal amounts of debt. As we now reflect on U.S. foreign policy during the cold war, and as America continues to try to define its role in a post–cold war world, presidents such as Truman and Kennedy can serve as sources of inspiration. But so can a number of their advisers who pointed the way to a different kind of international role for the United States, one blending restraint with the demands of world leadership.

NOTES

INTRODUCTION

1. Bob Woodward, "Cheney Was Unwavering in Desire to Go to War," *Washington Post*, April 20, 2004 (washingtonpost.com).

2. A rare exception to the lack of attention paid to the issue of dissent is Thomas G. Paterson, ed., *Cold War Critics: Alternatives to American Foreign Policy in the Truman Years* (Chicago: Quadrangle Books, 1971).

1. THE GHOST OF FDR

1. Oral history of Matthew J. Connelly, p. 127, Harry S. Truman Library, Independence, Missouri (hereafter HSTL); David S. McLellan and David C. Acheson, eds., *Among Friends: Personal Letters of Dean Acheson* (New York: Dodd Mead, 1980), p. 51.

2. Winston Churchill, *Triumph and Tragedy* (London: Cassell, 1954), p. 412; W. Averell Harriman and Elie Abel, *Special Envoy: Churchill and Stalin, 1941–1946* (New York: Random House, 1975), p. 443.

3. Journal entry, April 12, 1945 (midnight), Papers of Joseph E. Davies, box 16, Library of Congress, Washington, D.C.

4. Hopkins to Stalin, Hopkins to Churchill, both April 13, 1945, in Papers of Harry Hopkins, box 338, Franklin D. Roosevelt Library, Hyde Park, New York (hereafter FDRL); Hopkins to Truman, April 13, 1945, Official File, Papers of Harry S. Truman, box 1059, HSTL.

5. Elizabeth Kimball MacLean, *Joseph E. Davies: Envoy to the Soviets* (Westport, Conn.: Praeger, 1992), is a commendably lucid and comprehensive biography. See also Keith David Eagles, *Ambassador Joseph E. Davies and American-Soviet Relations, 1937–1941* (New York and London: Garland, 1985).

6. "Profiles—House Great I and II," *New Yorker*, August 7 and 14, 1943, in Hopkins Papers, box 338; Henry H. Adams, *Harry Hopkins* (New York: Putnam, 1977), passim; George McJimsey, *Harry Hopkins: Ally of the Poor and Defender of Democracy* (Cambridge, Mass., and London: Harvard University Press, 1987), passim.

7. "Profiles—House Great I and II."

8. "Profiles—House Great I"; Elizabeth Kimball MacLean, "Joseph E. Davies and Soviet-American Relations, 1941–1943," *Diplomatic History* 4 (Winter 1980), 73–93.

9. Truman has generated a vast literature. The many detailed, insightful biographies include David McCullough, *Truman* (New York: Simon and Schuster, 1992); Alonzo L. Hamby, *Man of the People: A Life of Harry S. Truman* (New York: Oxford University Press, 1995); and Robert H. Ferrell, *Harry S. Truman: A Life* (Columbia: University of Missouri Press, 1994).

10. Richard C. Lukas, *Bitter Legacy: Polish-American Relations in the Wake of World War II* (Lexington: University Press of Kentucky, 1982), p. 2; Vojtech Mastny, *Russia's Road to the Cold War: Diplomacy, Warfare, and the Politics of Communism, 1941–1945* (New York: Columbia University Press, 1979), pp. 24–25, 40–41.

11. Robert Dallek, *Franklin D. Roosevelt and American Foreign Policy, 1932–1945* (New York: Oxford University Press, 1979), p. 437.

12. Mastny, *Russia's Road to the Cold War*, p. 167; Dallek, *Franklin D. Roosevelt*, pp. 400, 463, 504.

13. Report of the Crimea Conference, February 12, 1945, in U.S. Department of State, *Foreign Relations of the United States* (hereafter *FRUS*), *1945* (Washington, D.C.: U.S. Government Printing Office, 1955), *The Conferences at Malta and Yalta, 1945*, p. 973. The old standard on the Yalta Conference is Diane Shaver Clemens, *Yalta* (New York: Oxford University Press, 1970).

14. Report of the Crimea Conference, February 12, 1945, *FRUS: Malta and Yalta*, p. 974.

15. Ibid., p. 973.

16. Harriman and Abel, *Special Envoy*, p. 444; entry for April 12, 1945, diary of Adolf A. Berle, FDRL. See also Lloyd C. Gardner, *Spheres of Influence: The Great Powers Partition Europe, from Munich to Yalta* (Chicago: Ivan R. Dee, 1993).

17. Roosevelt to Churchill, March 29, 1945, in U.S. Department of State, *FRUS, 1945* (Washington, D.C.: U.S. Government Printing Office, 1967), vol. V, *Europe*, 189.

18. Roosevelt to Stalin, April 1, 1945, in ibid., V, 194–196.

19. Stalin to Roosevelt, April 7, 1945, in ibid., V, 202–204.

20. Roosevelt to Churchill, April 11, 1945, in ibid., V, 210.

21. State Department memorandum for the president, April 13, 1945, in Harry S. Truman, *Memoirs: Year of Decisions* (Garden City, N.Y.: Doubleday, 1955), I, 15.

22. Truman to Churchill, April 13, 1945, and Truman and Churchill to Stalin, April 18, 1945, *FRUS, 1945*, V, 212, 220–221.

23. Truman and Churchill to Stalin, April 18, 1945, *FRUS, 1945*, V, 220–221.

24. Hopkins to Charles A. Ward, April 13, 1945, Hopkins Papers, roll 20 (microfilm).

25. Calendar notes, April 13, 1945, in Thomas M. Campbell and George C. Herring, eds., *The Diaries of Edward R. Stettinius* (New York: New Viewpoints, 1975), p. 317.

26. Truman, *Memoirs*, I, 30–31; Merle Miller, *Plain Speaking: An Oral Biography of Harry S. Truman* (New York: Berkley Publishing, 1974), pp. 207–208.

27. Truman, *Memoirs*, I, 31.

28. Ibid., pp. 31–32; Hopkins to Joseph T. McNarney, February 26, 1945, Hopkins Papers, box 337.

29. Newspaper clipping, "Hopkins Lunches with Truman," Hopkins Papers, roll 20 (microfilm).

30. Halifax to Churchill, April 16, 1945, in Churchill, *Triumph and Tragedy*, pp. 419–420.

31. Memorandum of conversation, April 20, 1945, Record Group 59, Decimal File 760C.61/4-2045, Department of State Records, National Archives, Washington, D.C.; Truman, *Memoirs*, I, 70.

32. Memorandum of conversation, April 20, 1945.

33. Stettinius memorandum for the president, April 22, 1945, president's secretary's files, box 187, HSTL; memorandum of conversation, April 22, 1945, RG 59, Decimal File 760C.61/4-2245, Department of State Records.

34. Journal entry, April 23, 1945, Davies Papers, box 16.

35. Memorandum of meeting at the White House, April 23, 1945, RG 59, Decimal File 760C.61/4-2345, Department of State Records.

36. Ibid.

37. Memorandum of conversation, April 23, 1945, RG 59, Decimal File 760C.61/4-2345, Department of State Records; Truman, *Memoirs*, I, 79–80.

38. Charles E. Bohlen, *Witness to History, 1929–1969* (New York: Norton, 1973), p. 213; William D. Leahy, *I Was There: The Personal Story of the Chief of Staff to Presidents Roosevelt and Truman* (New York: Whittlesey House, 1950), p. 352; Truman, *Memoirs*, I, 82, 85–86; memorandum of conversation, April 23, 1945, and Stalin to Truman, April 24, 1945, in *FRUS, 1945*, V, 257, 263–264; Eben A. Ayers, assistant press secretary to Truman, wrote in his diary on April 24: "In our conference with the president this morning, there was again some talk of the president's discussion with Molotov late yesterday. The president indicated he talked strongly to the foreign minister. The president seemed serious about it but hopeful of good effects from the meeting." See Robert H. Ferrell, ed., *Truman in the White House: The Diary of Eben A. Ayers* (Columbia: University of Missouri Press, 1991), p. 14.

39. Bohlen memorandum, April 24, 1945, in *FRUS, 1945*, I, *General: The United Nations*, 381–382; Bohlen, memorandum of conversation, May 4, 1945, in *FRUS, 1945*, V, 281–284; Arthur H. Vandenberg, Jr., ed., *The Private Papers of Senator Vandenberg* (Boston: Houghton Mifflin, 1952), p. 181.

40. Memorandum of conversation, April 22, 1945, RG 59, Decimal File 760C.61/4-2245, Department of State Records.

41. Notable explanations of the economic motives behind U.S. foreign policy during this period include Lloyd C. Gardner, *Architects of Illusion: Men and Ideas in American Foreign Policy, 1941–1949* (Chicago: Quadrangle Books, 1970); Walter La Feber, *America, Russia, and the Cold War, 1945–1966* (New York: Wiley, 1967); and Thomas G. Paterson, *Soviet-American Confrontation: Postwar Reconstruction and the Origins of the Cold War* (Baltimore: Johns Hopkins University Press, 1973).

42. For an analysis of the impact of the Polish American constituency on U.S. policy toward Poland, see Peter H. Irons, "'The Test Is Poland': Polish Americans and the Origins of the Cold War," *Polish American Studies* 30:2 (1973), 5–63. Roosevelt's politically motivated avoidance of the Polish question before the 1944 presidential election is explored in Jack L. Hammersmith, "Franklin Roosevelt, the Polish Question and the Election of 1944," *Mid-America* 59:1 (1977), 5–17.

43. "Realist" scholars, among others, have depicted American foreign policy as idealistic and moralistic, though they have criticized it for being so. For this point

of view, see Norman A. Graebner, *Cold War Diplomacy: American Foreign Policy, 1945–1960* (Princeton, N.J.: Von Nostrand, 1962); Hans J. Morgenthau, *In Defense of the National Interest: A Critical Examination of American Foreign Policy* (New York: Knopf, 1951).

44. Gaddis Smith, *Dean Acheson* (New York: Cooper Square Publishers, 1972), pp. 414–424; Lane to Grew, May 4, 1945, in *FRUS, 1945*, V, 279. For other explorations of the way U.S. policymakers drew analogies between Soviet ambitions at the end of World War II and German aggression before it, see Ernest R. May, *"Lessons" of the Past: The Use and Misuse of History in American Foreign Policy* (New York: Oxford University Press, 1973); and Les K. Adler and Thomas G. Paterson, "Red Fascism: The Merger of Nazi Germany and Soviet Russia in the American Image of Totalitarianism, 1930s–1950s," *American Historical Review* 75:4 (1970), 1046–1064.

45. Churchill to Stalin, April 28, 1945, *FRUS, 1945*, V, 267.

46. Oral history of Samuel I. Rosenman, p. 55, HSTL; Joseph C. Grew, *Turbulent Era: A Diplomatic Record of Forty Years, 1904–1945* (Boston: Houghton Mifflin, 1952), II, pp. 1447–1448.

47. Monte M. Poen, ed., *Letters Home by Harry Truman* (New York: Putnam, 1984), p. 189.

48. Davies to Truman, April 15, 1945, and Truman to Davies, April 19, 1945, in Davies Papers, box 16.

49. Journal entry, April 30, 1945, Davies Papers, box 16.

50. Ibid.

51. Ibid.

52. Diary entry, "Truman takes over," n.d., Davies Papers, box 16.

53. Journal entries, May 21, 1945, box 17, May 13, 1945, box 16, and April 30, 1945, box 16; all in Davies Papers.

54. Harriman and Abel, *Special Envoy*, p. 459; Bohlen, *Witness to History*, p. 215.

55. Harriman and Abel, *Special Envoy*, p. 459; Bohlen, *Witness to History*, p. 215.

56. Truman, *Memoirs*, I, 257–258; transcript of telephone conversation between Truman and Stettinius, May 10, 1945, in Campbell and Herring, eds., *Diaries of Edward R. Stettinius*, p. 358.

57. Journal entry, "Sustaining Opinion from Justice Frankfurter," May 13, 1945, Davies Papers, box 16.

58. Journal entry, "A Sunday Evening with President Truman," May 13, 1945, Davies Papers, box 16.

59. Ibid.; Davies to Truman, May 12, 1945, Davies to Molotov, May 2, 1945, Molotov to Davies, May 9, 1945—all in Davies Papers, box 16.

60. Journal entry, "A Sunday Evening with President Truman."

61. Ibid.

62. Davies to Molotov, May 14, 1945, Davies Papers, box 17.

63. Memorandum, "The Hopkins-Davies Missions May–June 1945," n.d., Papers of Eben A. Ayers, box 7, HSTL.

64. Entry for May 19, 1945, Ayers Papers, box 9; Truman to Stalin, May 19, 1945, and Stalin to Truman, May 20, 1945, in *FRUS, The Conference of Berlin, 1945* (Washington, D.C.: U.S. Government Printing Office, 1960), I, 21–22.

65. Entry for May 20, 1945, Diaries of James Forrestal, box 1, Seely Mudd Library, Princeton, New Jersey.

66. Harriman and Abel, *Special Envoy*, p. 463; journal entry, May 21, 1945, Davies Papers, box 17.

67. Journal entry, May 21, 1945, Davies Papers, box 17. At this meeting Davies showed Truman a cable he had received from Molotov saying Stalin was in favor of another Big Three meeting and thought the Berlin area would be the most suitable site. See Molotov to Davies, May 20, 1945, Davies Papers, box 17.

68. Diary and journal entries, May 22, 1945, Davies Papers, box 17.

69. White House release, May 23, 1945, Truman Papers, Official File, box 1059, Truman Library; calendar notes, May 23, 1945, in Campbell and Herring, eds., *Diaries of Edward R. Stettinius*, p. 378.

70. Journal entry, May 24, 1945, Davies Papers, box 17; Harriman and Abel, *Special Envoy*, p. 463.

71. Diary entries, May 24 and 25, 1945, Davies Papers, box 17.

2. TALKING WITH CHURCHILL AND STALIN

1. Davies to Marjorie Davies, May 28, 1945, and memorandum beginning "Worked on letter," May 26, 1945; both in Davies Papers, box 17.

2. Davies, full report to Truman on mission to Churchill, June 12, 1945, Davies Papers, box 17.

3. Ibid.

4. Churchill, *Triumph and Tragedy*, p. 502; Davies, full report to Truman on mission to Churchill.

5. Diary entry, May 26, 1945, and memorandum beginning "Worked on letter"—both in Davies Papers, box 17.

6. Davies, full report to Truman on mission to Churchill.

7. Ibid.

8. Ibid.

9. Ibid.

10. Ibid.; Davies diary entry, May 26, 1945; Davies to Marjorie Davies, May 28, 1945.

11. Davies to Marjorie Davies, May 28, 1945; Davies, full report to Truman on mission to Churchill.

12. Diary entry, May 27, 1945, in Anthony Eden, *The Reckoning: The Eden Memoirs* (London: Cassell, 1965), p. 539.

13. Diary entry, May 27, 1945, Davies Papers, box 17; Davies, full report to Truman on mission to Churchill.

14. Davies to Marjorie Davies, May 28, 1945; Davies, full report to Truman on mission to Churchill.

15. Note by the prime minister on Mr. Davies' message, May 27, 1945, in Churchill, *Triumph and Tragedy*, p. 504.

16. Davies to Marjorie Davies, May 30, 1945, Davies Papers, box 17; Eden, *Reckoning*, p. 539.

17. Davies to Marjorie Davies, May 30, 1945; Eden, *Reckoning*, p. 539.

18. Davies to Marjorie Davies, May 30, 1945.

19. Ibid.; diary entry, May 29, 1945, in Eden, *Reckoning*, p. 539.

20. Davies to Marjorie Davies, May 30, 1945; diary entry, May 29, 1945, Davies Papers, box 17.

21. Davies to Marjorie Davies, May 30, 1945.

22. Ibid.; diary entries, May 30 and 31, June 3, 1945, Davies Papers, box 17.

23. Memorandum of 1st Hopkins-Stalin conversation, May 26, 1945, Hopkins Papers, box 338.

24. Ibid.

25. Ibid.

26. Memorandum of 2nd Hopkins-Stalin conversation, May 27, 1945, Hopkins Papers, box 338.

27. Ibid.

28. Ibid.

29. Ibid.

30. Ibid.

31. Hopkins to Truman, May 28, 1945, Hopkins Papers, box 338.

32. George F. Kennan, *Memoirs: 1925–1950* (Boston: Little, Brown, 1967), pp. 212–213.

33. Memorandum of 4th Hopkins-Stalin conversation, May 30, 1945, Hopkins Papers, box 338. The emphasis in the quotation is my own.

34. Ibid.; Hopkins to Truman, May 30, 1945, Hopkins Papers, box 338.

35. Memorandum of 5th Hopkins-Stalin conversation, May 31, 1945, Hopkins Papers, box 338.

36. Ibid.

37. Hopkins to Truman, May 31, 1945, Hopkins Papers, box 338.

38. Harriman and Abel, *Special Envoy*, pp. 469, 475.

39. Memorandum of conversation between Hopkins and Stalin, June 1, 1945, Hopkins Papers, box 338.

40. Entry for June 1, 1945, in Ferrell, ed., *Diary of Eben A. Ayers*, p. 39; Truman, *Memoirs*, I, 263; Truman to Churchill, June 1, 1945, and telegram from Foreign Office to Moscow and Washington, June 4, 1945—both in Hopkins Papers, box 338.

41. Hopkins to Truman, June 3, 1945, and Truman to Hopkins, June 5, 1945—both in Hopkins Papers, box 338.

42. Churchill to Truman, June 4, 1945, Hopkins Papers, box 338.

43. Memorandum of 6th Hopkins-Stalin conversation, June 6, 1945, Hopkins Papers, box 338.

44. Ibid.

45. Memorandum, "The Hopkins-Davies Missions May–June 1945," Papers of Eben A. Ayers, box 7, HSTL; Hopkins to H. H. Arnold, June 18, 1945, Hopkins Personal Papers, roll 20, FDRL; David Eisenhower, *Eisenhower: At War, 1943–1945* (New York: Random House, 1986), p. 818; Hopkins to Harriman, June 25, 1945, Hopkins Personal Papers, roll 20; Mrs. Dan Hollingsworth to Truman, July 5, 1945, Official File, box 1059, Papers of Harry S. Truman, HSTL.

46. Harriman to Truman, June 8, 1945, Decimal File 711.61/6-1145, box 3332, Department of State Records; Paul Mazur to Hopkins, June 15, 1945, and Beaverbrook to Hopkins, June 29, 1945—both in Hopkins Personal Papers, roll 20.

47. Diary entries, June 4 and 5, 1945, Davies to Truman, June 8, 1945, Davies, full report to Truman on mission to Churchill, journal entry, June 13, 1945—all in Davies Papers, box 17; Leahy, *I Was There*, p. 446.

48. Journal entries for June 13, 1945, Davies Papers, box 17; statement regarding the group of Poles who are invited to Moscow, June 12, 1945, Ayers Papers, box 9, HSTL.

49. Entry for June 13, 1945, in Ferrell, ed., *Diary of Eben A. Ayers*, p. 43; president's news conference, June 13, 1945, in *Public Papers of the Presidents of the United States: Harry S. Truman, 1945* (Washington, D.C.: U.S. Government Printing Office, 1961), p. 120.

50. President's news conference, June 13, 1945, pp. 121, 123.

51. Ibid., pp. 126–127.

52. Harriman to Stettinius, June 17 and 21, 1945, in *FRUS, 1945*, V, 346, 352–354; Harriman and Abel, *Special Envoy*, pp. 479–481.

53. Harriman to Stettinius, June 21, 1945, p. 354; Grew to Harriman, June 22, 1945; Harriman to Grew, June 23, 1945; Grew to Harriman, June 23, 1945—all in *FRUS, The Conference of Berlin*, pp. 720, 722–724.

54. Harriman to Stettinius, June 18, 1945, in *FRUS, 1945*, V, 348–351, including note 26.

55. U.S. Department of State, *Department of State Bulletin*, XIII (July 8, 1945), 47; Truman, *Memoirs*, I, 321–322; Truman to Churchill, July 2, 1945; Churchill to Truman, July 3, 1945; Truman to Churchill, July 3, 1945; White House press release, July 5, 1945—all in *FRUS, 1945, The Conference of Berlin*, I, 733–735.

56. Protocol of the proceedings of the Berlin Conference, August 1, 1945, *FRUS: Potsdam*, II, 1490–1492.

57. Connelly to Earl of Halifax, July 3, 1945, Official File, Truman Papers, box 1382.

58. Hopkins to Truman, July 2, 1945, Official File, Truman Papers, box 1059; Hopkins to Pierce Williams, July 6, 1945, Hopkins Personal Papers, roll 21, FDRL.

3. TROUBLED BY TRUMAN

1. Quoted in Miller, *Plain Speaking*, p. 206.

2. Diary entry, April 14, 1945, in Vandenberg, Jr., ed., *The Private Papers of Senator Vandenberg*, p. 168.

3. For a good summary of Wallace's early years, see Graham White and John Maze, *Henry A. Wallace: His Search for a New World Order* (Chapel Hill and London: University of North Carolina Press, 1995), pp. 1–15.

4. Ibid., pp. 36–37, 39–41, 44–46, 137–138.

5. Norman D. Markowitz, *The Rise and Fall of the People's Century: Henry A. Wallace and American Liberalism, 1941–1948* (New York: Free Press, 1973), pp. 28–30; White and Maze, *Henry A. Wallace*, pp. 194–197.

6. White and Maze, *Henry A. Wallace*, pp. 153–154, 194.

7. Markowitz, *Rise and Fall of the People's Century*, pp. 91–114, 126–135.

8. Oral history of Henry A. Wallace, p. 3692, Columbia University (copy in the Wallace Papers, University of Iowa, Iowa City), New York, New York. All subsequent references to the Wallace Papers are to the Iowa City collection (and not the Franklin Roosevelt Library collection in Hyde Park) unless otherwise specified.

9. Ibid., p. 3694.

10. Diary, April 27, 1945, Wallace Papers, box 12.

11. Ibid.

12. Ibid.

13. Ibid.

14. Ibid.

15. John C. Culver and John Hyde, *American Dreamer: The Life and Times of Henry A. Wallace* (New York and London: Norton, 2000), p. 389.

16. J. Samuel Walker, *Henry A. Wallace and American Foreign Policy* (Westport, Conn., and London: Greenwood Press, 1976), pp. 121–122, 137.

17. Diary, May 6, 1945, Wallace Papers, box 12.

18. Diary, May 2, 1945, Wallace Papers, box 12. Many words in the original source are in capital letters; these have been removed here and from some later paragraphs.

19. Ibid.

20. Ibid.

21. Ibid. The original memorandum reads: "But it is obvious there IS A CHANCE"—obviously a typographical error.

22. Diary (beginning, "More on the Russian thing"), May 2, 1945, Wallace Papers, box 12; Columbia oral history of Wallace, p. 3715.

23. Diary, May 3, 1945, Wallace Papers, box 12.

24. Walker, *Henry A. Wallace*, p. 119.

25. Diary, May 7, 1945, Wallace Papers, box 12; telephone conversations, Wallace to Dick Gilbert, May 7, 1945, Wallace Papers, box 65; Columbia oral history of Wallace, p. 3751.

26. Henry A. Wallace, *Sixty Million Jobs* (New York: Reynal and Hitchcock, 1945); Culver and Hyde, *American Dreamer*, p. 396; Walker, *Henry A. Wallace*, p. 117; Edward L. and Frederick H. Schapsmeier, *Prophet in Politics: Henry A. Wallace and the War Years, 1940–1965* (Ames: Iowa State University Press, 1970), p. 134.

27. Diary, May 2, 8, 10, 16, 1945, Wallace Papers, box 12.

28. Diary, May 16, 1945, Wallace Papers, box 12.

29. Ibid.

30. Diary, May 17, 1945, Wallace Papers, box 12.

31. Ibid.

32. Ibid.

33. Diary, May 18, 1945, Wallace Papers, box 12.

34. Ibid.

35. Diary, May 29, 1945, Wallace Papers, box 12.

36. Ibid.

37. Ibid.

38. Telephone conversations, Jim Patton to Wallace, May 30, 1945, Wallace Papers, box 65.

39. Transcript of phone conversation, Corcoran to Senator Hill, June 9, 1945, President's Secretary's Files, box 335, HSTL. See also Kai Bird and Max Holland, "Truman and Corcoran: The Tapping of 'Tommy the Cork,'" *Nation* (February 8, 1986), copy in the Truman Library.

40. Transcript of phone conversation, Corcoran to Hill, June 9, 1945.

41. Truman, *Memoirs*, I, 324–325, 326; Culver and Hyde, *American Dreamer*, pp. 389–390. See also Clark M. Clifford, *Counsel to the President: A Memoir* (New

York: Random House, 1991), p. 78; oral history of Samuel I. Rosenman, pp. 71–74, HSTL.

42. Diary, July 6, 1945, Wallace Papers, box 12; quoted in Richard J. Walton, *Henry Wallace, Harry Truman, and the Cold War* (New York: Viking, 1976), p. 50.

43. Wallace to Davies, June 19, 1945, Papers of Henry A. Wallace, reel 35, FDRL; telephone conversations, Wallace to Davies, June 26, 1945, Wallace Papers (Iowa City), box 65; Columbia oral history of Wallace, p. 3960.

4. THE BOMB

1. Truman, *Memoirs*, I, 421; McCullough, *Truman*, pp. 454–455.

2. Columbia oral history of Wallace, pp. 3977–3979; diary, August 7, 1945, Wallace Papers, box 12.

3. Columbia oral history of Wallace, pp. 4371–4372.

4. Ibid., pp. 3977, 4372–4373.

5. Ibid., pp. 4373–4376.

6. Ibid., pp. 4376–4377.

7. Ibid., p. 3808.

8. Ibid., p. 4378.

9. Wallace to Truman, August 21, 1945, and Truman to Wallace, August 24, 1945, Wallace Papers (Hyde Park), reel 59.

10. Diary, August 10, 1945, Wallace Papers, box 12.

11. Stimson to Truman, September 11, 1945, Papers of Henry L. Stimson, Sterling Library, Yale University, New Haven, Connecticut (microfilm edition of this collection at Roosevelt Study Center, Middelburg, Netherlands), reel 113.

12. Stimson memorandum for the president, "Proposed Action for Control of Atomic Bombs," September 11, 1945, Stimson Papers, reel 113.

13. Ibid.

14. Truman, *Memoirs*, I, 525.

15. Diary, September 18, 1945, Wallace Papers, box 12; diaries, September 18, 1945, Papers of James V. Forrestal, box 2, Seely G. Mudd Library, Princeton University, Princeton, New Jersey.

16. Diary, September 18, 1945, Wallace Papers; diaries, September 18, 1945, Forrestal Papers, box 2.

17. Truman to Stimson, September 19, 1945, Stimson Papers, reel 113; Truman to Bess Truman, September 22, 1945, in Robert H. Ferrell, ed., *Dear Bess: The Letters from Harry to Bess Truman, 1910–1959* (New York: Norton, 1983), p. 523; diaries, September 21, 1945, Forrestal Papers, box 2; diary, September 21, 1945, Wallace Papers, box 12; Connelly, notes of cabinet meeting, September 21, 1945, Papers of Matthew J. Connelly, box 2, HSTL.

18. Connelly notes, Wallace Diary, Forrestal Diaries, September 21, 1945.

19. Forrestal Diaries, September 21, 1945; Arthur Krock, *Memoirs: Sixty Years on the Firing Line* (New York: Funk and Wagnalls, 1968), pp. 248–249.

20. Wallace diary, September 21, 1945. Emphasis in the quotation is my own.

21. Felix Belair, Jr., "Plea to Give Soviet Atom Secret Stirs Debate in Cabinet," *New York Times*, September 22, 1945, Papers of Arthur Krock, box 60, Seely Mudd Library, Princeton University.

22. Connelly notes, September 21, 1945; Truman to Bess Truman, September 22, 1945.

23. Columbia oral history of Wallace, pp. 4104–4105, 4107; Forrestal to Wallace, June 2, 1945, Wallace Papers, box 64; diary, October 1, 1945, Wallace Papers, box 12.

24. Columbia oral history of Wallace, pp. 4108–4109.

25. Wallace to Truman, September 24, 1945, diary, Wallace Papers, box 12.

26. Diary, October 15, 1945, and Wallace memorandum, "The Significance of the Atomic Age," October 15, 1945, Wallace Papers, box 12.

27. Wallace memorandum, "The Significance of the Atomic Age."

28. White and Maze, *Henry A. Wallace*, pp. 16–43, 224.

29. Diary, October 15, 1945, Wallace Papers; Wallace to Truman, October 17, 1945, diary, Wallace Papers, box 12.

30. Diary, October 19, 1945, Wallace Papers, box 12.

31. Diary, October 23, 24, 26, 1945, Wallace Papers, box 12.

32. Diary, October 26, 1945, Wallace Papers.

33. Ibid. When Wallace recommended to Will Clayton that a loan be granted to Moscow, the assistant secretary of state curiously claimed that Russia did not need one. See Culver and Hyde, *American Dreamer*, p. 406.

34. Diary, October 26, 1945, Wallace Papers.

35. Ibid.

36. Culver and Hyde, *American Dreamer*, pp. 405–406; Walker, *Henry A. Wallace*, pp. 127–128.

37. Diary, November 28, 1945, and December 4, 1945, Wallace speech, "Peaceful Atomic Abundance," December 4, 1945, Wallace Papers, box 13.

38. Diary, October 23, 1945, Wallace Papers, box 12; diary, November 7, 21, 1945, Wallace Papers, box 13.

39. Diary, October 24, 1945, Wallace Papers.

40. Diary, December 29, 1945, Wallace Papers, box 13.

5. FIGHTING THE COLD WAR CONSENSUS

1. Insightful coverage of the emerging cold war in the early months of 1946 is provided by Fraser J. Harbutt, *The Iron Curtain: Churchill, America, and the Origins of the Cold War* (Oxford and New York: Oxford University Press, 1986).

2. Truman, *Memoirs*, I, 551–552.

3. James F. Byrnes, *All in One Lifetime* (New York: Harper, 1958), p. 346; Harriman and Abel, *Special Envoy*, p. 530; Campbell and Herring, eds., *Diaries of Edward R. Stettinius*, p. 459; Robert L. Messer, *End of an Alliance: James F. Byrnes, Roosevelt, Truman, and the Origins of the Cold War* (Chapel Hill: University of North Carolina Press, 1982), pp. 158, 162, 165; Truman, *Memoirs*, I, 552.

4. Vandenberg, Jr., ed., *Private Papers of Senator Vandenberg*, pp. 247–250; *New York Times*, February 28, 1946, p. 4.

5. U.S. Department of State, *Making the Peace Treaties, 1941–1947* (Washington, D.C.: U.S. Government Printing Office, 1947), p. 20; *Times* (London), March 1, 1946, p. 4.

6. *New York Times*, March 1, 1946, p. 1; Vandenberg, Jr., ed., *Private Papers of Senator Vandenberg*, p. 251; Vandenberg to Dewey, May 29, 1946, Papers of

Thomas E. Dewey, series 10, box 45, Rush Rhees Library, University of Rochester, Rochester, New York; Byrnes, *Lifetime*, p. 349.

7. Josef V. Stalin, "election speech," February 9, 1946, in Y. H. Kim, ed., *Twenty Years of Crises: The Cold War Era* (Englewood Cliffs, N.J.: Prentice-Hall, 1968), pp. 15–16.

8. Quoted in Hugh DeSantis, *Diplomacy of Silence: The American Foreign Service, the Soviet Union and the Cold War, 1933–1947* (Chicago: University of Chicago Press, 1980), p. 172; Dean Acheson, *Present at the Creation: My Years in the State Department* (New York: Norton, 1969), p. 150.

9. Messer, *End of an Alliance*, pp. 175–176; Harriman and Abel, *Special Envoy*, p. 547.

10. Kennan, *Memoirs, 1925–1950*, pp. 293, 547–559.

11. Acheson, *Present at the Creation*, p. 151; Kennan, *Memoirs, 1925–1950*, pp. 294–295.

12. Diary, January 2, 1946, Wallace Papers, box 13.

13. Ibid.

14. Columbia oral history of Wallace, p. 4682.

15. Diary, February 12, 1946, Wallace Papers, box 13.

16. Ibid.

17. Ibid.

18. Ibid.

19. McJimsey, *Harry Hopkins*, pp. 396–397; Truman, *Memoirs*, I, 553–554.

20. For the text of the speech, see *Congressional Record*, 79th Cong., 2nd Sess., A, pp. 1145–1147.

21. Walker, *Henry A. Wallace*, p. 136.

22. Diary, March 5, 1946, Wallace Papers, box 13.

23. Ibid.

24. Columbia oral history of Wallace, p. 4608.

25. Diary, March 12, 1946, Wallace Papers, box 13.

26. *New York Times* clipping, March 6, 1946, in diary, March 12, 1946, Wallace Papers, box 13.

27. Quoted in Patricia Dawson Ward, *The Threat of Peace: James F. Byrnes and the Council of Foreign Ministers, 1945–1946* (Kent, Ohio: Kent State University Press, 1979), pp. 82–83.

28. Diary, March 14, 1946, Wallace Papers, box 13.

29. Ibid.

30. Diary, March 15, 1946, and Wallace to Truman, March 14, 1946, Wallace Papers, box 13.

31. Wallace, memorandum for the president, March 15, 1946, Wallace Papers, box 13.

32. Wallace, diary, March 15, 1946, Wallace Papers, box 13; Columbia oral history of Wallace, p. 4642.

33. Wallace, address in honor of Averell Harriman, March 19, 1946, Wallace Papers, box 13.

34. Ibid.

35. Truman to Wallace, March 20, 1946, Wallace Papers, box 13.

36. Wallace to Truman, March 21, 1946, Wallace Papers, box 13; diary, March 22, 1946, Wallace Papers, box 13; Truman, *Memoirs*, I, 556.

37. Wallace, telephone call to Truman, and Wallace letter to Truman, both February 8, 1946, Wallace Papers, reels 66, 39, FDRL; diary, March 22, 1946, Wallace Papers, box 13; entry for March 23, 1946, in Ferrell, ed., *Diary of Eben A. Ayers*, p. 143.

38. Text of amendment to the McMahon Bill, March 13, 1946, in diary, Wallace Papers, box 13; Wallace to Truman, March 15, 1946, in Wallace Papers, reel 39, FDRL; Wallace telegram to Eleanor Roosevelt, March 19, 1946, Papers of Eleanor Roosevelt, box 3775, FDRL; Walker, *Henry A. Wallace*, p. 141.

39. Ward, *Threat of Peace*, p. 83.

40. Ibid., p. 84.

41. Wallace to Truman, March 20, 1946, in diary, Wallace Papers, box 13.

42. Diary, March 21, 1946, Wallace Papers, box 13.

43. Diary, March 22, 1946, Wallace Papers, box 13; Columbia oral history of Wallace, p. 4733.

44. *Chicago Tribune* clipping, May 29, 1946, in diary, Wallace Papers, box 14. When introduced on April 12 to a rally to commemorate Franklin Roosevelt on the anniversary of his death, Wallace was greeted by shouts from the crowd of "Wallace in '48." See Walton, *Henry Wallace, Harry Truman, and the Cold War*, p. 85.

45. *New York Herald Tribune* and *Wall Street Journal* clippings, June 2 and 14, 1946, Wallace Papers, box 14.

46. Wallace address, June 14, 1946, Wallace Papers, box 14.

47. Diary, July 16, 1946, Wallace Papers, box 14.

6. ELEVEN DAYS IN SEPTEMBER

1. Diary, July 18, 1946, Wallace Papers, box 14.

2. Ibid.

3. Ibid.

4. Diary, July 23, 1946, Wallace Papers, box 14.

5. Wallace to Truman, July 23, 1946, Wallace Papers, box 14.

6. Ibid.

7. Ibid. See, also, Markowitz, *Rise and Fall of the People's Century*, p. 178.

8. Wallace to Truman, July 23, 1946.

9. Ibid.

10. Ibid.

11. John T. Connor to Forrestal, September 18, 1946, Forrestal Papers, box 71.

12. Clifford, *Counsel to the President*, p. 114.

13. Ibid., pp. 114–115.

14. Truman to Wallace, August 8, 1946, Wallace Papers, box 14.

15. *Washington Post* clipping in diary, June 18, 1946, Wallace Papers, box 14; Walker, *Henry A. Wallace*, pp. 133–134, 145.

16. Clifford, *Counsel to the President*, pp. 113–114.

17. Ferrell, ed., *Diary of Eben A.* Ayers, pp. 156–157; memorandum, "Mexican Trip," August 29–September 10, 1946, Wallace Papers, box 14; Columbia oral history of Wallace, pp. 4941–4942.

18. Daily sheet for the president's appointments, September 10, 1946, President's Secretary's Files, box 84, HSTL; diary, September 10, 1946, Wallace Papers, box 14.

19. Truman, *Memoirs*, I, 557.

20. Diary, September 10, 1946, Wallace Papers. Graham White and John Maze argue that it is conceivable, though unlikely, that Wallace falsified his diary account of his meeting with Truman to cover himself in case a controversy ensued over what had been said. See White and Maze, *Henry A. Wallace: His Search for a New World Order*, p. 231.

21. Columbia oral history of Wallace, pp. 4953–4954.

22. Diary, September 10, 1946, Wallace Papers; Truman, *Memoirs*, I, 557.

23. Transcript, White House press conference, September 12, 1946, in diary, Wallace Papers, box 14; portion of transcript of same conference, Papers of Clark M. Clifford, box 20, HSTL.

24. Oral history of James W. Riddleberger, pp. 39–40, HSTL; John L. Sullivan memorandum for James Forrestal, September 12, 1946, in diaries, Forrestal Papers, box 3; Clifford, *Counsel to the President*, p. 118.

25. Clifford, *Counsel to the President*, p. 118.

26. Columbia oral history of Wallace, pp. 4955, 5036.

27. Ibid., p. 4985.

28. Wallace, text of Madison Square Garden address as delivered, September 12, 1946, Wallace Papers, box 14.

29. Ibid.

30. Ibid.

31. Telegram, Daniels to Wallace, September 13, 1946, Wallace Papers, box 42; Clifford, *Counsel to the President*, p. 119; Walker, *Henry A. Wallace*, p. 153.

32. Transcript of telephone call, Corcoran to Ickes, September 13, 1946, President's Secretary's Files, box 338, HSTL.

33. Clifford, *Counsel to the President*, p. 119.

34. Ibid.

35. Ibid.; statement by the president, September 14, 1946, Papers of George M. Elsey, box 105, HSTL.

36. Vandenberg, Jr., ed., *Private Papers of Senator Vandenberg*, p. 301.

37. Truman to Bess, September 15, 1946, in Ferrell, ed., *Dear Bess*, p. 537.

38. *New York Times* clipping, September 17, 1946, Elsey Papers, box 105, HSTL; diary (including record of the Wallace-Truman phone conversation), September 16, 1946, Wallace Papers, box 14; Columbia oral history of Wallace, p. 4984.

39. Record of Wallace-Truman phone conversation, September 16, 1946.

40. Columbia oral history of Wallace, pp. 4985–4986.

41. Wallace, statement, September 16, 1946, in diary, Wallace Papers, box 14; *New York Times*, September 17, 1946.

42. Diary, September 16, 17, 1946, Wallace Papers, box 14; Elsey memorandum, "L'Affaire Wallace," September 17, 1946, Elsey Papers, box 105; Ross to Wallace, telephone conversation, September 17, 1946, Wallace Papers, box 66.

43. Elsey memorandum, "L'Affaire Wallace."

44. Ibid.

45. Transcript of phone conversation, Panuch to Corcoran, September 17, 1946, President's Secretary's Files, box 338, HSTL.

46. Diary, September 18, 1946, Wallace Papers, box 14; president's engagements, September 18, 1946, President's Secretary's Files, box 79, HSTL.

47. Diary, September 18, 1946, Wallace Papers; Clifford, *Counsel to the President*, p. 120.

48. Diary, September 18, 1946, Wallace Papers.

49. Ibid.

50. Ibid.

51. Ibid.

52. *New York Times* clipping, September 19, 1946, in diary, Wallace Papers, box 14.

53. Truman, *Memoirs*, I, 559; James F. Byrnes, *Speaking Frankly* (New York: Harper, 1947), p. 240.

54. Byrnes, *Speaking Frankly*, p. 240.

55. Ibid.; Clifford, *Counsel to the President*, p. 120.

56. Transcript, teletype conference between Byrnes and Truman, September 19, 1946, President's Secretary's Files, box 84, HSTL.

57. Clifford, *Counsel to the President*, p. 120; transcript, teletype conference, September 19, 1946.

58. Transcript, teletype conference, September 19, 1946.

59. Ibid.; Byrnes, *Speaking Frankly*, p. 242.

60. Transcript, teletype conference, September 19, 1946; Clifford, *Counsel to the President*, pp. 120–121.

61. Oral history of George M. Elsey, p. 33, HSTL.

62. Clifford, *Counsel to the President*, p. 121; Columbia oral history of Wallace, p. 5028.

63. Columbia oral history of Wallace, p. 5028; diary entry for September 20, 1946, in Ferrell, ed., *Diary of Eben A. Ayers*, p. 159; Clifford, *Counsel to the President*, p. 121.

64. Truman, *Memoirs*, I, 560; Wallace to Truman, September 20, 1946, Wallace Papers, box 42.

65. Record of White House press conference, September 20, 1946, diary, Wallace Papers, box 14.

66. Ibid.; entry for September 20, 1946, in Ferrell, ed., *Diary of Eben A. Ayers*, p. 158.

67. Columbia oral history of Wallace, p. 5033.

68. Ibid., pp. 5033–5034.

69. Culver and Hyde, *American Dreamer*, p. 428; Walker, *Henry A. Wallace*, p. 159.

70. Truman, *Memoirs*, I, 560.

71. Melvyn P. Leffler, *A Preponderance of Power: National Security, the Truman Administration, and the Cold War* (Stanford: Stanford University Press, 1992), pp. 141–200.

72. Culver and Hyde, *American Dreamer*, pp. 456–502.

73. Ibid., pp. 502–531; Leffler, *Preponderance of Power*, pp. 217–518 passim.

74. Leffler, *Preponderance of Power*, pp. 217–518 passim.

7. A NEW WILSONIANISM

1. Stephen E. Ambrose, *Eisenhower: Soldier, General of the Army, President-Elect, 1890–1952* (London: George Allen and Unwin, 1984), p. 571.

2. Ibid., pp. 13–410.

3. Ibid., pp. 432–571.

4. The extensive literature on Dulles includes Townsend Hoopes, *The Devil and John Foster Dulles* (Boston: Little, Brown, 1973); Leonard Mosley, *Dulles: A Biography of Eleanor, Allen and John Foster Dulles* (London: Hodder and Stoughton, 1978); Frederick W. Marks, *Power and Peace: The Diplomacy of John Foster Dulles* (Westport, Conn., and London: Praeger, 1993); and Richard H. Immerman, *John Foster Dulles: Piety, Pragmatism, and Power in U.S. Foreign Policy* (Wilmington, Del.: Scholarly Resources, 1999).

5. Dwight D. Eisenhower, *Mandate for Change, 1953–1956: The White House Years* (Garden City, N.Y.: Doubleday, 1963), p. 86.

6. Entry for Charles Erwin Wilson, in John A. Garraty, ed., *Dictionary of American Biography* (New York: Charles Scribner's Sons, 1981), Supplement Seven: 1961–1965, pp. 793–794.

7. Ibid., pp. 793–794.

8. *Detroit News*, November 21, 1952, in scrapbook no. 8, Papers of Charles E. Wilson, Anderson University, Anderson, Indiana.

9. *New York Herald Tribune*, November 21, 1952, in scrapbook no. 8, Wilson Papers.

10. *New York Herald Tribune*, November 21, 1952; Henry Cabot Lodge, *As It Was: An Inside View of Politics and Power in the '50s and '60s* (New York: Norton, 1976), pp. 49–50.

11. Arthur W. Radford, *From Pearl Harbor to Vietnam: The Memoirs of Admiral Arthur W. Radford* (Stanford: Hoover Institution Press, 1980), pp. 303–304; Robert J. Donovan, *Eisenhower: The Inside Story* (New York: Harper and Bros., 1956), p. 18.

12. Donovan, *Eisenhower*, pp. 24–26; Eisenhower, *Mandate for Change*, pp. 110–112; *Washington Evening Star*, January 16, 1953, scrapbook no. 8, Wilson Papers.

13. Robert A. Divine, *Eisenhower and the Cold War* (Oxford and New York: Oxford University Press, 1981), pp. 13–17; Stephen E. Ambrose, *Eisenhower: The President, 1952–1969* (London: George Allen and Unwin, 1984), pp. 355–356, 367.

14. Ambrose, *Eisenhower: The President*, pp. 110–111, 171, 183.

15. Ibid., pp. 51–52, 109–112, 129–130, 183, 192–197, 209–210, 625–626.

16. Stephen G. Rabe, "Eisenhower Revisionism: A Decade of Scholarship," *Diplomatic History* 17 (Winter 1993), 97–115.

17. Ibid.

18. David L. Anderson, *Trapped by Success: The Eisenhower Administration and Vietnam, 1953–1961* (New York: Columbia University Press, 1991), pp. 5, 8–9; Lloyd C. Gardner, *Approaching Vietnam: From World War II Through Dienbienphu* (New York and London: Norton, 1988), pp. 64–65, 68.

19. George C. Herring, *America's Longest War: The United States and Vietnam, 1950–1975* (New York: Knopf, 1979), pp. 7–8.

20. Ibid., p. 9.

21. Anderson, *Trapped by Success*, pp. 9–11, 14–16; Gardner, *Approaching Vietnam*, p. 107; Stanley Karnow, *Vietnam: A History* (London: Century Publishing, 1983), p. 177.

22. E. Bruce Geelhoed, *Charles E. Wilson and Controversy at the Pentagon, 1953 to 1957* (Detroit: Wayne State University Press, 1979), pp. 18, 181–182; Donovan,

Eisenhower, p. 18; *Chicago Tribune*, January 23, 1956, in scrapbook no. 13, Wilson Papers.

23. *Chicago Tribune*, January 23, 1956.

24. Geelhoed, *Charles E. Wilson*, pp. 16–17; Maxwell D. Taylor, *Swords and Plowshares* (New York: Norton, 1972), p. 169.

25. Oral history of Dillon Anderson, pp. 46–47, Dwight D. Eisenhower Library, Abilene, Kansas (hereafter DDEL).

26. Ibid., p. 48.

27. Emmet John Hughes, *The Ordeal of Power: A Political Memoir of the Eisenhower Years* (New York: Atheneum, 1963), p. 75; Matthew B. Ridgway, *Soldier: The Memoirs of Matthew B. Ridgway* (New York: Harper and Bros., 1956), pp. 274, 283; William Bragg Ewald, *Eisenhower the President: Crucial Days, 1951–1960* (Englewood Cliffs, N.J.: Prentice-Hall, 1981), p. 192.

28. Ewald, *Eisenhower the President*, p. 193.

29. Geelhoed, *Charles E. Wilson*, p. 19; Ewald, *Eisenhower the President*, p. 192; Sherman Adams, *First-Hand Report: The Inside Story of the Eisenhower Administration* (New York: Harper, 1961), pp. 294–295.

30. Geelhoed, *Charles E. Wilson*, pp. 18–19.

31. Oral history of Thomas S. Gates, p. 4, John Foster Dulles oral history project, Princeton University Library. For the polite Dulles-Wilson correspondence referred to, see boxes 88, 112, 137, 143, Papers of John Foster Dulles, Princeton University Library.

32. John Foster Dulles, memorandum of conversation, March 24, 1953, and minutes of meeting between Eisenhower and Mayer, March 26, 1953, in U.S. Department of State, *FRUS, 1952–1954*, XIII, *Indochina*, 419–420, 429–432.

33. Paul H. Nitze, with Steven L. Rearden and Ann M. Smith, *From Hiroshima to Glasnost* (New York: Weidenfeld and Nicolson, 1989), p. 143; Adams, *First-Hand Report*, p. 91.

34. Allison memorandum for Dulles, April 3, 1953, *FRUS, 1952–1954*, XIII, 456; Radford, *From Pearl Harbor to Vietnam*, pp. 374–375.

35. Diary entry, May 14, 1953, in Robert H. Ferrell, ed., *The Eisenhower Diaries* (New York: Norton, 1981), p. 237.

36. Herring, *America's Longest War*, p. 25; Eisenhower, *Mandate for Change*, p. 169.

37. Memorandum, 161st NSC meeting, September 9, 1953, Ann Whitman File, NSC Series, box 4, DDEL; answers to the 32 questions asked by Senator Margaret Chase Smith, June 11, 1953, Public Statements of Secretary of Defense Wilson, 1953, vol. II, DDEL.

38. Herring, *America's Longest War*, pp. 25–26.

39. Radford, *From Pearl Harbor to Vietnam*, pp. 381–383.

8. "NOTHING BUT GRIEF": CONTESTING A COMMITMENT

1. Robert D. Schulzinger, *A Time for War: The United States and Vietnam, 1941–1975* (New York and Oxford: Oxford University Press, 1997), pp. 58–61; Anderson, *Trapped by Success*, p. 25.

2. Anderson, *Trapped by Success*, pp. 25–27.

3. Ambrose, *Eisenhower: The President*, p. 177.

4. Anderson, *Trapped by Success*, pp. 30–31.

5. Herring, *America's Longest War*, pp. 30–32.

6. Wilson to Dulles, March 23, 1954, p. 471, and Erskine to the special committee of the National Security Council, March 17, 1954, in *FRUS, 1952–1954*, XVI, 471, 475–479; Radford memorandum for Wilson, March 12, 1954, National Security Council Staff Papers, OCB Central File Series, box 37, DDEL.

7. Memorandum, 183rd National Security Council meeting, February 4, 1954, Ann Whitman File, NSC Series, box 5, DDEL; Wilson press conference, February 9, 1954, Public Statements of Secretary of Defense Wilson, 1954, vol. I, DDEL.

8. Memorandum, 190th National Security Council meeting, March 25, 1954, *FRUS, 1952–1954*, XIII, 1167–1168.

9. Wilson press conference, May 4, 1954, Public Statements of Secretary of Defense Wilson, 1954, vol. III, DDEL.

10. MacArthur, memorandum of conversation on May 10, May 11, 1954, *FRUS, 1952–1954*, XIII, 1527; Wilson press conference, May 11, 1954, Public Statements of Secretary of Defense Wilson, 1954, vol. III, DDEL.

11. Wilson press conference, June 2, 1954, Public Statements of Secretary of Defense Wilson, 1954, vol. III, DDEL; memorandum, 201st NSC meeting, June 9, 1954, Ann Whitman File, NSC Series, box 5, DDEL; Lacy to Department of State, May 25, 1954, *FRUS, 1952–1954*, XIII, 1612–1613.

12. Wilson press conference, June 2, 1954.

13. Herring, *America's Longest War*, pp. 38–40; Schulzinger, *Time for War*, pp. 71–75.

14. Memorandum, 202d National Security Council meeting, June 17, 1954, *FRUS, 1952–1954*, XIII, 1717; telephone call from Wilson to Dulles, June 30, 1954, Papers of John Foster Dulles, JFD Chronological Series, box 8, DDEL.

15. Ambrose, *Eisenhower: The President*, pp. 208–209; Herring, *America's Longest War*, pp. 40–41.

16. Schulzinger, *Time for War*, p. 77.

17. Minutes of a meeting on Southeast Asia, July 24, 1954, *FRUS, 1952–1954*, XII, 666–668.

18. Memorandum, 210th NSC meeting, August 12, 1954, Ann Whitman File, NSC Series, box 5, DDEL.

19. Ibid.

20. Ibid.

21. Ibid.

22. Ibid.

23. Wilson to Dulles (two letters), August 17, 1954, *FRUS, 1952–1954*, XII, 737–740, incl. 740n.

24. Memorandum, 215th NSC meeting, September 24, 1954, *FRUS, 1952–1954*, XIII, 2059.

25. Ambrose, *Eisenhower: The President*, pp. 209–210; Herring, *America's Longest War*, pp. 44–45.

26. David L. Anderson, "Dwight D. Eisenhower and Wholehearted Support of Ngo Dinh Diem," in Anderson, ed., *Shadow on the White House: Presidents and the Vietnam War, 1945–1975* (Lawrence: University Press of Kansas, 1993), p. 50.

27. Gardner, *Approaching Vietnam*, pp. 292–294, 318–319.

28. Memorandum, 216th NSC meeting, October 6, 1954, Ann Whitman File, NSC Series, box 6, DDEL.

29. Cutler, memorandum for the record, October 19, 1954, White House Office, Office of the Special Assistant for National Security Affairs: Records, 1952–1961, NSC Series, Briefing Notes Subseries, box 11, DDEL.

30. Memorandum, 219th NSC meeting, October 26, 1954, Ann Whitman File, NSC Series, box 6, DDEL.

31. Ibid.

32. Wilson press conference, November 30, 1954, Public Statements of Secretary of Defense Wilson, 1954, IV, 25–26, DDEL.

33. Stassen memorandum for Eisenhower, February 3, 1955, *FRUS, 1955–1957*, I, 72–74.

34. Memorandum, telephone conversation between Dulles and Wilson, May 4, 1955, pp. 355–356; memorandum, 251st NSC meeting, June 9, 1955, p. 443; letter from Wilson to Dulles, December 13, 1955, p. 615n—all in *FRUS, 1955–1957*, vol. I.

35. Donovan, *Eisenhower*, pp. 276–277.

36. Diary entry, March 12, 1955, in Ferrell, ed., *The Eisenhower Diaries*, p. 296.

37. Ambrose, *Eisenhower: The President*, pp. 223, 441.

9. THE RIVALS

1. The best studies of JFK's early life are Nigel Hamilton, *JFK: Reckless Youth* (New York: Random House, 1992), and Herbert S. Parmet, *Jack: The Struggles of John F. Kennedy* (New York: Dial, 1980).

2. Solid biographical studies of Stevenson include John Bartlow Martin, *Adlai Stevenson of Illinois: The Life of Adlai E. Stevenson* (Garden City, N.Y.: Doubleday, 1977), and Porter McKeever, *Adlai Stevenson: His Life and Legacy* (New York: Morrow, 1989).

3. McKeever, *Adlai Stevenson*, passim; John Bartlow Martin, *Adlai Stevenson and the World: The Life of Adlai E. Stevenson* (Garden City, N.Y.: Doubleday, 1977), passim.

4. Parmet, *Jack*, pp. 334–336, 345, 356–362, 374, 379–381; Edwin O. Guthman and Jeffrey Shulman, eds., *Robert Kennedy in His Own Words: The Unpublished Recollections of the Kennedy Years* (New York: Bantam, 1988), p. 445.

5. Parmet, *Jack*, pp. 405–406, 440.

6. Theodore H. White, *The Making of the President, 1960* (New York: Atheneum, 1961), pp. 62–63, 65–66, 73.

7. Oral history of Barbara Ward Jackson, p. 6, John F. Kennedy Library, Boston, Massachusetts (hereafter JFKL).

8. White, *Making of the President*, pp. 137–140; Arthur M. Schlesinger, Jr., *A Thousand Days: John F. Kennedy in the White House* (London: Mayflower-Dell reprint, 1967), p. 36.

9. Krock memorandum, May 26, 1960, Papers of Arthur Krock, box 31, Seely Mudd Library, Princeton University.

10. Schlesinger, *A Thousand Days*, p. 34.

11. George W. Ball, *The Past Has Another Pattern: Memoirs* (New York: Norton, 1982), p. 158; Charles Bartlett, "Portrait of a Friend," in Kenneth W. Thompson, ed., *The Kennedy Presidency: Seventeen Intimate Perspectives of John F. Kennedy* (Lanham, Md.: University Press of America, 1985), p. 10. Bartlett refers in this article to the aftermath of the West Virginia primary, but other evidence indicates that this episode took place after the Oregon primary.

12. Ball, *Past Has Another Pattern*, p. 158.

13. Schlesinger, *A Thousand Days*, p. 35; Bartlett, "Portrait of a Friend," p. 10.

14. Edward P. Doyle, ed., *As We Knew Adlai: The Stevenson Story by Twenty-Two Friends* (New York: Harper and Row, 1966), p. 162.

15. Memorandum of conversation, August 5, 1958, and editorial note, in Walter Johnson, ed., *The Papers of Adlai E. Stevenson* (Boston: Little, Brown, 1977), VII, 256–271, 363–364.

16. George F. Minde II and Michael Hennessey, "Reform of the Soviet Military Under Khrushchev and the Role of America's Strategic Modernization," in Robert O. Crummey, ed., *Reform in Russia and the U.S.S.R.: Past and Prospects* (Urbana and Chicago: University of Illinois Press, 1989), pp. 182–206.

17. Ibid., p. 183; William T. Lee, *The Estimation of Soviet Defense Expenditures, 1955–1975: An Unconventional Approach* (New York: Praeger, 1977), p. 98; Vasilii D. Sokolovskii, ed., *Soviet Military Strategy*, trans. and intro. Herbert S. Dinerstein, Leon Goure, and Thomas W. Wolfe (Englewood Cliffs, N.J.: Prentice-Hall, 1963), pp. 14–15.

18. Nikita Khrushchev, *Khrushchev Remembers: The Last Testament* (Boston: Little, Brown, 1974), p. 488.

19. Martin, *Adlai Stevenson and the World*, pp. 471–472; Stevenson memorandum, January 25, 1960, Papers of Adlai E. Stevenson, box 791, Seely Mudd Library, Princeton University.

20. Stevenson memorandum, January 25, 1960, Stevenson Papers.

21. Ibid.; Stevenson to Menshikov, January 22, 1960, Stevenson Papers, box 791.

22. White, *Making of the President*, pp. 144–145.

23. Martin, *Adlai Stevenson and the World*, pp. 524–525.

24. White, *Making of the President*, p. 191.

25. Ibid., pp. 190–192; Stevenson to Eugene McCarthy, August 10, 1960, in Johnson, ed., *Papers of Adlai E. Stevenson*, VII, 550.

26. Pierre Salinger, *With Kennedy* (Garden City, N.Y.: Doubleday, 1966), p. 42; Johnson, ed., *Papers of Adlai E. Stevenson*, VII, 538.

27. Stevenson speech, July 15, 1960, in Johnson, ed., *Papers of Adlai E. Stevenson*, VII, 538–541; *New York Times*, July 16, 1960, p. 7; Kenneth P. O'Donnell and David F. Powers, with Joe McCarthy, *"Johnny, We Hardly Knew Ye": Memories of John Fitzgerald Kennedy* (Boston: Little, Brown, 1972), p. 183.

28. Guthman and Shulman, eds., *Robert Kennedy in His Own Words*, p. 38; Garry Wills, *The Kennedy Imprisonment: A Meditation on Power* (Boston: Little, Brown, 1982), p. 99; Richard J. Walton, *The Remnants of Power: The Tragic Last Years of Adlai Stevenson* (New York: Coward-McCann, 1968), p. 15.

29. Martin, *Adlai Stevenson and the World*, p. 531.

30. Eleanor Roosevelt to Mary Lasker, August 15, 1960, and Kennedy to Eleanor Roosevelt, August 26, 1960, in President's Office Files, box 32, JFKL; oral

history of Chester Bowles, p. 10, JFKL; O'Donnell and Powers, *"Johnny, We Hardly Knew Ye,"* p. 236.

31. Doyle, ed., *As We Knew Adlai*, pp. 177–178.

32. Walton, *Remnants of Power*, pp. 15–16; *New York Times*, October 21, 1960, p. 18; Stevenson to Lady Barbara Jackson, October 28, 1962, in Johnson, ed., *Papers of Adlai E. Stevenson*, VII, 573; Trumbull Higgins, *The Perfect Failure: Kennedy, Eisenhower, and the CIA at the Bay of Pigs* (New York: Norton paperback ed., 1989), p. 60.

33. Khrushchev, *Khrushchev Remembers: The Last Testament*, p. 488; Michael R. Beschloss, *The Crisis Years: Kennedy and Khrushchev, 1960–1963* (New York: Edward Burlingame Books, 1991), pp. 15–16.

34. Beschloss, *Crisis Years*, p. 14.

35. Khrushchev, *Khrushchev Remembers: The Last Testament*, pp. 489–491.

36. Ibid., p. 491.

37. Martin, *Adlai Stevenson and the World*, pp. 550–551; White, *Making of the President*, p. 393.

38. Martin, *Adlai Stevenson and the World*, p. 561.

39. Ibid., p. 562.

40. Ibid., pp. 561–563.

41. Athan Theoharis, ed., *From the Secret Files of J. Edgar Hoover* (Chicago: Ivan R. Dee, 1991), pp. 282–291, esp. 291; quoted in Thomas C. Reeves, *A Question of Character: A Life of John F. Kennedy* (New York: Free Press, 1991), p. 152; oral history of George A. Smathers, interview III, tape 2, p. 7, JFKL.

42. JFK, inaugural address, January 20, 1961, U.S. National Archives and Records Service, *Public Papers of the Presidents of the United States: John F. Kennedy, 1961* (Washington, D.C.: U.S. Government Printing Office, 1962), p. 1.

43. McKeever, *Adlai Stevenson*, p. 480.

10. OPERATION CASTRATION

1. Doyle, ed., *As We Knew Adlai*, p. 254.

2. See Martin, *Adlai Stevenson and the World*; McKeever, *Adlai Stevenson*; Rodney M. Sievers, *The Last Puritan?: Adlai Stevenson in American Politics* (Port Washington, N.Y.: Associated Faculty Press, 1983); Kenneth S. Davis, *The Politics of Honor: A Biography of Adlai E. Stevenson* (New York: Putnam, 1967)—all passim.

3. Martin, *Adlai Stevenson and the World*, pp. 585–590; oral history of Harlan Cleveland, pp. 38–40, JFKL.

4. Martin, *Adlai Stevenson and the World*, pp. 586–587.

5. Oral history of Bowles, pp. 40–41, JFKL.

6. Oral history of W. Averell Harriman, p. 37, JFKL; Higgins, *Perfect Failure*, pp. 70–71, 79–80.

7. Stevenson to Kennedy, November 22, 1960, in Johnson, ed., *Papers of Adlai E. Stevenson*, VII, 585.

8. Stevenson, report on conference with Ambassador Menshikov, November 28, 1960, in Johnson, ed., *Papers of Adlai E. Stevenson*, VII, 587–591.

9. Stevenson, report on conference with Ambassador Menshikov, November 29, 1960, and Stevenson to Rusk, December 21, 1960, in Johnson, ed., *Papers of Adlai E. Stevenson*, VII, 591, 602.

10. Stevenson to Kennedy, November 22, 1960; Stevenson to Ball, November 29, 1960, in Johnson, ed., *Papers of Adlai E. Stevenson*, VII, 587–591; Stevenson to Rusk, December 21, 1960.

11. Telephone conversation with President Elect John F. Kennedy, January 13, 1961, in Johnson, ed., *Papers of Adlai E. Stevenson*, VII, 615–616.

12. Ibid., pp. 616–617.

13. Stevenson to Sorensen, December 30, 1960, in Johnson, ed., *Papers of Adlai E. Stevenson*, VII, 604–605.

14. Quoted in Mark J. White, *The Cuban Missile Crisis* (London and Basingstoke: Macmillan, 1996), p. 34.

15. Allen W. Dulles to Eisenhower, August 3, 1960, Papers of Allen W. Dulles, box 88, Seely Mudd Library, Princeton University; Dulles memorandum for the record, September 21, 1960, Dulles Papers, box 89; memorandum of meeting with the president on Cuba, February 8, 1961, National Security Files, box 35A, JFKL; Higgins, *Perfect Failure*, pp. 92–96.

16. Bowles to Rusk, March 13, 1961, in U.S. Department of State, *FRUS, 1961–1963* (Washington, D.C.: U.S. Government Printing Office, 1997), X, *Cuba, 1961–1962*, 178–181; Dean Rusk, as told to Richard Rusk, *As I Saw It* (New York: Norton, 1990), pp. 209–210; Wills, *Kennedy Imprisonment*, p. 236.

17. Schlesinger, *A Thousand Days*, pp. 229–230.

18. Salinger, *With Kennedy*, p. 147; Walter Johnson, ed., *Papers of Adlai E. Stevenson*, VIII, 53.

19. Martin, *Adlai Stevenson and the World*, p. 624.

20. Oral history of Harlan Cleveland, p. 21, JFKL; oral history of Francis T. P. Plimpton, p. 10, JFKL; Salinger, *With Kennedy*, p. 147.

21. Martin, *Adlai Stevenson and the World*, p. 624; oral history of Cleveland, p. 23, JFKL.

22. Higgins, *Perfect Failure*, pp. 126, 129.

23. Ibid., pp. 126, 130.

24. Ibid., pp. 89, 102, 131–132.

25. United Nations, General Assembly, *Official Records*, Plenary Meetings, 15th Session (Part 2), 984th meeting, April 15, 1961, p. 297.

26. Walter Johnson, ed., *The Papers of Adlai E. Stevenson* (Boston: Little, Brown, 1979), VIII, 53; Martin, *Adlai Stevenson and the World*, p. 626.

27. United Nations, General Assembly, *Official Records*, First Committee, 15th Session (Part 2), 1149th meeting, 3 p.m., April 15, 1961, p. 55.

28. Ibid., pp. 55–56.

29. Harris Wofford, *Of Kennedys and Kings: Making Sense of the Sixties* (New York: Farrar, Straus and Giroux, 1980), p. 348.

30. Martin, *Adlai Stevenson and the World*, p. 628; Higgins, *Perfect Failure*, pp. 130–131.

31. Martin, *Adlai Stevenson and the World*, pp. 579–580, 628.

32. Ibid., p. 628.

33. United Nations, General Assembly, *Official Records*, First Committee, 15th Session (Part 2), 1150th meeting, 11 a.m., April 17, 1961, pp. 57–60.

34. Ibid., p. 60.

35. Doyle, ed., *As We Knew Adlai*, p. 286.

36. Higgins, *Perfect Failure*, pp. 131–132, 139–140, 149.

37. See White, *Cuban Missile Crisis*, pp. 36–37.

38. Richard N. Goodwin, *Remembering America: A Voice from the Sixties* (Boston: Little, Brown, 1988), p. 187.

39. For JFK's concern over Berlin, see Richard M. Nixon, *Six Crises* (New York: Simon and Schuster reprint, 1990), pp. 234–235.

40. Khrushchev to Kennedy, and Kennedy to Khrushchev, both April 18, 1961, in U.S. Department of State, *FRUS, 1961–1963*, X, 264–265, 283–284.

41. JFK, speech, April 20, 1961, *Public Papers of the Presidents, 1961*, pp. 304–306; Goodwin, *Remembering America*, pp. 180–181.

42. United Nations, General Assembly, *Official Records*, First Committee, 15th Session (Part 2), 1154th meeting, 8:30 p.m., April 18, 1961, pp. 76–77, and 1159th meeting, April 20, 1961, pp. 99–100.

43. United Nations, General Assembly, *Official Records*, First Committee, 15th Session (Part 2), 1159th meeting, April 20, 1961, p. 99, and 1161st meeting, April 21, 1961, pp. 108–110; UN, General Assembly, *Official Records*, Plenary Meetings, 15th Session (Part 2), 995th meeting, April 21, 1961, p. 497; UN, General Assembly, *Official Records*, 15th Session, Supplement No. 16A, p. 3.

44. Stevenson to Eugene McCarthy, May 6, 1961, and to Mrs. Eugene Meyer, May 14, 1961, in Johnson, ed., *Papers of Adlai E. Stevenson*, VIII, 57, 59.

45. Doyle, ed., *As We Knew Adlai*, p. 178.

46. Goodwin, *Remembering America*, p. 188; Bowles to Kennedy, April 20, 1961, Papers of Chester Bowles, box 297, Sterling Library, Yale University, New Haven, Conn.

47. Stevenson to JFK, "Some lessons from Cuba," April 23, 1961, President's Office Files, box 114a, JFKL.

48. Ibid.

49. Ibid.

50. Ibid.

51. Ibid.

52. Stevenson to JFK, May 27, 1961, President's Office Files, box 33, JFKL.

53. Ibid.

54. National Security Action Memorandum No. 2422, "U.S. Policy Toward Cuba," May 5, 1961, National Security Files, box 313, JFKL.

55. Stevenson to Barbara Jackson, May 31, 1961, in Johnson, ed., *Papers of Adlai E. Stevenson*, VIII, 70.

56. Stevenson to White House, June 14, 1961, National Security Files, box 250, JFKL; Stevenson report to JFK on South America mission, June 27, 1961, in Johnson, ed., *Papers of Adlai E. Stevenson*, VIII, 75–83; JFK to Stevenson, July 6, 1961, President's Office Files, box 33, JFKL.

57. Theodore C. Sorensen, *The Kennedy Legacy* (London: Weidenfeld and Nicolson reprint, 1970), pp. 185–186; Beschloss, *Crisis Years*, pp. 134–135; David C. Martin, "The CIA's 'Loaded Gun': The Life and Times of 'America's James Bond,' William King Harvey," *Washington Post*, October 10, 1976, p. C1; Wofford, *Of Kennedys and Kings*, p. 362.

58. John F. Kennedy, *Why England Slept*, 2nd ed. (New York: W. Funk, 1961).

59. Goodwin, *Remembering America*, pp. 187–188; CIA paper on covert actions against Cuba, undated (but probably drafted in early August 1961), in *FRUS, 1961–1963*, X, 636–637.

60. Robert Kennedy, notes on White House meeting, November 3, 1961, and Richard Helms to John McCone, January 19, 1962, in *FRUS, 1961–1963*, X, 666, 719–720.

61. Memorandum from President Kennedy, November 30, 1961, in *FRUS, 1961–1963*, X, 688–689; James G. Hershberg, "Before 'The Missiles of October': Did Kennedy Plan a Military Strike Against Cuba?" *Diplomatic History* 14 (Spring 1990), 176; "Guidelines for Operation Mongoose," March 14, 1962, in *FRUS, 1961–1963*, X, 771–772.

62. "Guidelines for Operation Mongoose," p. 771; Jean R. Moenk, "USCONARC Participation in the Cuban Crisis 1962 (U)," October 1963, pp. 1–3, document no. 3164, 'The Cuban missile crisis, 1962' collection, National Security Archive (NSA), Washington, D.C.; Dennison, "CINCLANT Historical Account of Cuban Crisis 1963 (U)," April 29, 1963, pp. 17–21, document no. 3087, NSA; Robert McNamara to Lyman Lemnitzer, April 20, 1961, and Lansdale, "The Cuba Project," January 18, 1962, in *FRUS, 1961–1963*, X, 306–307, 714, 717.

63. Hershberg, "Before 'The Missiles of October,'" p. 181; "Big Maneuver Opens," *New York Times*, April 10, 1962; "President Sees Atlantic Fleet Hunt and Destroy 'Enemy' Submarine," *New York Times*, April 15, 1962.

64. U.S. Senate Select Committee to Study Governmental Operations with Respect to Intelligence Activities, interim report, S.Rept. 94-465, 94th Congress, 1st session, *Alleged Assassination Plots Involving Foreign Leaders*, pp. 71–77.

65. Ibid., pp. 79–84.

66. Ibid., pp. 119–120, 138; oral history of Smathers, interview 1, tape 2, pp. 6–7, JFKL; Goodwin, *Remembering America*, p. 189; Lansdale to Harriman, February 26, 1977, Papers of Edward G. Lansdale, box 3, Hoover Institution, Stanford, California.

67. Various resolutions in Council on Foreign Relations, *Documents on American Foreign Relations, 1962* (New York: Harper, 1963), pp. 336–348; newspaper clipping of a John Crosby article, "Shiny Words and Dollars," Stevenson Papers, box 846; White House statement concerning the embargo on trade with Cuba, February 3, 1962, *Public Papers of the Presidents of the United States: John F. Kennedy, 1962* (Washington, D.C.: U.S. Government Printing Office, 1963), p. 106.

68. UN General Assembly, *Official Records*, Plenary Meetings, 16th Session, 1032nd plenary meeting, October 10, 1961, p. 379.

69. Journal entry, November 14, 1961, in John Kenneth Galbraith, *Ambassador's Journal: A Personal Account of the Kennedy Years* (Boston: Houghton Mifflin, 1969), p. 254.

70. See Mark J. White, *Missiles in Cuba: Kennedy, Khrushchev, Castro and the 1962 Crisis* (Chicago: Ivan R. Dee, 1997), pp. 30–39, for a fuller discussion of this issue.

71. Thomas G. Paterson and William J. Brophy, "October Missiles and November Elections: The Cuban Missile Crisis and American Politics, 1962," *Journal of American History* 73 (June 1986), 87–119.

72. Transcript, news conference, September 4, 1962, National Security Files, box 36, JFKL; president's news conference, September 13, 1962, *Public Papers of the Presidents, 1962*, pp. 674–681 passim.

73. National Security Action Memorandum No. 181, August 23, 1962, in *FRUS, 1961–1963*, X, 957; McCone, memorandum of Mongoose meeting, October 4, 1962, in U.S. Department of State, *FRUS, 1961–1963* (Washington, D.C.: U.S. Government Printing Office, 1996), XI, *Cuban Missile Crisis and Aftermath*, 11–13; Hershberg, "Before 'The Missiles of October,'" pp. 185–192; oral history of William P. Mack, p. 390, document no. 3285, NSA.

74. Entry for October 15, 1962, National Security Archive Chronology, p. 54, NSA; Hershberg, "Before 'The Missiles of October,'" pp. 186–187.

75. Beschloss, *Crisis Years*, p. 4.

11. WAR OR PEACE

1. Beschloss, *Crisis Years*, pp. 4–5, 450.

2. ExComm transcript, 11:50 a.m., October 16, 1962, in Ernest R. May and Philip D. Zelikow, eds., *The Kennedy Tapes: Inside the White House During the Cuban Missile Crisis* (Cambridge, Mass., and London: Belknap Press of Harvard University Press, 1997), pp. 71–72.

3. Fritchey to Stevenson, April 13, 1965, Stevenson Papers, box 846; Elie Abel, *The Missile Crisis* (Philadelphia: Lippincott, 1966), p. 49; Johnson, ed., *Papers of Adlai E. Stevenson*, VIII, 299.

4. ExComm transcript, 6:30 p.m., October 16, 1962, in *Kennedy Tapes*, pp. 94, 100.

5. Ibid., pp. 105, 107.

6. ExComm transcript, 11:50 a.m., October 16, 1962, p. 66; ExComm transcript, 6:30 p.m., October 16, 1962, p. 102.

7. ExComm transcript, 6:30 p.m., October 16, 1962, pp. 113, 115.

8. Raymond L. Garthoff, *Reflections on the Cuban Missile Crisis*, rev. ed. (Washington, D.C.: Brookings Institution, 1989), p. 52; James G. Blight and David A. Welch, *On the Brink: Americans and Soviets Reexamine the Cuban Missile Crisis* (New York: Noonday, 1990), p. 359n.

9. Stevenson memorandum, "Notes and Questions," October 17, 1962, Stevenson Papers, box 846.

10. Ibid.

11. Stevenson to JFK, October 17, 1962, in Johnson, ed., *Papers of Adlai E. Stevenson*, VIII, 299–301.

12. Johnson, ed., *Papers of Adlai E. Stevenson*, VIII, 299n; Theodore C. Sorensen, *Kennedy* (New York: Harper, 1965), pp. 695–696.

13. Fritchey to Stevenson, April 13, 1965; Robert F. Kennedy, *Thirteen Days: A Memoir of the Cuban Missile Crisis* (New York: Norton, 1969), p. 25; Elie Abel, *The Missiles of October*, rev. ed. (London: MacGibbon and Kee, 1969), p. 55.

14. ExComm transcript, 11 a.m., October 18, 1962, in *Kennedy Tapes*, pp. 135, 137, 138, 142, 143, 144, 146.

15. Dean Acheson, "Dean Acheson's Version of Robert Kennedy's Version of the Cuban Missile Affair: Homage to Plain Dumb Luck," *Esquire* 71 (February 1969), 76–77; oral history of Dean Acheson, p. 24, JFKL; Abel, *Missiles of October*, p. 66.

16. Transcript, JFK dictation, October 18, 1962, in *Kennedy Tapes*, p. 172.

17. Entry for October 19, 1962, President's Appointment Book, JFKL; Leonard C. Meeker, minutes of 11 a.m. ExComm meeting, October 19, 1962, document no. 699, NSA.

18. Meeker, minutes of 11 a.m. ExComm meeting, October 19, 1962.

19. Abel, *Missiles of October*, p. 88; minutes of ExComm meeting, 2:30–5:10 p.m., October 20, 1962, in *FRUS, 1961–1963*, XI, 126–136; Stevenson memorandum for JFK, "Political Program to Be Announced by the President," October 20, 1962, in Johnson, ed., *Papers of Adlai E. Stevenson*, VIII, 301–302; Ball, *Past Has Another Pattern*, p. 295.

20. Abel, *Missile Crisis*, p. 96; minutes of ExComm meeting, 2:30–5:10 p.m., October 20, 1962, pp. 128, 133.

21. O'Donnell and Powers, *"Johnny, We Hardly Knew Ye,"* pp. 322–323; Arthur M. Schlesinger, Jr., *Robert Kennedy and His Times* (New York: Ballantine, 1979), p. 516.

22. O'Donnell and Powers, *"Johnny, We Hardly Knew Ye,"* p. 326.

23. Stevenson memorandum, October 21, 1962, in Johnson, ed., *Papers of Adlai E. Stevenson*, VIII, 304–306.

24. Minutes of ExComm meeting, 2:30–4:50 p.m., October 21, 1962, in *FRUS, 1961–1963*, XI, 145, 148.

25. McNamara, notes on meeting with President Kennedy, October 21, 1962, in *FRUS, 1961–1963*, XI, 139; transcript of meeting between JFK and the Joint Chiefs, October 19, 1962, in *Kennedy Tapes*, p. 175; minutes of ExComm meeting, 2:30–5:10 p.m., October 20, 1962, p. 131; Fritchey to Stevenson, April 13, 1965.

26. ExComm transcript, 11:30 a.m., October 22, 1962, in *Kennedy Tapes*, p. 222.

27. JFK, radio and television report to the American people on the Soviet arms buildup in Cuba, October 22, 1962, *Public Papers of the Presidents, 1962*, pp. 806–809.

28. ExComm transcripts, 10 a.m. and 6 p.m., October 23, 1962, in *Kennedy Tapes*, pp. 289–340 passim; Khrushchev to Kennedy, October 23, 1962, and Kennedy to Khrushchev, October 23, 1962, in *FRUS, 1961–1963*, XI, 170–171, 174–175; Kennedy, *Thirteen Days*, p. 41; memorandum from Robert Kennedy to JFK, October 24, 1962, in *FRUS, 1961–1963*, XI, 175–177.

29. Quoted in White, *Missiles in Cuba*, p. 118.

30. ExComm transcript, 10 a.m., October 24, 1962, in *Kennedy Tapes*, pp. 347–366 passim.

31. Ibid., pp. 353, 361.

32. ExComm transcript, 5 p.m., October 25, 1962, in *Kennedy Tapes*, pp. 432–433, 436–437; unauthored memorandum, "Political Path," October 25, 1962, National Security Files, box 315, JFKL; Khrushchev to Kennedy, October 24, 1962, in Ronald R. Pope, ed., *Soviet Views on the Cuban Missile Crisis: Myth and Reality in Foreign Policy Analysis* (Washington, D.C.: University Press of America, 1982), pp. 32–36; Kennedy to Khrushchev, October 25, 1962, in *FRUS, 1961–1963*, XI, 198.

33. U Thant, *View from the UN* (Garden City, N.Y.: Doubleday, 1978), pp. 154, 157–158.

34. Stevenson, "The Cuban Crisis: A Base for Communist Aggression," *Vital Speeches of the Day* 29:3 (November 15, 1962), 70–76; Martin, *Adlai Stevenson and*

the World, pp. 728–729; Stevenson, statement to the press, 8:45 p.m., October 23, 1962, Stevenson Papers, box 846.

35. Abel, *Missile Crisis*, p. 149.

36. Doyle, ed., *As We Knew Adlai*, p. 265; Blight and Welch, *On the Brink*, p. 366n.

37. Stevenson and Zorin, "Has the U.S.S.R. Missiles in Cuba? United Nations Debate," *Vital Speeches of the Day* 29:3 (November 15, 1962), 77–80.

38. Doyle, ed., *As We Knew Adlai*, p. 287; Stevenson and Zorin, "Has the U.S.S.R. Missiles in Cuba?," pp. 80–83.

39. Miscellaneous letters to Stevenson, Stevenson Papers, box 847; Martin, *Adlai Stevenson and the World*, p. 735; newspaper clipping, "The New Adlai," *Chicago Tribune*, in Stevenson Papers, box 847.

40. Charles Bartlett, "Portrait of a Friend," in Thompson, ed., *The Kennedy Presidency*, pp. 16–17.

41. Fritchey to Stevenson, April 13, 1965; Kennedy, *Thirteen Days*, pp. 59–60.

42. ExComm transcript, 10 a.m., October 26, 1962, in *Kennedy Tapes*, pp. 451, 462–464.

43. Ibid., p. 464.

44. Khrushchev to Kennedy, October 26, 1962, in *FRUS, 1961–1963*, XI, 235–241.

45. Ibid.; Beschloss, *Crisis Years*, pp. 514–515.

46. Khrushchev to Kennedy, October 27, 1962, in *FRUS, 1961–1963*, XI, 257–260.

47. Kennedy, *Thirteen Days*, pp. 79–80; ExComm transcript, 10 a.m., October 27, 1962, pp. 497–498, 499, 501–502, and ExComm transcript, 4 p.m., October 27, 1962, pp. 554–555, in *Kennedy Tapes*.

48. Kennedy to Khrushchev, October 27, 1962, in *FRUS, 1961–1963*, XI, 268–269; ExComm transcript, 4 p.m., October 27, 1962, pp. 550–551, 562–563; Sorensen, *Kennedy*, p. 714.

49. ExComm transcript, 10 a.m., October 27, 1962, pp. 498–499; ExComm transcript, 4:00 p.m., October 27, 1962, pp. 550, 563.

50. ExComm transcript, 4 p.m., October 27, 1962, pp. 548, 602.

51. Kennedy, *Thirteen Days*, p. 84; memorandum from Robert Kennedy to Rusk, October 30, 1962, in *FRUS, 1961–1963*, XI, 270–271 (including footnote 2); Anatoly Dobrynin to the Soviet Foreign Ministry, October 27, 1962, in Woodrow Wilson International Center, *Cold War International History Project Bulletin* 5 (Spring 1995), 79–80.

52. ExComm transcript, 4 p.m., October 27, 1962, pp. 545, 546, 564; Blight and Welch, *On the Brink*, pp. 83–84; Patrick Dean to the (British) Foreign Office, October 25, 1962, Foreign Office Records, 371/162387, Public Record Office, Kew, United Kingdom.

53. *Kennedy Tapes*, p. 629; CIA memorandum, "The Crisis: USSR/Cuba," 6 a.m., October 28, 1962, National Security Files, box 316, JFKL; Kennedy, *Thirteen Days*, p. 75; I. J. M. Sutherland to R. I. T. Cromartie, October 26, 1962, Foreign Office Records 371/162391, Public Record Office; Castro to Khrushchev, October 26, 1962, in Laurence Chang and Peter Kornbluh, eds., *The Cuban Missile Crisis: A Documents Reader* (New York: New Press, 1992), pp. 81, 189.

54. Anatoly Dobrynin, "The Caribbean Crisis: An Eyewitness Account," *International Affairs* 8 (August 1992), 58; Oleg Troyanovski, "The Caribbean Crisis: A View from the Kremlin," *International Affairs* 4–5 (April–May 1992), 155; Khrushchev to Kennedy, October 28, 1962, in *FRUS, 1961–1963*, XI, 279–283.

55. Summary record of ExComm meeting, 11:10 a.m., October 28, 1962, in *FRUS, 1961–1963*, XI, 283–285; quoted in White, *Missiles in Cuba*, pp. 144–145; JFK, statement by the president following the Soviet decision to withdraw missiles from Cuba, October 28, 1962, *Public Papers of the Presidents, 1962*, p. 815; Kennedy to Khrushchev, October 28, 1962, in *FRUS, 1961–1963*, XI, 285–286; Dobrynin to Soviet Ministry of Foreign Affairs, October 28, 1962, in *Cold War International History Project Bulletin* 5 (Spring 1995), 76.

56. Benjamin C. Bradlee, *Conversations with Kennedy* (New York: Norton, 1975), pp. 120–121.

57. Stewart Alsop and Charles Bartlett, "In Time of Crisis," *Saturday Evening Post*, December 8, 1962, pp. 15–20.

58. Entry for November 11, 1962, President's Appointment Book, JFKL; Bartlett to Kennedy, October 29 and 31, 1962, President's Office Files, box 28, JFKL; Johnson, ed., *Papers of Adlai E. Stevenson*, VIII, pp. 351–352.

59. Kennedy to Stevenson, December 4 and 5, 1962, and excerpts from JFK's press conference, December 12, 1962; both in Stevenson Papers, box 850; Stevenson to Salinger, December 10, 1962, President's Office Files, box 33, JFKL; oral history of Harlan Cleveland, p. 29, JFKL.

60. W. LeRoy Garth to Stevenson, December 13, 1962, Stevenson Papers, box 847; oral history of Cleveland, p. 43, JFKL.

61. Television and radio interview, December 17, 1962, *Public Papers of the Presidents, 1962*, p. 898.

62. Beschloss, *Crisis Years*, pp. 602, 627, 646; Kennedy, commencement address at American University in Washington, D.C., June 10, 1963, *Public Papers of the Presidents of the United States: John F. Kennedy, 1963* (Washington, D.C.: U.S. Government Printing Office, 1964), pp. 459–464; CIA, paper for the Standing Group of the National Security Council, June 8, 1963; memorandum for the record, June 19, 1963; memorandum from William Attwood to Gordon Chase, November 8, 1963; and memorandum from Chase to McGeorge Bundy, November 25, 1963, in *FRUS, 1961–1963*, XI, 828–834, 837–838, 879–883, 891–893.

63. Lawrence J. Bassett and Stephen E. Pelz, "The Failed Search for Victory: Vietnam and the Politics of War," in Thomas G. Paterson, ed., *Kennedy's Quest for Victory: American Foreign Policy, 1961–1963* (New York and Oxford: Oxford University Press, 1989), pp. 223–252.

64. McKeever, *Adlai Stevenson*, p. 563.

12. The Accidental President and the Tardy Rebel

1. Lyndon B. Johnson, *The Vantage Point: Perspectives of the Presidency, 1963–1969* (London: Weidenfeld and Nicolson, 1971), pp. 1–2, 4–5, 8–10.

2. Ibid., pp. 10–15; Ball, *Past Has Another Pattern*, pp. 312–313.

3. John McCone memorandum for the record, November 25, 1963, meeting notes file, presidential papers of LBJ, box 1, Lyndon Baines Johnson Library,

Austin, Texas (hereafter LBJL); quoted in Fredrik Logevall, *Choosing War: The Lost Chance for Peace and the Escalation of War in Vietnam* (Berkeley, Los Angeles, London: University of California Press, 1999), p. 77.

4. Lyndon Johnson, address before a Joint Session of Congress, November 27, 1963, *Public Papers of the Presidents of the United States: Lyndon B. Johnson, 1963–64* (Washington, D.C.: U.S. Government Printing Office, 1965), I, 8–10.

5. Key writings on Ball include David L. DiLeo, *George Ball, Vietnam, and the Rethinking of Containment* (Chapel Hill and London: University of North Carolina Press, 1991), and James A. Bill, *George Ball: Behind the Scenes in U.S. Foreign Policy* (New Haven and London: Yale University Press, 1997).

6. Alan Bennett, *The History Boys* (London: Faber and Faber, 2004).

7. McCone memorandum for the record, November 25, 1963.

8. Key studies of Johnson's pre-presidential years include Robert Dallek, *Lone Star Rising: Lyndon Johnson and His Times, 1908–1960* (New York and Oxford: Oxford University Press, 1991), and the following works by Robert A. Caro: *The Years of Lyndon Johnson: The Path to Power* (New York: Knopf, 1982); *The Years of Lyndon Johnson: Means of Ascent* (New York: Knopf, 1990); and *The Years of Lyndon Johnson: Master of the Senate* (New York: Knopf, 2002).

9. Caro, *Path to Power*, pp. 141–201.

10. Caro, *Means of Ascent*, passim; Dallek, *Lone Star Rising*, pp. 422–425, 462–463; Irwin Unger and Debi Unger, *LBJ: A Life* (New York: John Wiley, 1999), pp. 186–187.

11. Dallek, *Lone Star Rising*, passim.

12. Ibid., passim.

13. Ibid., pp. 544–546, 559–588.

14. Unger and Unger, *LBJ*, pp. 254–278.

15. Robert Dallek, *Flawed Giant: Lyndon Johnson and His Times, 1961–1973* (Oxford and New York: Oxford University Press, 1998), pp. 12–13; Bassett and Pelz, "The Failed Search for Victory," in Paterson, ed., *Kennedy's Quest for Victory*, pp. 228–230.

16. Dallek, *Flawed Giant*, pp. 17–18.

17. Johnson, *Vantage Point*, pp. 43–44.

18. Bill, *George Ball*, pp. 21–29.

19. Ibid., pp. 29–36.

20. Ball, *Past Has Another Pattern*, pp. 24, 37, 41, 61–62.

21. Bill, *George Ball*, pp. 40–42.

22. Ball, *Past Has Another Pattern*, pp. 152–153.

23. Bill, *George Ball*, pp. 56–57, 60, 64.

24. Ball, *Past Has Another Pattern*, pp. 164, 168.

25. David Halberstam, *The Best and the Brightest* (New York: Penguin ed., 1983), p. 598; Ball, *Past Has Another Pattern*, p. 168.

26. Halberstam, *Best and the Brightest*, p. 598; Ball, *Past Has Another Pattern*, pp. 145–148, 152.

27. White, *Missiles in Cuba*, p. 84; Halberstam, *Best and the Brightest*, p. 598.

28. Ball, *Past Has Another Pattern*, p. 183.

29. Ibid., pp. 163–164.

30. Ibid., pp. 365–366.

31. Ibid., p. 366; DiLeo, *George Ball*, p. 56.

32. Ball, *Past Has Another Pattern*, p. 367; Larry Berman, *Planning a Tragedy: The Americanization of the War in Vietnam* (New York and London: Norton, 1982), pp. 21–22.

33. Wills, *The Kennedy Imprisonment*, p. 236.

34. DiLeo, *George Ball*, p. 57; Bill, *George Ball*, p. 153; Kaysen-Ball telcon and Rusk-Ball telcon, July 1, 1963, Papers of George Ball, box 7, LBJL.

35. Ball, *Past Has Another Pattern*, p. 370.

36. Ibid., pp. 371–372.

37. Robert S. McNamara, *In Retrospect: The Tragedy and Lessons of Vietnam* (New York: Vintage, 1996 edition), p. 57; Bill, *George Ball*, p. 155.

38. Bromley Smith, memorandum of conference with the president, August 28, 1963, Papers of Bromley Smith, box 16 (temporary box), LBJL.

39. Dallek, *Flawed Giant*, p. 98.

13. DEVIL'S ADVOCATE

1. Johnson, *Vantage Point*, p. 62; Schulzinger, *Time for War*, pp. 128–129; McNamara, *In Retrospect*, pp. 103–106. For an outstanding account of Johnson's policies in Vietnam, see Lloyd C. Gardner, *Pay Any Price: Lyndon Johnson and the Wars for Vietnam* (Chicago: Ivan R. Dee, 1995).

2. Schulzinger, *Time for War*, pp. 134–135.

3. Dallek, *Flawed Giant*, p. 100.

4. Ibid., pp. 101–102.

5. Quoted in PBS documentary, *American Experience: LBJ* (1991).

6. Johnson, *Vantage Point*, pp. 66–68; McNamara, *In Retrospect*, p. 109.

7. Schulzinger, *Time for War*, p. 138.

8. Ball to Rusk, May 31, 1964, *FRUS, 1964–1968* (Washington, D.C.: U.S. Government Printing Office, 1992), I, *Vietnam, 1964,* 400.

9. McNamara, *In Retrospect*, pp. 103, 104–105, 119–120.

10. Ibid., pp. 107–109, 110–111.

11. Ibid., p. 112.

12. Johnson, *Vantage Point*, pp. 65–67; summary record of the 524th Meeting of the National Security Council, March 17, 1964, *FRUS, 1964–1968*, I, 170–172.

13. Quoted in McNamara, *In Retrospect*, p. 119; summary record of the 532nd Meeting of the National Security Council, May 15, 1964, *FRUS, 1964–1968*, I, 328–330.

14. McNamara, *In Retrospect*, pp. 121–122; Dallek, *Flawed Giant*, p. 106.

15. Dallek, *Flawed Giant*, p. 106.

16. Ball, *Past Has Another Pattern*, p. 377.

17. Bill, *George Ball*, pp. 157–158.

18. Oral history of George Ball, interview II, pp. 16, 39, LBJL; Bill, *George Ball*, p. 168.

19. Transcripts, Ball-McGeorge Bundy telcon, December 15, 1963; Ball-Johnson telcon, January 29, 1964; Ball-McNamara telcon, January 29, 1964—all in Ball Papers, box 7, LBJL; Ball telegram to Lodge, January 29, 1964, *FRUS, 1964–1968*, I, 42.

20. Transcript, Johnson-Ball telcon, May 13, 1964, Ball Papers, box 7, LBJL; oral history of Dean Rusk, interview II, tape 1, p. 34, LBJL.

21. Transcripts, Alexis Johnson-Ball telcon, April 21, 1964, and McNamara-Ball telcon, May 14, 1964, Ball Papers, box 7, LBJL; Ball, *Past Has Another Pattern*, p. 376.

22. Ball, *Past Has Another Pattern*, p. 377.

23. Ball to Rusk, May 31, 1964, pp. 400–404; Bill, *George Ball*, p. 158.

24. Ball to Rusk, May 31, 1964, pp. 400–401.

25. Ibid., pp. 401–402.

26. Ibid., pp. 402–404.

27. Ball, *Past Has Another Pattern*, pp. 377–378; memorandum from LBJ to Ball, June 4, 1964, National Security File (NSF), Country File-Vietnam, box 53, LBJL.

28. Ball to LBJ and Rusk, June 5, 1964, NSF, Country File–Vietnam, box 53, LBJL.

29. Ibid.

30. Ibid.

31. Ball to LBJ and Rusk, June 5, 1964, NSF, Country File–Vietnam, box 53, LBJL.

32. Ball, *Past Has Another Pattern*, p. 378.

33. Johnson, *Vantage Point*, pp. 112–113; John Prados, "40th Anniversary of the Gulf of Tonkin Incident," August 4, 2004, National Security Archive website (www.gwu.edu/~nsarchiv); McNamara, *In Retrospect*, pp. 129–130; Schulzinger, *Time for War*, pp. 150–151.

34. Johnson, *Vantage Point*, p. 113; Rusk, *As I Saw It*, p. 444; editorial note, *FRUS, 1964–1968*, 1, 597.

35. Prados, "40th Anniversary of the Gulf of Tonkin Incident."

36. Edwin E. Moise, *Tonkin Gulf and the Escalation of the Vietnam War* (Chapel Hill and London: University of North Carolina Press, 1996); Logevall, *Choosing War*, p. 198; Schulzinger, *Time for War*, p. 151; Prados, "40th Anniversary of the Gulf of Tonkin Incident."

37. Summary notes of 538th NSC meeting, August 4, 1964, 6:15–6:40 p.m., pp. 611–612, and notes of the Leadership meeting, August 4, 1964, 6:45 p.m., pp. 615–621, both in *FRUS, 1964–1968*, vol. I; radio and television report to the American people following renewed aggression in the Gulf of Tonkin, August 4, 1964, *Public Papers of the Presidents of the United States: Lyndon B. Johnson, 1963–1964* (Washington, D.C.: U.S. Government Printing Office, 1965), II, 927–928.

38. Dallek, *Flawed Giant*, p. 150.

39. Johnson, *Vantage Point*, p. 115; Rusk, *As I Saw It*, p. 445.

40. Johnson, *Vantage Point*, pp. 117–118.

41. Memorandum for the record of a meeting, August 10, 1964, in *FRUS, 1964–1968*, 1, 662–663.

42. Radio and television report to the American people, August 4, 1964, p. 927; notes of the Leadership meeting, August 4, 1964, p. 618; Schulzinger, *Time for War*, p. 151.

43. Oral history of George Ball, interview I, pp. 24–25, LBJL.

44. Johnson, *Vantage Point*, pp. 118–119.

45. Transcript, McNamara-Ball telcon, August 3, 1964, 9:55 a.m., and transcript, Bundy-Ball telcon, August 3, 1964, 10:15 a.m.—both in Ball Papers, box 7, LBJL.

46. Oral history of Ball, interview I, p. 23, LBJL; Ball, *Past Has Another Pattern*, p. 380.

47. Johnson, *Vantage Point*, pp. 117–118; oral history of William Bundy, tape 1, p. 28, LBJL; memorandum of a telephone conversation between Rusk and William Bundy, August 5, 1964, 2:22 p.m., *FRUS, 1964–1968*, I, 634.

48. Johnson, *Vantage Point*, p. 116.

49. Ball, "How Valid Are the Assumptions Underlying Our Vietnam Policies," October 5, 1964, NSF, Country File–Vietnam, box 222, LBJL.

50. Oral history of George Ball, interview I, p. 20, LBJL.

51. Memorandum for the record by McGeorge Bundy, September 20, 1964, *FRUS, 1964–1968*, I, 778–779.

52. Ibid., pp. 779–780; Ball, *Past Has Another Pattern*, pp. 379–380.

53. Memorandum for the record by McGeorge Bundy, September 20, 1964, p. 780.

54. Oral history of George Ball, interview I, pp. 15–16, LBJL; Ball, *Past Has Another Pattern*, p. 380; Ball to Rusk, McNamara, and Bundy, October 5, 1964, National Security File, Country File–Vietnam, box 222, LBJL.

55. Ball, "How Valid Are the Assumptions Underlying Our Vietnam Policies?," October 5, 1964.

56. Ibid.

57. Ibid.

58. Ibid.

59. Ibid.

60. Ibid.

61. Oral history of Ball, I, 16–17; Ball, *Past Has Another Pattern*, p. 383.

62. McNamara, *In Retrospect*, pp. 156, 158.

63. Forrestal-Ball telcon, October 8, 1964, Ball Papers, box 7, LBJL; Ball, *Past Has Another Pattern*, pp. 384–385.

64. Johnson, *Vantage Point*, p. 121.

65. Ibid., pp. 121–122.

14. CROSSING THE RUBICON

1. Johnson, *Vantage Point*, pp. 122–123; McNamara, *In Retrospect*, p. 170.

2. Summary notes of and the attendance list for the 545th NSC meeting, February 6, 1965, NSF, NSC Meetings File, box 1, LBJL.

3. Summary notes of 545th NSC meeting, February 6, 1965.

4. Ball, *Past Has Another Pattern*, p. 389; summary notes of 545th NSC meeting, February 6, 1965.

5. Johnson, *Vantage Point*, p. 125.

6. Ibid., pp. 126–128; summary notes of 547th NSC meeting, February 8, 1965, NSF, NSC Meetings File, box 1, LBJL.

7. Summary notes of 547th NSC meeting, February 8, 1965.

8. Clifford, *Counsel to the President*, p. 406.

9. Summary notes of 547th NSC meeting, February 8, 1965.

10. Ball to Saigon, February 13, 1965, NSF, NSC History—Deployment of Major U.S. Forces to Vietnam, July 1965, box 40, LBJL; McNamara, *In Retrospect*, p. 174.

11. Minutes, meeting of principals, 1:30 p.m., February 10, 1965, and summary record of NSC meeting no. 548, 2:10 p.m., February 10, 1965; both in NSF, NSC Meetings File, box 1, LBJL.

12. Ball, *Past Has Another Pattern*, pp. 390–391; Ball, memorandum for Johnson, February 13, 1965, NSF, NSC History—Deployment of Major U.S. Forces to Vietnam, July 1965, box 40, LBJL.

13. Ball, *Past Has Another Pattern*, pp. 391–392.

14. Transcript, Johnson-Ball telcon, February 15, 1965, 10 a.m., Ball Papers, box 7, LBJL.

15. Ball, *Past Has Another Pattern*, p. 392; quote from Berman, *Planning a Tragedy*, p. 48; transcript, Moyers-Ball telcon, February 25, 1965, 10:30 a.m., Ball Papers, box 7, LBJL.

16. Ball, *Past Has Another Pattern*, p. 392.

17. Berman, *Planning a Tragedy*, pp. 52–53.

18. Chronology of Presidential Decisions, NSF, NSC History—Deployment of Major U.S. Forces to Vietnam, July 1965, box 43, LBJL; Ball, *Past Has Another Pattern*, p. 393.

19. Clifford, *Counsel to the President*, p. 408; Dallek, *Flawed Giant*, pp. 257–258; Johnson, *Vantage Point*, pp. 132–133.

20. Johnson, address at Johns Hopkins University: "Peace Without Conquest," April 7, 1965, U.S. Government, *Public Papers of the Presidents of the United States: Lyndon B. Johnson, 1965* (Washington, D.C.: U.S. Government Printing Office, 1967), pp. 394–399; Johnson, *Vantage Point*, p. 134.

21. Chronology of Presidential Decisions, NSC History, July 1965; McNamara, *In Retrospect*, pp. 182–183; Johnson, *Vantage Point*, p. 141.

22. Transcripts, Fulbright-Ball telcon, March 4, 1965, 9:35 a.m., and LBJ-Ball telcon, April 6, 1965, 8:45 a.m., both in Ball Papers, box 7.

23. Oral history of Ball, interview II, p. 3, LBJL; Ball, *Past Has Another Pattern*, p. 393.

24. Ball memorandum for Johnson, "Should We Try to Move Toward a Vietnamese Settlement Now?," April 21, 1965, NSF, Country File–Vietnam, box 213, LBJL.

25. Ibid.

26. Ibid.

27. Johnson, *Vantage Point*, p. 142; transcript, Moyers-Ball telcon, April 23, 1965, 11:05 a.m., Ball Papers, box 7; transcript, Moyers-Ball telcon, April 24, 1965, 9:45 a.m., Ball Papers, box 7.

28. Ball, *Past Has Another Pattern*, p. 394; oral history of Ball, interview II, pp. 3–4, LBJL.

29. Transcript, LBJ-Ball telcon, June 14, 1965, 8:50 p.m., Ball Papers, box 7; Clifford, *Counsel to the President*, p. 410.

30. Clifford, *Counsel to the President*, p. 410; Hubert H. Humphrey, *The Education of a Public Man: My Life and Politics* (Garden City, N.Y.: Doubleday, 1976), pp. 319, 327.

31. Ball memorandum for Johnson, "Keeping the Power of Decision in the South Viet-Nam Crisis," June 18, 1965, NSF, Country File-Vietnam, box 19, LBJL.

32. Ibid.

33. Transcript, Moyers-Ball telcon, June 21, 1965, 3:30 p.m., Ball Papers, box 7.

34. McNamara, *In Retrospect*, pp. 192–193.

35. Ibid., p. 193; Ball memorandum for Rusk, McNamara et al., "Cutting Our Losses in South Viet-Nam," June 28, 1965, Papers of Paul C. Warnke, John Mc-Naughton Files, box 1, LBJL.

36. Ball memorandum for Rusk, McNamara et al., "Cutting Our Losses in South Viet-Nam," June 28, 1965.

37. Ibid.

38. McGeorge Bundy, notes of meeting, June 29, 1965, 3:30 p.m., Papers of McGeorge Bundy, box 1, LBJL.

39. Ball memorandum for LBJ, "A Compromise Solution for South Viet-Nam," July 1, 1965, Warnke Papers, John McNaughton Files, box 1, LBJL.

40. McGeorge Bundy, memorandum for LBJ, July 1, 1965, 8:20 p.m., NSF, Memos to the President, box 4, LBJL; McNamara, *In Retrospect*, p. 193.

41. McGeorge Bundy memorandum for LBJ, July 1, 1965, 5:50 p.m., NSF, Memos to the President, box 4, LBJL.

42. Johnson, *Vantage Point*, pp. 144–146.

43. Minutes of Cabinet Room meeting, July 21, 1965, 10:40 a.m., Presidential Papers of LBJ, Meeting Notes File, box 1, LBJL.

44. Ibid.

45. Ibid.

46. Bill, *George Ball*, p. 11.

47. Minutes of Cabinet Room meeting, July 21, 1965, 2:45 p.m., Presidential Papers of LBJ, Meeting Notes File, box 1, LBJL.

48. Ibid.

49. Ibid.

50. Ibid.

51. Ibid.

52. Ibid.

53. Clifford, *Counsel to the President*, p. 415.

54. Ibid., pp. 415–416.

55. Ibid., p. 416; transcript, Clifford-Ball telcon, July 23, 1965, 7:30 p.m., Ball Papers, box 7.

56. Minutes of Camp David meeting, July 25, 1965, 5:00 p.m., Presidential Papers of LBJ, Meeting Notes File, box 1, LBJL.

57. Summary notes of 553d Meeting of the NSC, July 27, 1965, *FRUS, 1964–1968*, III (electronic version); Clifford, *Counsel to the President*, p. 417.

58. President's news conference, July 28, 1965, *Public Papers of the Presidents, 1965*, pp. 794–803.

59. President's address to the nation announcing steps to limit the war in Vietnam and reporting his decision not to seek reelection, March 31, 1968, *Public Papers of the Presidents of the United States: Lyndon B. Johnson, 1968–69* (Washington, D.C.: U.S. Government Printing Office, 1970), pp. 469–476.

INDEX

A NOTE ON THE AUTHOR

Mark J. White was born in Holbrook, England, and studied at the University of Nottingham, the University of Wisconsin–Milwaukee, and Rutgers University, where he received a Ph.D. in American history. He has taught at six universities in Britain and North America and is now a Reader in History at the University of London (Queen Mary).